CRIMINAL LITIGATION

CRIMINAL LITIGATION

John Holtam, LLB (Southampton), LLM (Edinburgh), Solicitor

Published by

College of Law Publishing,
Braboeuf Manor, Portsmouth Road, St Catherines, Guildford GU3 1HA

British Library Cataloguing-in-Publication Data

A catalogue record for this book is available from the British Library.

ISBN 0 905835 91 3

Typeset by Style Photosetting Ltd, Mayfield, East Sussex

Printed in Great Britain by Ashford Colour Press Ltd, Gosport.

Preface

This book has been written primarily for use by students on the Legal Practice Course. The content and depth of subject covered are determined by the requirements of the course. The aim of the book is to provide the framework upon which the criminal litigation course is built. Because students are expected to carry out their own research in some aspects of the course and will receive further tuition in others, the book is not intended as a standard textbook on the subject.

Each chapter contains suggestions on further reading. These are intended as examples of primary and secondary sources to which the reader should refer to follow up a subject.

Although I am responsible for this edition of *Criminal Litigation*, I remain indebted to John Clegg (now District Judge Clegg) for his valuable contributions in previous years.

I have endeavoured to state the law as at 31 May 2005.

JOHN HOLTAM
Guildford

Contents

Table of Cases

S

W

Table of Statutes

Table of Statutory Instruments, Circulars and Guidance

Table of International Legislation

Table of Abbreviations

CJA 2003	Criminal Justice Act 2003
CPIA 1996	Criminal Procedure and Investigations Act 1996
CPO	community punishment order
CPS	Crown Prosecution Service
CrimPR	Criminal Procedure Rules 2005
EAH	early administrative hearing
EFH	early first hearing
MCA 1980	Magistrates' Courts Act 1980
PACE	Police and Criminal Evidence Act 1984
PCC(S)A 2000	Powers of Criminal Courts (Sentencing) Act 2000
PCMA	plea and case management hearing
PH	preparatory hearing
PTR	pre-trial review
RDCO	recovery of defence costs order
TIC	(offences) taken into consideration

Chapter 1

Introduction to Criminal Procedure

1.1 The solicitor's role

Solicitors are involved at every stage of the prosecution of a criminal offence, from police investigation to trial. Solicitors (and their unqualified representatives) are frequently called upon to advise suspects being held in the police station before they are charged. Difficult decisions have to be made with the client. Should police questions be answered? Should the client agree to stand on an identification parade?

Following the commencement of criminal proceedings, a solicitor may be involved in applying for a representation order for a client and in trying to secure his release from custody on bail. Criminal proceedings in a magistrates' court will usually be prosecuted and defended by solicitors, although barristers sometimes appear. If a case is to be dealt with in the Crown Court, most solicitors have limited rights of audience. Their major role is in preparing the case for trial and briefing a barrister (counsel) to represent the client.

Finally, where necessary, a solicitor will advise a client on rights of appeal, will prepare the appeal and, usually, will brief a barrister to represent the client at the appeal hearing.

This chapter provides an introduction to the criminal justice system and covers the basic information required to understand the progress of a criminal case from investigation to trial.

1.2 Classification of criminal offences

Criminal offences are divided into three categories:

(a) summary offences;

(b) offences triable either way;

(c) offences triable only on indictment.

Summary offences may be tried only in a magistrates' court.

Offences triable either way may be tried in a magistrates' court or in the Crown Court before a judge and jury. The place of trial will be determined at a plea before venue and mode of trial hearing in a magistrates' court.

Offences triable only on indictment must be tried in the Crown Court.

1.3 The courts and court personnel

1.3.1 Magistrates' courts

Business

The prosecution of all criminal offences starts in the magistrates' court even if the case will ultimately be tried in the Crown Court. The functions of a magistrates' court include:

(a)   to issue search and arrest warrants;

(b)   to issue warrants of further detention under the Police and Criminal Evidence Act 1984;

(c)   to issue summonses to defendants to appear before the court to answer a criminal charge;

(d)   to try summary offences and some either way offences;

(e)   to hold committal proceedings in respect of either way offences (not related to indictable only offences) which are to be tried in the Crown Court;

(f)   to send indictable only offences (and related either way and summary offences) to the Crown Court for trial;

(g)   to deal with applications for a representation order;

(h)   to deal with applications for bail.

Personnel

Most magistrates are not legally qualified. Between two and four magistrates will usually sit in court. The magistrates are advised on points of law, practice and procedure by the clerk to the justices. The clerk should not advise magistrates on questions of fact. In some courts, a legally qualified magistrate known as a district judge (magistrates' court) will sit alone.

1.3.2 Youth courts

Youth courts are courts set up to deal with defendants who are under 18 years of age. Lay magistrates and district judges (magistrates' court) sit in youth courts.

1.3.3 The Crown Court

Business

The functions of the Crown Court include:

(a)   to try and to sentence offences triable only on indictment and either way offences committed for trial by a magistrates' court;

(b)   to determine questions of bail and representation;

(c)   to hear appeals against conviction and/or sentence from a magistrates' court and youth court.

Personnel

The judges of the Crown Court are recorders, circuit judges and High Court judges. The judge sits with a jury on not guilty pleas and with magistrates when dealing with appeals from a magistrates' court.

1.3.4   High Court (Queen's Bench Division)

Business

The Queen's Bench Division of the High Court hears appeals on points of law from magistrates' courts and youth courts and appeals on law from re-hearings in the Crown Court (appeals by way of case stated). It also has power to quash a decision by making a quashing order, to order the court to try a case by making a mandatory order, or to stop a court hearing a case by making a prohibiting order.

Personnel

The judges are judges of the Queen's Bench Division of the High Court chosen on an ad hoc basis.

1.3.5   The Court of Appeal

Business

The Court of Appeal (Criminal Division) hears appeals against conviction and/or sentence from the Crown Court.

Personnel

The judges in the Court of Appeal will be drawn from the Lord Chief Justice, Lords Justices of Appeal and High Court judges.

1.3.6   The House of Lords

Business

The House of Lords is the final appeal court. It hears appeals from the Court of Appeal and High Court but only where a point of law of general public importance is involved.

Personnel

The judges in the House of Lords are usually five Lords of Appeal.

1.4   The prosecution and the defence

1.4.1   The prosecution

Once the police have instituted proceedings, full responsibility for the prosecution will pass to the Crown Prosecution Service (CPS). The CPS will review the evidence and surrounding circumstances of each case and decide whether and how the prosecution should proceed. In appropriate cases the CPS can discontinue proceedings. There is a Code for Crown Prosecutors which gives guidelines on discontinuance and other matters.

Joint charging standards have been drawn up by the police and the CPS. The purpose of joint charging standards is to make sure that the most appropriate charge is selected, in the light of the evidence which can be proved, at the earliest possible opportunity. To date, three joint charging standards have been published: Offences Against the Person (26 April 1996), Public Order Offences (26 April 1996) and Driving Offences (March 1996).

The CPS is now responsible for determining the charge in all but the most routine cases. The police will charge minor or routine cases without reference to the CPS.

The Director of Public Prosecutions has issued guidance on what can be charged without reference to the CPS and what must be referred pre-charge to the CPS

1.4.2 The defence

A defendant has the right to conduct his own defence (*R v Woodward* [1944] KB 118; see also the European Convention for the Protection of Human Rights and Fundamental Freedoms 1950, art 6(3), and **1.8**). There are restrictions on cross-examination by defendants in person (see **9.3.2**). A defendant may, however, be represented by a solicitor whom he will pay privately, or who will be paid under a representation order. If the services of a barrister (counsel) are needed, the solicitor instructs a barrister. The defendant cannot instruct a barrister direct.

A solicitor has a right of audience in a magistrates' court. For most solicitors, rights of audience in the Crown Court are limited to:

(a) applications in chambers, for example, bail applications;

(b) appeals against conviction and/or sentence from a magistrates' court, provided a member of the solicitor's firm conducted the proceedings in the magistrates' court;

(c) on committal by a magistrates' court to the Crown Court for sentence, provided a member of the solicitor's firm conducted the hearing in the magistrates' court;

(d) preliminary hearings in the Crown Court where the defendant has been sent for trial for an indictable defence.

Thus, solicitors cannot normally conduct a trial by jury in the Crown Court. However, in certain Crown Courts, solicitors enjoy extended rights of audience, including the right to conduct some jury trials. A number of solicitors have now been granted full rights of audience in the Crown Court and higher appeal courts.

1.4.3 Criminal Defence Service

The Criminal Defence Service was created by the Access to Justice Act 1999 (ss 12–18 and Sch 3). The purpose of the Criminal Defence Service is to 'secure the provision of advice, assistance and representation, according to the interests of justice, to people suspected of a criminal offence, or facing criminal proceedings' (*Legal Services Commission Manual* (Sweet & Maxwell, 1D-004)).

The Legal Services Commission funds the Criminal Defence Service and secures the provision of advice, assistance and representation under a General Criminal Contract with solicitors in private practice, or by providing them through salaried public defenders. All contractors are expected to meet quality assurance standards and provide the full range of services from arrest until the case is completed. Only those solicitors with a General Criminal Contract with the Legal Services Commission are able to undertake publicly funded defence work.

The following advice and assistance may be granted without reference to the financial resources of the individual:

(1) advice and assistance (including advocacy assistance) provided by a solicitor acting as a court duty solicitor;

(2) police station advice and assistance to a client who is arrested and held at a police station or who is a volunteer;

(3) advocacy assistance on an application for a warrant of further detention or for an extension to such a warrant (Criminal Defence Service (General) (No 2) Regulations 2001 (SI 2001/1437)).

Where a representation order is requested an applicant will need to satisfy the interests of justice test set out in Access to Justice Act 1999, Sch 3 (see **3.3.2**).

1.5   An overview of criminal procedure

See **Appendix 1(A)** for a flowchart giving an overview of criminal procedure.

1.5.1   Police investigations

Police investigation includes arrest, search and the detention and questioning of a suspect (see **Chapter 2**).

1.5.2   Commencement of criminal proceedings

The commencement of criminal proceedings will be by way of charge or summons. A charge is normally used when a suspect has been arrested and taken to the police station. A summons is normally used for relatively minor offences that may not involve arrest at all (eg, motoring offences). The summons will be served by post and will notify the defendant of the date, time and place of the hearing (see **Chapter 3**).

1.5.3   Magistrates' courts

All cases begin in a magistrates' court. At the initial hearing, questions of adjournments, representation and bail are likely to arise (see **Chapter 3**).

If the offence before the court is a summary offence, it must be dealt with by a magistrates' court. The defendant will plead guilty or not guilty and on conviction will be sentenced (see **Chapter 8**).

If the offence is an either way offence (which is not related to an indictable only offence), the prosecution begins with the determination of plea before venue before the magistrates. If the defendant refuses to indicate a plea, or indicates a not guilty plea, the magistrates will proceed to mode of trial, to determine whether the case should be dealt with by a magistrates' court or by the Crown Court (see **Chapter 4**). If the offence proceeds in the magistrates' court and the defendant is convicted, then the magistrates may commit him to the Crown Court for sentencing in certain circumstances (see **Chapter 10**). If the case is to proceed to the Crown Court, there will be committal proceedings in the magistrates' court. At committal, the defence can require the prosecution to show that there is a case to answer. Alternatively, the defence may not dispute that there is a case to answer. If so, the committal may be a formality (see **Chapter 6**). Following committal, the defendant will be tried by judge and jury. Following conviction, the defendant is sentenced by a judge.

If the offence is an indictable only offence, the magistrates must send the defendant to the Crown Court to be tried. The magistrates must also send related summary only and either way offences to the Crown Court (see **Chapter 6**).

1.5.4   Disclosure of prosecution evidence

In all cases, the defendant has a statutory right to receive a copy of certain documents such as his custody record and the record of an identification parade.

If the defendant is charged with a summary offence, the defendant has no statutory right to see the prosecution evidence before it is presented at the trial. However, the prosecution is usually prepared to disclose its evidence on a voluntary basis.

If the defendant is charged with an either way offence, then prior to the mode of trial decision, he has a right to receive either a summary or a copy of the prosecution witness statements.

If the defendant's case is to be committed to the Crown Court, the prosecution must serve copies of its evidence on the defence before the case is committed from the magistrates' court to the Crown Court.

If the defendant's case is sent to the Crown Court for trial, the prosecution must serve copies of its evidence on the defence at the Crown Court.

These rules are dealt with in more detail at **5.2**.

1.5.5 Appeal

There are rights of appeal against conviction and/or sentence from the magistrates' court and the Crown Court (see **Chapter 11**).

1.5.6 The rules governing criminal procedure

Solicitors need to be familiar not only with the statutes governing criminal procedure (eg, the Police and Criminal Evidence Act 1984, the Magistrates' Courts Act 1980, the Criminal Procedure and Investigations Act 1996, the Crime and Disorder Act 1998, the Criminal Justice Act 2003), but also the Criminal Procedure Rules (SI 2005/384) (CrimPR) and the *Practice Direction (Criminal Proceedings: Consolidation)* [2002] 3 All ER 904.

The first Criminal Procedure Rules to be made under s 72 of the Courts Act 2003 came into force on 4 April 2005. The Criminal Procedure Rules consolidated the rules governing criminal proceedings and provided a new framework for the management of criminal cases.

The rules introduced an overriding objective.

> **1.1   The overriding objective**
>
> (1)   The overriding objective of this new code is that criminal cases be dealt with justly.
>
> (2)   Dealing with a criminal case justly includes—
>
> (a)   acquitting the innocent and convicting the guilty;
>
> (b)   dealing with prosecution and defence fairly;
>
> (c)   recognising the rights of a defendant, particularly those under Article 6 of the European Convention on Human Rights;
>
> (d)   respecting the interests of witnesses, victims and jurors, and keeping them informed of the progress of the case;
>
> (e)   dealing with the case efficiently and expeditiously;
>
> (f)   ensuring that appropriate information is available to the court when bail and sentence are considered; and
>
> (g)   dealing with the case in ways that take into account—
>
> (i)   the gravity of the offence alleged,
>
> (ii)   the complexity of what is in issue,
>
> (iii)   the severity of the consequences for the defendant and others affected, and
>
> (iv)   the needs of other cases.
>
> **1.2   The duty of the participants in a criminal case**
>
> (1)   Each participant, in the conduct of each case, must—

    (a)   prepare and conduct the case in accordance with the overriding objective;

    (b)   comply with these Rules, practice directions and directions made by the court; and

    (c)   at once inform the court and all parties of any significant failure (whether or not the participant is responsible for that failure) to take any procedural step required by these Rules, any practice direction or any direction of the court. A failure is significant if it might hinder the court in furthering the overriding objective.

    (2)   Anyone involved in any way with a criminal case is a participant in its conduct for the purposes of this rule.

1.3   The application by the court of the overriding objective

The court must further the overriding objective in particular when—

    (a)   exercising any power given to it by legislation (including these Rules);

    (b)   applying any practice direction; or

    (c)   interpreting any rule or practice direction.

Part 3 of the Criminal Procedure Rules 2005 deals with case management and sets out the obligation of all parties. At the beginning of the case each party must nominate a case progression officer and notify the other parties of that person's identity. It is the duty of the case progression officer to:

(a)   monitor compliance with directions;

(b)   make sure that the court is kept informed of events that may affect the progress of the case;

(c)   make sure that he can be contacted during normal business hours;

(d)   act promptly and reasonably in response to communications about the case; and

(e)   if he will be unavailable appoint a substitute to fulfil his duties and inform the other case progression officers.

Practice Direction (Criminal Proceedings: Consolidation) was issued by the Lord Chief Justice on 8 July 2002 and has subsequently been amended by him. The Practice Direction consolidated all previous practice directions, practice statements and practice notes affecting proceedings in the Court of Appeal (Criminal Division), the Crown Court and the magistrates' court. The Lord Chief Justice issued amendments to the Practice Direction in relation to case management on 22 March 2005.

1.6 Substantive criminal law

This book has been designed as a constituent part of the Legal Practice Course. As such, it will not generally address questions of substantive criminal law. However, an outline knowledge of the offences which have been used to illustrate points of practice, procedure and evidence is necessary. It is also necessary to know how each offence is classified for trial purposes and the maximum penalties that can be imposed on conviction. The offences which are illustrated in this book are summarised below.

1.6.1 Theft

(a)   Classification – triable either way.

(b)   Theft is an arrestable offence within the meaning of the Police and Criminal Evidence Act 1984, s 24.

(c)   Maximum penalties – Crown Court: 7 years' imprisonment and/or unlimited fine. Magistrates' court: 6 months' imprisonment and/or £5,000 fine. If theft of a motor vehicle: discretionary disqualification from driving.

(d)   Definition – Theft Act 1968, s 1:

Dishonest appropriation of property belonging to another with the intention of permanently depriving the other of it.

1.6.2 Burglary

(a)   Classification – triable either way if involving theft or intention to steal, unless burglary of a dwelling and any person in the dwelling is subjected to violence or the threat of it, in which case triable only on indictment.

(b)   Burglary is an arrestable offence within the meaning of the Police and Criminal Evidence Act 1984, s 24.

(c)   Maximum penalties – Crown Court: 14 years' imprisonment and/or unlimited fine (maximum 10 years if not of a dwelling). Magistrates' court: 6 months' imprisonment and/or £5,000 fine.

(d)   There is a minimum sentence of 3 years' imprisonment for the third conviction of burglary of a dwelling. The court need not impose the minimum term if it is of the opinion that there are particular circumstances which:

(i)   relate to any of the offences or the offender; and

(ii)   would make the prescribed minimum sentence unjust in all the circumstances (Powers of Criminal Courts (Sentencing) Act 2000 (PCC(S)A 2000), ss 111–115).

(e)   Definition – Theft Act 1968, s 9:

(1)   A person is guilty of burglary if—

(a)   he enters any building or part of a building as a trespasser and with intent to commit any such offence as is mentioned in subsection (2) below; or

(b)   having entered any building or part of a building as a trespasser he steals or attempts to steal anything in the building or that part of it or inflicts or attempts to inflict on any person therein any grievous bodily harm.

(2)   The offences referred to in subsection (1)(a) above are offences of stealing anything in the building or part of a building in question, of inflicting on any person therein any grievous bodily harm, and of doing unlawful damage to the building or anything therein.

1.6.3 Robbery

(a)   Classification – triable only on indictment.

(b)   Robbery is an arrestable offence within the meaning of the Police and Criminal Evidence Act 1984, s 24.

(c)   Maximum penalties – life imprisonment and/or unlimited fine.

(d)   Definition – Theft Act 1968, s 8(1):

A person is guilty of robbery if he steals and immediately before or at the time of doing so, and in order to do so, he uses force on any person or puts or seeks to put any person in fear of being then and there subjected to force.

1.6.4 Obtaining property by deception

(a)   Classification – either way.

(b)   The offence is an arrestable offence within the meaning of the Police and Criminal Evidence Act 1984, s 24.

(c) Maximum penalties – Crown Court: 10 years' imprisonment and/or unlimited fine; Magistrates' court: 6 months' imprisonment and/or £5000 fine.

(d) Definition – Theft Act 1968, s 15:

   (1) A person who by any deception dishonestly obtains property belonging to another, with the intention of permanently depriving the other of it ...

   (4) For the purposes of this section 'deception' means any deception (whether deliberate or reckless) by words or conduct as to fact or as to law, including a deception as to the present intentions of the person using the deception or any other person.

1.6.5 Handling stolen goods

(a) Classification – triable either way.

(b) Handling is an either way offence within the meaning of the Police and Criminal Evidence Act 1984, s 24.

(c) Maximum penalties – Crown Court: 14 years' imprisonment and/or unlimited fine. Magistrates' court: 6 months' imprisonment and/or unlimited fine.

(d) Definition – Theft Act 1968, s 22(1):

A person handles stolen goods if (otherwise than in the course of the stealing) knowing or believing them to be stolen goods he dishonestly receives the goods, or dishonestly undertakes or assists in the retention, removal, disposal or realisation by or for the benefit of another person, or if he arranges to do so.

1.6.6 Common assault

(a) Classification – summary only.

(b) The offence is not an arrestable offence within the meaning of the Police and Criminal Evidence Act 1984, s 24.

(c) Maximum penalties – 6 months' imprisonment and/or £5000 fine.

(d) Definition:

There are two ways of committing a common assault; a simple assault or a physical assault (sometimes referred to as a battery). A simple assault is committed when the defendant, intentionally or recklessly, causes the victim to apprehend immediate and unlawful personal violence. A physical assault consists of the infliction of unlawful personal violence, either intentionally or recklessly, by the defendant upon the victim.

All common assaults are offences contrary to the Criminal Justice Act 1988, s 39 and the wording of the charge should make clear whether the prosecution is alleging a simple assault ('assault') or a physical assault ('assault by beating').

1.6.7 Assault occasioning actual bodily harm

(a) Classification – either way.

(b) The offence is an arrestable offence within the meaning of the Police and Criminal Evidence Act 1984, s 24.

(c) Maximum penalties – Crown Court: 5 years' imprisonment and/or unlimited fine. Magistrates' court: 6 months' imprisonment and/or £5,000 fine.

(d) Definition – Offences Against the Person Act 1861, s 47:

... assault occasioning actual bodily harm.

Any injury can be classified as actual bodily harm. However, the Crown Prosecution Service *Charging Standards* document (issued in April 1996) makes it clear that a s 47 charge is not appropriate if the injuries amount to no more than 'grazes, scratches, abrasions, minor bruising, superficial cuts or a black eye'. For such minor injuries, the appropriate charge is common assault. A verdict of assault occasioning actual bodily harm may be returned on proof of an assault together with proof that actual bodily harm was occasioned by the assault. The prosecution do not have to prove that the defendant intended to cause some actual bodily harm or was reckless as to whether such harm would be caused (*R v Savage; R v Parmenter* [1991] 4 All ER 698).

1.6.8   Wounding or inflicting grievous bodily harm

(a)   Classification – either way.

(b)   The offence is an arrestable offence within the Police and Criminal Evidence Act 1984, s 24.

(c)   Maximum penalties

Crown Court: 5 years' imprisonment and/or unlimited fine.

Magistrates' court: 6 months' imprisonment and/or £5000 fine.

(d)   Definition – Offences Against the Person Act 1861, s 20:

> Whosoever shall unlawfully and maliciously wound or inflict grievous bodily harm upon any other person, either with or without any weapon or instrument, shall be guilty of [an offence], and being convicted thereof shall be liable to [imprisonment for not more than five years].

A wound requires the breaking of two layers of skin. In theory, even trivial wounds may qualify, but the Charging Standards urge that minor wounds should not, in practice, be charged under s 20. Grievous bodily harm means really serious harm (*Director of Public Prosecutions v Smith* [1961] AC 290). The Charging Standards list examples of injuries which should normally be prosecuted under s 20, for example, injury resulting in permanent disability or permanent loss of sensory function; injury which results in more than minor permanent, visible disfigurement; broken or displaced limbs or bones, including fractured skull; compound fractures, broken cheek bone, jaw, ribs, etc; injuries which cause substantial loss of blood, usually necessitating a transfusion; and injuries resulting in lengthy treatment or incapacity.

The prosecution must prove that either the defendant intended, or actually foresaw, that the act would cause some harm. It is not necessary to prove that the defendant intended or foresaw that the unlawful act might cause the physical harm described in s 20. It is enough that the defendant foresaw that some physical harm to some person, albeit of a minor character, might result (*R v Savage; R v Parmenter*).

1.6.9   Secondary participation

A person who aids, abets, counsels or procures the commission of an offence is a secondary party. Basically, aiding is giving assistance, abetting is giving encouragement at the time of the commission of the offence, counselling is giving encouragement earlier, and procuring is bringing about the offence.

An accomplice will often be jointly charged with a principal offender.

Example

John Smith steals goods while Alan Jones keeps a lookout.

Alan Jones' charge may read:

'Jointly with John Smith stole ...' etc.

The charge reads as though Alan Jones is a principal offender. This is permissible by virtue of the Accessories and Abettors Act 1861, s 8.

1.7   Professional ethics

A solicitor involved in criminal litigation faces many ethical problems. Should a prosecutor reveal information to the defence which will assist the defence case? Can you act for a client who tells you that he is guilty but who wishes to plead not guilty? How should you react to a major change of story by your client? This section seeks to identify the major ethical problems which are likely to arise in a criminal case and suggests solutions to them.

1.7.1   Duty not to mislead the court

The general principle for a solicitor involved in criminal proceedings is that, while he owes a duty to his client to do his best for him, a solicitor must not mislead or deceive the court.

1.7.2   The prosecution

Prosecuting advocates are under a duty to ensure that all material evidence supporting the prosecution case is put before the court in a dispassionate and fair manner. In particular:

(a)   all relevant facts known to the prosecution should be put before the court including, after conviction, facts relevant to mitigation;

(b)   if a prosecution witness gives evidence in court which is inconsistent with any earlier statement made, there is a duty to disclose this fact to the defence.

When arguing a point of law, all relevant legal authorities should be cited, including those which are against the prosecution.

1.7.3   The defence

A number of ethical problems can arise when conducting a criminal defence. Always bear in mind the duty not to mislead the court (see **1.7.1**). In addition, the following guidelines may be of assistance.

(a)   The client who admits his guilt. This may happen before or during the course of proceedings. If the client insists on giving evidence in the witness box denying his guilt, then a solicitor should decline to act. It is, however, proper to act on a not guilty plea if the defence merely intends to put the prosecution to proof of its case without calling defence evidence.

(b)   Occasionally, a client will wish to plead guilty notwithstanding that his instructions indicate that he has a defence. Such a client should be advised of the defence available. If he insists on pleading guilty, the solicitor may continue to act but should advise the client that in mitigation it will not be possible to rely on facts that may constitute a defence.

(c)   The client who gives inconsistent instructions. The mere fact that a client makes inconsistent statements to his solicitor does not make it improper for the solicitor to continue to act. If it becomes clear that the client is changing his instructions with a view to putting forward false evidence to the court, the solicitor should refuse to act.

(d)   Disclosure of the defence case. A solicitor should not, without the express consent of his client, disclose details of his client's case to any other party. Requests for disclosure sometimes come, for example, from the solicitors acting for a co-defendant. Such requests should be treated with caution and the client's instructions taken.

(e)   Arguing a point of law. All relevant authorities should be cited, including those which are against the advocate. This is a positive duty to assist the court in contrast to matters of fact where the duty is a negative one – not to mislead the court.

(f)   The client who gives a false name to the court. A solicitor should not act for a client who, to the knowledge of the solicitor, gives a false name, address or date of birth to the court. If faced with this problem the solicitor should try to persuade the client to change his mind. If the client refuses to do so then the solicitor should cease to act.

(g)   Knowledge of previous convictions. On occasion, the list of previous convictions of a defendant produced to the court by the prosecution will be inaccurate. If asked to confirm the accuracy of the list, a solicitor should decline to comment. To confirm the list as accurate would amount to a positive deception of the court. A solicitor should not mislead the court. On the other hand, disclosing previous convictions without the client's express consent is a breach of the duty of confidentiality to the client. The solicitor should, wherever possible, obtain a list of previous convictions from the police or CPS sufficiently in advance of going to court so that he can discuss any problems with the client. The client should be warned of the dangers of misleading the court. If the client insists that, if asked, he will pretend the list is accurate, the solicitor must cease to act (see the *Guide to the Professional Conduct of Solicitors* (The Law Society, 1999), Annex 21F).

(h)   Conflicts of interest. A solicitor must not continue to act for two or more defendants where a conflict of interest arises between them. Within the context of criminal proceedings, a conflict can arise, for example, where one defendant decides to blame the other and changes his plea to not guilty. Even where pleas are consistent it may not be possible to act for the defendants if one is seeking to implicate the other or to allege that one played a larger role in the offence than the other. If a conflict arises while a solicitor is acting for both defendants then he should consider withdrawing from the case altogether. This would be appropriate where the solicitor has information in his possession about one defendant which could be used to assist the other defendant in the case.

(i)   Interviewing prosecution witnesses. Although there is no property in a witness, defence solicitors should proceed with caution when intending to interview a prosecution witness. The best course of action is to notify the prosecution of the fact that a witness is to be interviewed and to invite a representative to attend as an observer. This will avoid suspicion of an attempt to pervert the course of justice and allegations that a witness has been pressured in some way to change his evidence.

(j)   If circumstances arise which require a solicitor to withdraw from a case (for example, see (f) and (g) above), the reason for withdrawal should not normally be given to the court. The solicitor should simply explain that a matter has arisen which makes it impossible for him to continue to act in the case.

1.8 European Convention on Human Rights

The Human Rights Act 1998 gives effect in domestic law to the rights and freedoms guaranteed by the European Convention for the Protection of Human Rights and Fundamental Freedoms (the Convention), to which the UK is a party.

(a)   All legislation must, if possible, be interpreted so as to be compatible with the Convention (s 3(1)). Domestic courts must strive to find a construction consistent with the intentions of Parliament and the wording of legislation which is nearest to Convention rights. Courts should proceed on the basis that Parliament is deemed to have intended its statutes to be compatible with the Convention. The only basis for the courts concluding that Parliament has failed to carry that intention into effect is where it is impossible to construe a statute so as to be compatible with the Convention (Lord Chancellor, 18 November 1997, House of Lords Committee Stage, *Hansard,* col 535).

(b)   Where it is not possible to interpret primary legislation so as to be compatible with the Convention, the courts will have no power to strike it down. However, the House of Lords, the Judicial Committee of the Privy Council, the Court of Appeal and the High Court will have power to make a 'declaration of incompatibility' which (in theory) should prompt government action. Such a declaration does not affect the validity, continuing operation or enforcement of the provision in respect of which it is made (s 4(6)(a)). Nor does it bind the parties to the proceedings in which it is made (s 4(6)(b)). It is intended to operate as a clear signal to Parliament that an incompatibility has been found.

The government envisages that a declaration of incompatibility will 'almost certainly' prompt legislative change (White Paper, 'Rights Brought Home: The Human Rights Bill' (Cm 3782), para 2.9). The Act provides a 'fast track' procedure for amending the law so as to bring it into conformity with the Convention (s 10).

(c)   Where it simply is not possible to interpret subordinate legislation so as to be compatible with the Convention, the courts have power to disapply it. The only exception is where primary legislation prevents the removal of any incompatibility (s 4(4)(b)).

(d)   All public authorities, including all courts and tribunals, must, if possible, act in a way which is compatible with the Convention. Public authorities include (but are not limited to) courts, tribunals and 'any person certain of whose functions are functions of a public nature' (s 6(3)). The definition is in wide terms and is intended to cover the police.

(e)   Individuals who believe that their Convention rights have been infringed by a public authority can rely on their rights as a defence in civil and criminal proceedings or as the basis of an appeal, alternatively seek judicial review, or bring civil proceedings for damages (s 7 and s 8).

(f)   Section 8(1) of the Act provides that:

In relation to any act (or proposed act) of a public authority which the court finds is (or would be) unlawful, it may grant such relief or remedy, or make such order, within its powers as it considers just and appropriate.

As a result, criminal courts will have the power to stay proceedings as an abuse of process, quash an indictment or charge, rule evidence inadmissible, quash convictions and even recognise new defences where Convention rights have been violated.

(g)   In resolving Convention issues, all courts and tribunals must take into account the case-law of the European Court of Human Rights, Commission of Human Rights and the Committee of Ministers established under the Convention (s 2).

Since the Act came into force, practitioners have been able to rely on the Convention in criminal proceedings. Practitioners can test domestic law and practice for compliance with the Convention, particularly:

Article 3

Prohibition of torture

No one shall be subjected to torture or to inhuman or degrading treatment or punishment. ...

Article 5

Right to liberty and security

1.   Everyone has the right to liberty and security of person. No one shall be deprived of his liberty save in the following cases and in accordance with a procedure prescribed by law:

   (a)   the lawful detention of a person after conviction by a competent court;

   (b)   the lawful arrest or detention of a person for non-compliance with the lawful order of a court or in order to secure the fulfilment of any obligation prescribed by law;

   (c)   the lawful arrest or detention of a person effected for the purpose of bringing him before the competent legal authority on reasonable suspicion of having committed an offence or when it is reasonably considered necessary to prevent his committing an offence or fleeing after having done so;

   (d)   the detention of a minor by lawful order for the purpose of educational supervision or his lawful detention for the purpose of bringing him before the competent legal authority;

   (e)   the lawful detention of persons for the prevention of the spreading of infectious diseases, of persons of unsound mind, alcoholics or drug addicts or vagrants;

   (f)   the lawful arrest or detention of a person to prevent his effecting an unauthorised entry into the country or of a person against whom action is being taken with a view to deportation or extradition.

2.   Everyone who is arrested shall be informed promptly, in a language which he understands, of the reasons for his arrest and of any charge against him.

3.   Everyone arrested or detained in accordance with the provisions of paragraph 1(c) of this Article shall be brought promptly before a judge or other officer authorised by law to exercise judicial power and shall be entitled to trial within a reasonable time or to release pending trial. Release may be conditioned by guarantees to appear for trial.

4.   Everyone who is deprived of his liberty by arrest or detention shall be entitled to take proceedings by which the lawfulness of his detention shall be decided speedily by a court and his release ordered if the detention is not lawful.

5.   Everyone who has been the victim of arrest or detention in contravention of the provisions of this Article shall have an enforceable right to compensation.

Article 6

Right to a fair trial

1.   In the determination of his civil rights and obligations or of any criminal charge against him, everyone is entitled to a fair and public hearing within a reasonable time by an independent and impartial tribunal established by law. Judgment shall be pronounced publicly but the press and public may be excluded from all or part of the trial in the interest of morals, public order or national security in a democratic society, where the interests of juveniles or the

protection of the private life of the parties so require, or to the extent strictly necessary in the opinion of the court in special circumstances where publicity would prejudice the interests of justice.

2.   Everyone charged with a criminal offence shall be presumed innocent until proved guilty according to the law.

3.   Everyone charged with a criminal offence has the following minimum rights:

    (a)   to be informed promptly, in a language which he understands and in detail, of the nature and cause of the accusation against him;

    (b)   to have adequate time and facilities for the preparation of his defence;

    (c)   to defend himself in person or through legal assistance of his own choosing or, if he has not sufficient means to pay for legal assistance, to be given it free when the interests of justice so require;

    (d)   to examine or have examined witnesses against him and to obtain the attendance and examination of witnesses on his behalf under the same conditions as witnesses against him;

    (e)   to have the free assistance of an interpreter if he cannot understand or speak the language used in court.

Article 7

No punishment without law

1.   No one shall be held guilty of any criminal offence on account of any act or omission which did not constitute a criminal offence under national or international law at the time when it was committed. Nor shall a heavier penalty be imposed than the one that was applicable at the time the criminal offence was committed.

2.   This Article shall not prejudice the trial and punishment of any person for any act or omission which, at the time when it was committed, was criminal according to the general principles of law recognised by civilised nations.

There is no rule under the Act requiring a Convention point to be taken at any given stage in criminal proceedings. Convention points can be taken before the trial (eg, by challenging the charge or indictment), at trial (by seeking to exclude evidence obtained in breach of the Convention or limiting the basis upon which adverse inferences can be drawn), or on appeal (eg, by quashing a conviction on the basis that it was obtained in breach of the Convention). It is possible that courts may also examine Convention issues of their own volition since they are 'public authorities' under s 6 and, accordingly, are obliged to act in accordance with the Convention.

1.9   Further reading

See, for example:

Archbold: Criminal Pleading, Evidence and Practice (Sweet & Maxwell, 2005)

Blackstone's Criminal Practice (Oxford University Press, 2005)

Pervasive and Core Topics

The Guide to the Professional Conduct of Solicitors (The Law Society, 1999)

J Wadham and H Mountfield, *Blackstone's Guide to the Human Rights Act 1998*, 3rd edn (Oxford University Press, 2003)

Chapter 2

The Suspect in the Police Station

2.1 Introduction

The police have wide powers to arrest and detain a person, without charge, if that person is suspected of having committed a criminal offence. A suspect who is detained in a police station has the right to legal advice. A solicitor's role in the police station involves advising a suspect of his rights, 'sitting in' on police interviews with a suspect, ensuring 'fair play' in the police station and attending identification parades. This chapter examines the law governing the detention, treatment and questioning of a suspect and considers the role of a solicitor in the police station. The law is contained primarily in the Police and Criminal Evidence Act 1984 (PACE 1984), the Codes of Practice issued under that Act and the Criminal Justice and Public Order Act 1994. References to section numbers in this chapter are, unless otherwise stated, to the Police and Criminal Evidence Act 1984. References to 'Code C' are to the Code of Practice on the Detention, Treatment and Questioning of Suspects (see **Appendix 6**), references to 'Code D' are to the Code of Practice on Identification Procedures (see **Appendix 6**) and references to 'Code E' are to the Code of Practice on Tape Recording of Interviews with Suspects. A diagram showing some of the ranks in the police appears at **Appendix 1(B)**.

2.2 The serious arrestable offence (PACE 1984, s 116 and Sch 5)

An important concept running through the Police and Criminal Evidence Act 1984 is the serious arrestable offence. It is relevant to the powers of the police to detain a suspect for more than 36 hours and to delay access to legal advice.

Of the offences covered in this book, the following are arrestable offences:

> Theft
>
> Burglary
>
> Robbery
>
> Assault occasioning actual bodily harm
>
> Wounding or inflicting grievous bodily harm

Obtaining property by deception

Handling stolen goods

An offence listed above will be a serious arrestable offence if:

(a)   it has led, inter alia, to the death of any person, serious injury of any person, substantial financial gain to any person, or serious financial loss to any person; or

(b)   it is intended or is likely to lead to any of the consequences in (a) above.

Serious financial loss is assessed subjectively. Thus, theft of a relatively small amount of money from a poor person can legitimately be treated as a serious arrestable offence. Substantial financial gain is assessed objectively.

The initial decision as to whether an offence under investigation is a serious arrestable offence will be taken by a superintendent at the police station where a suspect is being held. If necessary, the defence can challenge the decision in court. This may be done, for example, as part of an argument that a confession should not be admitted in evidence (see **Chapter 9**).

In practice, the detailed provisions of the Act must be consulted if there is doubt as to whether an offence is a serious arrestable offence.

2.3   Police powers of detention

A flowchart showing procedure at the police station is included at **Appendix 1(C)**.

2.3.1   Volunteers

A person sometimes attends a police station on a voluntary basis to assist the police with their enquiries. Section 29 of the Act provides that:

> Where for the purposes of assisting with an investigation a person attends
> voluntarily at a police station ... without having been arrested:
> (a)   he shall be entitled to leave at will unless he is placed under arrest;
> (b)   he shall be informed at once that he is under arrest if a decision is taken by a constable to prevent him from leaving at will.

The status of a suspect is likely to change from volunteer to arrested suspect if answers given to police questions give rise to a reasonable suspicion that the detainee may have committed an offence.

2.3.2   Persons under arrest

Where a suspect is arrested at any place other than a police station, he must be taken to a police station by a police officer as soon as practicable after the arrest (s 30) unless he is released on bail to attend a police station at a later date, sometimes referred to as 'street bail' (s 30A).

A person who is arrested and released on 'street bail' must be given a notice in writing stating the offence for which he is arrested, the grounds for his arrest and that he is required to attend a police station. It may also specify the police station that he is required to attend and the time when he is required to attend (s 30B). No other condition may be imposed as a condition of bail.

A person who is arrested and taken to a police station is taken before the custody officer. The custody officer is a police officer of at least the rank of sergeant. The custody officer:

shall determine whether he has before him sufficient evidence to charge that person with the offence for which he was arrested and may detain him at the police station for such period as is necessary to enable him to do so (s 37(1)).

To enable the custody officer to determine whether there is sufficient evidence to charge the arrested person, he will usually speak to the arresting officer. The test to be applied in determining whether there is sufficient evidence to charge is whether there is sufficient evidence to provide a realistic prospect of a conviction (Code C, para 16.1).

In all but the most trivial of offences there is unlikely to be sufficient evidence to charge the suspect at this stage.

> If the custody officer determines that he does not have such evidence before him the person arrested shall be released either on bail or without bail unless the custody officer has reasonable grounds for believing that his detention without being charged is necessary to secure or preserve evidence relating to an offence for which he is under arrest or to obtain such evidence by questioning him (s 37(2)).
>
> If the custody officer has reasonable grounds for so believing he may authorise the person arrested to be kept in police detention (s 37(3)).

A suspect can, therefore, be detained for samples to be taken or while premises are searched. The most common ground for detention without charge is to question the suspect.

The custody officer is required to open and maintain a custody record for each suspect taken to the police station. The grounds for detention without charge must be recorded in the custody record and a chronological record of events occurring during the suspect's period of detention must be kept. An example of a custody record appears at **Appendix 2(A)**.

A legal representative attending the police station to advise a suspect is entitled to inspect the custody record (Code C, para 2.4). A copy of the custody record must be given to the suspect or his legal representative on request when the suspect is taken before a court or upon the suspect's release from police detention.

2.3.3 Periods of detention without charge

The basic detention process can conveniently be illustrated in chart form (see **Appendix 1(D)**).

The following points in particular should be noted.

(a) The basic maximum period of detention without charge is 24 hours. Normally, this runs from the time the arrested person arrives at the police station. If the person went to the police station on a voluntary basis, then time runs from when he is arrested at the police station.

(b) If the offence under investigation is an arrestable offence further detention up to 36 hours on the detention clock can be authorised by a superintendent on certain specified grounds (s 42).

(c) Detention beyond 36 hours can only be authorised by a magistrates' court on the granting of a warrant of further detention. A warrant of further detention is only available if the offence is a serious arrestable offence (s 43). A warrant may initially be granted for a period not exceeding 36 hours but can be extended for further periods until 96 hours have expired on the detention clock. This is the absolute maximum period of detention without charge.

(d) A review of detention must be carried out by an inspector within 6 hours of detention being first authorised and thereafter at 9-hourly intervals. This is to ensure that the initial grounds for detention still exist. Details of the reviews must be recorded in the custody record.

2.3.4 The decision to charge

The CPS is responsible for determining the charge in all but the most routine cases. The police will charge minor or routine cases without reference to the CPS. The Director of Public Prosecutions has issued guidance on what can be charged without reference to the CPS and what must be referred pre-charge to the CPS.

2.3.5 Bail following charge

When a person has been charged with an offence, the custody officer must decide whether to keep that person in custody until his court appearance. Section 38(1) provides that:

> Where a person arrested for an offence ... is charged with an offence, the custody officer shall ... order his release from police detention, either on bail or without bail, unless—
>
> (a)   ...
>> (i)   his name or address cannot be ascertained or the custody officer has reasonable grounds for doubting whether a name or address furnished by him as his name or address is his real name or address;
>> (ii) the custody officer has reasonable grounds for believing that the person arrested will fail to appear in court to answer to bail;
>> (iii) in the case of a person arrested for an imprisonable offence, the custody officer has reasonable grounds for believing that the detention of the person arrested is necessary to prevent him from committing an offence;
>> (iv) in the case of a person arrested for an offence which is not an imprisonable offence, the custody officer has reasonable grounds for believing that the detention of the person arrested is necessary to prevent him from causing physical injury to any other person or from causing loss of or damage to property;
>> (v)   the custody officer has reasonable grounds for believing that the detention of the person arrested is necessary to prevent him from interfering with the administration of justice or with the investigation of offences or of a particular offence; or
>> (vi) the custody officer has reasonable grounds for believing that the detention of the person arrested is necessary for his own protection.'

The custody officer, in deciding whether grounds (ii)–(v) apply, must have regard to the same factors as a court is required to consider when taking a bail decision (see **3.4.3**).

The custody officer has power, when granting bail, to impose the same conditions as a court (with the exception of residence at a bail hostel) (Bail Act 1976, s 3A). A full discussion of conditions of bail and when they may be appropriate can be found at **3.4.3**.

2.3.6 Release without charge on bail

The police may decide that there is insufficient evidence to charge a person with an offence but require him to return to the police station at a later date. This may happen for example, if the police have further enquires to make or where they are waiting for the results of forensic tests or they need to refer the matter to the CPS for a decision on whether or not to charge. In such a case, the person is released on bail with or without conditions (Police and Criminal Evidence Act 1984, s 37). Where a person has been released on bail to return to the police station on a specified date, he may be arrested without a warrant if he fails to attend at the appointed time (Police and Criminal Evidence Act 1984, s 46A).

Section 34 of the Police and Criminal Evidence Act 1984 provides that where a person returns to the police station to answer bail (or is arrested for failing to do so) he is to be regarded as having been arrested for the original offence at that moment. Therefore, the person is in the same position as a person who is being detained without charge and so the rules governing detention without charge set out in **2.3.3** apply.

2.4 The right to legal advice

2.4.1 Volunteers

A person who is attending a police station on a voluntary basis and who is not under arrest has an absolute right to legal advice in private or to communicate with anyone outside the police station at any time (Code C, note 1A). These rights are confirmed in a written notice given to the suspect (see **Appendix 2(B)**).

2.4.2 Persons under arrest → entitled to 2 phone calls.

> Where a person has been arrested and is being held in custody in a police station, or other premises, he shall be entitled, if he requests, to have one friend or relative or other person who is known to him or is likely to take an interest in his welfare told, as soon as practicable ... , that he has been arrested and is being detained there. (s 56(1))
>
> A person arrested and held in custody in a police station or other premises shall be entitled, if he so requests, to consult a solicitor privately at any time. (s 58)

On arrival at the police station, the suspect will be informed by the custody officer of the right to legal advice and that it is free of charge, the right to have someone informed of his arrest and the right to consult the Codes of Practice. These rights are confirmed in a written notice given to the suspect (see **Appendix 2(C)** and **(D)**). The suspect is then asked to sign the custody record to indicate whether or not he wishes to exercise his rights (see the custody record referred to at **2.3.2**). Even if the suspect indicates that he does not want to exercise his rights, he is entitled to change his mind at any time while he is in police detention.

The suspect is entitled to advice in person, in writing or by telephone (Code C, para 6.1) from his own solicitor, if available, or the duty solicitor. Duty solicitor schemes operate throughout most of the country to ensure that a solicitor is available on a 24-hour basis to attend police stations to advise suspects who are being detained. The advice and assistance given is free of charge, irrespective of the suspect's means, and the solicitor attending the police station is paid under contract on a fixed hourly rate by the Legal Services Commission.

2.4.3 Delaying access to legal advice

The right of access to legal advice can be delayed for a period not exceeding 36 hours from the time of the suspect's arrival at the police station if:

(a)   ... a person is in police detention ... for a serious arrestable offence; and

(b)   if an officer of at least the rank of superintendent authorises it. (s 58(6))

A superintendent can authorise the delaying of access to legal advice only if he has reasonable grounds for believing that the exercise of the right:

(a)   will lead to interference with or harm to evidence connected with a serious arrestable offence or interference with or physical injury to other persons; or

(b)   will lead to the alerting of other persons suspected of having committed such an offence but not yet arrested for it; or

(c)   will hinder the recovery of any property obtained as a result of such an offence. (s 58(8))

In effect, a superintendent may lawfully authorise delaying access to legal advice only if he has reasonable grounds to believe that the specific solicitor seeking access will, inadvertently or otherwise, pass on a message from the suspect which will lead to any of the consequences listed above coming about. Even if the superintendent has such grounds, he is required to offer the suspect access to a different solicitor (see Code C, Annex B, para A3).

Access to legal advice cannot be delayed on grounds that:

(a)   the solicitor might advise the suspect not to answer questions (Code C, Annex B, para A4); or

(b)   the solicitor was initially instructed by a third party, provided the suspect wishes to see the solicitor. The suspect must be told that the solicitor has come to the police station and must be asked to sign the custody record to signify whether or not he wishes to see the solicitor (Code C, para 6.15 and Code C, Annex B, para A4).

The statutory right for a suspect to have a friend or relative notified of his arrest can be delayed on similar grounds to those for delayed access to legal advice.

2.5 Interviewing the suspect

2.5.1 What is an interview?

An interview is the questioning of a person regarding his involvement or suspected involvement in a criminal offence or offences which, under paragraph 10.1 must be carried out under caution (Code C, para 11.1A).

Example

A police officer notices a young man standing on a street corner with a large bag. He asks the man what he is doing. The replies are evasive. This will not be an interview. The officer then notices a broken window in the shop on the corner and that the man has fragments of glass on his clothing. Any further questioning will constitute an interview. The significance of this is that the rules on the conduct of interviews must be followed (see 2.5.2–2.8).

Questioning solely to establish identity or ownership of a vehicle, or 'in furtherance of the proper and effective conduct of a search' is not an interview (Code C, para 10.1).

2.5.2 Interview following arrest

Following a decision to arrest a suspect, that suspect must not be interviewed about the relevant offence except at a police station (or other authorised place of detention) unless the consequent delay would be likely to:

(a)   lead to interference with, or harm to, evidence connected with an offence or interference with, or physical harm to, other people; or serious loss of, or damage to, property; or

(b)   lead to the alerting of other persons suspected of having committed such an offence but not yet arrested for it; or

(c)   hinder the recovery of property obtained in consequence of the commission of such an offence (Code C, para 11.1).

2.5.3   Interview after charge

Following charge, no further questions relating to the offence charged may be put unless further questioning is necessary to:

(a)   prevent or minimise harm or loss to some other person or to the public; or

(b)   clear up an ambiguity in a previous answer or statement; or

(c)   give the suspect an opportunity to comment on information concerning the offence which has come to light since he was charged (Code C, para 16.5).

If any statement or interview record involving another person is to be put to the suspect, no reply or comment should be invited (Code C, para 16.4).

2.6   Methods of interview

2.6.1   Tape recording

All interviews at the police station except those concerning purely summary offences should be tape recorded. The purpose of the tape-recording procedures is to provide an impartial and accurate record of police interviews with suspects in the police station (Code E, para 3.1).

Two tapes are used at an interview. When an interview comes to an end, the master tape should be sealed and signed by the suspect or by an interviewing officer. The other tape is the working copy from which a summary of the tape-recorded interview will be prepared by the police (Code E, para 2.2).

A summary of the tape-recorded interview will be sent to the defence. The defence has a right of access to a working copy of the tape and the defence solicitor will often listen to the tape to check the accuracy of the summary prepared by the prosecution.

If the defence agrees that the summary served by the prosecution is acceptable then it will be admissible in evidence at the trial (subject to any argument over the admissibility of any confession that may have been made (see **9.6.2.3**)). See the example of a record of a tape-recorded interview at **Appendix 2(E)**.

If the defence does not agree with the summary then the tape can be transcribed in full for use at the trial. If necessary, the tape can be played at the trial. The tape to be played in court will be the master copy and the seal will be broken in court. It may be necessary to play the tape in court where the manner in which something has been said is relevant; for example, if the admissibility of a confession is being challenged because of the conduct of the police during the interview, the way in which questions have been put may be relevant.

2.6.2   Non-taped interviews

Not all interviews will be tape recorded. A suspect may, on occasions, be interviewed somewhere other than a police station. An interview concerning a purely summary offence may be conducted at a police station off-tape. Any conversation between a police officer and suspect which falls within the definition of an interview and which is not tape recorded is subject to the following rules.

(a)   An accurate record must be made of each interview whether or not the interview takes place at the police station (Code C, para 11.7(a)).

(b)   The record must be made during the course of the interview, unless in the investigating officer's view this would not be practicable or would interfere with the conduct of the interview, and must constitute either a verbatim record of what has been said, or failing this, an account of the interview which adequately and accurately summarises it (Code C, para 11.7(c)). Compiling such a record will usually involve writing down each question and answer during the interview.

(c)   If an interview record is not made during the course of the interview, it must be made as soon as practicable after completion of the interview (Code C, para 11.8).

(d)   Unless it is impracticable, the person interviewed must be given the opportunity to read the interview record and to sign it as correct, or to indicate the respects in which he considers it inaccurate (Code C, para 11.11).

(e)   A record of an interview which has not been taped will be served on the defence. If the interview record has been signed by the defendant or his solicitor then it will be admissible in evidence (subject to the admissibility of any confession that may have been made being challenged (see **9.6.2.3**)). If the record is not signed by the defence then it is not admissible in evidence. Instead, the interviewing officer will give oral evidence of what happened at the interview, using any contemporaneous notes made to refresh his memory (see **9.3.2.2**).

(f)   Rather than be interviewed, a suspect may offer to make a 'written statement under caution'. This is simply a prepared statement setting out the suspect's version of events or a confession. See the example of a statement at **Appendix 2(F)**. Note the caution at the top of the page. There is nothing to prevent the police from asking further questions on the written statement made by the suspect.

2.6.3   Comments outside interview

A written record should also be made of any comments made by a suspected person, including unsolicited comments, which are outside the context of an interview but which might be relevant to the offence. Any such record must be timed and signed by the maker. Where practicable, the person shall be given the opportunity to read that record and to sign it as correct or to indicate the respects in which he considers it inaccurate. Any refusal to sign should be recorded (Code C, para 11.14).

Example

A police officer arrests a suspect on suspicion of an assault occasioning actual bodily harm. On the way to the police station, the suspect says, 'I hit him but I was provoked'. The suspect volunteered this information; it was not in response to any question put by the police officer. Such a statement by the suspect does not constitute an interview. The police officer, on arrival at the police station, should make a record of what the suspect said and the time he said it. He should then sign the record and give the suspect the opportunity to read it and to sign it as correct or to indicate the respects in which he considers it inaccurate.

At the beginning of an interview carried out in a police station, the interviewing officer, after cautioning the suspect, should put to the suspect any significant statement or significant silence which has occurred before the suspect's arrival at the police station. The interviewing officer should ask the suspect whether he confirms or denies that earlier statement or silence, and whether he wishes to add anything. A 'significant' statement or silence is one which appears capable of being used against a suspect (Code C, para 11.4A).

2.7 The right to have a solicitor present at interviews

A detainee who has asked for legal advice may not be interviewed or continue to be interviewed until he has received such legal advice (Code C, para 6.6).

Exceptions to this rule are where:

(a) the right to legal advice can lawfully be delayed (see **2.4.3**); or

(b) a superintendent has reasonable grounds to believe that:

   (i) delay will involve immediate risk of harm to persons or serious loss of, or damage to, property; or

   (ii) a solicitor has agreed to attend but waiting for his arrival would cause unreasonable delay to the process of investigation; or

(c) a nominated solicitor cannot or will not attend and the suspect has declined the duty solicitor or the duty solicitor is unavailable and an inspector has authorised the interview; or

(d) the suspect has changed his mind and agrees in writing or on tape to the commencement of the interview and an inspector has authorised the interview.

In addition, no police officer shall at any time do or say anything with the intention of dissuading a detainee in detention from obtaining legal advice (Code C, para 6.4).

2.8 Safeguards for the suspect

2.8.1 Reminders of the right to legal advice

A suspect must be reminded of the right to free legal advice:

(a) immediately prior to the commencement or recommencement of any interview at a police station;

(b) before a review of detention takes place;

(c) after charge, if a police officer wishes to draw the attention of the suspect to any written or oral statement made by another person;

(d) after charge, if further questions are to be put to a suspect about the offence (see **2.5.3** as to when this is possible);

(e) before an identification parade, group identification or video identification takes place;

(f) before an intimate body sample is requested.

If, on being informed or reminded of the right to legal advice, the suspect declines to speak to a solicitor in person, the suspect should be informed of the right to communicate with a solicitor by telephone.

If a suspect continues to waive his right to legal advice, he should be asked his reasons for doing so. Any reasons should be recorded on the custody record or interview record, as appropriate.

2.8.2 The caution

A caution must be given by a police officer to a suspect in the following terms:

You do not have to say anything. But it may harm your defence if you do not mention when questioned something which you later rely on in court. Anything you do say may be given in evidence (Code C, para 10.5).

A caution is required:

(a)   on or immediately before arrest;

(b)   before an interview;

(c)   following a break in questioning (if there is any doubt as to whether the suspect appreciates that he is still under caution) (Code C, paras 10.1 and 10.8).

2.8.3   Detention conditions

In any period of 24 hours, a detained person must be allowed a continuous period of at least 8 hours' rest. This period should normally be at night (Code C, para 12.2).

Before a detained person is interviewed the custody officer must assess whether he is fit enough to be interviewed. The custody officer must not allow a detained person to be interviewed if the custody officer considers it would cause significant harm to the detained person's physical or mental state (Code C, para 12.3 and Annex G). See also Code C, Annex H.

Interview rooms should be adequately heated, lit and ventilated (Code C, para 12.4).

Persons being questioned or making statements must not be required to stand (Code C, para 12.6).

Breaks in interviewing should be made at recognised meal times (Code C, para 12.8).

Short breaks for refreshments shall be provided at intervals of approximately 2 hours (Code C, para 12.8).

2.8.4   Suspects at risk

2.8.4.1   Juveniles (under 17) (Code C, paras 1.5 and 1.7)

An 'appropriate adult' must be informed that the juvenile has been arrested and should be asked to attend the police station.

An 'appropriate adult' should be the parent or guardian of the juvenile. If the parent or guardian is unsuitable (eg, because he or she is also involved in the offence), a social worker should be called. If a social worker is unavailable, another responsible adult aged 18 or over (who is not a police officer or employed by the police) should be called. A solicitor who is present at the police station in his professional capacity may not act as 'appropriate adult'.

The purpose of the 'appropriate adult' attending is to ensure the presence of an impartial adult to safeguard the rights of the juvenile. The appropriate adult's role, according to Code C, para 11.17, is not merely to act as an observer, but also to advise the juvenile and, if necessary, to 'facilitate communication with him'.

2.8.4.2   Mentally disordered/handicapped suspects (Code C, paras 1.4 and 1.7)

If an officer has any suspicion, or is told in good faith, that a person of any age may be mentally disordered or otherwise mentally vulnerable, in the absence of clear evidence to dispel that suspicion, the person should be treated as such for the purposes of this Code.

An 'appropriate adult' must be informed that the suspect has been arrested and should be asked to attend the police station.

An 'appropriate adult' should be a relative, guardian or other person responsible for the custody of the suspect. Failing this, a specialist social worker should be called. If a social worker is unavailable, another responsible adult aged 18 or over (who is not a police officer or employed by the police) should be called. A solicitor who is present at the police station in his professional capacity may not act as an 'appropriate adult'.

The purpose of the 'appropriate adult' is as for juveniles.

2.9   Tactical considerations

2.9.1   Purpose of solicitor's attendance

The solicitor's only role in the police station is to protect and advance the legal rights of their client (Code C, note 6D).

2.9.2   Record of attendance

A solicitor's presence in the police station makes him a potential witness in the case. It is essential, therefore, that the solicitor makes a contemporaneous record of everything that happens at the police station. This record should include details of initial contact with the custody officer, information given by the investigating officer, advice given to the client and any other matter that seems to be of significance. (See sample form at **Appendix 2(G)**.)

2.9.3   Custody record

On arrival at the police station, a solicitor should speak to the custody officer and ask to inspect the custody record. A solicitor has a right to inspect the custody record as soon as practicable after arrival at the police station (Code C, para 2.4). Matters such as reasons for detention, periods of detention, review periods and details of any interviews should be noted by the solicitor from the custody record.

2.9.4   The investigating officer

After speaking to the custody officer, a solicitor should, wherever possible, speak to the investigating officer about the offence. The investigating officer should be asked what evidence the police have against the suspect. A careful record should be made of information given. If the investigating officer is not forthcoming about the evidence available this is something that should be borne in mind when formulating advice to the client (see **2.9.5**).

2.9.5   Advising the suspect

A suspect held in the police station may be frightened, disorientated and suspicious of anyone who comes to see him. The solicitor should explain to the suspect the role of the solicitor who has been called to see him and, as far as possible, attempt to put him at ease.

The solicitor should take instructions from the suspect (see sample form at **Appendix 2(G)**. The solicitor should then consider the information given to him by the police and his instructions from his client and formulate advice to the client.

2.9.6 Criminal Justice and Public Order Act 1994 – the right to remain silent

Section 34 – failure to mention facts when questioned or charged

> (1) Where in any proceedings against a person for an offence, evidence is given that the accused—
>
>   (a) at any time before he was charged with the offence, on being questioned under caution by a constable trying to discover whether or by whom the offence had been committed, failed to mention any fact relied on in his defence in those proceedings; or
>
>   (b) on being charged with the offence or officially informed that he might be prosecuted for it, failed to mention any such fact,
>
> being a fact which in the circumstances existing at the time the accused could reasonably have been expected to mention when so questioned, charged or informed, as the case may be ...
>
> the court or jury ... may draw such inferences from the failure as appear proper.'

Example 1

Joe is being questioned about a suspected assault. He refuses to answer the questions put by the police. At his trial, Joe raises self-defence. Under s 34, a court may draw inferences from Joe's failure to mention self-defence when being interviewed or when charged.

Example 2

Joanne is being questioned about a suspected theft. She does not answer questions put by the police at interview. At her trial, Joanne raises an alibi defence: she was at home at the time of the theft. Under s 34, a court may draw inferences from Joanne's failure to mention the alibi when being interviewed or when charged.

The following points should be noted about s 34.

(a) The section does not take away the right of a suspect to remain silent. It simply enables a court to draw inferences from silence if facts are raised in court in the defence of the suspect. If a suspect remains silent and does not raise facts in his defence then s 34 has no effect.

(b) The section states that a court may draw inferences from silence. Such inferences are not mandatory and may only be drawn if the magistrates or jury are satisfied that in the circumstances existing at the time of the interview it would have been reasonable to expect the suspect to mention the relevant facts (see 'Advising the client' below for examples of when a court may decide not to draw adverse inferences).

(c) In *R v Argent (Brian)* [1997] 2 Cr App R 27, the Court of Appeal said that before a jury could draw such inferences as appear proper under s 34(1)(a), the following six formal conditions had to be met.

   (i) There had to be proceedings against a person for an offence.

   (ii) The alleged failure had to occur before a defendant was charged.

   (iii) The alleged failure had to occur during questioning under caution by a constable or other person authorised under s 34(4).

   (iv) The questioning had to be directed to trying to discover whether or by whom the alleged offence had been committed.

   (v) The alleged failure by the defendant had to be to mention any fact relied on in his defence in those proceedings.

   (vi) The fact which the defendant failed to mention was a fact which, in the circumstances existing at the time, he could reasonably have been expected to mention when so questioned.

(d)   It was generally thought that the inference which the prosecution seeks to draw from failure to mention facts in interview is that they have been subsequently fabricated. In *R v Randall* [1998] 6 *Archbold News* 1, the Court of Appeal held that s 34 could apply where a defendant had an account to give but did not want it subject to scrutiny. A similar approach was taken in *R v Daniel (Anthony Junior)* [1998] 2 Cr App R 373, where the court held that s 34 was not confined to cases of recent fabrication but was apt to cover 'a reluctance to be subject to questioning and further enquiry' (at 383). The same approach was followed by the Court of Appeal in *R v Beckles and Montague* [1999] Crim LR 148, *R v McGuiness (Cyril)* [1999] Crim LR 318, *R v Taylor* [1999] Crim LR 75 and *R v Mitford* [2001] Crim LR 330.

(e)   In those cases where the judge has ruled that there is no evidence on which a jury could properly conclude that the defendant had failed to mention any fact relied on in his defence, and that therefore no question arises of leaving the possibility of drawing inferences to the jury, the judge should specifically direct the jury that they should not draw any adverse inference from the defendant's silence (*R v McGarry* [1999] 1 Cr App R 377).

(f)   In *Condron and Another v United Kingdom* [2000] Crim LR 679, the European Court of Human Rights held that a trial judge had not properly directed the jury on the issue of the defendants' silence during police interview. As a consequence, the applicants had not received a fair trial within the meaning of art 6 of the European Convention on Human Rights. In the court's opinion, as a matter of fairness, the jury should have been directed that if it was satisfied that the applicants' silence at the police interview could not sensibly be attributed to their having no answer to the police's allegations or none that could stand up to cross-examination, it should not draw an inference. The court considered that a direction to that effect was more than merely 'desirable' as found by the Court of Appeal.

The court noted that the responsibility for deciding whether or not to draw an inference rested with the jury. It was impossible to ascertain what weight, if any, was given to the applicants' silence since a jury did not provide reasons for its decisions.

The court did not accept the government's submission that the fairness of the applicants' trial was secured by the appeal process. The Court of Appeal had no means of ascertaining whether or not the defendants' silence played a significant role in the jury's decision to convict. The Court of Appeal was concerned with the safety of the defendants' conviction, not whether they had received a fair trial. Since the jury was not properly directed, the imperfection in the direction could not be remedied on appeal.

(g)   In *R v Betts and Hall* [2001] EWCA Crim 244, [2001] 2 Cr App R 257, a bare admission at trial of part of the prosecution case was held incapable of constituting a fact for the purposes of s 34. Consequently, the jury was not entitled to draw an adverse inference from the defendant's failure to mention it in interview. The Court of Appeal also confirmed that if a defendant remains silent during the first interview, yet answers questions during the second interview, the jury can still draw inferences from the defendant's failure to answer questions during the first interview.

Section 36 – failure to account for objects, substances or marks → also consequences of not doing so.

(1)   Where:

(a)   a person is arrested by a constable, and there is:

(i)   on his person; or

(ii)   in or on his clothing or footwear; or

(iii)   otherwise in his possession; or

(iv)   in any place in which he is at the time of his arrest, any object, substance or mark, or there is any mark on any such object; and

(b)   that or another constable investigating the case reasonably believes that the presence of the object, substance or mark may be attributable to the participation of the person arrested in the commission of an offence specified by the constable; and

(c)   the constable informs the person arrested that he so believes, and requests him to account for the presence of the object, substance or mark; and

(d)   the person fails or refuses to do so,

then ... the court or jury ... may draw such inferences from the failure or refusal as appear proper.

Example

Fred is arrested on suspicion of assaulting John. On being interviewed, he is asked to account for the fact that on arrest his shirt was covered in blood and he had cut knuckles. Fred does not reply. Under s 36, a court may draw inferences from Fred's failure to account for the bloodstains and cuts.

The following points should be noted about s 36:

(a)   There is a degree of overlap between ss 34 and 36. However, whilst s 34 can only apply if a suspect later raises facts in his defence, s 36 will operate irrespective of any defence put forward. It can apply even if no defence is raised at the trial.

Example

Following a street fight, Joe is arrested nearby. His shirt is badly torn. The police inform Joe that he is suspected of assault at the street fight and ask him to account for his torn shirt. Joe refuses to answer any questions.

If Joe gives evidence at his trial that he was walking home from a night club and tripped up, tearing his shirt, s 34 will apply. Joe did not mention the facts at the interview.

As Joe failed to account for his torn shirt, s 36 will apply irrespective of any defence put forward by Joe.

(b)   As with s 34, the court may draw inferences but there is no obligation to do so (see **2.9.6.2**).

(c)   The section can apply only if the accused has been told, in ordinary language, by the officer requesting the explanation, the effect of failure to comply with the request (s 36(4)). The following points must be brought to the attention of the suspect ('the special warning'):

(i)   what offence is under investigation;

(ii)   what fact the suspect is being asked to account for;

(iii)   that the officer believes this fact may be due to the suspect's taking part in the commission of the offence in question;

(iv)   that a court may draw an inference from failure to comply with the request;

(v)   that a record is being made of the interview and that it may be given in evidence if the suspect is brought to trial (Code C, para 10.11).

Section 37 – failure to account for presence at a particular place

(1)   Where—

(a)   a person arrested by a constable was found by him at a place at or about the time the offence for which he was arrested is alleged to have been committed; and

(b)   that or another constable investigating the offence reasonably believes that the presence of the person at that place and at that time may be attributed to his participation in the commission of the offence; and

(c)   the constable informs the person that he so believes, and requests him to account for that presence; and

(d)   the person fails or refuses to do so,

then ... the court or jury ... may draw such inferences from the failure or refusal as appear proper.

Example

Denis is arrested on suspicion of theft. He is found by a police officer standing close to a shop which has a window broken. Goods are missing from the shop. When questioned about the alleged offence, Denis is asked to account for his presence by the shop window. Denis does not reply. A court may draw inferences from Denis's refusal to account for his presence outside the shop.

The following points should be noted about s 37.

(a)   There is a degree of overlap between ss 34 and 37. However, while s 34 can apply only if a suspect later raises facts in his defence, s 37 will operate irrespective of any defence put forward. It can apply even if no defence is raised at the trial.

Example

Following a burglary, Joan is arrested walking down a passageway close to the scene of the crime. Joan is interviewed by the police who tell her that she is suspected of committing the burglary. Joan is asked to account for her presence in the passageway. She remains silent at the interview.

If, at her trial, Joan explains that she was in the passageway as she was taking a short cut home, s 34 will apply. Joan did not mention the facts at the interview.

As Joan failed to account for her presence in the passageway, s 37 will apply irrespective of any defence put forward by Joan.

(b)   As with s 34, the court may draw inferences but there is no obligation to do so (see **2.9.6.2**).

(c)   As with s 36, this section can apply only if the accused has been told in ordinary language by the officer requesting the explanation, the effect of failure to comply with the request ('the special warning' – see further Code C, para 10.11 above).

2.9.6.1   Points common to ss 34, 36 and 37

The following points apply to ss 34, 36 and 37.

(a)   The sections will normally apply only to interviews at a police station (it is important to remember the general prohibition on interviewing outside a police station (see **2.5.1**)). The suspect will have been cautioned and given the opportunity of taking legal advice.

(b)   By s 38(3), 'a person shall not have the proceedings against him committed to the Crown Court for trial, have a case to answer or be convicted of any offence solely on an inference' drawn under s 34, s 36 or s 37. In other words, the prosecution must always have some other evidence. A defendant cannot be convicted solely because he refused to answer questions.

(c) No inferences can be drawn from silence when a suspect is questioned at a police station while denied access to legal advice (Youth Justice and Criminal Evidence Act 1999, s 58).

This provision brings the law into compliance with the judgment of the European Court of Human Rights in the case of *Murray v United Kingdom (Right to Silence)* (1996) 22 EHRR 29. In this case, the court held that there was a breach of art 6 of the European Convention on Human Rights as a result of denying the applicant access to legal advice in circumstances where inferences could be drawn from his silence during police questioning.

(d) The Judicial Studies Board (JSB) specimen directions on ss 34, 36 and 37 are available on the JSB website (www.jsboard.co.uk).

2.9.6.2 Advising the client

In formulating advice to a client on whether to remain silent, a legal adviser must balance the potential effects of the law against good reasons for not answering questions. If a court finds that there were good reasons for remaining silent then inferences should not be drawn from the exercise of that right. In *R v Roble (Ali Hersi)* [1997] Crim LR 449, the Court of Appeal indicated that good reasons for advising silence might be that the interviewing officer had disclosed little or nothing of the nature of the case against the defendant, so that the legal adviser cannot usefully advise his client, or where the nature of the offence, or the material in the hands of the police is so complex, or relates to matters so long ago, that no immediate response is feasible. In *R v Argent (Brian)* [1997] 2 Cr App R 27, the Court of Appeal stated that a court should not interpret the expression 'in the circumstances' in s 34(1) restrictively. Matters such as the time of day, the suspect's age, experience, mental capacity, state of health, sobriety, tiredness, personality and legal advice were all relevant circumstances.

In particular, a legal adviser at the police station should consider:

(a) The extent of the evidence disclosed by the police. If there is little or no evidence then silence is likely to remain the best advice. All that the suspect is likely to achieve by answering questions is to incriminate himself.

If the police refuse to disclose the evidence available then, normally, a suspect should be advised to remain silent. This is because it is not possible to assess the strength of the case against the suspect and provide proper advice.

(b) The ability of the suspect to deal with an interview. If a suspect is highly emotional, inarticulate or otherwise unfit to deal with an interview then silence is likely to be the best course of action.

(c) Whether there is any other good explanation for remaining silent. For example, a suspect may be afraid of associates or may wish to protect another person.

In *R v Beckles* [2004] EWCA Crim 2766 the Court of Appeal, in a judgment delivered by Lord Woolf CJ, held that in a case where the solicitor's advice was relied upon by the defendant in the police interview, the ultimate question for the jury, under s 34, remained whether the facts relied upon at the trial were facts which the defendant could reasonably have been expected to mention at interview. If the jury considered that the defendant had genuinely relied on the advice, it would not necessarily be the end of the matter. If it was possible to say that the defendant had genuinely acted on the advice but had done so because it suited his purpose that might mean that he had acted unreasonably in mentioning the facts. The jury had to make a determination on his

often used where pre-interview disclosure is incomplete, but more often may be likely where the suspect has an account that will not withstand cross-examination.

2.9.6.9 Handing in the statement on charge

Alternatively, the written statement may be handed in on charge. Handing in the written statement on charge may be useful if the legal adviser believes that the police will not have enough evidence to charge. A written statement given to the police during the interview may give the police sufficient evidence to charge. Thus, the legal adviser may consider advising a no comment interview and submitting the written statement only if the police decide to charge the suspect. Such a course of action avoids inferences under s 34(1)(b) but inferences may still be drawn under s 34(1)(a).

2.9.6.10 Making a confession

If the police evidence appears to be strong and the suspect admits his guilt then there may be advantages in making a confession at the police interview. This can be good mitigation when the suspect is being sentenced, particularly if he implicates others or gives information that leads to the recovery of stolen property.

The Criminal Law Committee of The Law Society has issued guidance to help solicitors decide whether it is in the best interests of their client to answer police questions (see **Appendix 4**).

Whatever advice is given to a client, the final decision as to whether or not to answer police questions is that of the client.

2.9.7 Preparing the suspect for the interview

It is important to explain to a suspect the procedure to be followed at a tape-recorded interview and to warn him about likely police tactics. The following points should be covered:

(a) That the interview will be tape recorded and all parties will be asked to identify themselves on tape.

(b) That the interview can be stopped at any time if the suspect wants further advice.

(c) If the suspect is to remain silent he should be advised to use a stock phrase such as 'No comment'. Most suspects find this easier than remaining in total silence.

(d) Police tactics – a suspect who wishes to remain silent should be warned:

(i) that the police may try to get him to talk by asking apparently innocuous questions;

(ii) that the police may try to alienate him from his solicitor by suggesting that poor advice has been given;

(iii) that the police may make threats such as of arresting members of his family unless he speaks.

The suspect should be advised to ignore any of these tactics and remain silent.

(e) That the legal adviser is present to protect the suspect's interests and will intervene in the interview as and when necessary.

2.9.8 The solicitor's role at an interview

It is important to understand that a solicitor is not at an interview simply as an observer. It may be necessary for the solicitor to intervene to object to improper questioning or to give the client further advice in private. The following points should be noted.

(a) At the start of a tape-recorded interview, a legal adviser should make an opening statement explaining the role he intends to play in the interview. This will leave the police in no doubt about the reason for the adviser's presence. It also gives an opportunity to state the advice given to the client and the reasons for that advice. A suggested form of statement is:

I am ... a solicitor/authorised representative with [firm name]. I am now required to explain my role. My role is to protect my client's rights. I shall continue to advise my client throughout the interview.

I shall intervene in the interview if:

•   my client asks for, or needs legal advice; or

•   your questioning is inappropriate; or

•   you raise matters which are not based on matters that have been made known to me.

After receiving legal advice my client has decided:

[either]

•   to exercise the right to silence [if you consider it appropriate to give a reason] because [reason]. Please respect that decision.

[or]

•   to answer questions which you may raise which are relevant to my client's arrest/voluntary attendance.

(Shepherd, *Police Station Skills for Legal Advisers; a Pocket Reference* (The Law Society, 1997))

(b) A client may need further advice if, for example, matters that the legal adviser was not aware of are raised in the interview. It may also be necessary to give further advice if a client is becoming agitated or uncertain about the conduct of the interview.

(c) Examples of improper questioning include:

(i)   where questions are put in a confusing manner, for example, two or three questions rolled into one;

(ii)   where questions are put in an aggressive or bullying fashion;

(iii) where questions are put which are not based on evidence of which the solicitor is aware. Advice given to the client will have been on the basis of the evidence disclosed to the solicitor. If evidence has been held back it may be necessary to take further instructions.

(d) The police sometimes threaten to exclude legal advisers who have intervened in an interview. It is therefore important to be familiar with the provisions of the Code of Practice in this area:

The solicitor may intervene in order to seek clarification or to challenge an improper question to their client or the manner in which it is put, advise their client not to reply to particular questions, or if they wish to give their client further legal advice. (Code C, note 6D)

The Code further provides that an adviser may be excluded only:

> ... if the solicitor's approach or conduct prevents or unreasonably obstructs proper questions being put to the suspect or the suspect's response being recorded. Examples of unacceptable conduct include answering questions on a suspect's behalf or providing written replies for the suspect to quote. (Code C, note 6D)

An investigating officer has no power to exclude a legal adviser from an interview. The investigating officer must:

> ... stop the interview and consult an officer not below the rank of superintendent. ... After speaking to the solicitor, the officer consulted will decide if the interview should continue in the presence of that solicitor. (Code C, para 6.10)

(e)   If a suspect, against advice, breaks his silence during the interview and begins to answer questions, it is permissible for a legal adviser to remind the suspect of his earlier advice to remain silent. It is also possible to stop the interview to remind the client of the earlier advice. However, continuous interruptions for this purpose would constitute misconduct which could lead to the adviser being excluded from the interview.

(f)   The police may seek to dictate the seating positions of parties at an interview:

> The solicitor should be positioned in such a way that there can be no natural eye contact between him and the suspect, nor should he be in a position where he can easily catch the eye of the main interviewer. This makes it much more difficult for him to support the suspect non-verbally and, because he cannot have eye contact with the main interviewer, it is more difficult for him to interject and interrupt the interview verbally.
>
> (John Walkley, *Police Interrogation* (Police Review Publishing Co Ltd, 1987))

Needless to say, any attempt to do this should be resisted. It is important for a legal adviser to be seated in a position whereby he has eye contact with his client and is properly able to advise him.

2.10   Identification

2.10.1   Finding a suspect

Where a witness has seen an offence being committed, that witness may be able to give a description of the culprit to the police. The Code of Practice on Identification Procedures (Code D) prescribes two possible courses of action:

(a)   A police officer may take a witness to a particular neighbourhood or place to see whether he can identify the person whom he said he saw on the relevant occasion (Code D, para 3.2).

(b)   A witness may be shown photographs, computerised or artist's composite likeness or similar likeness or pictures (including 'E-fit' images) (Code D, para 3.3 and Annex E). Any identification from photographs will not normally be admissible in evidence.

2.10.2   Cases where the suspect is known

In a case that involves disputed identification evidence the following identification procedures may be used:

(1)   video identification;

(2)   identification parade;

(3)   group identification;

(4)   confrontation.

All four identification methods must be organised by an officer of at least inspector rank (the identification officer). No officer involved with the investigation of the case may take part (Code D, para 3.11).

The purpose of any method of identification is to test the reliability of an eye-witness who saw someone committing an offence and to obtain admissible evidence of identification for use in court.

2.10.3   Circumstances on which an identification procedure must be held

Whenever a suspect disputes an identification made or purported to be made by a witness, an identification procedure shall be held if practicable. Such a procedure may also be held if the officer in charge of the investigation considers that it would be useful (Code D, para 3.13).

An identification procedure need not be held if, in all the circumstances, it would serve no useful purpose in proving or disproving whether the suspect committed the offence. For example, where the suspect is already known to the witness who saw the suspect commit the crime (see *R v Harris* [2003] EWCA Crim 174) or where there is no reasonable possibility that the witness would be able to make an identification (Code D, para 3.12).

2.10.4   Selecting an identification procedure

The officer in charge of the case has a free choice between a video identification or an identification parade.

A group identification may be offered initially if the officer in the case considers that it would be more satisfactory than a video identification or identification parade and the identification officer considers it practicable to arrange. Otherwise it should only be offered if a video identification or identification parade are refused or considered impracticable.

If none of these methods are practicable then the identification officer has discretion to make arrangements for a covert video identification or covert group identification to take place. A confrontation is the last resort (Code D, paras 3.21–3.24).

2.10.5   Video identification

A video identification is where the witness is shown moving images of the suspect together with similar images of other people who resemble the suspect.

The suspect should be asked for his consent to a video identification. However, where such consent is refused, the identification officer has a discretion to proceed with a covert video identification.

If a video identification is to be used, a video should be made of the suspect and at least eight other persons of similar age, height, general appearance and position in life (Code D, Annex A, para 2).

The participants should all be videoed in the same positions and carrying out the same activity under identical conditions (Code D, Annex A, para 3).

Only one witness may see the video at a time. The video may be frozen and there is no limit on the number of times that a witness may see the video (Code D, Annex A, para 11).

2.10.6 Identification parade

An identification parade is where the witness sees the suspect in a line of other people who resemble the suspect.

The parade must consist of at least eight persons in addition to the suspect who so far as possible, resemble the suspect in age, height, general appearance and position in life (Code D, Annex B, para 9).

Witnesses must be properly segregated both before and after the parade and the person conducting a witness to a parade must not discuss with him the composition of the parade and, in particular, must not disclose whether a previous witness has made any identification (Code D, Annex B, para 15).

2.10.7 Group identification

A group identification is where the witness sees the suspect in an informal group of people.

The suspect should be asked for his consent to a group identification. However, where consent is refused, the identification officer has a discretion to proceed with a covert group identification if it is practicable to do so (Code D, Annex C, para 2).

There is no set format for a group identification. A group identification may be arranged, for example, in a room of people, a railway station, a bus station, or a shopping parade. The suspect may be asked to stand anywhere in a group or to walk through a busy shopping area. The witness will be asked whether or not he saw the person he thinks committed the offence.

2.10.8 Confrontation

If no group identification, identification parade or video identification procedure is possible the witness may confront the suspect. The consent of the suspect is not required.

A confrontation involves taking the witness to the suspect and asking whether the suspect is the person in question.

Confrontation must take place in the presence of the suspect's solicitor or friend unless this would cause unreasonable delay (Code D, Annex D, para 4).

A confrontation is only to take place if none of the other procedures are practicable. It should be a last resort (Code D, para 3.23).

2.10.9 Notice to suspect

Before a video identification, identification parade or group identification, the identification officer must explain a number of things to the suspect, including:

(a) that he is entitled to free legal advice and is entitled to have a solicitor or friend present;

(b) that he does not have to take part but his refusal may be given in evidence and the police may proceed covertly without his consent or arrange a confrontation identification;

(c) that he or his solicitor will be provided with details of the description as first given by any witnesses that are to take part in an identification procedure;

(d) whether the witnesses have been shown photographs or other pictures.

This information must also be contained in a written notice that must be handed to the suspect (Code D, para 3.18).

2.10.10 Identification record

The identification officer must make a record of the video identification, identification parade, group identification or confrontation on forms provided for the purpose.

2.10.11 Tactical considerations

A suspect may wish to be advised as to whether or not it is in his best interests to agree to take part in a video identification or an identification parade. It will normally be in his best interests to do so. A refusal can lead to one of the other methods of identification being used. If the police decide that a video identification or an identification parade or group identification is not practicable then a confrontation may take place. A confrontation is the least satisfactory method of identification as it involves a witness being asked whether the suspect is the person who was seen at the relevant time. Refusal to take part in an identification procedure may be given in evidence at any subsequent trial.

A solicitor attending the police station is entitled to be given details of the description of a suspect as first given by a potential witness. The police are obliged to keep a record of this description (Code D, para 3.1).

A solicitor attending a video identification must be given a reasonable opportunity to see the complete set of images before it is shown to any witness. A suspect can object to any of the images or any of the participants (Code D, Annex A, para 7). Similarly a suspect can object to the composition of the parade (Code D, Annex B, para 12). Relevant considerations will include whether the participants satisfy the requirements as to age, height, appearance and position in life. Bear in mind that too many objections may force the police into using an alternative method of identification.

All relevant matters should be recorded and the solicitor and suspect will be given an opportunity to comment on any relevant matter that occurred during the course of the parade. The identification officer will record any comments made.

2.11 Evidential considerations

2.11.1 Challenging inferences from silence

In the Crown Court, any arguments over the admissibility of the defendant's silence when being interviewed will take place in the absence of the jury.

The defence may seek to argue that evidence of the defendant's silence should not go before the jury because of a breach of the Codes of Practice such as a failure to caution the defendant. Such a breach will not automatically render the evidence inadmissible but will be a relevant factor for the court to consider.

If a judge rules that evidence of the silence is inadmissible the jury will not hear the evidence. If the evidence is ruled admissible then the judge will direct the jury on the inferences that they are entitled to draw. It will be for the jury to decide whether or not actually to draw the inferences.

In a magistrates' court, it will be for the magistrates to rule on the admissibility of a defendant's silence and to decide whether or not to draw inferences.

2.11.2 Confessions and identification evidence

Evidence of a confession and the outcome of an identification parade, group identification, video identification or confrontation will usually be admissible in evidence.

A breach of the Codes of Practice will not automatically render any evidence obtained inadmissible. However, a breach may be relevant to a challenge by the defence at the trial to the admissibility of evidence such as an identification parade or a confession (see **9.2.5** and **9.6.2.3**).

2.12 Samples

2.12.1 Intimate samples (s 62)

Intimate body samples are samples of blood, semen or any tissue, fluid, urine or pubic hair, a dental impression, or a swab taken from a person's body orifice other than the mouth.

An intimate sample may be taken:

(a)   if the suspect consents; and

(b)   if a superintendent authorises the taking of the sample on the basis that the offence under investigation is a recordable offence and that samples will tend to confirm or disprove the suspect's involvement in the offence.

A recordable offence includes an offence punishable by imprisonment.

If a suspect refuses to consent to the taking of an intimate sample then inferences can be drawn from that refusal. A refusal of consent is also capable of amounting to corroboration of any evidence against the person in relation to which the refusal is material.

Example
John is being questioned about a rape. He denies having intercourse with the victim and refuses to give a sample of semen. This refusal is capable of corroborating the evidence of the victim that intercourse took place.

2.12.2 Non-intimate samples (s 63)

Non-intimate body samples include samples of hair, saliva and samples taken from fingernails or toenails.

The consent of a suspect is not required provided a superintendent's authority is given (the grounds are the same as for intimate samples).

A non-intimate sample can also be taken from a person without consent if he has been convicted of a recordable offence or if he is in police detention following arrest for a recordable offence and he has not had a non-intimate sample of the same type and from the same part of his body taken in the course of the investigation of the offence. If a sample had been taken but proved insufficient a further sample can be taken

2.13 Alternatives to prosecution

2.13.1 Formal cautioning

Instead of prosecuting, the police or the CPS may decide to issue a formal caution. A caution can only be used for adults as there is a system of reprimands and warnings introduced for juveniles under the Crime and Disorder Act 1998. A caution is usually administered in the police station by an officer of the rank of inspector or above. Although a caution does not constitute a conviction, records are kept of them for at least five years and they may be cited in court as evidence of the defendant's character should he subsequently be convicted of an offence. Cautioning practice is governed by a Home Office Circular 18/1994 which incorporates revised National Standards for Cautioning.

The major conditions for issuing a caution are that the evidence is strong enough to justify a prosecution and the offender must admit the offence. Where these conditions are satisfied, consideration should then be given as to whether a caution is in the public interest. In deciding whether a caution is in the public interest the following factors should be considered:

(a)   The public interest principles in the Code for Crown Prosecutors should be taken into account.

(b)   Cautions should not be used for indictable only offences, other than in the most exceptional circumstances.

(c)   Other offences may be too serious for a caution. In deciding this, the harm resulting from the offence, whether it was racially motivated, whether it involved a breach of trust and whether it was carried out in an organised way are all relevant factors.

(d)   The victim's view of the offence and whether a caution is appropriate should be sought but is not conclusive.

(e)   Only where the subsequent offence is trivial or where there has been a sufficient lapse of time since the first caution to suggest that it had some affect should an offender be cautioned for a second time.

(f)   There should be a presumption in favour of cautioning rather than prosecuting certain categories of offender, for example, the elderly and those who suffer from mental illness or impairment or a severe physical illness.

(g)   The offender's attitude to the offence must be considered.

(h)   If the offence was carried out by a group, each offender must be separately considered.

2.13.2 Conditional cautioning

The Criminal Justice Act 2003 (ss 22–27) gives the CPS the power to impose a conditional caution. Under a conditional caution, conditions may be attached to the caution for facilitating rehabilitation or reparation for the offence. A conditional caution may be given to an offender who is 18 or over provided each of the five requirements in s 23 of the Act are satisfied:

(a)   there is evidence that the offender has committed the offence;

(b)   there is sufficient evidence to charge the offender with the offence, however, it is decided that a conditional caution should be given instead;

(c)   the offender admits the offence;

(d)   the effect of the conditional caution is explained to the offender and the offender is warned that failure to comply with any of the conditions attached to the caution may result in prosecution for the offence;

(e)   the offender signs a document containing;

(i)   details of the offence;

(ii)   an admission that he committed the offence;

(iii) his consent to the conditional caution;

(iv) the conditions attached to the caution.

If the offender fails, without reasonable excuse, to comply with any of the conditions attached to the conditional caution then criminal proceedings may be instituted against the offender for the offence in question.

There is a Code of Practice governing the detailed operation of the scheme.

2.13.3 Oral warning

The police may in some cases issue an oral warning (sometimes referred to as 'an informal caution'). Such a warning has no official status and may not be cited in subsequent court proceedings.

2.14 Further reading

See, for example:

Ed Cape with Jawaid Luqmani, *Defending Suspects at Police Stations* (Legal Action Group, 2003)

Andrew Keogh, *CLSA Duty Solicitors' Handbook* (The Law Society, 2002)

Chapter 3

Commencement of Criminal Proceedings

3.1 Preliminary considerations

3.1.1 Time-limits

In this chapter, section numbers refer to the Magistrates' Courts Act 1980 unless otherwise indicated.

If the offence to be prosecuted is a summary offence, a magistrates' court cannot deal with the prosecution if the information is laid more than six months after the alleged offence was committed (s 127). An information is laid when it is received at the court office by an authorised officer (see **3.2.2**).

For most indictable offences (including offences triable either way) there are no statutory time-limits for commencing criminal proceedings. It should be noted, however, that a defendant has a common law right to be protected from undue delay. Courts have a discretion to dismiss proceedings which constitute an abuse of process of the court. The defendant would have to show either substantial delay in bringing the prosecution which cannot be justified, or bad faith on the part of the prosecution. In practice, both are very difficult to establish.

3.1.2 The Road Traffic Offenders Act 1988 (as amended by the Road Traffic Act 1991)

Subject to section 2 of this Act a person shall not be convicted of an offence to which this section applies unless—

(a) he was warned at the time the offence was committed that the question of prosecuting him for some one or other of the offences to which this section applies would be taken into consideration, or

(b) within 14 days of the commission of the offence a summons for the offence was served on him, or

(c) within 14 days of the commission of the offence a notice of the intended prosecution specifying the nature of the alleged offence and time and place where it is alleged to have been committed was ...

served on him or on the person, if any, registered as the keeper of the vehicle at the time of the commission of the offence. (s 1(1))

The requirement of section 1(a) of this Act does not apply in relation to an offence if, at the time of the offence or immediately after it, an accident occurs owing to the presence on a road of the vehicle in respect of which the offence was committed. (2(1))

The offences to which these sections apply include dangerous driving and careless driving.

3.2 Commencing the prosecution

The prosecution usually begins in one of two ways: by charge or by summons. A flowchart summarising the two ways in which criminal proceedings may be commenced is included at **Appendix 1(E)**.

Section 29 of the Criminal Justice Act 2003 will introduce a new method of commencing proceedings: 'written charge' and 'requisition'. Once this section is in force public prosecutors will have no power to apply for a summons.

3.2.1 Charge

Having been arrested, the defendant will be taken to a police station, charged and either released on bail to appear before the next available magistrates' court sitting (Police and Criminal Evidence Act 1984, s 47(3A)) or kept in police custody and taken before a magistrates' court 'as soon as practicable' (Police and Criminal Evidence Act 1984, s 46(2)). An example of a charge sheet appears at **Appendix 2(H)**.

Following charge, the CPS lawyer in the police station will review the police file and determine which one of the following hearings will be necessary.

3.2.1.1 Defendant charged with a summary offence or an offence triable either way

Bailed to attend court

Early first hearing (EFH)

This hearing is where the defendant is likely to enter a 'simple guilty plea'. A 'simple guilty plea' is where the defendant admits all the elements of the offence, or the offence is witnessed by the police and there is no indication that the defendant intends to deny it. In addition, the offence must involve no complex issues, meaning that there must be no more that two defendants or three key witnesses.

The CPS lawyer will prepare an abbreviated file which will be disclosed to the solicitor representing the defendant at court. The file must contain the charge sheet and key witness statements.

If the court is informed that a case is likely to be a 'simple guilty plea' it will list it before a full bench so that the defendant can be sentenced that day or the case can be adjourned for the court to obtain a pre-sentence report. The prosecution will usually be represented by a designated case worker, a non-legally qualified CPS representative.

Early administrative hearing (EAH)

If the case is not likely to be a 'simple guilty plea' the defendant's first appearance before a magistrates' court may take the form of an early administrative hearing (EAH) (Crime and Disorder Act 1998, s 50). An EAH may occur when the plea is not known, a not guilty plea is expected, or guilty pleas are expected but the case is not one that can be classified as a 'simple guilty plea'. The prosecution will usually be represented by a CPS lawyer.

The main purpose of the EAH is to enable arrangements to be made for the defendant to obtain representation and to consult a solicitor. Sometimes it may be possible at the EAH for the pleas to be entered, and if the defendant enters a not guilty plea a trial date will be set. If that is not possible, the case will be adjourned for a pre-trial review (PTR) (see **8.4.2**).

At the EAH, the case will be adjourned. A single justice may remand the defendant on bail or in custody. A justices' clerk cannot remand the defendant in custody.

Detained to attend court

The defendant will be kept in custody and taken before a magistrates' court 'as soon as practicable'. The magistrates, at a remand hearing, will decide how the case is to proceed.

3.2.1.2 Defendant charged with an indictable only offence

The first hearing for an indictable only offence will take the form of a preliminary hearing (see **6.7.2**).

3.2.2 Summons

For less serious offences (which may not involve an arrest at all, for example, careless driving), the prosecution will lay an information. This involves informing a magistrate or magistrates' clerk of the alleged offence with a request for a summons to be issued. Normally an information will be in writing and must specify one offence only. An information which alleges more than one offence is bad for duplicity. An example would be an information alleging that D assaulted A on 15 October and B on 15 October. Assuming that the assaults were two separate acts, two informations are required. This is an important rule as once the trial has commenced there is no power to amend the information to cure the defect. In practice, arguments over duplicity on informations are often complex and the detail involved is beyond the scope of this book.

Following the laying of an information, the magistrate or the magistrates' clerk will issue a summons. A single summons may cover more than one information. The summons will usually be served by posting it to the defendant's last-known or usual address. An example of a summons and certificate of service appears at **Appendix 2(I)**.

3.3 Financing the defence – Criminal Defence Service

Only firms who have a contract with the Legal Services Commission (or public defenders) are able to undertake Criminal Defence Service work funded by the Legal Services Commission.

Criminal Defence Service work falls into two categories:

(a)   advice and assistance; and

(b)   representation orders.

3.3.1 Advice and assistance

The law relating to advice and assistance is to be found in the Access to Justice Act 1999, s 13 and the Criminal Defence Service (General) (No 2) Regulations 2001, regs 5 and 6.

A solicitor will claim under this part of the contract with the Legal Services Commission if he is advising a suspect at the police station, appearing as a duty solicitor at court or representing a suspect in an application for a warrant of further detention or for an extension of such a warrant. Such advice and assistance (including advocacy assistance) is non-means tested.

Solicitors are remunerated for advice and assistance by a fixed hourly rate paid by the Legal Services Commission. There is an upper financial limit on the amount that can be claimed. The upper financial limit can be extended on application to the Legal Services Commission. In general authority to extend the upper limit may only be granted where the work carried out to date and the further work proposed is reasonable. If an extension is refused there is a right of review to the Funding Review Committee of the Legal Services Commission Regional Office.

A claim for payment should be made on the prescribed form and submitted to the Legal Services Commission Regional Office.

3.3.2   Representation orders

Representation in court in a criminal case is normally financed by a representation order.

The law relating to representation orders is largely to be found in the Access to Justice Act 1999, s 14 and the Criminal Defence Service (General) (No 2) Regulations 2001 (SI 2001/1437).

A representation order is available to cover representation in a magistrates' court, the Crown Court, the High Court, the Court of Appeal and the House of Lords.

> Any question as to whether a right to representation should be granted shall be determined according to the interests of justice. (Access to Justice Act 1999, Sch 3, para 5(1))

There is no means test. The Government has, however, announced its intention to re-introduce a means test for magistrates' court proceedings.

3.3.2.1   The interests of justice test

The factors to be taken into account in determining whether it is in the interests of justice for representation to be granted are contained in the Access to Justice Act 1999, Sch 3, para 5(2). They are:

> Whether the individual would, if any matter arising in the proceedings is decided against him, be likely to lose his liberty or livelihood or suffer serious damage to his reputation, (para 5(2)(a)

Loss of liberty may, for example, be apparent from the nature and seriousness of the offence. Loss of livelihood will be relevant, for example, where on conviction the applicant will lose his job. Serious damage to reputation will include a person of previous good character who is charged with a criminal offence involving something like dishonesty or violence.

> Whether the determination of any matter in the proceedings may involve consideration of a substantial question of law, para 5(2)(b)

A substantial question of law will include difficult points of substantive criminal law connected with the offence charged. It may also include points of evidence such as the admissibility of a confession or consideration of the rules relating to cases involving disputed identification evidence.

> whether the individual may be unable to understand the proceedings or to state his own case, (para 5(2)(c)
>
> whether the proceedings may involve the tracing, interviewing or expert cross-examination of witnesses on behalf of the individual, para 5(2)(d).

Expert cross-examination of a prosecution witness will include cross-examination of identification witnesses, cross-examination of police officers as to what happened at a police station and generally any cross-examination that requires an element of legal knowledge.

Whether it is in the interests of another person that the individual be represented (para 5(2)(e))

A defendant is prohibited from personally cross-examining certain witnesses (see **9.3.2**). In such cases, it is likely that the court will determine that it is in the interests of justice for representation to be granted.

3.3.2.2 Guidelines

In 2001 the Lord Chancellor's Department issued guidelines (Guidance to Courts from the Lord Chancellor's Department – Interests of Justice Test) with the intention of effecting greater consistency of approach when considering the interests of justice test. The guidelines do not replace the statutory criteria set out above but should be used as an aid to their application.

The guidelines include the following.

The Schedule 3 criteria

The Sch 3 criteria are not exhaustive. For example, the fact that a community punishment order is a possibility may be a relevant factor.

Deprivation of liberty

(a)   Reference should be made to the Magistrates' Association Sentencing Guidelines (see **Appendix 3**) which provide examples of aggravating factors and mitigating factors for various types of offence. These will assist in deciding whether there is a real and practical risk of loss of liberty.

(b)   Conviction should be assumed.

(c)   Representation should normally be granted upon a committal to the Crown Court for sentence.

Loss of livelihood

(a)   This should be a direct consequence of the conviction or sentence.

(b)   This will normally refer to current livelihood.

(c)   'Assertions that disqualification from driving will result in a loss of livelihood should be examined critically ... Though a grant could be justified in exceptional circumstances (eg, if the applicant could show that the disqualification would result in a real risk of dismissal), representation would not usually be justified where the accused sought to avoid a "totting up" disqualification, having acquired twelve or more penalty points.'

Serious damage to reputation

(a)   'This would relate to those cases in which the offence, or the offender's circumstances, are such that the disgrace of conviction, or consequent damage to the applicant's standing, would greatly exceed the direct effect of the penalty which might be imposed.'

(b)   'Reputation, for these purposes, is a question of good character, including honesty and trustworthiness.'

(c)   'The loss of reputation on a conviction for dishonesty is absolute and not relevant to the amount.'

(d)   'Consideration should be given to whether an accused who is undertaking vocational or professional training might suffer damage to reputation so serious that there is a risk that future livelihood might be lost.'

Substantial question of law

'Representation should only be granted under this criterion if a question of law is raised which the applicant cannot be expected to deal with unaided and is a substantial question and is relevant to the applicant's case.'

Tracing and interviewing witnesses

'Details of the witnesses and why there is a necessity for representation to trace and/or interview them, should be included in the application. If details of witnesses are not included, consideration of the application for representation should be deferred until the applicant has provided the court with sufficient information to make a determination.'

Expert cross-examination of a prosecution witness

(a)   This 'refers to expert cross-examination of a witness and not only to cross-examination of an expert witness'.

(b)   'Representation should be granted ... when there is a need for professional cross-examination of a witness. This may very likely be the case where the evidence is provided by an expert since an accused person would rarely be capable, for example, of cross-examining a medical or handwriting expert. It may also apply in other cases, such as those where shades of emphasis in the evidence can make an action appear more sinister than it was in fact.'

3.3.2.3   Where to apply for representation

If a case is before a magistrates' court, any application for a representation order should be made to that court.

A magistrates' court which sends a person to the Crown Court for trial or commits a person to the Crown Court for trial or sentence or from which a person appeals to the Crown Court against his conviction or sentence may grant a representation order for the proceedings before the Crown Court (Criminal Defence Service (General) (No 2) Regulations 2001, reg 9).

The Crown Court may grant a representation order for any case that has been sent for trial or has been committed or appealed to it.

3.3.2.4   'Through representation orders'

If the case is going to be sent to the Crown Court for trial under s 51 of the Crime and Disorder Act 1998 (see **6.7**), a solicitor should apply for a 'through representation order' which will enable the solicitor to claim for work done that is relevant to proceedings before a magistrates' court and the Crown Court.

3.3.2.5   How to apply for representation

An application for a representation order in respect of proceedings in a magistrates' court may be made orally or in writing to the justices' clerk (Criminal Defence Service (General) (No 2) Regulations 2001, reg 8).

The more common method of application is in writing using Form A (**Appendix 2(J)**). Particular care should be taken in completing the section of the application form dealing with the 'interests of justice test'. As much information as possible should be given to convince the court that a representation order should be granted to the applicant.

3.3.2.6   The scope of a representation order

If a representation order is granted, a certificate will be issued to the solicitor. An example of a representation order appears at **Appendix 2(K)**.

The following points should be noted in relation to the scope of the certificate.

(a)   Representation orders covering proceedings in a magistrates' court or the Crown Court extend not merely to preparation and representation but also to advice on, and assistance in, preparing a notice of appeal. A separate representation order is necessary, however, for the conduct of the appeal itself.

(b)   A representation order in the magistrates' court will normally consist of representation by solicitor only. Where there is more than one defendant, the same solicitor will act for all defendants unless there is a conflict of interest. If there is a conflict, separate representation is permitted.

(c)   In a magistrates' court, representation by both solicitor and advocate (barrister or solicitor with higher rights of audience) is permitted if the offence is an indictable offence which is unusually grave or difficult and, in the opinion of the court it is desirable to have representation by solicitor and advocate.

(d)   In a magistrates' court, where the order does not provide for representation by an advocate, the solicitor can still instruct an advocate to conduct the proceedings in court. However, the solicitor will not be paid for dictating and delivering the brief to an advocate and no payment will be made for accompanying an advocate in court.

(e)   Representation in the Crown Court normally consists of representation by a solicitor and advocate. For guidance on when an advocate need be attended by a solicitor's representative at the Crown Court, see Solicitor's Professional Conduct Rule 20.04. The principles contained in Rule 20.04 match the provisions restricting the circumstances in which remuneration can be paid for attendance at the Crown Court.

(f)   Representation orders are not generally retrospective. However, pre-order work may be claimed under a representation order (once granted) provided certain conditions are met.

3.3.2.7   Refusal of representation

An applicant who is refused representation can always make another application to the court (Criminal Defence Service (Representation Order Appeals) Regulations 2001 (SI 2001/1168)).

Where an application for a representation order is made and is refused, a claim for payment can still be made by the solicitor under the advice and assistance part of the contract with the Legal Services Commission. However, such a claim is restricted to a maximum of one hour's work. This work could include, for example, advising on whether an application for a representation order is likely to be successful, completing an application for a representation order and, if necessary, advocacy at an early hearing.

3.3.2.8   Payment of fees under a representation order

Work carried out in a magistrates' court under a representation order is remunerated by a standard fee in most cases. At the conclusion of the case, a claim for payment should be made on the prescribed form and submitted to the Legal Services Commission Regional Office.

Certain complex cases are outside the standard fee scheme and are remunerated at fixed hourly rates on a 'work done basis'.

Work done in the Crown Court is in some cases remunerated by the payment of standard fees. In other cases, payment is on a 'work done basis' although fixed hourly rates are prescribed. A claim for payment should be made to the Crown Court Taxing Office.

3.3.3 Court duty solicitors

The court duty solicitor scheme aims to provide an emergency service to those appearing in a magistrates' court who would otherwise be unrepresented. Representation is available on that day only, is free of charge and is restricted to advising those who are in custody and those who are charged with imprisonable offences. A duty solicitor will apply for adjournments, make bail applications and present pleas in mitigation. The regulations do not permit a duty solicitor to conduct the trial of a not guilty plea or committal proceedings.

The court duty solicitor scheme is staffed by contracted solicitors on a rota basis. Remuneration is provided from the Legal Services Commission at fixed hourly rates for advice and assistance (including advocacy assistance). Subject to checking that the client does not want any other solicitor to handle the case and explaining that the client may choose any solicitor to act or a public defender, it is permissible, and indeed usual, for the duty solicitor to agree to take over the conduct of cases that will proceed further. Further work must be financed privately or under a representation order.

3.3.4 Further reading

The *Legal Services Commission Manual* (Sweet & Maxwell) is the standard reference work for publicly funded criminal work. See also Ede and Edwards, *Criminal Defence* (The Law Society, 2002).

3.4 Adjournments, remands and bail

3.4.1 Adjournments

Magistrates may adjourn a case at any time.

Common reasons for adjournments include:

(a)   to enable the prosecution or defence to prepare their case. Examples include enabling the prosecution to receive a full file from the police or for the defence to be provided with advance disclosure of the prosecution case;

(b)   to fix a date for committal proceedings or trial;

(c)   to obtain reports to assist the court in sentencing.

3.4.2 Remands → hold in custody until next crt hearing

When a court adjourns a case, it will also consider whether or not to remand the defendant. If the case is adjourned without a remand, the court has not taken any steps to ensure that the defendant attends the next hearing. A remand is an adjournment upon which the court decides to attempt to ensure the defendant's attendance at the next hearing.

A remand may be in custody until the adjourned hearing date or on bail. Magistrates may remand the defendant in any case. Unless the offence is very trivial (eg, careless driving), the defendant is likely to be remanded on an adjournment.

3.4.2.1 Individual duration of remands

Before conviction or committal for trial

The general rule is that a defendant may not be remanded in custody for more than eight clear days at a time. Where the defendant is remanded on bail, subject to his consent, there is no time-limit (Magistrates' Courts Act 1980, s 128).

Where there are successive remands in custody, a defendant need only be brought before the court on every fourth remand, provided he has consented (and such consent has not been withdrawn) and has a solicitor acting for him (whether present in court or not) (Magistrates' Courts Act 1980, s 128(3A)).

Further, a court has power under s 128A to remand a defendant in custody for up to 28 days if it has previously remanded him in custody for the same offence, he is before the court, and it can set a date to remand him to on which it expects the next stage of the proceedings to take place (this may be within the 28-day remand period).

After conviction

After conviction by magistrates, adjournments may be for successive periods of four weeks unless the defendant is remanded in custody, in which case the maximum period is three weeks (s 10(3)).

Following committal to the Crown Court

If a defendant is committed to the Crown Court for trial or sentence, he is remanded on bail or in custody until the case is due to be heard.

3.4.2.2 Time-limits

Under the Prosecution of Offences Act 1985, s 22(1), the Home Secretary has the power to make regulations which lay down time-limits for the prosecution to complete any stage in criminal proceedings and the maximum overall period that a defendant may be remanded in custody.

The Prosecution of Offences (Custody Time Limits) Regulations 1987 (SI 1987/2299) lay down maximum overall periods for which a defendant can be remanded in custody awaiting completion of a particular stage in the proceedings.

The maximum overall periods of remand in custody at the magistrates' court are:

(a) 70 days before summary trial (56 days for a summary offence) unless the decision for summary trial is taken within 56 days, in which case the limit is reduced to 56 days;

(b) 70 days before committal proceedings (regs 4(2) and 4(4)).

When the time-limits have expired, the defendant must be released on bail unless the court considers it reasonable to extend the period.

Example 1

Sarah appears before the magistrates for the first time charged with a complicated theft. She is remanded in custody for 7 days. At the next hearing, Sarah is remanded in custody for a further 28 days, after which plea before venue and mode of trial are to take place. Twenty-eight days later, Sarah is back before the court. She indicates a not guilty plea, the magistrates accept jurisdiction and Sarah enters a not guilty plea. The case is adjourned for 7 days for a pre-trial review and Sarah is remanded in custody. At the pre-trial review, a not guilty hearing date is set for 14 days' time and Sarah is remanded in custody. By the time of the next hearing, Sarah will have been in custody for 56 days (7 + 28 + 7 + 14). If the prosecution is not ready to proceed with the not guilty hearing on that date, Sarah must be released on bail unless the magistrates agree that it is reasonable to extend the custody time-limit.

Example 2

Joe appears before the magistrates, for the first time, on a charge of assault occasioning actual bodily harm. He is remanded in custody for 7 days. At the next hearing, Joe is remanded in custody for a further 28 days, after which committal proceedings are to take place. Twenty-eight days later, Joe is back before the court. The prosecution asks for a further 28-day remand as it is not ready to proceed to committal. The magistrates agree, on the basis that the committal will take place at the next hearing. By the time of the next hearing, Joe will have been in custody for 63 days (7 + 28 + 28). If the prosecution is not ready to proceed with committal on that date, then Joe can only be remanded in custody for a further 7 days (and then must be released on bail) unless the magistrates agree that it is reasonable to extend the custody time-limit.

The maximum overall periods for remands in custody at the Crown Court (for indictable only or either way offences) are:

(a)   182 days from sending the case for trial and the start of the trial less any period (or the aggregate of any periods) during which the defendant has been in the custody of the magistrates' court since that first appearance for the offence (reg 5(6B), as amended by the Prosecution of Offences (Custody Time Limits) (Modification) Regulations 1998 (SI 1998/3037));

(b)   112 days from committing the case for trial and the start of the trial (reg 5(3)(a)).

3.4.3   Bail

3.4.3.1   The nature of bail

Whenever magistrates adjourn a case and decide to remand the defendant, they must also decide whether the remand should be in custody or on bail.

A defendant who is granted bail is under a duty to surrender to custody at the time and place appointed (Bail Act 1976, s 3(1)).

A defendant who fails, without reasonable cause, to surrender to custody is guilty of the offence of absconding. The burden of proving reasonable cause lies on the defendant (Bail Act 1976, s 6).

The offence of absconding is punishable on summary conviction in a magistrates' court with up to 3 months' imprisonment and/or a £5000 fine. In the Crown Court, the matter is dealt with as a criminal contempt and is punishable with up to 12 months' imprisonment and/or an unlimited fine.

If a defendant fails to surrender to bail, the court may issue a warrant for his arrest (Bail Act 1976, s 7(1), (2)).

3.4.3.2   Limitations on bail (Criminal Justice and Public Order Act 1994, s 25)

A court may, only in exceptional circumstances, grant bail to a person charged with:

(a)   murder;

(b)   attempted murder;

(c)   manslaughter;

(d)   rape; or

(e)   attempted rape

if that person has been previously convicted of any one of these offences. There is no requirement that the previous conviction be for the same offence as the current charge before the court.

3.4.3.3   The right to bail (Bail Act 1976, s 4)

A court has an obligation to grant bail (except in the 'limited bail' cases above, and as provided in Sch 1 (see below)):

(a)   prior to conviction, to all defendants;

(b)   after conviction, to a defendant whose case is then adjourned for reports or enquiries;

(c)   to offenders brought before a magistrates' court for breach of a community rehabilitation order or community punishment order.

The basic right to bail does not apply:

(a)   where magistrates having convicted a defendant commit him to the Crown Court for sentence (see **10.2.16**);

(b)   when a person is appealing against conviction or sentence.

3.4.3.4   Exceptions to the right to bail for a defendant charged with an imprisonable offence (Bail Act 1976, Sch 1, Part I)

A defendant need not be granted bail if:

(2)   ... the court is satisfied that there are substantial grounds for believing that the defendant, if released on bail ... would:

    (a)   fail to surrender to custody, or

    (b)   commit an offence while on bail, or

    (c)   interfere with witnesses or otherwise obstruct the course of justice, whether in relation to himself or any other person,

(3)   ... the court is satisfied that the defendant should be kept in custody for his own protection or, if he is a child or young person, for his own welfare.

(4)   the defendant is ... in custody in pursuance of the sentence of a court ...

(5)   ... the court is satisfied that it has not been practicable to obtain sufficient information for the purpose of taking the decisions required ... for want of time since the institution of the proceedings against him.

(7)   ... the case is adjourned for inquiries or a report, ... if it appears to the court that it would be impracticable to complete the inquiries or make the report without keeping the defendant in custody.

Paragraph 2A and paragraph 6 provide further exceptions to the defendant's right to bail:

2A(1)   If the defendant falls within this paragraph, he may not be granted bail unless the court is satisfied that there is no significant risk of his committing an offence while on bail (whether subject to bail conditions or not).

(2)   The defendant falls within this paragraph if—

    (a)   he is aged over 18 or over, and

    (b)   it appears to the court that he was on bail in criminal proceedings at the date of the offence.

6(1)   If the defendant falls within this paragraph, he may not be granted bail unless the court is satisfied that there is no significant risk that, if released on bail (whether subject to conditions or not), he would fail to surrender to custody.

(2)   Subject to subparagraph (3) below, the defendant falls within this paragraph if—

(a)   he is aged 18 or over, and

(b)   it appears to the court that, having been released on bail in or in connection with the proceedings for the offence, he failed to surrender to custody.

(3)   Where it appears to the court that the defendant had reasonable cause for his failure to surrender to custody, he does not fall within this paragraph unless it also appears to the court that he failed to surrender to custody at the appointed place as soon as reasonably practicable after the appointed time."

Should the prosecution apply for the defendant's remand in custody the above exceptions to bail will become the prosecution's objections to bail. There are restrictions on the granting of bail for drug users in paragraphs 6C–6F. Those provisions are beyond the scope of this book.

3.4.3.5 Factors

In considering whether the para 2, para 2A or para 6 exceptions set out above apply, a court should take into account the following factors:

(a)   the nature and seriousness of the offence or default (and the probable method of dealing with the defendant for it),

(b)   the character, antecedents, associations and community ties of the defendant,

(c)   the defendant's record as respects the fulfilment of his obligations under previous grants of bail in criminal proceedings,

(d)   except in the case of a defendant whose case is adjourned for inquiries or a report, the strength of the evidence of his having committed the offence or having defaulted. (Bail Act 1976, Sch 1, Pt I, para 9)

These factors are not exceptions to the defendant's right to bail. They are factors that the court takes into account when deciding whether to grant bail. Such factors can be used by the prosecution to explain why a particular exception to the defendant's right to bail applies or by the defence in support of the defendant's bail application.

These factors are considered below.

The nature and seriousness of the offence and the probable method of dealing with it

This factor is particularly relevant to an argument that, if released on bail, the defendant will fail to surrender to custody. If the offence is a serious one the prosecution may say that a custodial sentence is likely to follow conviction and if released on bail the defendant will not wish to face that possibility. The defence will sometimes argue that the very fact that an offence is serious will mean that the defendant is likely to answer bail as he will not wish to make matters any worse for himself than they are already. Furthermore, the defence may acknowledge that the offence is serious, state that the defendant is pleading not guilty and is anxious to attend court to clear his name.

The defendant's character and antecedents

The defendant's criminal record is admissible on an application for bail. A history of offending may be relevant to an argument that the defendant would commit an offence while on bail. If he has a history of committing the particular type of offence with which he is charged then, if released on bail, he may offend again. A defendant's previous good character will also be relevant.

The defendant's associations

This factor may be relevant to arguments that the defendant will commit an offence while on bail or interfere with witnesses. If it is alleged that the defendant associates with known criminals or is perhaps a member of an organised gang this could indicate that he will commit further offences. If a prosecution witness is known to the defendant or is perhaps a relative then an argument may be put forward that he will attempt to interfere with that witness by persuading him to change his evidence.

The defendant's community ties

This is likely to be relevant in relation to an argument that the defendant will fail to surrender to custody. If the defendant is of no fixed abode, has no relatives in the area, or has no job then it can be argued that if released on bail there is little to keep him in the area. Conversely, if he has a fixed residence, family ties or secure employment this may indicate that he will stay in the area and surrender to custody.

The defendant's record in relation to previous grants of bail

Any history of failing to surrender to custody or committing offences while on bail will be relevant. Conversely, a defendant with a criminal record who has no history of failure to surrender or of committing offences while on bail is entitled to have this taken into account when a court decides whether there are substantial grounds for believing that he would fail to surrender to custody or would commit an offence while on bail.

Strength of evidence

Except where the case has been adjourned for enquiries or report, the strength of the evidence against the defendant will be a consideration.

If the prosecution alleges that the evidence against the defendant is strong, this will support an argument of probable failure to surrender to custody. This factor is unlikely to be used in isolation but, if combined with a serious offence which indicates a custodial sentence on conviction, it can be very persuasive. Equally, the defence can argue that the evidence against the defendant is not strong (eg, it may consist of disputed identification evidence) and that as a result the defendant is anxious to attend the trial to clear his name.

The arguments cited above are illustrative only and the factors can be used in any way by the prosecution or defence to support or oppose an application for a remand in custody.

3.4.3.6 Exceptions to the right to bail for a defendant charged with a non-imprisonable offence (Bail Act 1976, Sch 1, Part II)

If the defendant is charged with a non-imprisonable offence, the prosecution will not normally oppose bail. The exceptions for refusing bail are:

(a) it appears to the court that, having been previously granted bail in criminal proceedings, the defendant has failed to surrender to custody in accordance with his obligations under the grant of bail and the court believes, in view of that failure, that the defendant, if released on bail (whether subject to conditions or not), would fail to surrender to custody;

(b)   the defendant ought to be kept in custody for his own protection or, if he is a child or young person, for his own welfare;

(c)   the defendant is in custody in pursuance of the sentence of a court;

(d)   the defendant, having been released on bail in the proceedings, has been arrested for absconding or breaking conditions of bail.

These exceptions are largely self-explanatory.

3.4.3.7   Conditions of bail (Bail Act 1976, s 3)

A defendant may be required by a court:

> ... to comply, before release on bail or later, with such requirements as appear to the court to be necessary to secure that—
> (a)   he surrenders to custody,
> (b)   he does not commit an offence while on bail,
> (c)   he does not interfere with witnesses or otherwise obstruct the course of justice whether in relation to himself or any other person,
> (d)   he makes himself available for the purpose of enabling enquiries or a report to be made to assist the court in dealing with him for the offence,
> (e)   before the time appointed for him to surrender to custody, he attends an interview with an authorised advocate or authorised litigator, as defined by s 119(1) of the Courts and Legal Services Act 1990. (s 3(6))

'Authorised advocate' includes a barrister or solicitor and 'authorised litigator' includes a solicitor.

Conditions may be suggested by the defence when attempting to persuade a court to grant bail or they may be imposed by the court of its own volition. Such conditions include sureties, security, reporting regularly to a police station, a curfew and a condition of non-communication with named prosecution witnesses. This list is not exhaustive, and any condition may be imposed which appears to be realistic.

Sureties

A surety is a person who enters into a recognisance of money (eg, X stands surety for Y in the sum of £10,000) and is under an obligation to use every reasonable effort to ensure the defendant's appearance at court. The surety is not required to pay over any money at this stage.

If the defendant fails to appear, the court is required to declare the immediate and automatic forfeiture of the recognisance (Magistrates' Courts Act 1980, s 120(1A)). After declaring the recognisance forfeited, the court must issue a summons to the surety to appear before the court to explain why he should not pay the sum. The court will then decide whether all, part or none of the sum should be paid.

In considering the suitability of a proposed surety the Bail Act 1976, s 8(2) states that:

> ... regard may be had (amongst other things) to—
> (a)   the surety's financial resources;
> (b)   his character and any previous convictions of his; and
> (c)   his proximity (whether in point of kinship, place of residence or otherwise) to the person for whom he is to be surety.

Thus a person without any assets or with a substantial criminal record or who lives a long way from the defendant is unlikely to be acceptable. As a matter of professional conduct, a solicitor should not stand surety for his client.

A court may indicate that it is prepared to grant bail subject to a suitable surety being found. In such a case, the amount of the recognisance should be fixed by the court and the suitability of any surety who is found can be determined by a magistrate, a magistrates' clerk or an inspector at a police station. If a surety is rejected in these circumstances, it is possible to apply to the court for a final decision (see Bail Act 1976, s 8(4), (5)).

Sureties may be put forward to overcome a prosecution objection that the defendant will fail to surrender to custody.

Security → passport

The defendant may be required to give security for his surrender in the form of money or chattels.

This condition is again relevant to a prosecution objection to bail on the basis that the defendant will fail to surrender to custody. Deposit of a sum of money is an example of security.

Reporting to a police station

This condition can again be used to overcome a prosecution objection that the defendant will fail to surrender to custody. Reporting to a police station can be daily or even twice daily, where appropriate.

Curfew

An example of the imposition of a curfew is that the defendant shall not leave his place of residence between the hours of 6 pm and 7 am. The condition is frequently used to overcome an objection to bail that the defendant will commit further offences while on bail. It may be particularly relevant where the defendant is charged with or has a history of night-time offending.

Non-communication with prosecution witnesses

This condition can be used to overcome a prosecution objection to bail that the defendant will interfere with witnesses. If the named witness is a relative with whom the defendant resides it will, of course, be necessary to find the defendant alternative accommodation.

Residence

A condition of residence, frequently expressed as a condition to live and sleep at a specified address, can be used to overcome a prosecution objection to bail that the defendant will fail to surrender to custody. It can be used where the defendant has a known address or where he is allegedly of no fixed abode. If the defendant is of no fixed abode, it may be possible to find a place for him at a bail hostel. These are institutions (often run by the Probation Service) which can provide accommodation for people who would otherwise be refused bail on the basis of no fixed abode. Strict conditions, for example as to hours kept, have to be complied with.

3.4.3.8 Variation and breach of conditions

The court may vary conditions or, subsequent to the granting of bail, impose them on application by either party.

The police have power to arrest without warrant for breach of bail conditions (Bail Act 1976, s 7). Breach of condition is not, of itself, an offence but will create an exception for a court to refuse bail in the present proceedings.

3.4.3.9 Bail procedure

If the prosecution is objecting to bail, the following procedure will apply.

(a) The prosecutor will make an application for a remand in custody and will hand in to the court a list of the defendant's previous convictions. The prosecutor will identify the exceptions to bail which apply. The prosecutor will argue the exceptions as objections to bail being granted and will cite relevant facts of the case in support.

(b) The defence advocate will make an application for bail. A good application for bail will deal with each of the prosecution objections in turn, offering conditions of bail where appropriate.

(c) Evidence may be called at a bail hearing. The court may wish to hear from a prospective employer or someone who is prepared to offer a home to the defendant. However, the usual rules of evidence do not apply and the court may accept hearsay from witnesses and mere assertions of fact from the advocates.

(d) The court decides whether to remand in custody or on bail. If bail is granted subject to a surety, the court will hear evidence on oath from the surety in order to be satisfied as to the suitability of the surety.

A court which grants or withholds bail or which imposes or varies conditions must make a record of the decision in the prescribed form. A copy will then be given to the defendant.

Further, a magistrates' court or Crown Court must give reasons (and include a note of them in the record) for withholding bail or for imposing or varying conditions and it must normally give the defendant a copy of the note.

If bail is opposed by the prosecutor and a magistrates' court or a Crown Court grants bail, reasons for granting bail must be given (and a note of them included in the record of decision). A copy of the record must be given to the prosecutor if he so requests (Bail Act 1976, s 5).

An example of the prescribed form appears at **Appendix 2(L)**. A chart summarising the above procedure is included at **Appendix 1(F)**.

In preparing for a bail application, it is useful for the defence solicitor to discuss the grounds for objection with the prosecutor and to see whether or not the objections can be overcome by the imposition of suitable conditions.

3.4.3.10 Further applications when bail is refused

To the magistrates' court

If a court refuses bail, it is under a duty at each subsequent hearing to consider the question of bail, provided that:

(a) the defendant is still in custody; and

(b) the right to bail still applies.

This does not necessarily mean that the court must hear another full bail application. Part IIA of Sch 1 to the Bail Act 1976 provides:

2. At the first hearing after that at which the court decided not to grant the defendant bail he may support an application for bail with any argument as to fact or law that he desires (whether or not he has advanced that argument previously).

3. At subsequent hearings the court need not hear arguments as to fact or law which it has heard previously.

Example

Daniel is remanded in custody for 7 days on 7 June following a bail application by his solicitor. The solicitor may make a further application on 14 June using the same arguments. If Daniel is remanded in custody again, new arguments will be necessary before the court will hear a further application. New arguments could include matters such as the availability of a job or a surety.

In applying this rule, the court should ignore a hearing at which bail was refused on the basis that it has not been practicable to obtain sufficient information about the defendant (*R v Calder Justices, ex p Kennedy* [1992] Crim LR 496). In the example above, if Daniel was remanded in custody on 7 June on the insufficient information ground, he would still be entitled to bail applications at his next two hearings.

If a magistrates' court remands a person in custody after a fully argued bail application, it must issue a certificate confirming that it has heard full argument. An example of a full argument certificate appears at **Appendix 2(L)**.

To the Crown Court (Supreme Court Act 1981, s 81, as amended by the Criminal Justice Act 1982, s 60)

A defendant who has been remanded in custody by a magistrates' court may apply to the Crown Court for bail provided that the magistrates have issued a full argument certificate on the bail application which has been refused.

A defendant who has been committed in custody to the Crown Court for trial or sentence or who has appealed to the Crown Court can apply to the Crown Court for bail. No full argument certificate is required as the magistrates no longer have jurisdiction to hear applications in the case.

The rights to apply to the Crown Court above are entirely separate. The test is whether or not the case has yet been sent to the Crown Court for trial, sentence or appeal. If it has not, then a full argument certificate is required. If it has been sent to the Crown Court, a full argument certificate is not required.

Representation

A grant of representation in criminal proceedings will cover representation in related bail proceedings (Access to Justice Act 1999, Sch 3, para 2(2)). This means that representation in Crown Court bail proceedings falls within the scope of the original grant of representation in the magistrates' court.

3.4.3.11   Challenging grants of bail

By s 1(1) of the Bail (Amendment) Act 1993:

> Where a magistrates' court grants bail to a person who is charged with or convicted of an offence punishable by a term of imprisonment the prosecution may appeal to a judge of the Crown Court against the granting of bail.

Such an appeal can be made only if the prosecution objected to the magistrates granting bail to the defendant.

3.4.3.12   Prosecution request for reconsideration of bail (Bail Act 1976, s 5B)

If a defendant is charged with an indictable or either way offence and a magistrates' court has granted him bail, the prosecution can ask the magistrates to reconsider their decision. This power can be exercised only if information has come to light which was not available to the court when the decision to grant bail was taken.

A magistrates' court which reconsiders a bail decision may:

(a)   vary conditions of bail;

(b)   impose new conditions of bail; or

(c)   withhold bail.

3.5   Bail and the Human Rights Act 1998

In June 2001 the Law Commission published *Bail and the Human Rights Act 1998* (Paper No 269) accompanied by the Guidance. The Guidance has been disseminated to the judiciary and justice's clerks and is reproduced in **Appendix 5**.

3.6   Further reading

Further details on the law of bail can be found in numerous publications including:

Archbold: Criminal Pleading, Evidence and Practice (Sweet & Maxwell, 2005)

Blackstone's Criminal Practice (Oxford University Press, 2005)

John Sprack, *Emmins on Criminal Procedure* (Oxford University Press, 2004)

Practical guidance can be found in:

Ede and Edwards, *Criminal Defence* (The Law Society, 2002)

Chapter 4

The Prosecution of an Offence Triable Either Way

4.1 Introduction

An offence triable either way can be tried either in a magistrates' court or in the Crown Court before a judge and jury. The first substantive step in the prosecution will be plea before venue. If the defendant indicates a not guilty plea or refuses to indicate a plea, the mode of trial enquiry will take place. The purpose of this procedure is to determine whether the case will be dealt with by a magistrates' court or by the Crown Court.

4.2 Advance disclosure of the prosecution case

Under the Criminal Procedure Rules 2005, Part 21, a defendant charged with an either way offence is entitled to advance disclosure of the prosecution case. Before a decision is made as to plea before venue and mode of trial, the defence should usually request advance disclosure from the prosecution. Advance disclosure will usually include copies of written statements of prosecution witnesses.

4.3 The plea before venue procedure

The procedure is as follows. (This is summarised in chart form at **Appendix 1(J)**.)

(a) The charge is read out by the clerk to the justices.

(b) The clerk to the justices will ensure that the defendant is aware of his right to advance disclosure of the prosecution case. If necessary, the hearing will be adjourned to a future date to enable advance disclosure to take place.

(c) (i) The clerk to the justices will explain to the defendant that he may indicate how he would plead if the matter were to proceed to trial.

(ii) The clerk will tell the defendant that if he indicates that he intends to plead guilty he will be treated as having pleaded guilty before the magistrates who may then sentence him. However, the magistrates could still commit him to the Crown Court to be sentenced if they feel that their powers of sentencing are inadequate.

(iii) The clerk will then ask the defendant for his plea.

(iv) If the defendant indicates a guilty plea, the court will proceed as though he had just pleaded guilty at summary trial (see **10.3.2**).

(v) If the defendant refuses to indicate a plea or indicates that he intends to plead not guilty, the procedure in 4.4 below will be followed.

4.4 The mode of trial procedure → No indication of plea or if Not Guilty plea.

The procedure is as follows. (This is summarised in chart form at **Appendix 1(J)**.)

(a)   The prosecutor will address the court. He will outline the nature of the charge and will indicate in which court the prosecution feels that the case should be tried.

(b)   The defence advocate may then address the court. He may indicate where the defence feels the case should be tried.

(c)   The magistrates then announce whether they are prepared to deal with the case or whether they feel that the case is suitable only for trial in the Crown Court. The Magistrates' Courts Act 1980, s 19(3) states that the magistrates, in reaching their decision, must take into account:

   (i)   the nature of the offence;

   (ii)   whether the circumstances make the offence one of serious character;

   (iii)   whether the punishment which a magistrates' court would have power to inflict for it would be adequate; and

   (iv)   any other circumstances which appear to the court to make it more suitable for the offence to be tried in one way rather than the other.

   The defendant's previous convictions are irrelevant for the purpose of deciding mode of trial (*R v Colchester Justices, ex p North East Essex Building Co Ltd* [1977] 1 WLR 1109).

(d)   If the magistrates decide that the case is not suitable for summary trial then the defendant has no choice. The case will be adjourned to a future date for committal proceedings to take place.

(e)   If the magistrates are prepared to deal with the case then:

   (i)   the clerk to the justices will explain to the defendant that he has the right to elect for trial in the Crown Court;

   (ii)   the clerk will inform the defendant that if he consents to be tried by the magistrates and is convicted, the magistrates may commit him to the Crown Court to be sentenced if they feel that their powers of sentencing are inadequate. (Magistrates cannot imprison a defendant for more than 6 months or, if two or more either way offences are committed, for more than a total of 12 months.) Such a decision may be taken, for example, if facts emerge after mode of trial has been determined (ie, usually at a trial of a not guilty plea or a sentencing hearing):

   –   that show that the offence is so serious that only a custodial sentence would be justified; and

   –   that the powers of the magistrates to pass a custodial sentence are inadequate.

   Otherwise, if the magistrates feel at the mode of trial hearing that their powers of sentence are likely to be inadequate they will commit to the Crown Court for trial;

   (iii)   the defendant makes his decision. If he consents to magistrates' court trial and pleads guilty (having earlier indicated no plea or now having changed his plea), his case may be dealt with immediately. If he consents to magistrates' court trial and pleads not guilty, the court will fix a date for trial. Alternatively, the case may be adjourned for a pre-trial review (PTR). At the PTR, the magistrates will set a date for trial (see **8.4.2**). If the defendant asks for Crown Court trial, he will not be asked to plead. The case will be adjourned to a future date for committal proceedings to take place.

4.5   Practical points on mode of trial procedure

4.5.1   Guidelines

In reaching a decision as to whether or not a case should be sent to the Crown Court, the magistrates will bear in mind the guidelines issued in *Practice Direction (Criminal Proceedings: Consolidation)* [2002] 3 All ER 904, para 51, *Mode of trial*. The purpose of the guidelines is to help magistrates decide whether or not to commit either way offences for trial in the Crown Court. Their objective is to provide guidance, not direction. They are not intended to impinge upon a magistrate's duty to consider each case individually and on its particular facts.

4.5.2   Observations in the guidelines

The following general observations are made in the guidelines.

(a)   The prosecution version of the facts should be assumed to be correct.

(b)   Where cases involve complex questions of fact or law, committal for trial should be considered.

(c)   Where two or more defendants are jointly charged with an offence each has an individual right to elect his mode of trial.

Example

Christine and Dorothy are jointly charged with assault. Both defendants indicate not guilty pleas. The magistrates are prepared to deal with the case. Christine elects trial by jury. Dorothy consents to a summary trial. According to *R v Ipswich, Justices ex p Callaghan* (1995) 159 JP 748, each defendant has the right to elect mode of trial even if it results in not guilty trials before separate courts.

(d)   The presumption is that cases will be tried summarily unless:

(i)   one of the relevant circumstances listed below is present; and

(ii)   the sentencing powers of the magistrates are considered insufficient.

The guidelines identify certain features of specific either way offences which may make them unsuitable for trial by magistrates.

Burglary

Burglary of dwelling-houses involving daytime entry of occupied house; night-time entry of a house normally occupied; part of a series of offences; soiling, ransacking, damage or vandalism; professional hallmarks; unrecovered property of high value (at least £10,000).

Note that if any person in the dwelling is subjected to violence or the threat of violence, the offence cannot be tried by magistrates (Magistrates' Courts Act 1980, Sch 1, para 28(c)).

Non dwellings – entry of a pharmacy or doctor's surgery; fear caused or violence done to anyone lawfully on the premises; professional hallmarks; substantial vandalism; unrecovered property of high value (at least £10,000).

Wounding/inflicting grievous bodily harm and assault occasioning actual bodily harm

Use of a weapon of a kind likely to cause serious injury; violence to the vulnerable, for example, the elderly or infirm; more than minor injury caused by kicking, headbutting; serious violence on those whose work brings them into contact with the public, for example, police, bus drivers, shopkeepers, publicans; the offence has clear racial motives.

Theft and fraud

Breach of trust by person in a position of substantial authority or in whom a high degree of trust placed; committed in a sophisticated manner; committed by an organised gang; vulnerable victim, for example, elderly or infirm; unrecovered property of high value (see 'Burglary' above).

Handling stolen goods

Dishonest handling of stolen property by a receiver who has commissioned the theft; the offence has professional hallmarks; the property is of high value (at least £10,000).

4.5.3 Representations by the defence

Although the defence is given an opportunity to address the court on mode of trial, in many cases this will not be necessary. If the prosecution requests Crown Court trial and the defence agrees, then there is unlikely to be any reason to address the court. This will also be the case if the defence agrees with the prosecution's request for magistrates' court trial. Representations may be necessary if the defence does not agree with the prosecution's arguments. The defence may, for example, request that the magistrates deal with the case, whilst the prosecution requests Crown Court trial.

4.5.4 Defendant changes his mind

A defendant who consents to trial by magistrates may wish to change his mind and go to the Crown Court. This point sometimes arises where the defendant was not legally represented when he made his original decision. The magistrates have a discretion to permit the defendant to change his mind and elect for Crown Court trial at any time before the conclusion of the prosecution evidence (Magistrates' Courts Act 1980, s 25(2)). This discretion may, for example, be exercised in the defendant's favour where he did not understand his legal position or the significance of the choice which he was making. See *R v Birmingham Justices, ex p Hodgson and Another* [1985] 2 All ER 193.

4.5.5 Magistrates' discretion

The magistrates have a discretion to change from Crown Court trial to magistrates' court trial at any time before the conclusion of committal proceedings (see **Chapter 7**), provided the defendant consents (Magistrates' Courts Act 1980, s 25(3)). This is unlikely to happen very often in practice.

4.6 Advising the client

If the defendant indicates a guilty plea, the case will be dealt with in the magistrates' court and the defendant will have no choice. If the defendant indicates a not guilty plea, the decision as to whether a case will be tried in a magistrates' court or in the Crown Court will rest with the defendant if the magistrates indicate that they are prepared to deal with the matter. A defendant is entitled to expect advice from his solicitor as to the appropriate court for his case. In formulating this advice, the following factors may be relevant.

4.6.1   Factors in favour of the Crown Court

4.6.1.1   Likelihood of conviction

Whilst this is subject to knowledge of a local court, it is generally felt that there is a better chance of acquittal in the Crown Court. This may be the case where the defendant is relying on a common defence, such as 'I forgot to pay' in a theft by way of shoplifting case. Magistrates tend to hear the same stories on numerous occasions and may become 'case hardened'. Most jurors are new to the criminal justice system and may be more inclined to believe the defendant's story. If police evidence is to be challenged, magistrates may be familiar with the officer in question and the question may be better raised in the Crown Court before a jury.

4.6.1.2   Procedure for dealing with the admissibility of evidence

If the admissibility of evidence is to be challenged, the Crown Court provides the better procedure for doing so. Questions of admissibility are decided by the judge in the absence of the jury, so if evidence is ruled inadmissible, the jury will not hear it. In the magistrates' court, the justices are arbiters of fact and law, therefore they will have to hear the evidence (eg, that the defendant has made a confession) before ruling on its admissibility.

4.6.2   Factors in favour of the magistrates' court

4.6.2.1   Speed and stress

A case is likely to be dealt with more quickly in a magistrates' court. The proceedings are less formal than in the Crown Court and may, therefore, be less stressful for the defendant.

4.6.2.2   Cost

If the defendant is convicted the prosecution will apply for a contribution towards prosecution costs. A Crown Court trial is likely to be more costly than a hearing in the magistrates' court.

If the defendant is represented under a representation order the judge has the power at the conclusion of the case in the Crown Court to order a defendant to pay all or some of the costs of his defence (see **10.2.10.4**). No such power is available in the magistrates' court.

4.6.2.3   Sentence

Magistrates' powers of sentencing are limited; six months imprisonment for one either way offence (subject to such a maximum being prescribed for the offence) and 12 months for two or more either way offences (Magistrates Courts' Act 1980, s 133). A higher sentence may be imposed in the Crown Court. However, it is also necessary to bear in mind the power of a magistrates' court to commit a defendant to the Crown Court for sentencing if the court feels that its powers of sentencing are inadequate. (As to the exercise of this power, see **10.2.12.1**.)

The advice given to a client as to the appropriate trial court will depend on the facts of the case and which of the factors listed above are considered to be the most important.

4.7   Criminal Justice Act 2003

Section 41 and Sch 3 to the Criminal Justice Act 2003 make substantial changes to the way cases are allocated between courts. The Act amends the plea before venue and mode of trial procedures significantly. These changes are expected to be introduced in September 2006.

4.8 Further reading

See, for example:

Archbold: Criminal Pleading, Evidence and Practice (Sweet & Maxwell, 2005)

Blackstone's Criminal Practice (Oxford University Press, 2005)

John Sprack, *Emmins on Criminal Procedure* (Blackstone Press, 2004)

Chapter 5

Disclosure

5.1 Introduction

In this chapter, the prosecution's duty of disclosure is considered. This duty has two purposes:

(a) the obligation to notify the defence of the evidence upon which the prosecution intend to rely ('advance information');

(b) the obligation to make available to the defence any material of relevance to the case upon which the prosecution does not intend to rely ('unused material').

Both purposes are efforts to ensure a fair trial for the defendant and to achieve 'equality of arms' as far as possible between the prosecution and the defence.

A solicitor cannot advise a defendant properly until he knows the extent of the prosecution case against the defendant. Neither is the solicitor in a position to expose the weaknesses in the prosecution case, or fully investigate the defence case, unless he has access to all the relevant material.

5.2 Duty to provide advance information

This is the obligation on the prosecution to notify the defence of its case (ie, the evidence upon which it intends to rely at trial). The duty applies to all criminal offences but the authority for such a duty and when such a duty arises depends on the classification of offence.

5.2.1 Summary offences

There is no statutory obligation on the prosecution to provide advance information for summary offences. In *R v Stratford Justices, ex p Imbert* [1999] 2 Cr App R 276, the Divisional Court stated that as a matter of good practice disclosure should normally be given. This is recognised in the Attorney-General's Guidelines on Disclosure of Information in Criminal Proceedings (29 November 2000), para 43:

> The prosecutor should ... provide to the defence all evidence upon which the Crown proposes to rely in a summary trial. Such provision should allow the accused or their legal advisers sufficient time to properly consider the evidence before it is called. Exceptionally, statements may be withheld for the protection of witnesses or to avoid interference with the course of justice.

5.2.2   Either way offences

Under CrimPR, Part 21, a defendant charged with an either way offence is entitled to advance information of the prosecution case. Before a decision is made as to plea before venue and mode of trial, the defence should usually request advance information from the prosecution. Advance information will usually include copies of written statements of prosecution witnesses.

If the defendant's case is to be committed to the Crown Court, the prosecution must serve copies of its evidence on the defence before the case is committed from the magistrates' court to the Crown Court.

5.2.3   Indictable only offences

If the defendant's case is sent to the Crown Court for trial, the prosecution must serve copies of its evidence on the defence at the Crown Court.

All evidence that the prosecution seek to adduce at the Crown Court trial must be disclosed to the defence.

5.3   Duty to disclose 'unused material'

This is the obligation on the prosecution under the Criminal Procedure and Investigations Act 1996 (CPIA 1996) to make available to the defence any material of relevance upon which it does not intend to rely – 'unused material'.

In order for disclosure of such prosecution 'unused material' to be effective, proper procedures must be followed during the criminal investigation so that information, documents and objects are properly recorded and retained. These procedures are set out in the Criminal Procedure and Investigations Act 1996 Code of Practice (the Code).

The Code provides that all material which is obtained in a criminal investigation and which may be relevant to the investigation is retained and revealed to the prosecution.

The Code is admissible in evidence in all criminal and civil proceedings. If a court considers that any provision of the Code or any breach of the Code is relevant to any question arising in the proceedings, the court must take that into account when deciding the question (s 23).

The Attorney General's Guidelines on Disclosure of Information in Criminal Proceedings, issued on 29 November 2000, are also of importance.

The scheme for disclosure is described below.

5.4   Disclosure by the prosecution (CPIA 1996, s 3)

The prosecution's duty of disclosure of 'unused material' will apply when the defendant pleads not guilty in the magistrates' court or when the defendant is committed for trial to the Crown Court or sent to the Crown Court for trial.

In such a case, the prosecution must either:

(a)   disclose to the defence any previous undisclosed prosecution material which might reasonably be considered capable of undermining the case for the prosecution case against the defendant or of assisting the case for the defendant, or

(b)   give to the defendant a written statement that there is no such material.

The test for disclosure is an objective one, albeit one exercised by the prosecutor.

5.4.1   Time-limit (CPIA 1996, ss 12 and 13)

The prosecution must make disclosure as soon as is reasonably practicable after the defendant pleads not guilty in the magistrates' court or is committed to the Crown Court for trial.

Example

David is charged with theft. He intends to plead not guilty. Prior to the plea before venue and mode of trial proceedings the prosecution serves the defence with advance disclosure of the prosecution case under the Magistrates' Courts (Advance Information) Rules 1985. At plea before venue, David pleads not guilty. At mode of trial, the magistrates accept jurisdiction and David consents to summary trial. The prosecution must make disclosure to the defence of material it does not wish to rely on (unused material) as soon as practicable.

For cases sent to the Crown Court for trial the prosecution must make disclosure as soon as practicable after the prosecution has served its evidence on the defence (see **7.4.3**).

When the prosecutor makes disclosure, the prosecutor should send the defendant a notice setting out his rights and duties (Home Office Circular 11/1997, Criminal Procedure and Investigations Act 1996, paras 12 and 13).

5.4.2   Examples of matters which may fall under the duty of primary disclosure

Some examples of undermining material are found in para 7.3 of the Code:

—   information provided by a defendant which indicates an explanation for the offence with which he has been charged;

—   any material casting doubt on the reliability of a confession;

—   any material casting doubt on the reliability of a witness;

—   any other material which the investigator believes may fall within the test for prosecution disclosure in the Act.

Other examples of undermining material were given in the White Paper Disclosure (Cm 2864).

(a)   If part of the prosecution case is a statement by a witness that he saw the defendant near the scene of the crime shortly after it was committed, it will be necessary to disclose a statement by another witness that he saw a person of a different description from the defendant at the same time and place.

(b)   If the defendant has told the police in an interview that he was acting in self-defence, it will be necessary to disclose the statement of any witness who supports this but whom the prosecution does not regard as truthful.

(c)   If the victim died of a hammer blow and part of the prosecution case is a forensic test showing that the blood stains on a hammer found buried in the defendant's back garden matched those of the victim, it will be necessary to disclose a negative test showing that the fingerprints on the hammer did not match those of the defendant.

(d) If the prosecution is aware that its main witness has a previous conviction, it must disclose it to the defence, since it may affect the weight to be placed on his testimony.

(e) If the prosecution is in possession of a psychiatric report showing that its main witness has a history of psychiatric disorder with a tendency to fantasise, it should disclose the report since it clearly undermines the credibility of that witness.

(f) If the prosecution is aware that a prosecution witness has applied for a reward for information leading to the conviction of a person for a criminal offence, it must disclose this to the defence.

(g) If previous versions of witness statements are inconsistent with the final version served on the defence, they must be disclosed.

Further examples are noted by Ede in his book *Active Defence* (The Law Society, 2000):

(a) the fact of a witness having been hypnotised;

(b) the fact of a witness having been coached or rehearsed for a TV programme;

(c) the fact of a payment to a witness other than as a reward.

The prosecutor's duty also extends to material which might assist the defendant's case.

Example

Cathryn is charged with theft. The prosecution allege that the offence took place at about 11 pm on a Saturday evening. Cathryn says nothing when interviewed by the police. The prosecution has evidence that Cathryn was seen entering her flat at 3 am on the Sunday morning but not that she was seen leaving it earlier in the evening. The prosecution is under an obligation to disclose the evidence that Cathryn was seen entering her flat at 3 am.

5.5 Defence disclosure (CPIA 1996, ss 5 and 6)

Where the defendant pleads not guilty at summary trial, once the prosecution has made disclosure the defendant may give a defence statement if he wishes but he has no duty to do so.

If the case has been committed to the Crown Court for trial or sent to the Crown Court for trial, once the prosecution has made disclosure the defendant must give a defence statement.

The defence statement must be in writing, and must:

(a) set out the nature of the defendant's defence, including any particular defences on which he intends to rely;

(b) indicate the matters of fact on which the defendant takes issue with the prosecution; and

(c) set out, in the case of each such matter, the reason why the defendant takes issue with the prosecution; and

(d) indicate any point of law (including any point as to the admissibility of evidence or an abuse of process) which the defendant wishes to take, and any authority on which he intends to rely for that purpose.

If the defence statement discloses an alibi, the defendant must give particulars of it, including:

(a)   the name and address and date of birth of any witness the defendant believes is able to give evidence in support of the alibi, or as many of those details as are known to the defendant when the statement is given (includes evidence of alibi given by the defendant himself); and

(b)   any information in the defendant's possession which might be of material assistance in identifying or finding any such witnesses in whose case any of the details mentioned in paragraph (a) are not known to the defendant when the statement is given.

Evidence in support of an alibi is 'evidence tending to show that by reason of the presence of the accused at a particular place or in a particular area at a particular time he was not, or was unlikely to have been, at the place where the offence is alleged to have been committed at the time of its alleged commission' (s 6(A)(3)).

For an example of a defence statement, see **Appendix 2(T)**.

For sanctions to which the defendant will be liable if he is deficient in his duty of disclosure, see **5.11.2**.

5.5.1   Proving the defence statement (CPIA 1996, s 6E)

A defence statement given on behalf of a defendant by his solicitor shall, unless the contrary is proved, be deemed to be given with the consent of the defendant (s 6E(2)).

Presumably therefore if counsel drafts a defence statement and hands it into the court this deeming provision is not satisfied.

The Bar Council has issued guidance to counsel about the circumstances which should exist before counsel agrees to draft a defence statement. These remind counsel about the significance of this document and the need to obtain the client's informed agreement before it is sent (see Bar Counsel's Guidance on Drafting Defence Statements, as approved by the Professional Conduct and Complaints Committee, 24 September 1997).

5.5.2   Time-limit (CPIA 1996, s 12)

If the defendant chooses to give a defence statement it must be given to the prosecution and the court within 14 days of the prosecutor complying, or purporting to comply, with the obligation to provide prosecution disclosure (Criminal Procedure and Investigations Act 1996 (Defence Disclosure Time Limits) Regulations 1997 (SI 1997/684), reg 2)).

The period for making defence disclosure may be extended by as many days as the court specifies, but only if an application is made before the expiration of the relevant period (reg 3(2)).

An application for extension of the period must:

(a)   state that the defendant believes, on reasonable grounds, that it is not possible to give a defence statement during the relevant period;

(b)   specify the grounds for so believing; and

(c)   specify the number of days by which the defendant wishes the period to be extended (reg 3(3)).

There is no limit on the number of applications that may be made, but in each case the court may grant an extension only if satisfied that the defendant cannot reasonably give a defence statement within the relevant period (reg 4(2), (3)).

5.5.2.1 Updated defence disclosure (CPIA 1996, s 6B)

New regulations will prescribe a time limit for updated defence disclosure (provided that initial disclosure has been completed within the statutory time limits).

The updated statement must comply with all of the above requirements that apply to the initial defence case statement, but must be updated by reference to state of affairs at the time when the defence statement is given (s 6B(3)).

At the time of writing s 6B is not in force.

5.5.2.2 Service of updated defence case statement (CPIA 1996, s 12)

An updated defence statement must be given within the timescales set down under s 12 of the CPIA 1996 on both the court and the prosecution.

A court may also order, following application by any party of its own motion, the service of the updated defence statement on other parties to the proceedings (ie, co-defendants).

The updated defence statement must conform to s 6A of the CPIA 1996. As an alternative to an updated defence statement the defendant may give a written statement stating that he has no earlier changes to make to the earlier defence statement (s 6(B)).

5.6 Notices in relation to defence witnesses (CPIA 1996, s 6C)

Section 6C of the Act (not in force at the time of writing) provides for the service of a notice on the court and the prosecutor (within timescales to be prescribed) indicating whether the defendant intends to give or call any evidence at trial, and if so:

(a)   giving the name, address and date of birth of each proposed witness (other than the defendant himself), or as many of those details as are known to the defendant when the notice is given (save where these witnesses are in relation to alibi and the information has already been given);

(b)   providing any information in the defendant's possession which might be of material assistance in identifying, or finding any proposed witness in whose case any of the details mentioned in paragraph (a) are not known to the defendant when the notice is given.

5.6.1 Amended notices

If, following the giving of a notice, the defendant:

(a)   decides to call a person who is not included in the notice as a proposed witness, or decides not to call a person who is so included; or

(b)   discovers any information which he could have had to include in the notice if he had been aware of it when giving the notice;

he must give an appropriately amended notice to the court and to the prosecutor.

5.6.2 Code of Practice in relation to police interviews of witnesses notified by the defendant (CPIA 1996, s 21A)

Section 21A provides for the Secretary of State to issue a Code of Practice in relation to the interviewing of defence witnesses. The Code is designed to provide an important safeguard against police abuse of the requirement to identify defence witnesses, and will in particular contain guidance in relation to the following issues:

(a) information that should be provided to the interviewee and the defendant in relation to such an interview;

(b) the notification of the defendant's solicitor of such an interview;

(c) the attendance of the interviewee's solicitor at such an interview;

(d) the attendance of the defendant's solicitor at such an interview;

(e) the attendance of any other appropriate person at such an interview taking into account the interviewee's age or any disability of the interviewee.

The Code will be binding on the police who must have regard to it when interviewing witnesses (s 21A(3)).

If the police adopt the practice of interviewing defence witnesses and the only purpose in reality is to try to collate an account that might be inconsistent with any given in court, it will no doubt become defence practice to likewise seek to interview prosecution witnesses prior to trial. There is nothing in the Law Society rules of professional conduct that would prevent such a course of action, although guidance is given.

5.7 Notices in relation to defence experts (CPIA 1996, s 6D)

If the defendant instructs a person with a view to his providing any expert opinion for *possible* use as evidence at the defendant's not guilty trial, a notice must be served on the court and prosecutor specifying the person's name and address, unless that information has already been given as part of the defendant's notification of defence witnesses.

Section 12 of the Act will prescribe time limits for the service of such notices.

5.7.1 Sanctions

There is no sanction for failing to serve details of defence experts and in the absence of any professional conduct rules elsewhere it is difficult to see why any defence lawyer would wish to comply with this rule.

At the time of writing s 6D is not in force.

5.8 Public interest immunity

Certain material must not be disclosed to the defendant.

The most important example of this is where a court, on the application of the prosecution, has ruled that it is not in the public interest to disclose it. Such an application is likely to be on the basis that the material in question falls within one of the categories of 'sensitive' material.

Some examples of 'sensitive' material are found in para 6.12 of the Code:

(a) material relating to national security;

(b) material received from the intelligence and security agencies;

(c)   material relating to intelligence from foreign sources which reveals sensitive intelligence gathering methods;

(d)   material given in confidence;

(e)   material relating to the identity or activities of informants, under-cover police officers, witnesses, or other persons supplying information to the police who may be in danger if their identities are revealed;

(f)   material revealing the location of any premises or other place used for police surveillance, or the identity of any person allowing a police officer to use them for surveillance;

(g)   material revealing, either directly or indirectly, techniques and methods relied upon by a police officer in the course of a criminal investigation, eg, covert surveillance techniques, or other methods of detecting crime;

(h)   material whose disclosure might facilitate the commission of other offences or hinder the prevention and detection of crime;

(i)   material upon the strength of which search warrants were obtained;

(j)   material containing details of persons taking part in identification parades;

(k)   material supplied to an investigator during a criminal investigation which has been generated by an official of a body concerned with the regulation or supervision of bodies corporate or of persons engaged in financial activities, or which has been generated by a person retained by such a body;

(l)   material relating to a child witness (eg, material generated by a local authority social services department).

(m)   material relating to the private life of a witness.

5.9   Application to court for disclosure (CPIA 1996, s 8)

Where a defendant has served a defence statement (but not otherwise) and the prosecution has complied with its duty of disclosure, or purportedly complied, or failed, the defendant can, if he has reasonable cause to believe that there is prosecution material that is properly disclosable but has not been disclosed, apply to the court for an order of disclosure.

The requirement to serve a defence statement contradicts the intention of the initial test of disclosure and in theory means that if a prosecutor fails to disclose any information at all, the defendant could not challenge that failure until he himself has served a defence statement.

A court may also order, following an application by any party, or its own motion, the service of the defence statement on any party to the proceedings (eg, co-defendants) (s 5(5)(A)).

5.10   The prosecution's continuing duty of disclosure (CPIA 1996, s 7A)

This section requires the prosecution to keep under review the prosecution material.

The prosecutor must keep under review the question whether at any given time (and, in particular, following the giving of a defence statement) there is prosecution material which might reasonably be considered capable of undermining the case for the prosecution against the accused or of assisting the case for the accused (CPIA 1996, s 7A(2)).

This duty continues until the trial is over (as a result of a conviction or an acquittal or the prosecutor decides not to proceed with the case).

5.11 Consequences of failure to comply with disclosure requirements (CPIA 1996, ss 10 and 11)

5.11.1 By the prosecution

If the prosecution fails to comply with the time-limit for disclosure and, because of the delay, the defendant is denied a fair trial, this could constitute grounds for staying the proceedings for abuse of process.

5.11.2 By the defendant

If the defendant:

(a)   fails to make defence statement when obliged to do so (see **5.5**); or

(b)   does not comply with the time-limit for doing so; or

(c)   fails to give an updated defence statement after being required to do so; or

(d)   gives an updated defence statement out of time; or

(e)   sets out inconsistent defences in his defence statement;

the court, or with leave, any other party, may make such comments as appear appropriate; and the court may draw such inferences as appear proper when deciding whether the defendant is guilty. Where a defendant calls a witness who he has failed to notify or adequately identify, the court must have regard to whether there is a justification for the failure.

If the defendant at his trial:

(a)   puts forward a defence which was not mentioned in his defence statement or is different from any defence set out in that statement; or

(b)   relies on a matter which, in breach of the requirements about the contents of his defence statement was not mentioned in his defence statement; or

(c)   adduces evidence in support of an alibi, without having given particulars of the alibi in his defence statement; or

(d)   calls a witness to give evidence in support of an alibi without complying with the requirements as regards the witness in his defence statement;

then the court, or with leave, any other party, may make such comments as appear appropriate; and the court may draw such inferences as appear proper when deciding whether the defendant is guilty. Where a defendant calls an alibi witness who he has failed to notify or adequately identify in his defence statement, the court must have regard to whether there is a justification for the failure.

If the defendant has put forward a defence at trial which is different from a defence in the defence statement, the court must look at the extent of the difference and whether there is any justification for it, before commenting, granting leave to comment, or drawing an inference.

Example

Melanie is charged with burglary and pleads not guilty. The prosecution makes initial disclosure. Melanie's defence statement indicates a defence of alibi and names Duncan as an alibi witness. At her trial Melanie wishes to call three witnesses Duncan, Nick and Lisa to support her alibi. As no reference was made to Nick and Lisa in her defence statement, by name or otherwise, the court, or, with leave, the prosecution, may comment on this and the court may draw such inferences as appear proper.

If a defendant:

(a)   gives a witness notice out of time; or

(b)   at his trial calls a witness not included or adequately identified in a witness notice;

the court or any other party may, with leave of the court, make such comment as appears appropriate and the court may draw such inferences as proper in deciding whether the defendant is guilty of the offence.

A defendant cannot be convicted solely on an inference drawn from his failure to comply with the disclosure provisions (s 11(5)).

5.11.3 Warning to the defendant

If it appears to the judge at a pre-trial hearing in the Crown Court that the defendant has failed to comply with defence obligations to disclose, such that there is a possibility of comment being made or inferences being drawn, then the judge must warn the defendant accordingly (s 6E(2)).

5.12 Admissibility of defence statements (CPIA 1996, s 6E)

A judge on his own motion, or following an application by a party, may direct that the jury be given copies of the defence statement (including any updated defence statement). If the judge does so, he may direct that the defence statement be edited so as not to include references to inadmissible evidence (s 6E(4)). Before the defence statement is made available to the jury the judge must be of the opinion that seeing a copy of the defence statement would help the jury understand the case or resolve an issue in the case.

5.13 Further reading

Archbold: Criminal Pleading, Evidence and Practice (Sweet & Maxwell, 2005)

Blackstone's Criminal Practice (Oxford University Press, 2005)

Ede, *Active Defence* (The Law Society, 2000)

Chapter 6

Committal Proceedings and Sending for Trial

6.1 Introduction

Offences triable either way (which are not related to indictable only offences) will be the subject of committal proceedings before a magistrates' court. The purpose of committal proceedings is to ensure that there is a case for the defendant to answer in the Crown Court.

There is power to bypass committal proceedings in serious fraud cases and certain sexual or violent offences involving a child witness. Additionally, the prosecution could avoid the holding of committal proceedings by applying to a High Court judge for a voluntary bill of indictment (see Administration of Justice (Miscellaneous Provisions) Act 1933, s 2). Such cases are beyond the scope of this book.

6.2 Types of committal proceedings

Offences triable either way (which are not related to indictable only offences) will be subject to committal proceedings.

There are two types of committal proceedings:

(a) committal without consideration of the evidence under Magistrates' Courts Act 1980, s 6(2); and

(b) committal with consideration of the evidence under Magistrates' Courts Act 1980, s 6(1), at which the prosecution must satisfy the magistrates that there is sufficient evidence to put the defendant on trial in the Crown Court.

6.3 Preliminary points

Whichever type of committal proceedings takes place, the following points will always apply.

6.3.1 Conduct of proceedings

Proceedings may be conducted by a single magistrate.

6.3.2 Reporting restrictions (Magistrates' Courts Act 1980, s 8)

Committal proceedings usually take place in open court. The press may be present but any report is restricted to the formal part of the proceedings, that is to say, the names of the defendants and witnesses, the offence charged, and the result of the proceedings. The press are not allowed to report the evidence given at committal proceedings. The main reason for reporting restrictions is to prevent a jury from being prejudiced by what they may read in the newspapers and to attempt to ensure that they decide the case in the Crown Court on the evidence presented at the trial.

A single defendant can insist that reporting restrictions be lifted. A defendant may wish to exercise this right, for example, if publicity is needed to trace a witness whose identity is not known.

6.3.3 Evidence which is admissible at committal proceedings

Only the prosecution can adduce evidence at committal proceedings. To be admissible the evidence must fall within one of the categories set out in Magistrates' Courts Act 1980, ss 5B–5E.

6.3.3.1 Written statements under the Magistrates' Courts Act 1980, s 5B

The written statement of a prosecution witness is admissible if:

(a) it purports to be signed by the person who made it;

(b) it contains a declaration that it is true to the best of the maker's knowledge and belief and that it is made knowing that if it is tendered in evidence the maker would be liable to prosecution if he wilfully stated in it anything he knows to be false or did not believe to be true; and

(c) before being tendered in evidence a copy of the statement is given to each of the other parties.

Any documents or exhibits referred to in the s 5B statements are also admissible at committal proceedings.

6.3.3.2 Depositions under the Magistrates' Courts Act 1980, s 5C

Depositions are used where a witness will not voluntarily make a written statement or produce a document or exhibit for the prosecution.

Where a magistrate considers that a person is likely to be able to make a written statement or produce a document or exhibit on behalf of the prosecution which will contain or is likely to be material evidence and the person will not do so voluntarily, the magistrate must issue a summons requiring that person to appear before him to give his evidence or produce the document or exhibit (Magistrates' Courts Act 1980, s 97A).

When that person attends court, his evidence will be taken down in writing by the magistrate in the form of a deposition. If that person fails to attend the magistrate can, in certain circumstances, issue a warrant for his arrest.

To be admissible evidence at committal proceedings, a copy of the deposition must be given to all the parties.

Any documents or exhibits included in the deposition are also admissible at committal proceedings.

6.3.3.3   Statements under the Magistrates' Courts Act 1980, s 5D

These are statements which the prosecution reasonably believes will only be admissible at trial under s 116 or s 117 of the Criminal Justice Act 2003.

In order for the statement to be admissible at committal proceedings, the prosecutor must notify the court and all the parties of his belief and provide them with a copy of the statement.

The magistrates at committal have no power to rule the statement inadmissible.

6.3.3.4   Documents under the Magistrates' Courts Act 1980, s 5E

These are documents which are admissible by some other enactment (eg, a certificate from the Driver and Vehicle Licensing Agency).

6.3.4   Defendant's right to object to written evidence being read at trial

At the same time as the prosecution serves on the defence the evidence to be adduced in committal proceedings, the prosecution must notify the defence of its right to object to written evidence which is admitted in committal proceedings being read at the Crown Court trial without further evidence (see **Appendix 2(O)**).

6.3.5   Pre-committal disclosure of unused material

The prosecution's duty of disclosure of 'unused material' under the Criminal Procedure and Investigations Act 1996 applies when the defendant is committed for trial or sent to the Crown Court for trial (see **7.5**). In *R v Director of Public Prosecutions, ex p Lee* [1999] 2 All ER 737, the Divisional Court held that the 1996 Act did not abolish pre-committal disclosure of 'unused material'. In most cases, prosecution disclosure can wait until after committal without jeopardising the defendant's right to a fair trial. However, the prosecutor must always be alive to the need to disclose material of which he is aware (either from his own consideration of the papers or because his attention has been drawn to it by the defence) and which he, as a responsible prosecutor, recognises should be disclosed at an earlier stage.

6.4   Committal without consideration of the evidence (Magistrates' Courts Act 1980, s 6(2))

The procedure is summarised in **Appendix 1(K)**.

6.4.1   Offer of committal

It is up to the prosecution to offer the defence a committal without consideration of the evidence.

The offer of a committal without consideration of the evidence will be made in virtually all cases and will normally be by letter. The prosecution will serve on the defence a bundle of prosecution documents complying with the requirements of ss 5B–5E of the Magistrates' Courts Act 1980. The defence solicitor will consider the statements with his client. Unless there is a good reason for asking for a committal with consideration of the evidence (see **6.6.2**), the defence will accept the prosecution's offer.

6.4.2   Procedure at committal without consideration of the evidence

The court's function is largely administrative and the proceedings will take only a few minutes.

The prosecution and defendant will attend court. A solicitor acting under a representation order will not receive payment for attending a committal without consideration of the evidence unless his presence is necessary. His presence may be necessary, for example, if there is to be a defence application for bail which will be opposed by the prosecution.

The committal proceedings commence with the charge being read to the defendant. No plea is entered as this is not a trial.

The court clerk asks whether the defence wants reporting restrictions to be lifted (see **6.3.2**).

The court clerk will then check that the formalities for a committal without consideration of the evidence have been complied with. The formalities are:

(a)   that all the prosecution's evidence falls within ss 5B–5E of the Magistrates' Courts Act 1980; and

(b)   copies of the statements and depositions have been served on the defence;

(c)   the defendant has a solicitor acting for him (whether present in court or not); and

(d)   the defence does not wish to make a submission of no case to answer (see **6.5.1**). If the defence does wish to make such a submission, a committal without consideration of the evidence is not appropriate.

The magistrates do not at any stage read the evidence contained in the prosecution statements.

The defendant is committed for trial to the Crown Court and reminded of his right to object to written evidence which was admitted in committal proceedings being read out at the Crown Court trial without further evidence.

A date will be set for a plea and directions hearing in the Crown Court.

The defence will then deal with the following ancillary matters.

6.4.2.1   Representation

The defence will make an application for representation to be extended to cover the Crown Court trial. Such an application will usually be granted.

6.4.2.2   Bail

If the defendant is already on bail, it will be usual for bail to be extended until the Crown Court trial. If the defendant has been in custody until committal proceedings, the defence may be able to make a further bail application to the magistrates (see **3.4.3.10**).

6.5   Committal with consideration of the evidence (Magistrates' Courts Act 1980, s 6(1))

If the defendant is to be committed for trial, the prosecution must show that there is a case to answer.

6.5.1   Procedure

The procedure is summarised in **Appendix 1(L)**.

The charge is read to the defendant but no plea is taken.

The court clerk will ask whether the defence wants reporting restrictions to be lifted.

The prosecution evidence will either be read aloud at the hearing or, if the court directs, orally summarised. No witnesses can be called to give oral evidence.

At the close of the prosecution case, the defence may make a submission of no case to answer. The test to be applied by the magistrates when considering a submission is laid down in the case of *R v Galbraith (George Charles)* [1981] 2 All ER 1060. The magistrates must ask themselves whether the prosecution evidence, taken at its highest, is such that a jury properly directed could not properly convict on it. The practical effect of this test was considered in Galbraith:

> ... where the prosecution evidence is such that its strength or weakness depends on the view to be taken of a witness's reliability or other matters which are generally speaking within the jury's province and where one possible view of the facts is that there is evidence on which the jury could properly convict,

then the submission of no case to answer will fail.

For a submission to succeed, therefore, the defence will have to show that the prosecution has failed to adduce evidence in support of an essential element of the offence or that, even taking the best possible view of the prosecution evidence, the case against the defendant is so unreliable that a jury could not convict on it.

If no submission is made or if the submission is rejected, the magistrates will announce that there is a case to answer and commit the defendant to the Crown Court for trial. The magistrates will then remind the defendant of his right to object to written evidence which has been adduced in committal proceedings being read out in the Crown Court without further evidence. If they uphold the submission the magistrates will announce that the submission has been upheld and discharge the defendant.

If the defendant is committed for trial, a date will be set for a plea and case management hearing at the Crown Court. Bail and representation will then be dealt with as on a s 6(2) committal.

6.5.1.1   Excluding evidence at committal

The Criminal Procedure and Investigations Act 1996 (Sch 1, paras 25 and 26) provides that the magistrates have no power to exclude prosecution evidence at committal proceedings under either s 76(2) or s 78 of the Police and Criminal Evidence Act 1984.

6.6   Deciding on the type of committal proceedings

6.6.1   Prosecution decides on committal with consideration of the evidence

If the prosecution decides to have a committal with consideration of the evidence then the defence does not have a choice.

Since the prosecution can no longer use committal proceedings to test its own witnesses by calling them to give oral evidence, it is now very unlikely ever to insist on a s 6(1) (MCA 1980) committal.

6.6.2   Prosecution decides on committal without consideration of the evidence

If the prosecution offers the defence a committal without consideration of the evidence, the choice as to the type of committal will rest with the defence. Reasons for insisting on a committal with consideration of the evidence include the following.

(a)   Making a submission of no case to answer

The circumstances in which this is a realistic possibility were discussed at **6.5.1**.

(b)   To try to persuade the court to commit the defendant for trial on a lesser charge than the one being dealt with at committal

For example, a charge of causing grievous bodily harm could be reduced to a charge of assault occasioning actual bodily harm.

If neither of the reasons described above applies to the case then a committal without consideration of the evidence is appropriate. This will be quicker than a s 6(1) committal.

Agreeing to a s 6(2) committal does not in any way prevent the defence from challenging the prosecution witnesses or the admissibility of their evidence at Crown Court.

6.7   Sending for trial procedure (Crime and Disorder Act 1998, ss 51, 52 and Sch 3)

6.7.1   Cases to which s 51 applies

Where an adult appears or is brought before a magistrates' court charged with an indictable only offence, the court must send him to the Crown Court for trial:

(a)   for that offence; and

(b)   for any either way offence or summary offence with which he is charged which fulfils the 'requisite conditions' (s 51(1)).

The 'requisite conditions' are that:

(a)   the either way or summary offence appears to the court to be related to the indictable only offence; and

(b)   in the case of a summary only offence, it is punishable with imprisonment or involves obligatory or discretionary disqualification from driving (s 51(11)).

An either way offence is related to an indictable only offence if the charge for the either way offence could be joined in the same indictment as the charge for the indictable only offence. A summary offence is related to an indictable only offence if it arises out of circumstances which are the same as or connected with those giving rise to the indictable only offence (s 51(12)).

An adult co-defendant who is charged with a related either way offence must also be sent to the Crown Court for trial (s 51(3)).

If a defendant is sent for trial for a summary offence, the trial of that offence in the magistrates' court shall be treated as if the court had adjourned it and had not fixed the time and place for its resumption (s 51(9)).

A juvenile (an offender under 18) is not liable to be sent to the Crown Court unless he is jointly charged with an indictable offence with an adult. When the adult is sent to the Crown Court under s 51, the magistrates may send the juvenile to the Crown Court as well if the magistrates consider that it is in the interests of justice for him to be tried jointly with the adult defendant. Where they do so, the magistrates may also send the juvenile to the Crown Court to be tried for related offences (s 51(5) and (6)).

6.7.2   The preliminary hearing in the magistrates' court

An adult defendant charged with an offence triable only on indictment will be sent straight to the Crown Court for trial, following a preliminary hearing in the magistrates' court. The purpose of the hearing is to determine whether there is an indictable only offence charged and whether there are related offences which should also be sent to the Crown Court. The court will also consider representation. The magistrates will set the date on which the first preliminary hearing will take place in the Crown Court and will remand the defendant in custody or on bail to appear at the Crown Court.

The preliminary hearing should be before two or more justices. The CPS must be represented by a Crown prosecutor. The preliminary hearing is likely to take place at the next available court sitting after the defendant has been charged.

Section 52(5) provides that the preliminary hearing in the magistrates' court may be adjourned but it is envisaged that, given the limited nature of the court's function under s 51, it will seldom be necessary to adjourn.

6.7.3   Representation

A magistrates' court has the power to grant a 'through representation order' (see **3.3.2.4**) for indictable only offences (and related offences or defendants) that are sent to the Crown Court under s 51.

If an application for representation has not been submitted already representation will be dealt with at the preliminary hearing. The magistrates or the justices' clerk will consider whether the case meets the interests of justice criteria and grant a representation order which covers both representation in the magistrates' court and the Crown Court.

6.7.4   Statement of means for the Crown Court

Only the interests of justice test has to be satisfied before granting a representation order: a representation order is non-means tested. At the conclusion of the case in the Crown Court the judge has the power to order a defendant to pay some or all the costs of his defence (see **10.2.14**).

When the defendant applies for representation to cover proceedings in the Crown Court, the magistrates' court will provide the defendant with Form B (see **Appendix 2(O)**). This form should be returned to the Crown Court at least four days before the first hearing at the Crown Court which will usually be the preliminary hearing (for cases sent to the Crown Court for trial) or the plea and case management hearing (for cases committed to the Crown Court for trial). Failure to return this form, which provides details of the defendant's means and those of a partner if the defendant has one, could result in a defendant's costs order being made at the conclusion of the case for the full defence costs.

6.8 Linked summary offences

If the defendant is to be tried in the Crown Court, a question sometimes arises as to what will happen to other offences with which he is charged but which are purely summary offences.

6.8.1 Criminal Justice Act 1988, s 40(1)

A count charging a person with a summary offence to which this section applies may be included in an indictment if the charge—

(a)   is founded on the same facts or evidence as a count charging an indictable offence; or

(b)   is part of a series of offences of the same or similar character as an indictable offence which is also charged,

but only if (in either case) the facts or evidence relating to the offence were disclosed to a magistrates' court inquiring into the offence as examining justices or are disclosed by material which, in pursuance of regulations made under paragraph 1 of Schedule 3 to the Crime and Disorder Act 1998 (procedure where person sent for trial under section 51, has been served on the person charged).

The offences to which this section applies are: taking a conveyance, common assault, driving while disqualified and certain offences of criminal damage.

The effect of s 40 is to enable the prosecution, when drafting the indictment for trial in the Crown Court, to include a purely summary offence provided the conditions in s 40 are satisfied.

Example 1

Imran is charged with theft of goods from a motor vehicle and with taking a conveyance. The facts are that he took a vehicle without the owner's consent and stole a quantity of tapes and a radio from the car while it was in his possession. The charges are therefore founded on the same facts. Imran is committed to the Crown Court for trial on the theft charge. Under s 40, the summary offence of taking a conveyance can also be tried in the Crown Court, provided evidence in support of the charge is included in the witness statements adduced in evidence in committal proceedings.

Example 2

Sean is charged with robbery and driving whilst disqualified. The facts are that Sean pushed Susan to the ground, stole her handbag and then made his getaway by car. The charges are therefore founded on the same facts. Sean is sent to the Crown Court for trial on the robbery charge. Under s 40, the summary offence of driving while disqualified can also be tried at the Crown Court, provided evidence of the charge is included in the prosecution evidence served on the defence at the Crown Court.

If the defendant is convicted of the summary offence, the Crown Court's sentencing powers are limited to those of the magistrates.

For summary only offences that are sent to the Crown Court for trial and do not satisfy the requirements of s 40, see **7.4.6**.

6.8.2 Criminal Justice Act 1988, s 41(1)

Where a magistrates' court commits a person to the Crown Court for trial on indictment for an offence triable either way or a number of such offences, it may also commit him for trial for any summary offence with which he is charged and which—

(a)   is punishable with imprisonment or involves obligatory or discretionary disqualification from driving; and

(b)   arises out of circumstances which appear to the court to be the same as or connected with those giving rise to the offence, or one of the offences, triable either way,

whether or not evidence relating to that summary offence appears on the depositions or written statements in the case;

Provided the offence committed for trial is triable either way, any summary offence which satisfies the conditions set out above may also be committed for trial.

If the defendant, on conviction for the either way offence, pleads guilty to the summary offence, the Crown Court can sentence for the summary offence, but its powers are limited to those of the magistrates. If the defendant pleads not guilty the summary offence must be remitted to the magistrates' court for trial. The Crown Court has no power to deal with the summary offence in these circumstances.

Example

Chris is committed for trial in the Crown Court on a charge of assault occasioning actual bodily harm. He also faces a charge of threatening behaviour, under the Public Order Act 1986, s 4, arising out of the same incident. This offence can be added to the indictment in the Crown Court. If Chris is convicted of the assault charge the Crown Court can sentence him for the public order offence, provided he pleads guilty. If Chris pleads not guilty to the public order offence or is acquitted on the assault charge, the Crown Court must remit the public order offence back to the magistrates.

The Crown Court is required to inform the clerk of the committing magistrates' court of the outcome of any proceedings under s 41, as proceedings in the magistrates' court in respect of the summary offence will have been adjourned.

6.8.3 Conclusion

Sections 40 and 41 are similar in that they both may allow the Crown Court to deal with linked summary offences. However, they have the following key differences.

(a)   Section 40 allows the summary offence to be tried in the Crown Court, along with the either way offence.

Section 41 only allows the Crown Court to sentence for the summary offence if the defendant pleads guilty to it. If he pleads not guilty, the trial must be held in the magistrates' court.

(b)   Section 40 applies if the defendant is committed to the Crown Court for trial for any either way offence or when an indictable offence is sent to the Crown Court for trial.

Section 41 only applies if the defendant is committed to the Crown Court for an either way offence.

(c)   Section 40 only enables the Crown Court to try a limited list of the more serious summary offences.

Section 41 may enable the Crown Court to sentence for any summary offence which is punishable with imprisonment or disqualification.

6.9 Criminal Justice Act 2003

Section 41 and Sch 3 to the Criminal Justice Act 2003 make substantial changes to the way cases are allocated between courts. The changes are likely to be introduced in September 2006.

6.10 Further reading

For further discussions on criminal proceedings, see, for example:

Archbold: Criminal Pleading, Evidence and Practice (Sweet & Maxwell, 2005)

Blackstone's Criminal Practice (Oxford University Press, 2005)

John Sprack, *Emmins on Criminal Procedure* (Oxford University Press, 2004)

Ede and Edwards, *Criminal Defence* (The Law Society, 2002)

Chapter 7

Preparations for Trial on Indictment

7.1 Introduction

This chapter deals with what happens to a case after it has been either committed to the Crown Court for trial or sent to the Crown Court for trial under s 51 of the Crime and Disorder Act 1998. The major procedural steps are summarised in chart form at **Appendix 1(R)** and **Appendix 1(S)**. This chapter also deals with the main preparatory steps for Crown Court trial.

Amendment 11 to the Consolidated Criminal Practice Direction (Case Management) amends the *Practice Direction (Criminal Proceedings: Consolidation)* [2002] 3 All ER 904 and applies to the sending for trial or committal for trial of cases by the magistrates' court to the Crown Court and the management of those cases in the Crown Court.

In all cases tried on indictment the case progression officer (see **1.5.6**) should complete the relevant case details forms:

(a) for cases sent to the Crown Court for trial the case progression form and the preliminary hearing (PH) form are set out in **Appendix 2(U)** with guidance notes. The forms provide a detailed timetable to enable the plea and case management hearing (PCMH) to be effective;

(b) for cases committed for trial the case progression form to be used in the magistrates' court is set out in **Appendix 2(V)** with guidance notes.

7.2 The indictment

The indictment is the formal document containing a list of charges against the defendant, to which he pleads guilty or not guilty at the beginning of the Crown Court trial. The offences alleged against the defendant are set out in separate counts of the indictment. Each count must allege only one offence. The indictment must be signed by an officer of the Crown Court. Until the indictment is signed, it is merely a 'bill of indictment'. Bills of indictment are usually drafted by the prosecution and the prosecution will have to deliver the bill to the Crown Court to be signed. Such delivery is known as 'preferment of the bill of indictment'.

The law on drafting indictments is contained principally in the Indictments Act 1915, the Indictment (Procedure) Rules 1971 (SI 1971/2084) and the Criminal Procedure Rules 2005 (CrimPR), Pt 14. CrimPR, r 14.2 provides that a bill of indictment must be preferred within 28 days of committal to the Crown Court or within 28 days of service of the prosecution case if the case is sent for trial. This period can be extended by application to the court.

7.3   Cases committed to the Crown Court for trial

7.3.1   Use of statements and depositions of prosecution witnesses at trial

The Criminal Procedure and Investigations Act 1996, s 68 and Sch 2, paras 1 and 2, provide that written statements and depositions which have been admitted in evidence in committal proceedings can be read at the Crown Court trial where all parties agree or where the court considers it to be in the interests of justice to do so (see **9.6.2.10**).

If the defendant intends to plead not guilty at the Crown Court, the defence must consider whether to object to this prosecution evidence being read to the court. Any objection to the reading out at the trial of a statement or deposition without further evidence shall be made in writing to the prosecutor and the Crown Court within 14 days of the defendant being committed for trial unless the court, at its discretion, permits such an objection to be made outside that period (CrimPR, Pt 27).

If the defence wishes to challenge the admissibility of the contents of the written statement or cross-examine the maker of the written statement or deposition, the defence should object.

7.3.2   First hearing

The first hearing for a defendant committed for trial at the Crown Court for an either way offence will be the plea and case management hearing (PCMH) (see 7.8). When committing a case to the Crown Court, a magistrates' court should order that a PCMH be held within about seven weeks after committal (*Practice Direction (Criminal Proceedings: Consolidation)* [2002] 3 All ER 904, para 41).

7.4   Cases sent to the Crown Court for trial

7.4.1   Preliminary hearing

The first hearing for a defendant sent for trial for an indictable only offence may be a preliminary hearing (PH). A preliminary hearing is any hearing which takes place before the prosecution has completed service of its case. A PH is not required in every case sent for trial and should be ordered by the magistrates' court or the Crown Court only when such a hearing is considered necessary. The PH should be held about 14 days after the case has been sent for trial.

The notice specifying the charges upon which the defendant is sent for trial (required by s 51(7) of the Crime and Disorder Act 1998), together with other documents, including the charge, must be sent by the magistrates' court to the Crown Court within four days of sending a person to be tried in the Crown Court (CrimPR, r 12.1). The first Crown Court appearance must then take place in accordance with any directions given by the magistrates' court (CrimPR, r 12.2).

The preliminary hearing allows a defendant, who has been sent for trial in custody, to apply to the Crown Court for bail, and allows the judge, having consulted the prosecution, to set a date by which the prosecution is to serve its case on the defence.

There is nothing to prevent a defendant from making a bail application before the date fixed for the preliminary hearing. It is then for the Crown Court to decide when to allow an earlier hearing to determine bail. If the court so decides, it will depend on the circumstances of the case whether at that hearing it is possible for the court to determine the timetable for the case (in effect bringing forward the date of the preliminary hearing), or whether it will still be necessary to hold a hearing for that purpose on the date originally fixed. If an earlier hearing is arranged, then the s 51(7) notice and associated documents should be sent to the Crown Court in time for the hearing and the CPS should be given as much notice of the hearing as possible.

The Criminal Procedure Rules, r 16.11 allows the preliminary hearing to take place in chambers. Normally the preliminary hearing (and any others which take place before the prosecution case is served) are heard in open court as chambers, with the defendant present and the court open to the public. The Crown may be represented at the hearing by a Crown prosecutor and the defence by a solicitor.

Whether or not a magistrates' court orders a PH it should order a PCMH to be held within about 14 weeks after sending for trial where a defendant is in custody and within about 17 weeks after sending for trial where a defendant is on bail.

7.4.2 Depositions from reluctant witnesses

A provision equivalent to that in s 97A of the Magistrates' Courts Act 1980 (see **6.3.3.2**) is available. The procedure allows for the taking (before service of the prosecution case) of depositions from reluctant witnesses and this is taken before a magistrate, notwithstanding that the case has been sent to the Crown Court (Crime and Disorder Act 1998, Sch 3, para 4).

7.4.3 Service of prosecution case

The Attorney-General is required to make regulations for the service of documents containing the prosecution evidence on which the charge or charges are based (Crime and Disorder Act 1998, s 51(7), Sch 3, para 1). The Crime and Disorder Act 1998 (Service of Prosecution Evidence) Regulations 1998 (SI 1998/3115) set a 'long stop' date of one year from the date the case is sent, for the judge to determine the date by which the evidence is to be served.

It will generally be convenient for the evidence to be served in one bundle. In a complex case, it may be appropriate to serve evidence as it becomes available. If so, the prosecution should notify the defence that more evidence is to be served later and advise the defence once the case has been fully served.

The evidence that is served will form the prima facie case.

The date of service of the prosecution case is relevant for the timing of applications for dismissal, disclosure of evidence the prosecution do not intend to rely on and the preferment of the indictment.

There will usually be another Crown Court hearing after service of the prosecution case (or to find out why the prosecution case has not yet been served). The purpose of this hearing will be to review the case to date and confirm the PCMH date. The timing of this hearing will be at the judge's discretion.

7.4.4 Applications for dismissal

Once the prosecution case has been served, the defence may make an application for dismissal (Crime and Disorder Act 1998, Sch 3, para 2). The judge shall dismiss the charge if it appears to him that the evidence against the defendant would not be sufficient for the jury to properly convict him. Detailed provision for this is made in CrimPR, Pt 13. The defence may give notice of intention to make an oral application, or make an application in writing (to which the prosecution may respond with a request for an oral hearing). The notice or written application, accompanied by copies of any material relied on, must be copied to the prosecution, which is allowed 14 days from receipt to make written comments or adduce further evidence. There is provision for the 14-day period to be extended.

The Rules include provision for evidence to be given orally, but only with the leave of the judge, which is to be given only when the interests of justice require.

Reporting restrictions apply which are modelled on the restrictions which apply to the reporting of committal proceedings (see **6.3.2**).

If a defendant succeeds in having the case against him dismissed, no further proceedings on the dismissed charge may be made (other than through a voluntary bill of indictment).

7.4.5 Related either way offences

Sending related either way offences for trial enables the Crown Court to deal with the indictable only offence and related either way offences in the one trial.

Where (following a successful application to dismiss or to discontinue or for any other reason) the indictable only offence which caused the case to be sent to the Crown Court in the first place is no longer on the indictment, consideration must be given to the outstanding related either way offences.

7.4.5.1 Adult defendants

The Crown Court should deal with outstanding either way offences where there is a guilty plea, or where the case appears suitable for trial on indictment, or where the defendant elects Crown Court trial.

The either way offences should be remitted to the magistrates for trial only where a not guilty plea is indicated (or no indication given), the case is suitable for summary trial and the defendant consents to be so tried (Crime and Disorder Act 1998, Sch 3, paras 7–12).

7.4.5.2 Procedure

The procedure amounts to an adapted mode of trial hearing, at which the Crown Court determines mode of trial in much the same way as magistrates would do.

(a) The outstanding counts on the indictment that charge either way offences are read to the defendant and the court will invite him to indicate a plea, explaining that if he indicates that he would plead guilty, the court will proceed to deal with him as if the trial had started and he pleaded guilty.

(b) If the defendant indicates that he would plead not guilty or fails to give any indication, the court must next consider whether the case is more suitable for summary trial or trial on indictment, having regard to any representations made by the prosecution or the defendant, the nature of the case, the seriousness of the offence, whether the magistrates' sentencing powers would be adequate, or any other relevant circumstances.

(c) If the court decides that the offence is more suitable for trial on indictment, the case will proceed in the usual way. If, on the other hand, it decides that the case is more suitable for summary trial, the court must give the defendant the option of electing Crown Court trial.

(d) If the defendant consents to summary trial, the case is remitted to the magistrates. The defendant will be remanded on bail or in custody to appear before the magistrates' court.

Example

Teja is sent for trial to the Crown Court on a robbery charge. He also faces a charge of assault occasioning actual bodily harm arising out of the same incident. This offence can be sent to the Crown Court as a related either way offence.

At the Crown Court, the robbery charge is dismissed following an application for dismissal. The court will conduct a mode of trial procedure in relation to the charge of assault occasioning actual bodily harm.

If Teja indicates a guilty plea, the court will deal with him as if the trial had started and he had pleaded guilty. The court will proceed to sentence.

If Teja indicates a not guilty plea, the court will have to decide whether the case is suitable for trial on indictment or summary trial. If the court decides that trial on indictment is more suitable, Teja has no choice; he will be tried on indictment. If the court decides that summary trial is more suitable then Teja has a choice. If he consents to summary trial, the case is remitted to the magistrates' court for trial. If not, he will be tried on indictment.

7.4.5.3 Juvenile defendants

Cases involving juveniles should be remitted to the magistrates' court unless it is necessary that they should be tried in the Crown Court. The circumstances in which the Crown Court should deal with juvenile defendants are where:

(a) the defendant is charged with an offence which is a grave crime for the purposes of s 91 of the Powers of Criminal Courts (Sentencing) Act 2000 and the court considers that it ought to be possible for him to be sentenced under that provision; or

(b) the juvenile is charged jointly with an adult with an either way offence and it is necessary in the interests of justice that they both should be tried at the Crown Court.

(Crime and Disorder Act 1998, Sch 3, para 13)

7.4.6 Related summary offences

Where a magistrates' court has sent a defendant for trial for offences which include a summary offence, the summary offence will not be included in the indictment and the defendant will not be asked to plead to the summary offence when the trial begins (unless the summary offence has been included in the indictment under s 40 of the Criminal Justice Act 1988, which only applies to a few summary offences; see **6.8.1**).

The Crown Court will deal with a summary offence only if the defendant pleads guilty to it and the defendant has been convicted of the indictable only offence to which it related; in so doing, the court's powers are restricted to those which would have been available to a magistrates' court. In any other circumstances, the summary offence will either be remitted to the magistrates for trial or (if the prosecution do not wish to proceed) be dismissed (Crime and Disorder Act 1998, Sch 3, para 6).

The Crown Court is required to inform the clerk of the 'sending magistrates' court' of the outcome of any proceedings in respect of the summary offence (Sch 3, para 6(7)) as proceedings in the magistrates' court in respect of the summary offence will have been adjourned.

Example

Dmitri is sent for trial in the Crown Court on a charge of robbery. He also faces a charge of threatening behavior, under the Public Order Act 1986, s 4, arising out of the same incident. The s 4 offence is sent to the Crown Court as a related summary offence. If Dmitri is convicted of the robbery charge, the Crown Court can sentence him for the public order offence, provided he pleads guilty. If he pleads not guilty to the public order offence or is acquitted of the robbery charge, the Crown Court must remit the public order offence back to the magistrates unless the prosecution decide not to proceed with the public order offence, in which case the Crown Court can dismiss the charge.

7.4.7   The Criminal Justice Act 2003

Section 41 of and Sch 3 to the Criminal Justice Act 2003 make substantial changes to the way cases will be allocated between courts. It is not expected that those changes will be introduced before September 2006.

7.5   Disclosure

7.5.1   Duty to provide advance information

If the case has been committed to the Crown Court for trial, this duty is met by the papers served on the defence prior to committal to the Crown Court. For those cases sent to the Crown Court for trial, the prosecution will disclose its case at the Crown Court (see **7.4.3**). Any additional evidence which the prosecution later decide to adduce as part of the prosecution case must be brought to the defendant's attention by way of notice of further evidence (see **7.6**).

7.5.2   Duty to disclose 'unused material'

The prosecution's duty of disclosure of 'unused material' will apply where the defendant is committed for trial to the Crown Court or sent to the Crown Court for trial under s 51 of the Crime and Disorder Act 1998. The defence must give a 'defence statement' to the prosecution. If the defendant discloses inconsistent defences or a defence inconsistent with that later advanced at trial, the court or, with leave, any other party, may make such comments as appear appropriate; and the court may draw such inferences as appear proper when deciding whether the defendant is guilty.

For guidance on the drafting of defence statements, see the Professional Conduct and Complaints Committee of the Bar Council Guidance dated 24 September 1997.

7.6   Notices of further evidence

A witness may be called to give evidence for the prosecution in the Crown Court even though his statement was not served on the defence at committal stage or not served by the prosecution at the Crown Court for cases sent to the Crown

Court for trial. It may be, for example, that the evidence only came to light after the plea and directions hearing in the Crown Court.

If the prosecution wishes to call additional evidence, a notice of intention to do so will be served on the defence and the Crown Court. The notice will be accompanied by a copy of the relevant witness statement.

7.7 Preparing for the plea and case management hearing

7.7.1 Guilty pleas

If a defendant intends to plead guilty, the defence solicitor should notify the Probation Service, the prosecution and the court as soon as this is known.

7.7.2 Not guilty pleas

The defence solicitor should ensure that the case is sufficiently prepared for the PCMH to enable the advocate who appears at the hearing to give the judge the information required to fix a trial date. The amount of information required is such that the case has to be almost ready for a full trial unless it is very complex, in which case further pre-trial hearings may be necessary. In particular:

(a)   the defence should have checked the availability of defence witnesses for the trial and served witness summonses;

(b)   any evidence sought to be admitted by the defence under Criminal Justice Act 1967, s 9 should be served on the prosecution;

(c)   any complex issues of law or issues of admissibility of evidence should have been identified;

(d)   any factors relevant to mitigation in the event of conviction should have been identified.

A copy of the PCMH form which has to be completed and handed in to the court prior to the commencement of the PCMH appears at **Appendix 2(P)**.

7.8 Plea and case management hearing

When committing a case to the Crown Court, a magistrates' court should order a PCMH to be held within about seven weeks after committal.

A PCMH will also take place in relation to cases sent to the Crown Court for trial. In cases sent for trial the magistrates' court should order a PCMH to be held within about 14 weeks after sending for trial where a defendant is in custody, and within about 17 weeks after sending for trial when a defendant is on bail.

At the PCMH, a defendant will be required to plead to the charge(s) against him. A defendant who has pleaded guilty may be sentenced at the PCMH. If a defendant pleads not guilty, the judge will require the following information:

(a)   a summary of the issues in the case;

(b)   number of witnesses to give oral evidence;

(c)   number of witnesses whose evidence will be given in writing;

(d)   any facts formally admitted;

(e)   any alibi which should have been disclosed to the prosecution;

(f)   any points of law or admissibility of evidence likely to arise at the trial;

(g)   estimated length of trial;

(h)   dates of availability of witnesses;

(i)   dates of availability of the advocates.

See *Practice Direction (Criminal Proceedings: Consolidation)* [2002] 3 All ER 904, para 41.

If a date is not fixed for the not guilty trial, then the case will be placed in the warned list. The warned list is the list of cases awaiting a not guilty trial date. Each Crown Court will send out warned lists for the coming weeks. The Crown Court will then contact the solicitor (usually the previous afternoon) to warn the solicitor that the case will be listed for hearing the next morning.

In the majority of cases committed for trial in the Crown Court, the only pre-trial hearing will be a PCMH.

7.9 Pre-trial hearings

Section 40 of the Criminal Procedure and Investigations Act 1996 allows a judge, before the trial begins, to rule on the admissibility of evidence and on any question of law relating to the case. For the purposes of this section, a trial begins when a jury is sworn or a guilty plea is accepted or a preparatory hearing starts (see **7.10**).

The ruling can be made on the application of the prosecution or the defence or on the judge's own motion.

It will bind the parties at trial unless it is discharged or varied.

A ruling can be discharged or varied on the judge's own motion or on an application by the prosecution or the defence if the judge considers that it is in the interests of justice to do so. The prosecution or defence can only apply for a discharge or variation if there has been a material change of circumstances since the ruling was made.

Example

The judge could be asked to rule on the admissibility of a written statement which the prosecution or the defence seeks to adduce at trial. If the judge ruled it to be inadmissible that ruling would be binding unless it was subsequently discharged in the interests of justice.

7.10 Preparatory hearings

Part III of the Criminal Procedure and Investigations Act 1996 creates a statutory scheme of preparatory hearings (PHs) for long or complex cases which are to be tried in the Crown Court.

A judge, on his own motion, or on the application of the prosecution or the defence, can order that a PH be held if he considers that it is likely to bring substantial benefits because of the complexity or likely length of the case.

The PH will take place before the jury are sworn in and can be used for any of the following purposes:

(a)   to identify important issues for the jury;
(b)   to help the jury's understanding of the issues;
(c)   to speed up the proceedings before the jury;
(d)   to help the judge's management of the trial.

The plea will be taken at the start of the PH unless it has already been taken.

At the PH, the judge can rule on the admissibility of evidence and on any other question of law.

Under s 31 of the CPIA 1996, the judge can also exercise powers to help identify, simplify and narrow the issues of dispute, for example, he can require the prosecution or the defence to provide a detailed case statement.

Any order or ruling made by the judge is binding throughout the trial unless he decides on the application of the prosecution or the defence that it is in the interests of justice to vary or discharge it.

Inferences

If either party departs from the case disclosed as a result of a requirement under s 31, or fails to comply with a s 31 requirement, the judge or, with leave of the judge, any other party, may comment on this at the trial and the jury may draw such inferences from it as appear proper.

Appeals

It is possible, in certain circumstances, to appeal against the judge's ruling on the admissibility of evidence or a question of law to the Court of Appeal and then to the House of Lords.

7.11 Briefing counsel

If counsel is to be instructed in the Crown Court, a brief to counsel should be prepared and sent to counsel's clerk as soon as the case has been committed to the Crown Court or sent for trial to the Crown Court.

On receipt of the brief, counsel may require a conference. The purpose of a conference is to enable the defendant to meet and be advised by counsel. A conference:

> should normally be held in the following cases:
> – where there is a not guilty hearing;
> – where the defendant needs to be advised about please;
> – where the case is complicated by a particular factor or involves serious consequences;
> – where the case requires careful consideration of tactics, evidence, plea, experts, exhibits and witnesses.
>
> (Ede and Edwards, *Criminal Defence* (The Law Society, 2002), p 198)

An example of a brief to counsel appears as **Appendix 2(Q)**. It covers counsel attending the PCMH and trial. A brief should be as full as possible and should be broken down into sections:

(a) Introduction – this deals with the defendant, the charge, the history of the case, bail arrangements and which prosecution witnesses must attend the trial to give oral evidence.

(b) Prosecution case – this contains a summary of the evidence to be given by each witness.

(c) Defence case – this contains a summary of the defence evidence.

(d) Evidence – any major point likely to arise at the trial should be highlighted for the benefit of counsel.

(e) Mitigation – any facts relevant to mitigation in the event of a conviction should be mentioned.

7.12 Trial on indictment

Procedure in the Crown Court on a not guilty plea is summarised in **Appendix 1(M)**.

A trial on indictment begins with the arraignment at the PCMH, which consists of putting the counts in the indictment to the defendant so that he can plead guilty or not guilty.

If there is a plea of not guilty the trial takes place before a judge and a jury in the presence of the defendant (unless, for example, he is disruptive). The order of proceedings is similar to that in a magistrates' court, except that the prosecution must make an opening speech and will also address the jury at the conclusion of the defence case before counsel for the defence. The judge will then sum up to the jury.

The judge hears argument on points of law and evidence in the absence of the jury and may direct the jury to acquit if, for example, there is a successful submission of no case to answer. The test to be applied by the judge when considering a submission is laid down in the case of *R v Galbraith (George Charles)* [1981] 2 All ER 1060 (see **6.5.1**).

The verdict whether guilty or not guilty is decided by unanimous vote of the jury, although a majority verdict of 11:1, or 10:2 will be accepted if, after two hours, unanimity is not possible. If the jury fails to agree there may be a new trial before a new jury.

The judge decides on sentence and has wider powers of sentencing than the magistrates.

7.13 Further reading

For further discussions on criminal proceedings, see, for example:

Archbold: Criminal Pleading, Evidence and Practice (Sweet & Maxwell, 2005)

Blackstone's Criminal Practice (Oxford University Press, 2005)

John Sprack, *Emmins on Criminal Procedure* (Oxford University Press, 2004)

Ede and Edwards, *Criminal Defence* (The Law Society, 2002)

Chapter 8
Summary Trial

8.1 Introduction

Magistrates must try a summary offence and have power to try an either way offence with the defendant's consent. This chapter distinguishes the right to advance information of the prosecution case from the rules relating to disclosure of unused material by the prosecution. It explains what happens at a pre-trial review and also gives an outline of the procedure followed at a trial in the magistrates' court. The procedure on a plea of guilty in the magistrates' court is examined separately in **Chapter 10**.

The major procedural steps in relation to a summary offence are summarised in chart form at **Appendix 1(T)**.

8.2 Disclosure

8.2.1 Duty to provide advance information

This is the obligation on the prosecution to notify the defence of its case, ie, the evidence upon which it intends to rely at trial.

The Criminal Procedure Rules 2005, Part 21, provides that if the defendant is charged with an offence triable either way, the prosecution must provide the defence either with copies of the prosecution witnesses' written statements or with a summary of the facts and matters about which evidence will be adduced during the course of the prosecution.

For summary only offences, it is CPS practice to give advance information (Attorney General's Guidelines: Disclosure of Information in Criminal Proceedings (29 November 2000), para 43).

For more detailed information, see **5.2**.

8.2.2 Duty to disclose 'unused material'

This is the obligation on the prosecution under the Criminal Procedure and Investigations Act 1996 to make available to the defence any material of relevance to the case upon which it does not intend to rely – 'unused material'. It applies when the defendant pleads not guilty in the magistrates' court.

In the magistrates' court there is no obligation on the defendant to provide a defence statement. It is probable that most defence solicitors will advise against providing a defence statement in the magistrates' court.

8.3 Preparing the case for trial

In preparing a case for trial by magistrates, the following steps should be considered.

8.3.1 Interviewing the client

Although outline instructions may have been taken at the police station or to enable a bail application or application for a representation order to be made, detailed instructions must now be taken from the defendant. A pro forma can be used to confirm the formal part of instructions such as name, address, date of birth, family details, etc, but a detailed statement will have to be taken as regards the offence. The solicitor should not be afraid to challenge the client's story in interview as it will most certainly be challenged by the prosecution at the trial.

If advance disclosure of the prosecution case has been given (as it must be with an either way offence, see **8.2.1**), the statement should also include comments on the prosecution evidence. The statement should be signed and dated by the client.

8.3.2 Interviewing witnesses

The defendant will have provided the names and addresses of relevant witnesses. Witnesses should be interviewed as soon as possible and a full proof of evidence taken from them. Again, when interviewing witnesses, the solicitor should not be afraid to challenge what they say. It is important that inconsistencies be ironed out or explained at this stage rather than in court. The witness's proof of evidence should be signed by the witness and dated.

8.3.3 Writing to the prosecution

A pro forma letter can be sent to the prosecution requesting such of the following information as is appropriate to the case.

(a)   In either way offences, advance disclosure of the prosecution case. There is no statutory right to advance disclosure if the offence is summary only. However, a request for voluntary disclosure in such cases will be looked upon favourably (see **5.2.1**).

(b)   Details of the defendant's criminal record. Although details will have been taken from the client, this cannot be relied upon. The prosecution will supply a copy of the record that it will be relying upon in court. This record should be checked against the information given by the client and any inconsistencies cleared up as soon as possible.

(c)   A record of any interviews with the defendant.

(d)   A copy of the custody record. In some areas the custody record is available directly from the police, but the initial approach may be to the CPS.

8.3.4 Location

If the location of the crime is important to the defence, a visit to the relevant scene should be made and plans and photographs prepared. This action may be necessary, for example, in road traffic cases and in cases where the defendant alleges that a prosecution witness, because of his position, could not possibly have seen the events which he alleges he has seen.

8.3.5 Expert evidence

If expert evidence is necessary, an expert should be instructed at the earliest possible opportunity to prepare a report. Expert evidence may be required on any technical matter that is outside the competence of the magistrates. Expert evidence should be disclosed to the prosecution before the trial. If the defendant is represented under a representation order, it is prudent to seek prior authority from the Legal Services Commission Regional Office before instructing the expert. Prior authority is sought by written application outlining the reason for instructing the expert and his fee. If prior authority is granted, the solicitor is certain to recover the cost involved from the Legal Services Commission. If prior authority is refused then the costs will still be recoverable, provided the solicitor can justify the expenditure at the end of the case.

8.3.6 Securing the attendances of witnesses

A witness summons can be issued only if the clerk to the justices or a magistrate is satisfied that a witness will not voluntarily attend or produce a document or thing (Magistrates' Courts Act 1980, s 97(1)). The magistrates' court has a discretion to refuse a witness summons if not satisfied that the application was made as soon as practicable after the defendant pleaded not guilty (Magistrates' Courts Act 1980, s 97(2B)).

Before applying for a witness summons to be issued, a witness should be asked in writing to confirm that he will attend the trial. If a negative response is received, or no response at all, this will be sufficient evidence for a witness summons to be issued. A letter to the court explaining that it has not been possible to secure the voluntary attendance of the witness will usually suffice.

A witness summons should be served personally on each witness.

If a magistrate is satisfied by evidence on oath that a witness summons is unlikely to be obeyed, he may, instead of issuing a witness summons, issue a warrant to arrest the witness (Magistrates' Courts Act 1980, s 97(2)).

8.3.7 Dispensing with attendance of witnesses

Criminal Justice Act 1967, s 9

Section 9 of the Criminal Justice Act 1967 provides that a witness's written statement is admissible at a summary trial provided that:

(a)   it is in the proper form;
(b)   a copy has been served before the hearing on each of the other parties; and
(c)   none of the parties has objected within 7 days.

The statement may only contain matters which would have been admissible if the witness had given evidence on oath.

An example of a s 9 statement illustrating the correct form is illustrated at **Appendix 2(M)**. Section 9 statements are used for matters not in dispute. If the other side wishes to challenge the admissibility of the contents of the statement or cross-examine the maker of the statement, they should object.

The s 9 procedure is available to the prosecution and defence.

Criminal Justice Act 2003, s 116

Section 116 of the Criminal Justice Act 2003, examined in detail at **9.6.2.1**, allows the admissibility of hearsay such as a witness statement provided that there is a prescribed reason for not calling the witness to give evidence.

8.4 Procedure on a not guilty plea

8.4.1 Preliminary matters

8.4.1.1 Defect in process

The defendant cannot object to an information, summons or warrant on the ground of any defect in substance or form or because of any variation between it and the prosecution evidence. If the variance has misled the defendant, the court must, on his application, adjourn the hearing (Magistrates' Courts Act 1980, s 123).

The practical effect of s 123 is that trivial errors in the information or summons will have no effect at all. This will include misspellings of names or places. Where there is a substantial difference between the information or summons and the evidence to be produced, the defendant is entitled to an adjournment. An example might be an information which alleges that an offence was committed on 1 July and the defendant has alibi evidence to refute the allegation but it transpires that the prosecution evidence will show that the offence was committed on 10 July. The defendant must be allowed an adjournment to reconsider his defence.

8.4.1.2 Joinder of offences and offenders

Two or more defendants can be charged in one information with having committed an offence jointly. They will normally be tried together.

Two or more defendants charged on separate informations may be tried together if the defence agrees. The same rule applies if one defendant is charged with more than one offence. If the defence does not agree, the court has power to try two or more informations together if it is of the opinion that it is in the interests of justice to do so because they are founded on the same facts or form part of a series of offences of the same or similar character (*Chief Constable of Norfolk v Clayton (Terence Edward); Chief Constable of Norfolk v Clayton (Eileen Annie); In re Clayton* [1983] 2 AC 473).

Example 1

Julie is charged with theft, assault and burglary. The offences are unrelated. Unless Julie consents (and she is unlikely to do so), the offences must be tried individually. They do not fall within the rule in *Clayton*.

Example 2

Kathy is charged with four offences of theft. The allegations all arise from separate incidents of alleged shoplifting, on separate dates, within the same shopping precinct. These cases could be tried together as forming part of a series of offences of the same character. In reaching a decision, the magistrates will have to balance the convenience to the prosecution against the prejudice caused to Kathy.

8.4.1.3 Exclusion of witnesses

During a criminal trial, witnesses for either side should not sit in court before having been called to give evidence. The reason for this is to minimise the risk of evidence being tailored to suit testimony which has already been given. This rule does not apply to the defendant or to expert witnesses.

8.4.2 Case management

When a defendant first enters a not guilty plea the court may be able to fix a date for trial. Alternatively the case may be adjourned for a pre-trial review (PTR). At the PTR the court will set a date for trial.

The PTR may be conducted by a justices' clerk.

The case progression form to be completed by the case progression officer (see **1.5.6**), when a defendant pleads not guilty to a summary offence or when a defendant pleads not guilty to an either way offence and it is determined that the case will be tried in the magistrates' court, is set out in **Appendix 2(V)** with guidance notes. The form, read with the notes, constitutes a case progression timetable for the effective progression of a case.

8.4.3 A not guilty trial

The procedure in the magistrates' court in a not guilty trial is summarised in **Appendix 1(I)**.

8.4.3.1 The plea

The charge will be read to the defendant and he will be asked whether he pleads guilty or not guilty. The plea must not be equivocal, ie, ambiguous. An example is a defendant charged with theft who says, 'Guilty, but I did not intend to steal anything'. When faced with an equivocal plea, the magistrates should endeavour to explain to the defendant in simple language the nature of the charge. The charge should then be put to the defendant again. If the plea remains equivocal, the magistrates should enter a not guilty plea on behalf of the defendant.

The court has a discretion to allow a change of plea from guilty to not guilty at any time before sentence.

8.4.3.2 Prosecution's opening speech

The prosecution may state the facts of the case and indicate the issues involved and the witnesses who will be called to prove them.

8.4.3.3 Prosecution calls evidence

This may consist of oral evidence and/or written evidence under the Criminal Justice Act 1967, s 9 or the Criminal Justice Act 2003, s 116 or s 117. Witnesses who give oral evidence will be examined-in-chief, cross-examined and re-examined as described at **9.3.2**.

8.4.3.4 Submission of no case to answer

The defence may, at the end of the prosecution case, be in a position to make a submission of no case to answer. The test to be applied was formerly laid down in *Practice Direction (Submission of No Case)* [1962] 1 WLR 227. This provided that a submission should be made and upheld where:

(a)   there has been no evidence to prove an essential element in the alleged offence; or

(b)   the evidence adduced by the prosecution has been so discredited as a result of cross-examination or is so manifestly unreliable that no reasonable tribunal could safely convict on it.

This Practice Direction was revoked by *Practice Direction (Criminal Proceedings: Consolidation)* [2002] 3 All ER 904 but nothing was put in its place. This leaves the magistrates' court with no clear guidance on the test to be applied when considering a submission of no case.

It seems likely that magistrates will continue to take the view that, if a submission of no case to answer is made, the decision should depend not so much on whether they would at that stage convict or acquit but on whether the evidence is such that a reasonable tribunal might convict. If a reasonable tribunal might convict on the evidence so far before it, there is a case to answer. The submission should succeed if a conviction would be perverse, in the sense that no reasonable magistrates' court could convict.

An important issue is the extent to which the magistrates' court may have regard to the credibility of prosecuting witnesses when considering a submission of no case to answer. In the Crown Court, the test to be applied by a judge when ruling on a submission of no case is set out in *Galbraith (George Charles)* [1981] 2 All ER 1060 (see **6.5.1** and **7.1.2**). The requirement that the Crown Court judge should 'take the prosecution evidence at its highest' is intended to leave questions of credibility to the jury. In *R v Barking and Dagenham Justices, ex p DPP* (1995) 159 JP 373, the Divisional Court said that questions of credibility should, except in the clearest cases, not normally be taken into account by the magistrates' court when considering a submission of no case. Nonetheless, it is submitted that some magistrates' courts may take the pragmatic view that it would be inappropriate for them to go through the motions of hearing defence evidence if they have already formed the view that the prosecution evidence is unconvincing that they will not convict on it in any event.

If a submission of no case to answer is made, the prosecution has a right of reply.

If the submission is accepted, the charge against the defendant is dismissed. If the submission is rejected, the defence may then present its case and call witnesses.

8.4.3.5   Defence opening speech

The defence may address the court either before or after calling evidence, but it is more usual for the defence advocate to make a closing speech.

8.4.3.6   Defence calls evidence

Defence witnesses may be called or their statements admitted in the same way as prosecution evidence. Remember that, if the defendant does give evidence, then he must be called before any other defence witnesses unless the court 'otherwise directs' (Police and Criminal Evidence Act 1984, s 79).

8.4.3.7   Further prosecution evidence

After the close of its case, the prosecution cannot usually call further evidence without leave. The court may, for example, grant leave for the prosecution to call rebutting evidence on a matter which it could not reasonably have foreseen and of which it had no warning, for example, alibi evidence.

8.4.3.8 Defence final speech

The defence addresses the court if it has not already made an opening speech. The only matters which can be covered in this closing speech are matters which have been revealed by admissible evidence.

When the defendant is of good character (having no previous convictions for criminal offences) this should be emphasised in the closing speech.

The prosecution may only address the court further with leave. The defence will always address the court last.

8.4.3.9 Points of law

Either side may address the court on matters of law at any stage in the proceedings as of right. The opponent always has a right of reply.

8.4.3.10 Verdict

The magistrates' verdict is by a majority. They may be advised by their clerk on matters of law but not on issues of fact.

If the defendant is found guilty, the court will then proceed to sentence (see **10.3**).

8.4.4 Costs

A defendant who is convicted can be ordered to pay all, or part, of the prosecution costs. If an order is made it will be for payment of a specified sum.

A defendant who is not represented under a representation order and who is acquitted should normally be awarded costs from central funds. There are exceptions, for example, a defendant who by his conduct has brought suspicion upon himself may find that costs are not awarded in his favour.

8.5 Further reading

See, for example:

Archbold: Criminal Pleading, Evidence and Practice (Sweet & Maxwell, 2005)

Blackstone's Criminal Practice (Oxford University Press, 2005)

John Sprack, *Emmins on Criminal Procedure* (Oxford University Press, 2004)

Ede, *Active Defence* (The Law Society, 2000)

Chapter 9

Criminal Evidence

9.1 Introduction

The law of evidence regulates the way in which a criminal case may be presented to a jury or to magistrates. The rules of evidence determine whether the prosecution must prove the guilt of the defendant or whether it is for the defendant to establish his innocence, the standard of proof required and the methods of proving a case.

It is not possible to understand evidence in isolation. The first step is to appreciate how the rules of evidence to be examined in this chapter fit into the procedural progress of a trial. A summary of the general principles appears at **9.1.1** below. Each of the principles referred to is dealt with later in some detail, but an initial overview is essential.

9.1.1   Presentation of evidence – An overview

Stage A

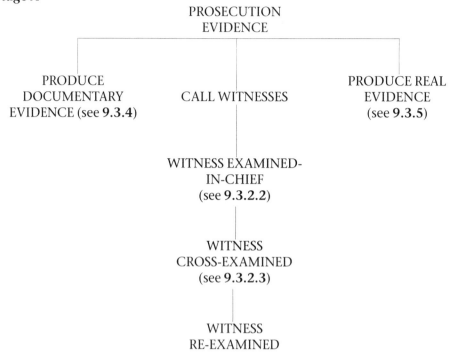

Note that at any stage of the prosecution case, the defence can challenge the admissibility of prosecution evidence. A challenge to the admissibility of prosecution evidence is likely to be on the grounds that the evidence infringes one of the following rules:

(a)   opinion evidence (see **9.5.4**);

(b)   self-made evidence (see **9.5.3**);

(c)   the bad character and previous criminal convictions of the defendant (see **9.8.3**);

(d)   hearsay evidence including confessions made by the defendant (see **9.6**).

The court also has a general discretion to exclude prosecution evidence where its admission would have an adverse effect on the fairness of the proceedings (see **9.2.5**).

Stage B: Defence submission of no case to answer

In certain circumstances, the defence may, at the close of the prosecution case, make a submission of no case to answer. If this succeeds then the prosecution case will have failed.

Stage C

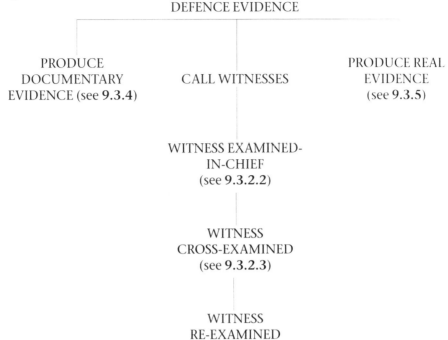

Note that at any stage of the defence case, the prosecution can challenge the admissibility of defence evidence. A challenge to the admissibility of defence evidence is likely to be on the ground that it is one of the following:

(a)   opinion evidence (see **9.5.4**);

(b)   self-made evidence (see **9.5.3**);

(c)   hearsay evidence including documentary hearsay (see **9.6**).

Stage D: Closing speeches (and, in the Crown Court, judge's summing up)

Relevant evidential considerations include:

(a)   burden and standards of proof (see **9.2.1**);

(b)   evidential burden (see **9.2.2**);

(c)   corroboration (see **9.4.1**);

(d)   identification evidence (see **9.4.2**).

Stage E: Verdict

When studying the rules of evidence which follow, the overall framework of a criminal trial should be borne in mind and, when necessary, reference back to the above summary should be made.

9.2   Preliminary points of evidence

This section will consider:

(a)   who must prove what;

(b)   to what standard;

(c)   whether there are any matters that a court can take into account without hearing evidence;

(d)   whether the law imposes any requirements as to the amount of evidence required.

9.2.1 Burden and standards of proof

As a general rule, the prosecution is required to prove the guilt of the defendant beyond reasonable doubt. This means that at the end of a case the magistrates or jury should be told to consider all of the evidence in the case (both prosecution and defence) and to convict only if they are sure of the defendant's guilt (*Woolmington v Director of Public Prosecutions* [1935] AC 462; *Walters (Henry) v The Queen* [1969] 2 AC 26).

In exceptional cases, the burden of proof falls on the defence. For example, if a defendant wishes to plead insanity he is required to prove that fact.

If the burden of proof rests with the defence, the standard of proof required is proof on a balance of probabilities. This is a lower standard of proof than proof beyond reasonable doubt. It was explained in *Miller v Ministry of Pensions* [1947] 2 All ER 372 as simply meaning 'more probable than not'.

Subject to *Woolmington* and *Walters*, a defendant who wishes to introduce a defence to a case (eg, alibi, self-defence, mechanical defect in a vehicle) does not have the burden of proving that defence. It is for the prosecution, as part of the requirement to prove the case beyond reasonable doubt, to satisfy the magistrates or jury that the defence is not true.

9.2.2 The evidential burden

The evidential burden arises in the following ways in a criminal case.

9.2.2.1 The burden on the prosecution

It has been seen at **9.1.1** that the prosecution will present its case first. At the end of the prosecution case, the defence should consider whether the prosecution has presented sufficient evidence to justify a finding of guilt (remember that the defence will not have adduced any evidence at this stage). A submission of no case to answer can be made at this stage. Such a submission will succeed if the prosecution has failed to adduce evidence in support of a material part of the offence. For example, on a charge of theft, if no evidence has been presented to prove that the goods taken 'belonged to another', a submission should succeed.

A submission of no case to answer is made to the judge in the Crown Court and to the magistrates at summary trial.

If no submission is made, or if it fails, then the prosecution has satisfied 'the evidential burden'. This does not mean that the prosecution is entitled to a conviction at this stage. It means that the case can proceed to the next stage where the defence has an opportunity to present evidence to the court.

9.2.2.2 The burden on the defence

The defence does not have to adduce any evidence. It can simply hope that the jury or magistrates will not accept that the prosecution evidence is sufficient to prove the case beyond reasonable doubt. However, if the defendant wishes to rely on a specific defence to a charge (eg, self-defence, alibi) then some evidence of that defence must be put before the magistrates or jury. To this extent there is an evidential burden on the defence. It is important to remember that the defendant is not required to prove his defence. All that is necessary is to put some evidence before the court and the evidential burden is satisfied. The prosecution must satisfy the magistrates or jury that the defence is not true.

In certain circumstances, courts are entitled to infer a fact against the defendant. Such cases again place an evidential burden on the defendant. See further **9.2.3.3**.

Example

Diana is charged with theft. Evidence is adduced to show that Diana was found in possession of recently stolen property. There is now an evidential burden on Diana to give an explanation for possession of the goods. In the absence of a credible explanation, the jury or magistrates are entitled to infer that Diana is the thief.

9.2.3 Proof by evidence

In deciding whether the prosecution has proved its case beyond reasonable doubt, a jury or magistrates can only take into account a fact which has been proved by evidence.

Example

Stuart is charged with assault. No admissible evidence is put forward in support of a defence of self-defence. During his closing speech at the end of the trial, Stuart's advocate raises the issue of self-defence. This cannot be taken into account as no evidence has been adduced in support of the fact.

This rule is subject to a number of exceptions.

9.2.3.1 Facts formally admitted

In order to narrow the issues to be decided at a criminal trial, it is possible for the prosecution or defence formally to admit certain facts. For example, on a charge of theft, the sole issue to be decided may be whether the defendant was acting dishonestly. The defence can make a formal admission to the effect that the defendant appropriated goods belonging to another with the intention to permanently deprive. This relieves the prosecution of the burden of adducing evidence of these facts and the trial can proceed solely on the issue of dishonesty.

A formal admission can be made either before or at the trial. If an admission is made out of court by the defendant, it must be made in writing and made by, or be approved by, the defendant's counsel or solicitor (Criminal Justice Act 1967, s 10).

A formal admission is not to be confused with admissions made to the police by a suspect when being questioned about suspected involvement in an offence.

9.2.3.2 Judicial notice

If a court takes judicial notice of a fact then evidence of that fact will not be required.

A court is obliged by law to take judicial notice of matters of law. Thus, there is no requirement to prove the content of a public Act of Parliament.

A court may take judicial notice of matters of common knowledge, including local knowledge. An example would be the rules of the road. On a driving charge, the prosecution would not be required to prove that, in Britain, motorists should drive on the left-hand side of the road. This would be a matter of common knowledge. The distance between towns and the time taken to travel between them are matters of local knowledge and may not have to be proved by evidence.

9.2.3.3 Inferences of fact

In many criminal cases, there will be no available direct evidence from eye witnesses to support the prosecution or defence case. A court, in reaching a verdict, will be entitled to draw inferences from the existence of other proven facts. The fact that the fingerprints of the defendant were found on burgled premises and that he was seen in the vicinity of the property around the time of the crime may lead to an inference that he committed the crime.

Two common examples of inferences arising in criminal cases are as follows.

The doctrine of recent possession

A court is entitled to infer that a person found in possession of recently stolen goods is the thief or a handler. Such an inference may only be drawn in the absence of a credible explanation from the defendant. If the prosecution gives evidence of possession of recently stolen property there is an evidential burden on the defendant to put forward an explanation (see **9.2.2.2**).

The doctrine of continuance

If evidence is adduced to prove that a certain state of affairs existed at a particular time, a court is entitled to infer that it continued to exist at another reasonably proximate time. For example, on a charge of dangerous driving, evidence may be given that the defendant was driving at great speed 500 yards from the scene of the accident, giving rise to the charge. The court may infer that this speed continued to the scene of the accident. Again, there may be an evidential burden on the defendant if he wishes to rebut the inference that may be drawn.

9.2.4 Improperly obtained evidence

At common law, evidence illegally or unfairly obtained was admissible. Courts would not exclude evidence which was relevant simply because it had been obtained by the police as a result of an illegal search (*Kuruma v The Queen* [1955] AC 197).

In relation to evidence obtained from the defendant which was tantamount to a self-incriminatory admission (eg, a confession or evidence from an identification parade), the court has a general discretion to exclude such evidence if it had been improperly obtained (*R v Sang* [1980] AC 402).

9.2.5 Court's discretion to exclude evidence

The Police and Criminal Evidence Act 1984, s 78(1) gives criminal courts a statutory discretion to exclude prosecution evidence:

> In any proceedings the court may refuse to allow evidence on which the prosecution proposes to rely to be given if it appears to the court that, having regard to all of the circumstances, including the circumstances in which the evidence was obtained, the admission of the evidence would have such an adverse effect on the fairness of the proceedings that the court ought not to admit it.

The section has been interpreted broadly in line with the existing common law. Thus the fact that evidence has been obtained as a result of an illegal search is unlikely to be a ground for exclusion under s 78.

In *Khan v United Kingdom* [2000] Crim LR 684, the European Court of Human Rights considered the relationship between s 78 and art 6 of the European Convention on Human Rights.

The court held that since domestic law did not regulate the use of covert listening devices at the time of the applicant's conviction, the applicant's right to respect for private and family life, as guaranteed by art 8 of the Convention, had been violated.

The applicant also alleged a breach of art 6(1) of the Convention. He argued that the use, as the sole evidence in his case, of the material which had been obtained in breach of art 8 was not compatible with the 'fair hearing' requirements of art 6.

The court noted that it was not its role to determine, as a matter of principle, whether particular types of evidence, for example, unlawfully obtained evidence, might be admissible or, indeed, whether the applicant was guilty or not.

In examining whether, in all the circumstances, including the way in which the evidence was obtained, the proceedings as a whole were unfair, the court observed that the recording of the applicant's conversation had not been unlawful in the sense of being contrary to domestic criminal law, even though it had been obtained in breach of art 8.

At each level of jurisdiction the domestic courts assessed the effect of admission of the evidence on the fairness of the trial and discussed, among other matters, the non-statutory basis for the surveillance. In the court's view it was clear that, had the domestic courts been of the view that the admission of the evidence would have given rise to substantive unfairness, they would have exercised their discretion under s 78 to exclude it. As a result, the court found that the use at the applicant's trial of the secretly taped material did not conflict with the requirements of a fair trial guaranteed by art 6(1).

There are two major areas of operation of s 78:

(a)   identification evidence; and

(b)   confessions.

Section 78 has no application to committal proceedings.

Confessions are examined at **9.6.2.3**; identification evidence and s 78 are discussed below.

9.2.5.1   Identification evidence

A breach of the Code of Practice D on identification does not automatically render evidence inadmissible. It is something that a court will take into account in determining an application to exclude such evidence under s 78. Examples include: *R v Gaynor* [1988] Crim LR 242, where evidence of a group identification was excluded because insufficient effort had been made to arrange an identification parade; *R v Gall* (1990) 90 Cr App R 64, breach of the rule that an investigating officer should take no part in the parade procedure; *R v Nagah (Jasant Singh)* (1991) 92 Cr App R 334, where a confrontation identification was disallowed because the defendant had requested an identification parade and it was practicable to hold one.

If evidence is to be excluded under s 78 because of a breach of the Code D, the defence will have to show why it would be unfair to admit it. The mere fact that there has been a technical breach which does not lead to unfairness will be insufficient to exclude evidence (*R v Grannell (Robert James Lawson)* (1990) 90 Cr App R 149).

9.3   Methods of proof

Evidence may be presented by:

(a)   calling witnesses;

(b)   adducing documentary evidence;

(c)   adducing real evidence.

Usually evidence is presented by calling witnesses to give oral evidence.

A number of technical rules must be borne in mind when presenting certain types of evidence.

9.3.1   Witnesses – competence and compellability

9.3.1.1   Competence

Competence means that the witness will be permitted to testify. The general rule is that all witnesses are competent to give evidence. Only if a witness cannot understand questions asked of him in court, or cannot answer them in a way that can be understood (with, if necessary, the assistance of special measures – see **9.3.2.1**), will the witness not be able to testify (Youth Justice and Criminal Evidence Act 1999, s 54).

The only exception to the general rule relates to the defendant. The defendant is not competent to give evidence for the prosecution in his own trial, nor is any co-defendant in the proceedings (see **9.7.1**).

9.3.1.2   Determining whether a witness is competent

A witness's competence to give evidence may be challenged by the prosecution, the defence or the court itself.

In assessing the witness's competence to give evidence, the court is required to take into account any special measures it has granted, or is planning to grant, to the witness (see **9.3.2.1**).

If the witness's competence is challenged, the court will ask questions of the witness (not the party that is calling or cross-examining the witness). Any such questioning will be done in the presence of both the prosecution and the defence. The court will be allowed to ask for expert advice about the witness's competence. It will be the responsibility of the party calling the witness to satisfy the court that the witness is competent.

9.3.1.3   Determining whether witnesses are to be sworn

References to swearing an oath include making an affirmation. The question of whether a witness is eligible to swear an oath may be raised by either the prosecution or the defence or by the court itself. The procedure used to determine this question will be the same as the procedure outlined above for determining competence (Youth Justice and Criminal Evidence Act 1999, s 55).

No witness under the age of 14 is to be sworn. A witness of 14 or over is eligible to give sworn evidence only if he understands the solemnity of a criminal trial and that taking an oath places a particular responsibility on him to tell the truth. If no evidence is offered suggesting that the witness does not understand those two matters there is a presumption that the witness is to give sworn evidence.

As with considerations of competence, the question of whether a witness should be sworn is to be considered in the absence of any jury (but in the presence of both the prosecution and the defence). Expert evidence can be received on this subject.

9.3.1.4 Unsworn evidence

Any witness who is competent to be a witness but is not allowed to give evidence on oath may give unsworn evidence (Youth Justice and Criminal Evidence Act 1999, ss 56 and 57).

9.3.1.5 Compellability

The general rule is that all witnesses can be compelled to attend court to give evidence by the service of a witness summons. The only exceptions relate to the defendant and the defendant's spouse (see **9.7.1**).

9.3.2 Oral evidence from witnesses

9.3.2.1 Special measures

There are a number of special measures available to help witnesses (other than the defendant) who might otherwise have difficulty giving evidence in criminal proceedings or who might be reluctant to do so (Youth Justice and Criminal Evidence Act 1999, ss 16–33).

The following can apply to the court for special measures to help them give evidence in court:

(a)   children under the age of 17;

(b)   those who suffer from a mental or physical disorder, or have a disability or impairment that is likely to affect their evidence; and

(c)   those whose evidence is likely to be affected by their fear or distress at giving evidence in the proceedings.

Witnesses who are alleged to be victims of a sexual offence will be considered to be eligible for help with giving evidence unless they tell the court that they do not want to be considered eligible. Otherwise, it is for the court to determine whether a witness falls into any of these categories. The court must also determine whether making particular special measures available to an eligible witness will be likely to improve the quality of the evidence given by the witness.

Both the prosecution and defence will be able to apply, normally before the trial, for the court to make a direction authorising the use of special measures for a witness they are calling. A court may also decide to make a direction even if no such application has been made.

The special measures that are available are:

(a)   screens, to ensure that the witness does not see the defendant;

(b)   allowing an interview with the witness, which has been video recorded before the trial, to be shown as the witness's evidence-in-chief at trial;

(c)   allowing a witness to give evidence from outside the court by live television link;

(d)   clearing people from the court so that evidence can be given in private;

(e)   not wearing the court dress of wigs and gowns;

(f)   allowing a witness to be cross-examined before the trial about their evidence and a video recording of that cross-examination to be shown at trial instead of the witness being cross-examined live at trial;

(g)   allowing an approved intermediary to help a witness communicate with legal representatives and the court;

(h)   allowing a witness to use communication aids.

Live links

Section 32 of the Criminal Justice Act 2003 permits a witness outside the UK to testify by means of a live TV link. Part 8 of the Criminal Justice Act 2003 (not in force at the time of writing) deals with live links. It confers a general power to give evidence through a live TV link in the proceedings defined by s 51. That includes all trials, whether summary or on indictment. The court must so direct.

9.3.2.2 Examination-in-chief

Leading questions

A witness is examined-in-chief by the party calling that witness. As a general rule, leading questions should not be asked on matters which are in dispute. It is, however, permissible to ask a leading question where the object is to elicit a denial of an opponent's case. For example, it would be permissible to ask a defendant, 'were you in the pub at the time of the assault?'.

A leading question is one which suggests the answer expected or assumes the existence of a fact which has not been proved.

Example

Gareth is called as a prosecution witness. He is to testify to the fact that he saw Tony, at 11 am on 6 October, steal some goods from Tescos.

The prosecutor cannot say to Gareth, 'Did you see Tony steal goods from Tescos at 11 am on 6 October?' This is a leading question.

Instead, the evidence should be elicited in this way:

Q   Where were you on 6 October at about 11 am?

A   In Tescos.

Q   Did you see anything unusual in the shop?

A   Yes, I saw Tony put some chocolate into his pocket.

Q   What happened then?

A   Tony walked out of the shop without paying for the chocolate.

Memory refreshing

A party calling a witness may apply to the court for the witness to refresh his memory in the witness-box from a document which was made or verified by him at an earlier time if—

(a)   he states in his oral evidence that the document records his recollection of the matters at that earlier time, and

(b)   his recollection of the matter is likely to have been significantly better at that time than it is at the time of his oral evidence.

(Criminal Justice Act 2003, s 139(1))

A document is made by a witness if he writes down what he saw and it is verified by him if he dictated what he saw to someone else and checked the accuracy of the document.

A document which is used to refresh the witness's memory does not become evidence in the case in its own right. However, the other party has the right to request and inspect a document used for this purpose.

Unfavourable witnesses

A witness who is called to give evidence may not give the evidence expected of him. He may be nervous, forgetful or stupid. However, if the failure to testify as expected is not deliberate, the party calling the witness is not allowed to contradict or to try to discredit that witness.

Hostile witnesses

If a witness appears to be unwilling to tell the truth on behalf of the party calling him then the party may apply to the judge or magistrates to declare that witness 'hostile'. If declared hostile, the witness may:

(a)   be cross-examined by the party calling him. Leading questions may now be asked of the witness to show that he is being untruthful; and, with leave of the court,

(b)   have any previous inconsistent statement put to him by the party calling him (Criminal Procedure Act 1865, s 3).

In practice, witnesses are commonly shown to be hostile by proving that they have made an earlier out-of-court statement from which they appear to be deliberately and dishonestly departing.

A previous inconsistent statement is admissible to prove the truth of anything contained in the statement. The statement can also be used to undermine the credibility of the witness.

Video recorded evidence in chief

Section 137 of the Criminal Justice Act 2003 (not in force at the time of writing) allows a video recording of the account of an eye-witness, given while the events were fresh in the mind of the witness to amount to the evidence-in-chief of that witness, with leave of the court. This section applies to indictable only offences and prescribed either way offences. This section does not apply to defendants but will apply to other defence witnesses.

In determining whether the admission of such evidence is in the interests of justice under s 137(4) the court must consider in particular:

(a)   the time interval between the events and the making of the video;

(b)   factors affecting the reliability of what is said in the video account (eg, if the video was made very shortly after the event it could be tainted by grief or anger);

(c)   the quality of the recording;

(d)   any view of the witness as to whether his account should be given orally or by way of video.

If the court concludes that admitting any part of the video would carry a risk of prejudice to the defendant, it should nevertheless go on to consider whether the interests of justice as a whole require it to be admitted in view of the desirability of showing the whole, or substantially the whole of the recorded video (s 138(3)).

Oral evidence cannot be given to supplement any matter which in the opinion of the court has been adequately dealt with in the video.

9.3.2.3 Cross-examination

Following examination-in-chief, a witness may be cross-examined by the other party (or all other parties). Leading questions may be asked.

The purposes of cross-examination include:

(a)   to put the case of the cross-examiner to the witness. A failure to challenge a witness's evidence implies acceptance of it;

(b)   to challenge the credibility of the witness;

(c)   to elicit information helpful to the cross-examiner.

9.3.2.4 Restrictions on the defendant's right to cross-examination

A defendant is prohibited from personally cross-examining witnesses in the following circumstances:

(a)   when the witness is the alleged victim of a sexual offence;

(b)   when the witness is a child who is either the alleged victim, or a witness to the commission of the alleged offence, in a case involving sexual offences, kidnapping or abduction, cruelty or physical assault. This includes child witnesses who are co-defendants;

(c)   in any other case, when the court is satisfied, upon an application or on its own initiative, that the circumstances of the case merit it.

In such circumstances, the defendant must appoint a legal representative to conduct the cross-examination on his behalf. Where the defendant refuses or fails to do so, the court must consider whether it is in the interests of justice to appoint a legal representative to test the witness's evidence (Youth Justice and Criminal Evidence Act 1999, ss 34–39).

9.3.2.5 Cross-examination as to credit – general rule

A witness called by another party may be cross-examined as to credit where it is relevant as to whether the witness's evidence should be believed. Questions as to credit may include questions as to the witness's character, criminal convictions, previous inconsistent statements and whether a witness is biased in relation to the proceedings because of, for example, a grudge or relationship with a party to the proceedings.

As a general rule, the answer given to a credit question is final. This means that the cross-examiner cannot pursue the matter raised any further by calling independent evidence to prove the fact, but there are exceptions.

9.3.2.6 Cross-examination as to credit – exceptions

With certain credit questions the answer given is not final. The cross-examining party is allowed to call other evidence to prove the matter denied by the witness in cross-examination. These exceptional cases include:

(a)   When it is alleged that a witness is biased.

(b)   When it is alleged that the witness has made a previous inconsistent statement (Criminal Procedure Act 1865, ss 4, 5). If a previous inconsistent statement is proved (either by the witness admitting that he made it or by independent evidence), it is admissible to prove the truth of anything stated in it. Thus the trial judge or magistrates can accept the previous inconsistent statement as true (unless the witness admits that it is true). It is relevant not only to the credibility of the witness.

(c)   When the question is to show that the witness has been convicted of a criminal offence (Criminal Procedure Act 1865, s 6). If a witness denies a conviction then it may be proved by producing a certificate signed by the clerk to the convicting court and proving that the person named in the certificate is the witness being cross-examined (Police and Criminal Evidence Act 1984, s 73).

9.3.3   Written statements from witnesses

As an alternative to a witness giving oral evidence, a written statement may be admissible in evidence. The major provisions enabling a witness statement to be admitted in evidence include:

(a)   Criminal Justice Act 2003, ss 116, 117;

(b)   Criminal Justice Act 1988, s 30;

(c)   Criminal Procedure and Investigations Act 1996, s 68 and Sch 2, paras 1 and 2;

(d)   Criminal Justice Act 1967, s 9.

These provisions require an appreciation of the rule against hearsay and are discussed at **9.6.1**.

9.3.4   Documentary evidence

A document must be authenticated by a witness if it is to be admitted in evidence. This will usually involve calling a witness to explain to the court how the document came into existence.

By the Criminal Justice Act 2003, s 133, a copy document is admissible even though the original is still in existence.

The content of a document may be hearsay evidence. The provisions governing the admissibility of hearsay evidence are discussed at **9.6**.

9.3.5   Real evidence

Items such as objects produced in court (exhibits) and places viewed by the court, are classified as real evidence. Items produced in court may include photographs, tape recordings and video recordings. Real evidence will normally require the additional testimony of a witness to explain the relevance of the evidence to the prosecution or defence case.

9.4   Corroboration and identification evidence

9.4.1   Corroboration

In determining the guilt or innocence of the defendant, the jury or magistrates will have regard to the cogency (or weight) of evidence before them. As a general rule, the law does not give specific weight to particular types of evidence, but in certain cases there are rules relating to corroboration of a witness's evidence.

9.4.1.1   The meaning of corroboration

Corroboration is other independent evidence which supports the evidence to be corroborated in a material particular and which implicates the defendant in the crime charged (*R v Baskerville* [1916] 2 KB 658).

9.4.1.2 Examples of corroboration

(a) The evidence of another witness.

(b) A confession by the defendant (see **9.6.2.3**).

(c) Lies told by the defendant. These are capable of amounting to corroboration provided the jury or magistrates are satisfied that:

    (i) the lie is deliberate and relates to a material issue in the case; and

    (ii) the lie is told because of realisation of guilt; and

    (iii) the lie is proved by evidence independent of the witness to be corroborated. An admission by the defendant would suffice (see *R v Lucas (Ruth)* [1981] QB 720).

(d) Circumstantial evidence, for example, possession of stolen property or forensic evidence linking the defendant to the crime, is capable of amounting to corroboration.

(e) The refusal of a defendant, without good cause, to give an intimate body sample to the police is capable of amounting to corroboration of any other evidence in the case to which the refusal is material. In a rape case, for example, the refusal of a semen sample could corroborate the prosecution case on an issue of whether intercourse took place between the victim and the defendant. It would not provide corroboration on an issue of consent (Police and Criminal Evidence Act 1984, s 62).

(f) The refusal of a defendant, without good cause, to stand on an identification parade is capable of amounting to corroboration of any other evidence in the case to which the refusal is material.

In the Crown Court, the judge directs the jury as to evidence which is capable, as a matter of law, of amounting to corroboration. It is for the jury to decide whether to accept or reject the evidence. In a magistrates' court, the magistrates, taking advice from their clerk if necessary, decide what is capable of amounting to corroboration. They also decide whether or not to accept the evidence.

9.4.1.3 Special rules

Cases where corroboration is essential

In a limited number of cases there cannot be a conviction on the evidence of a single witness. Corroboration is required. These include treason, perjury and the offence of speeding (unless the evidence is from a roadside camera).

If, at the close of the prosecution case, no evidence has been adduced which is capable of amounting to corroboration, a submission of no case to answer will succeed (see **9.2.2**). If there is evidence capable of amounting to corroboration then it is left to the jury or magistrates to decide, when considering their verdict, whether or not to accept the evidence as corroboration.

It is important to remember that a defendant cannot be convicted of any offence if the only evidence against him is an inference under ss 34, 36 or 37 of the Criminal Justice and Public Order Act 1994 (Criminal Justice and Public Order Act 1994, s 38(3)).

Other cases

If a judge feels that the evidence of any type of witness is suspect, for whatever reason, he may direct a jury on the special need for caution and the dangers of convicting on that evidence alone (*R v Makanjuola; R v E* [1995] 1 WLR 1348).

Examples of such cases include:

(a)   Witnesses with a purpose of their own to serve in giving false evidence. Such witnesses may be:

    (i)   other parties to the crime charged. They may be giving evidence for the prosecution (having pleaded guilty) or evidence in their own defence. In either case they may be trying to put the blame on a co-defendant or minimising their role to get a lighter sentence;

    (ii)   witnesses with a grudge against the defendant;

    (iii)   witnesses whom a defendant alleges committed the offence.

(b)   Where a prosecution witness is a mental patient (*R v Spencer (Alan Widdison); R v Smails (George Glenville)* [1986] 3 WLR 348).

In a magistrates' court, it is always open to an advocate, when making a closing speech, to address the bench on the dangers of convicting on the evidence of a 'suspect' witness alone.

9.4.2   Disputed identification evidence

Special guidelines apply when a prosecution witness's evidence visually identifies the defendant and the identification is disputed (*R v Turnbull* [1977] QB 224).

9.4.2.1   When the rules apply

The *Turnbull* guidelines apply where there is evidence that a witness visually identified the defendant. This will usually come:

(a)   from evidence that the person who committed the crime was picked out at an identification parade, group identification, video identification or confrontation; or

(b)   from evidence that the witness recognised the person who committed the crime as someone previously known to him, for example, 'It was Fred Smith'.

If the witness has simply given a description to the court of the person who committed the crime and there is no direct evidence that it was the defendant other than the fact that his physical appearance matches the description then the Turnbull guidelines do not apply.

Example 1

Joe is on trial for theft. A prosecution witness tells the court that he saw a man commit the crime and later identified Joe as that man at an identification parade.

(a)   If Joe denies being at the scene of the theft, the *Turnbull* guidelines apply.

(b)   If Joe admits to being at the scene of the theft but denies that he was the person who committed the crime, the *Turnbull* guidelines apply 'if there is a possibility of the witness being mistaken' (*R v Thornton* [1995] 1 Cr App R 598). This will depend on the facts of the case. If the defendant was the only person present then the Turnbull direction would seem to be inappropriate. If, however, there were a number of people present, the guidelines will apply (*R v Slater (Robert David)* [1995] 1 Cr App R 584).

(c)   If Joe admits taking the goods and pleads absence of *mens rea*, the *Turnbull* guidelines do not apply. The identification is not disputed.

Example 2

Jane is on trial for assault. A witness tells the court that he saw Jane commit the offence. He says that he knows Jane by sight and name as they live on the same road.

(a)   If Jane denies being at the scene of the assault, the Turnbull guidelines apply.

(b)   If Jane admits to being at the scene of the assault but claims that it was someone else who hit the victim, the Turnbull guidelines may apply (*R v Thornton* (above)).

(c)   If Jane admits hitting the victim but pleads self-defence, Turnbull does not apply as the identification is not in dispute.

Example 3

Peter is on trial for taking a conveyance. The victim of the crime tells the court that he saw a man 'about 6ft tall, with brown spiky hair and a moustache'. Peter matches this description but he was not picked out at an identification parade.

The *Turnbull* guidelines cannot apply as there is no direct evidence identifying Peter as the man who committed the offence.

9.4.2.2   The *Turnbull* guidelines — Crown Court cases

In Crown Court cases, the trial judge should assess the quality of the identification evidence, that is to say, he should look at the circumstances of the original sighting of the offender by the witness. Factors to be taken into account will include:

(a)   the length of observation;

(b)   distance;

(c)   lighting;

(d)   conditions;

(e)   whether the person identified was someone already known to the witness;

(f)   how closely the description given to the police matches the appearance of the defendant.

Identification poor and without support

If the evidence is assessed as being of poor quality and without support then the judge should stop the trial at the end of the prosecution case and direct an acquittal.

Identification good

If the judge considers the quality of the initial sighting to be good, he should, when summing up the case to the jury, point out the dangers of relying on identification evidence (including the fact that it is easy for an honest witness to be mistaken) and direct the jury to take into account the factors listed above when considering the quality of the evidence.

Identification poor but supported

If the judge considers the quality of the initial sighting to be poor, but supported by other evidence, then a similar warning should be given.

Supporting evidence is some independent evidence that suggests that the identification of the defendant may be correct. It may, for example, come via a confession, possession of stolen property, or lies told by the defendant. There is no requirement that supporting evidence should fulfil all the legal criteria of corroboration. In particular, it need not be independent of the identifying witness.

9.4.2.3   The *Turnbull* guidelines – magistrates' court cases

In magistrates' court cases, the same principles apply as in Crown Court cases. Therefore:

(a) if the case is one which appears to consist of poor quality identification evidence without support, a submission of no case to answer should be made (see **9.2.2**). This will be on the basis that the evidence is manifestly unreliable;

(b) in any other type of case, the defence advocate is likely to deal with Turnbull in his closing speech by pointing out the unreliability of identification evidence.

9.5 Particular rules of admissibility of evidence

This paragraph is concerned with the content of evidence to be given by witnesses or which is contained in a document. Even though a witness may be competent to give evidence or a document can be authenticated, it is open to the prosecution or defence to challenge the evidence on the basis that it infringes one of the general principles of admissibility. Evidence may be inadmissible due to its being:

(a) irrelevant;

(b) self-made;

(c) opinion;

(d) privileged.

9.5.1 Challenging the admissibility of evidence

9.5.1.1 By agreement

It may be possible to agree with an opposing advocate that evidence is inadmissible. If so, such evidence will not be given at the trial and the jury or magistrates will not know about it.

9.5.1.2 By application to the court

Crown court cases

A challenge to the admissibility of evidence is made to the judge in the absence of the jury. If the challenge is on agreed facts then the advocates present legal argument to the judge who will make a ruling. If the evidence is ruled inadmissible, the jury will never hear it. If the evidence is admissible, the witness will testify in front of the jury. If there is a factual dispute involved (eg, whether the police pressured the defendant into confessing) then the judge will hear evidence from relevant witnesses for the prosecution and defence in the absence of the jury before ruling on admissibility. This procedure is known as a trial within a trial. It is commonly used to challenge the admissibility of a confession and is examined in more detail at **9.6.2.3**.

Magistrates' court cases

As magistrates are arbiters of both fact and law they must rule on the admissibility of evidence. This will often mean that the magistrates will have heard details of evidence which they find inadmissible. Such evidence should be ignored when a verdict is being considered. The special problems involved in challenging the admissibility of a confession are discussed at **9.6.2.3**.

9.5.2 Relevance

Evidence of a fact is not admissible unless that fact is relevant to an issue to be decided by the court. Relevant evidence will include direct evidence from a witness who perceived an event. It will also include circumstantial evidence from which a fact can be inferred. Even though a fact may be relevant, it can still be ruled inadmissible because it offends one of the other principles of admissibility of evidence which follow.

9.5.3 Self-made evidence

9.5.3.1 General rule

As a general rule, a witness is not allowed to support the evidence given at a trial by introducing a statement which he has made on a previous occasion. For example, if the defendant is charged with assault and gives evidence of self-defence, he will not be allowed to tell the court that, 'I told my wife the day after the incident that I was acting in self-defence'. Similarly, the wife could not testify as to what her husband told her. In either case, the evidence adds nothing to the testimony given in court. The rule against self-made evidence is subject to a number of exceptions. These include:

(a)   rebutting a suggestion of recent fabrication;

(b)   statements forming part of the *res gestae*;

(c)   exculpatory statements made to the police.

9.5.3.2 Rebutting a suggestion of recent fabrication

If, during cross-examination of a witness, it is put to a witness that he has recently concocted his testimony, evidence of previous statements can be admitted to rebut the assertion. In the example given in relation to the general rule, the defendant could call his wife to prove that he raised the issue of self-defence the day after the incident. The evidence would be admissible not only to show that the suggestion of recent fabrication was incorrect but also of the truth of the facts stated (see **9.6.2.6**).

9.5.3.3 Statements forming part of the *res gestae*

If a statement is made 'in circumstances of spontaneity or involvement in the event so that the possibility of concoction can be disregarded' (see *Ratten (Leith McDonald) v The Queen* [1972] AC 378), it will be admissible in evidence under the *res gestae* principle. This is on the basis that a statement which is made at the time of a relevant act should be put before the court to help explain the event. The *res gestae* principle is well known in the United States by the graphic name 'the excited utterance rule'. In *R v Roberts* [1942] 1 All ER 187, the defendant testified to the fact that a gun had gone off accidentally, killing his girlfriend. He was not allowed to testify that while he was in police custody he had told his father that it was an accident. This was too far removed from the event to fall within the *res gestae* principle. The Court of Appeal held, however, that the defendant should have been allowed to call witnesses to recount the defendant's explanation which had been made contemporaneously with or within a few minutes of the shooting. Such evidence formed part of the *res gestae*. The *res gestae* principle is also an exception to the rule against hearsay and is defined in the Criminal Justice Act 2003, s 118(1), para 4 (see **9.6.2.3**).

9.5.3.4 Exculpatory statements made to the police

When being questioned by the police about an offence the defendant may put forward an explanation which, if accepted by a court, would exonerate him. Such statements are generally admissible in evidence but only to show consistency with testimony given at the trial. See *R v Pearce (David Anthony)* (1979) 69 Cr App R 365.

Example

Nicholas is charged with assault. When interviewed by the police he claims that he was elsewhere at the time of the commission of the offence. If Nicholas gives evidence at his trial in support of his alibi evidence, his statement made to the police is admissible to show consistency. If, however, he fails to testify, his statement made to the police is of no evidential value. It is not open to Nicholas to say to the court, 'my defence is in my statement to the police, please take it into account'.

Although the statement will not assist the prosecution case, as a matter of practice the interviewing officer will give evidence of the interview during the prosecution evidence and the statement will be received by the court as an exception to the rule against self-made evidence.

9.5.4 Opinion evidence

9.5.4.1 Ordinary witnesses

A witness may relate to the court any fact that he has personally perceived. Inevitably, parts of his evidence will include opinions such as the fact that a car was travelling at about 60 mph, or that a person appeared to be drunk. This is acceptable as the witness is simply relating to the court the facts as he saw them. However, the witness is not allowed to give an opinion on matters which it is the function of the court to decide. In particular, therefore, the witness cannot give his opinion on the ultimate issue to be determined, ie, the guilt or innocence of the defendant.

9.5.4.2 Expert witnesses

Expert opinion evidence is admissible in relation to matters which are outside the competence of a jury or magistrates. Examples include matters of science, medicine and technology.

It is for the judge or magistrates to decide who is an expert. There is no fixed test and the presence or absence of formal qualifications is not conclusive.

Any party to criminal proceedings who proposes to adduce expert evidence at the trial is required to give advance disclosure to all other parties of the substance of the evidence as soon as practicable following a plea of not guilty in a magistrates' court trial or committal to the Crown Court for trial or being sent to the Crown Court for trial. If advance disclosure is not given then expert evidence cannot be adduced without leave of the court (Criminal Procedure Rules 2005, Pt 24).

Expert evidence can be difficult for a lay person to understand. To assist magistrates and juries, s 30(1) of the Criminal Justice Act 1988 provides that:

> An expert report shall be admissible as evidence in criminal proceedings, whether or not the person making it attends to give oral evidence in those proceedings.

This provision enables the jury or magistrates to have a copy of the written report by the expert in front of them as they listen to his oral evidence.

The provision is drawn widely enough to enable a written report to be admissible in the absence of the expert. Section 30(2) states that:

> If it is proposed that the person making the report shall not give oral evidence, the report shall only be admissible with the leave of the court.

Even if such leave were given, the amount of weight attached to the report is likely to be less than if the author of the report testified in person.

The written report of a prosecution expert witness is admissible at committal proceedings. No leave is required to admit it (Criminal Justice Act 1988, s 4A).

9.5.5 Privilege

9.5.5.1 Public policy privilege

As a matter of public policy, evidence which discloses the identity of a police informant is normally inadmissible. The rule extends to prevent the identification of premises used for police surveillance (*R v Rankine* [1986] 2 All ER 566). The reason for this protection is that it is in the public interest for the identity of those who help the police to be kept secret. The protection can be overridden if disclosure is necessary to show the innocence of the defendant. Thus, if the defendant alleges that he has been 'set up' by a particular person, X, the prosecution could be forced to reveal whether or not its informant was X.

9.5.5.2 Legal professional privilege

Communications between a client and his solicitor are privileged if the purpose of the communication is the giving or receiving of legal advice. In a criminal case, the practical effect of this is that letters, telephone calls, statements, etc are privileged. The defence cannot be compelled to reveal the content of such communications to any other party.

Communications between the defendant or his solicitor and a third party are also privileged, provided they are made in contemplation of pending or anticipated proceedings and the purpose, or dominant purpose, was to prepare for the litigation. Witness statements are obvious examples. The defence cannot be compelled to reveal the content of such communications to any other party.

9.5.5.3 Privilege against self-incrimination

A witness is not bound to answer a question if, in the opinion of the court, the answer would tend to expose him to proceedings for a criminal offence. This privilege is limited in the case of a defendant who elects to go into the witness box to give evidence. He will be obliged to answer questions even though the answer may tend to incriminate him as to the offence for which he is charged (Criminal Evidence Act 1898, s 1(e)).

9.6 Hearsay evidence

9.6.1 Introduction

Hearsay is:

(a)   an oral or written statement
(b)   made out of court
(c)   which is now being repeated to the court
(d)   to try to prove the truth of the matter stated out of court.

Hearsay evidence is most likely to consist of a witness giving evidence and seeking to repeat what someone else has said out of court or a party seeking to adduce a document (including a witness statement) in evidence.

At common law such statements were inadmissible to prove the truth of the matters stated in the statement unless an exception to the hearsay rule applied. There were two main reasons for the hearsay rule:

(a)   as second-hand evidence (ie, evidence one removed from the witness who could give original evidence based on personal knowledge or recollection), hearsay was likely to be unreliable;

(b)   not being given on oath and not being subject to cross examination the evidence was more likely to be unreliable and, if admitted, it could not be tested so that it would be more difficult for the court to assess.

Not all such evidence will be hearsay. It is necessary to consider why the party is seeking to adduce the evidence. If the purpose is to prove that anything in the statement or document is true then it will be hearsay. If it is being adduced for some other purpose, for example to show the state of mind of the maker or hearer of the statement, irrespective of its truth, then it is not hearsay (*Subramaniam v Public Prosecutor* [1956] 1 WLR 965).

Example 1

PC Smith wants to say to the court:

'I arrived at Waitburys. I was met by a store detective who told me that the defendant had left the store without paying for goods.'

If the prosecution in a criminal trial for theft is asking the court to accept the truth of the store detective's statement (ie, that the defendant left the store without paying for goods) then it will be hearsay.

If, on the other hand, where the defendant is bringing a civil claim for wrongful arrest against PC Smith, PC Smith is simply asking the court to accept that the statement was made to him by the store detective (thereby giving him reasonable grounds to suspect that the defendant had committed an arrestable offence) then it will not be hearsay. The court is not being asked to accept the truth of the store detective's statement.

Example 2

Michael is charged with burglary by entering a dwellinghouse as a trespasser with intent to steal. His defence is that he was simply trying to recover some of his own property in the house. The prosecution wants to call a witness to say:

'The day before the offence Michael told me that there was some valuable jewellery in the house and that he was going to steal it.'

This will not be hearsay. The court is not being asked to accept the truth of anything said by Michael (ie, that there was some valuable jewellery in the house), merely that he intended to steal. It is relevant only to his state of mind when entering the house.

Example 3

Marie makes a written statement in Suzanne's defence confirming an alibi. Marie is not available to give evidence. Marie's written statement will be hearsay as the court is being asked to accept the truth of the statement.

Example 4

Philip is charged with stealing £300 in cash from the safe at his place of work. The prosecution wishes to put in evidence a ledger compiled by a clerk showing that on the day of the offence £300 was deposited in the safe. The ledger will be hearsay as the court is being asked to accept the truth of the statement made in it, ie, that £300 was deposited.

The Criminal Justice Act 2003, Pt 2, Chapter 2 has substantially remodelled the law relating to hearsay; hearsay evidence is now admissible as a general rule provided certain conditions are met.

9.6.2   Hearsay admissible

By s 114(1) of the Criminal Justice Act 2003 (CJA 2003), in criminal proceedings, a statement not made in oral evidence in the proceedings is admissible as evidence of any matter stated if, and only if:

(a)   it is admissible under either Chapter 2 of CJA 2003 or under any other statutory provision;

(b)   it is admissible under any rule of law preserved by s 118 of CJA 2003;

(c)   all parties to the proceedings agree to the evidence being admissible; or

(d)   the court is satisfied that it is in the interests of justice for it to be admissible

The effect of s 114 is to render admissible out-of-court statements which are not otherwise admissible so long as they are cogent and reliable. The section applies not just to first-hand hearsay but also multiple hearsay where business documents or inconsistent statements or other previous statements are concerned (see **9.6.2.7**).

Example 1

Joe witnesses a crime. He makes a statement in writing, relating what he saw.

Joe's statement is first-hand hearsay. Joe is the witness as to fact and he has reduced what he said into writing.

Example 2

Joe witnesses a crime. He tells Jenny what he saw. Jenny makes a statement in writing, relating what Joe told her.

Jenny's statement is multiple hearsay. Joes's evidence has now gone through two stages of reporting.

Example 3

Ann deposits £300 in a safe. She records the deposit in the ledger.

Assuming that the ledger is to be adduced to prove the truth of the statement in it, ie, the deposit of £300, this would be first-hand hearsay. Ann is the witness with first-hand knowledge. The record in the ledger has gone through one stage of reporting.

In addition, s 114(3) permits the exclusion of statements even if they fulfil the requirements of the section. For example, confessions must meet the additional requirements of the Police and Criminal Evidence Act 1984 before being admissible in evidence.

Section 115(1) provides that:

(1)   In this Chapter references to a statement or a matter stated are to be read as follows.

(2)   A statement is any representation of fact or opinion made by a person by whatever means; and it includes a representation made in a sketch, photofit or other pictorial form.

(3)   A matter stated is one to which this Chapter applies if (and only if) the purpose, or one of the purposes, of the person making the statement appears to the court to have been—

    (a)   to cause another person to believe in the matter, or

    (b)   to cause another person to act or a machine to operate on the basis that the matter is as stated.

Section 115 thus permits the admission of hearsay evidence where the maker does not intend to communicate any evidence at all. Previously such statements were inadmissible at common law. It also permits evidence of a failure to record an event (sometimes known as negative hearsay) to be admitted if it was the purpose of the person who failed to record the event to cause anyone to believe that the event did not occur.

The definition in s 115(2) ensures that statements which are not based on human input fall outside the ambit of the hearsay rule. Tapes, films or photographs that directly record the commission of an offence and documents produced by machines that automatically record a process or event or perform calculations are not hearsay. Documents produced by machines will have to satisfy s 129.

The principal categories of admissibility are:

(a)   where a witness is unavailable;

(b)   business and other documents;

(c)   where hearsay evidence was already admissible at common law;

(d)   inconsistent statements;

(e)   other previous statements;

(f)   other statutory provisions where hearsay evidence was already admissible.

9.6.2.1   Where a witness is unavailable

Section 116(1) of CJA 2003 provides that:

> In criminal proceedings a statement not made in oral evidence in the proceedings is admissible as evidence of any matter stated if—
>
> (a)   oral evidence given in the proceedings by the person who made the statement would be admissible as evidence of that matter,
>
> (b)   the person who made the statement (the relevant person) is identified to the court's satisfaction, and
>
> (c)   any of the five conditions mentioned in subsection (2) is satisfied.

The circumstances in which a witness is held to be unavailable are set out in s 116(2):

(a)   he is dead;

(b)   he is unfit to give evidence through his bodily or mental condition;

(c)   he is outside the UK and it is not reasonably practicable to secure his attendance;

(d)   he cannot be found;

(e)   he does not give evidence through fear.

The provisions are available to the prosecution and the defence (and apply to both oral and documentary evidence, ie, conversations and comments as well as written statements).

The preliminary requirements set out in s 116(1) should be noted. The evidence is only admissible:

(a)   if it would have been admissible as oral evidence (this will ensure that otherwise inadmissible evidence is not admitted under the section); and

(b)   the person who made the statement is identified to the court's satisfaction. The party seeking to have the evidence admitted will therefore have to comply with these two preliminary requirements.

This may be done by submissions, based on the statements or other material in the case. In some cases, it may be necessary to hold a trial within a trial.

Section 116 of CJA 2003 replaces s 23 of the Criminal Justice Act 1988 which applied only to statements in documents. However, it is submitted, a number of decisions under that Act and other legislation are still relevant and applicable to CJA 2003. The conditions laid down by the legislation for hearsay to be admitted must be proved to the court's satisfaction. Accordingly, the party seeking to adduce evidence must lay a foundation for doing so.

In *R v Nicholls* [1976] 63 Cr App R 187, the Court of Appeal said that a sufficient foundation must be laid for the judge to draw a reasonable inference to satisfy himself that the requirements of the section had been met. The judge may need to hold a trial within a trial in order to do so. If the prosecution is seeking to adduce the evidence, the criminal standard of proof applies: the prosecution must satisfy the court beyond reasonable doubt by admissible evidence that the requirements are met. On the other hand, if the defence is seeking to have a statement admitted under the section, the civil standard applies, ie, the court must be satisfied on the balance of probabilities.

Deliberate unavailability

By s 116(5):

> A condition set out in any paragraph of subsection (2) which is in fact satisfied is to be treated as not satisfied if it is shown that the circumstances described in that paragraph are caused—
>
> (a) by the person in support of whose case it is sought to give the statement in evidence, or
>
> (b) by a person acting on his behalf,
>
> in order to prevent the relevant person giving oral evidence in the proceedings (whether at all or in connection with the subject matter of the statement).

This provision is aimed at those who seek to manufacture pretexts for witnesses not to appear in court and thereby avoid potentially embarrassing cross-examination. It will apply to witnesses for both the prosecution and defence. It will be for the party opposing admission to establish that this has happened. It is submitted that if there is a real possibility of this having occurred, the court should not admit the evidence.

In any event, the court retains the discretion under s 78 of the Police and Criminal Act 1984 to exclude such evidence if it would have such an adverse effect on the fairness of the proceedings.

The circumstances in which the witness may be held to be unavailable are now considered.

The witness is dead: s 116(2)(a)

Evidence of this fact is usually established by a death certificate or calling a witness (eg, a police officer) to prove the circumstances of death. Much will depend on the circumstances of the case. Provided the court is satisfied that the witness is dead, the statement is admissible.

The witness 'is unfit to be a witness because of his bodily or mental condition': s 116(2)(b)

Evidence of this fact is usually established by way of a medical report setting out the condition and explaining why it renders the witness unfit. A mere certificate will not suffice.

The witness 'is outside the United Kingdom and it is not reasonably practicable to secure his attendance': s 116(2)(c)

A party seeking to adduce a statement under this heading must adduce evidence both that the witness is outside the country and that it is not reasonably practical to secure his attendance at court. The first requirement will usually not be difficult to prove. For example, it will usually appear from the statements, and be undisputed, that the witness is resident abroad. The second requirement may present more difficulties. In an age of air travel or video link evidence, it may be relatively simple to get a witness's evidence before the court. However, there may be cost implications. All will depend on the circumstances.

This paragraph replaces para (b)(i)(ii) of s 23(2) of the Criminal Justice Act 1988. There are a number of decisions under the previous legislation. It is submitted that they still apply (see *R v Hurst* [1995] 1 Cr App R 82; *R v Castillo* [1996] 1 Cr App R 438; *R v Bray* (1989) 88 Cr App R 354; *R v French and Gowhar* (1993) 97 Cr App R 421; and *R v Gonzales* (1993) 96 Cr App R 399).

The witness 'cannot be found although such steps as is reasonably practicable to take to find him have been taken': s 116(2)(d)

The party seeking to adduce the statement of a witness in these circumstances must prove that:

(a)   the witness cannot be found;

(b)   such steps as are reasonably practicable to take to find him, have been taken.

This provision is aimed at ensuring that the evidence of a witness who has disappeared is not lost to the court, which might result in injustice. It will require the party to provide evidence to establish the fact that the witness cannot be found and to set out the steps that have been taken to find him. What is 'reasonably practicable' will depend on the particular circumstances. However, considerations such as those in the case of the witness abroad (see above) may be applicable, adapted to the situation of the witness who has disappeared. Thus, it may be necessary to establish where the witness was last seen and in what circumstances, and what steps have been taken to trace him.

The witness does not give evidence through fear: s 116(2)(e)

Section 116(2)(e) provides that hearsay evidence is admissible if:

> . . . through fear the [witness] does not give (or does not continue to give) oral evidence in the proceedings, either at all or in connection with the subject matter of the statement, and the court gives leave for the statement to be given in evidence.

By s 116(3) '"fear" is to be widely construed and (for example) includes fear of the death or injury of another person or of financial loss.'

By s 116(4) leave may only be given under this subsection:

> if the court considers that the statement ought to be admitted in the interests of justice, having regard—
> (a)   to the statement's contents,
> (b)   to any risk that its admission or exclusion will result in unfairness to any party to the proceedings (and in particular to how difficult it will be to challenge the statement if the relevant person does not give oral evidence),
> (c)   in appropriate cases, to the fact that a direction under section 19 of the Youth Justice and Criminal Evidence Act 1999 (special measures for the giving of

evidence by fearful witnesses etc) could be made in relation to the relevant person, and

(d)   to any other relevant circumstances.

There were a number of cases decided under the previous legislation (Criminal Justice Act 1988, s 23(3)). It is submitted that they are still applicable. (See *R v Waters* [1997] Crim LR 823; *R v Greer* [1998] Crim LR 572; *R v Denton* [2001] 1 Cr App R 227.)

A flowchart summarising the admissibility of evidence under s 116 is included at **Appendix 1(G)**.

9.6.2.2   Business and other documents

Section 117(1) of CJA 2003 makes admissible as evidence in criminal proceedings a statement contained in a document of any matter stated if oral evidence given in the proceedings would be admissible as evidence of that matter.

Documents admitted under s 117(1) must fulfil the requirements of s 117(2); they must have been created or received in the course of a trade, business, etc. Moreover, where such documents were prepared for criminal proceedings or a criminal investigation, additional requirements are laid down by s 117(4) and (5).

Documents created, etc: in the course of a trade, business, etc.: s 117(2)(3)

Section 117(2) provides that the requirements of this subsection are satisfied if:

(a)   the document or the part containing the statement was created or received by a person in the course of a trade, business, profession or other occupation, or as the holder of a paid or unpaid office,

(b)   the person who supplied the information contained in the statement (the relevant person) had or may reasonably supposed to have had personal knowledge of the matters dealt with, and

(c)   each person (if any) through whom the information was supplied from the relevant person to the person [who created or received the document must have] received the information in the course of a trade, business, profession or other occupation, or as the holder of a paid or unpaid office.

The person who created or received the document that contains the statement may be the same person as whoever supplied the information that is in the statement (s 117(3)).

Example 1

Ann deposits £300 in a safe. She tells William, a clerk, who records the deposit in a ledger.

Ann .... William .... William's statement in ledger

The ledger, if adduced to prove the deposit of £300, will be multiple hearsay. As William creates it in the course of a business, it is admissible under s 117.

Example 2

Ann deposits £300 in a safe. She tells William, a clerk. William passes on the information to Julian, who records the deposit in a ledger.

Ann .... William .... Julian .... Julian's statement in ledger

The ledger, if adduced to prove the deposit of £300, will be multiple hearsay. As William passed on the information in the course of a business to Julian who, also acting in the course of a business, recorded the deposit in a ledger, it is admissible under s 117.

Example 3

Sarah witnesses a crime. She tells PC Smith what she saw. PC Smith makes a statement setting out what Sarah told him but does not get her to sign it.

Sarah .... PC Smith .... PC Smith's statement

The written statement of PC Smith, if adduced to prove the truth of anything contained in it, will be multiple hearsay. As PC Smith made the statement as the holder of a paid office, it is admissible under s 117.

Under the previous legislation there were numerous decisions some of which, it is submitted, may be of assistance in relation to the interpretation of s 117. (See *R v Minors* [1989] 1 WLR 441; *R v Foxley* [1995] 2 CR App R 523; *R v Jenkins and Starling* [2003] Crim LR 107.)

Practically all business records, correspondence and files are admissible. The party seeking to rely on the section must satisfy the court that the requirements of the section have been met.

If the prosecution seeks to rely on the section, the criminal standard of proof will apply. In the Crown Court the judge may need to hold a trial within a trial and (unless admissions are made or statements read by agreement) hear oral evidence to satisfy himself beyond reasonable doubt before admitting the statement.

Documents prepared for the purposes of criminal proceedings or a criminal investigation: s 117(4) and (5)

These subsections apply to documents 'prepared for the purposes of pending or contemplated criminal proceedings or for a criminal investigation' (s 117(4)(a)).

There are two exceptions provided in s 117(4)(b). First, documents prepared pursuant to a request under s 7 of the Crime (International Co-operation) Act 2003 and secondly, a document prepared in accordance with an order under para 6 of Sch 13 to the Criminal Justice Act 1988. Both of these relate to overseas evidence. Section 117(4) and (5) do not apply to either of these types of document.

Further requirements for documents prepared for criminal proceedings or a criminal investigation

Section 117(5) enacts two further requirements for documents prepared for criminal proceedings or a criminal investigation. The document must meet either one or other of the following requirements:

(a) By s 117(5)(a) the document must fulfil the conditions laid down in s 116(2) as follows:

   (i)   he is dead;
   (ii)   he is unfit to give evidence through his bodily or mental condition;
   (iii) he is outside the UK and it is not reasonably practicable to secure his attendance;
   (iv)   he cannot be found;
   (v)   he does not give evidence through fear.

(b) Alternatively, by s 117(5)(b): 'the relevant person cannot reasonably be expected to have any recollection of the matters dealt with in the statement (having regard to the length of time and all other circumstances)'. In determining whether this requirement has been met, the court will have to consider the circumstances in which the statement was made, the nature of the events to which it relates and the length of time which has elapsed since the witness made it, and then decide whether the witness would reasonably be expected to have any recollection of the matters dealt with.

A document that does not meet these requirements is inadmissible if it is sought to admit it as a document prepared for criminal proceedings. (See *R v Bedi* (1992) 95 Cr App R 21, a case decided under the previous legislation but still relevant.)

Therefore, in Examples 1 and 2 above, the ledgers will be admissible without a prescribed reason as they were not prepared for use in criminal proceedings or a criminal investigation. In Example 3, a prescribed reason is required for Sarah as the police officer's statement will have been prepared for such purpose.

The question whether the maker of a statement can reasonably be expected to have any recollection of matters dealt within it is not merely to be examined at the moment the trial opens but against the whole background of the case. The fact that the maker of a statement retains a recollection of some of the matters dealt with in it does not prevent part of the statement being admitted; part of a document may be treated as an independent statement for the purposes of the section.

The court's discretion to exclude otherwise admissible evidence under s 78 of the Police and Criminal Evidence Act 1984 and at common law applies to evidence under s 117 (Criminal Justice Act 2003 s 126).

Doubtful statements: s 117(6) and (7)

The court has an important power to exclude statements of doubtful reliability under s 117(6) and (7):

(6) A statement is not admissible under this section if the court makes a direction to that effect under subsection (7).

(7) The court may make a direction under this subsection if satisfied that the statement's reliability as evidence for the purpose for which it is tendered is doubtful in view of—

(a) its contents,

(b) the source of the information contained in it,

(c) the way in which or the circumstances in which the information was supplied or received, or

(d) the way in which or the circumstances in which the document concerned was created or received.

Thus, if the contents of the document or the circumstances of its supply, or the source or supply of the information contained give rise to doubts about its reliability as evidence for the purposes for which it is tendered, the court has a discretion to exclude it. Thus, it is not the general unreliability, but reliability for the purpose for which the statement is tendered, which will lead to exclusion.

These powers are in addition to the court's powers to exclude evidence under s 126 of the 2003 Act (see below), ss 76, 76A or 78 of the Police and Criminal Act 1984 and at common law.

A flowchart summarising the admissibility of business documents under s 117 is included at **Appendix 1(H)**.

9.6.2.3 Statements admissible at common law

Section 118(1) of the Criminal Justice Act 2003 expressly preserves certain common law categories of admissibility. These are the rules as to:

(a)   public information, etc;

(b)   reputation as to character;

(c)   reputation or family tradition;

(d)   *res gestae*;

(e)   confessions, etc;

(f)   admissions by agents, etc;

(g)   common enterprise;

(h)   expert evidence.

By s 118(2) all other common law rules governing the admissibility of hearsay evidence are abolished.

The effect of the section is that in the circumstances specified above an out-of-court statement will be admissible as evidence of any matters stated in it. The first three categories listed above do not make common appearances in criminal trials.

Public information

Section 118(1) public information, preserves the common law rule under which:

(a)   published works dealing with matters of a public nature (such as histories, scientific works, dictionaries and maps) are admissible as evidence of facts of a public nature stated in them,

(b)   public documents (such as public registers, and returns made under public authority with respect to matters of public interest) are admissible as evidence of acts stated in them,

(c)   records (such as the records of certain courts, treaties, Crown grants, pardons and commissions) are admissible as evidence of facts stated in them, or

(d)   evidence relating to a person's age or date or place of birth may be given by a person without personal knowledge of the matter.

Reputation as to character

Section 118(1) reputation as to character preserves:

Any rule of law under which in criminal proceedings evidence of a person's reputation is admissible for the purpose of proving his good or bad character.

Note

The rule is preserved only so far as it allows the court to treat such evidence as proving the matter concerned.

Reputation or family tradition

Section 118(1) reputation or family tradition preserves:

Any rule of law under which in criminal proceedings evidence of reputation or family tradition is admissible for the purpose of proving or disproving—

(a)   pedigree or the existence of a marriage,

(b)   the existence of any public or general right, or

(c)   the identity of any person or thing.

Note

The rule is preserved only so far as it allows the court to treat such evidence as proving or disproving the matter concerned.

Res gestae

The principles of admissibility of a statement under the *res gestae* principle have already been discussed at **9.5.3.3** as an exception to the self-made evidence rule.

Such statements are also admissible as an exception to the rule against hearsay evidence.

Res gestae is defined in s 118(1) as:

> Any rule of law under which in criminal proceedings a statement is admissible as evidence of any matter stated if—
> (a) the statement was made by a person so emotionally overpowered by an event that the possibility of concoction or distortion can be disregarded,
> (b) the statement accompanied an act which can be properly evaluated as evidence only if considered in conjunction with the statement, or
> (c) the statement relates to a physical sensation or a mental state (such as intention or emotion).

Confessions

> In any proceedings a confession made by an accused person may be given in evidence against him insofar as it is relevant to any matter in issue in the proceedings and is not excluded by the court in pursuance of this section. (Police and Criminal Evidence Act 1984, s 76(1))
>
> In any proceedings a confession made by an accused person may be given in evidence for another person charged in the same proceedings (a co-accused) in so far as it is relevant to any other matter in issue in the proceedings and is not excluded by the court in pursuance of this section. (Police and Criminal Evidence Act 1984, s 76(A)(1))

A confession includes:

> Any statement wholly or partly adverse to the person who made it, whether made to a person in authority or not and whether made in words or otherwise. (Police and Criminal Evidence Act 1984, s 82(1))

Only the defendant can make a confession.

The most common examples of confessions will be admissions of guilt made by a defendant, orally or in writing, when being interviewed by the police. However, a confession can be made to anyone. If a defendant says to a friend, 'I did the burglary at number 10 last night', that would constitute a confession.

As a general rule, confessions are admissible in evidence (but only against the maker – they are inadmissible against anyone else implicated in the confession) as an exception to the rule excluding hearsay evidence. If a defendant says to the police, 'I stole the goods', the interviewing officer will give evidence of the defendant's statement. The court will be asked to accept the truth of that statement. It will be hearsay but admissible as an exception to the general exclusionary rule. Sometimes a confession statement will include statements, which are favourable to the defendant.

Example

'I hit the victim in the face' (confession) '... but in self-defence' (favourable to the defence).

These are often referred to as 'mixed statements'. The whole statement is admissible as an exception to the rule excluding hearsay (*R v Sharp (Colin)* (1988) 86 Cr App R 274).

Challenging the admissibility of confessions

Although, as a general principle, confessions are admissible in evidence, by the Police and Criminal Evidence Act 1984, s 76(2)(a), (b):

> If, in any proceedings where the prosecution proposes to give in evidence a confession made by an accused person, it is represented to the court that the confession was or may have been obtained—
>
> (a)   by oppression of the person who made it; or
>
> (b)   in consequence of anything said or done which was likely, in the circumstances existing at the time, to render unreliable any confession which might be made by him in consequence thereof,
>
> the court shall not allow the confession to be given in evidence against him except insofar as the prosecution proves to the court beyond reasonable doubt that the confession (notwithstanding that it may be true) was not obtained as aforesaid.

The magistrates at committal proceedings have no power to exclude confession evidence (Police and Criminal Evidence Act 1984, s 76(9)).

> If, in any proceedings where a co-accused proposes to give in evidence a confession made by an accused person, it is represented to the court that the confession was or may have been obtained—
>
> (a)   by oppression of the person who made it; or
>
> (b)   in consequence of anything said or done which was likely, in the circumstances existing at the time, to render unreliable any confession which might be made by him in consequence thereof,
>
> the court shall not allow the confession to be given in evidence for the co-accused except in so far as it is proved to the court on the balance of probabilities that the confession (notwithstanding that it may be true) was not so obtained. (Police and Criminal Evidence Act 1984, s 76(A)(2))

Oppression

Oppression includes 'torture, inhuman or degrading treatment, and the use or threat of violence (whether or not amounting to torture)' (s 76(8)). In *R v Fulling* [1987] 2 WLR 923, the Court of Appeal considered the meaning of oppression (the statutory definition not being intended to be a complete definition). It was held that the word 'oppression' was to be given its ordinary dictionary meaning, ie, 'exercise of authority or power in a burdensome, harsh or wrongful manner; unjust or cruel treatment of subjects, inferiors, etc; the imposition of unreasonable or unjust burdens'. Deliberate police misconduct in the form of a serious breach of the Code of Practice or a course of misconduct may constitute oppression. Code C, para 11.5 provides that no police officer may try to obtain answers to questions or elicit a statement by the use of oppression.

Example

D was unlawfully held at the police station, unlawfully denied access to legal advice and questioned about an offence for which he had not been arrested. His confession was excluded on the oppression ground: *R v Davison* [1988] Crim LR 442.

The 'unreliability' ground

It is necessary to consider:

(a)   the thing said or done which is the subject of the application to exclude the confession;

(b)   whether that thing said or done is likely to render any confession which might have been made by the defendant unreliable.

The thing said or done will usually involve a breach of Code C. Such breaches may include denial of access to legal advice, inducements to confess and failure to summon an independent adult in cases involving juveniles or the mentally disordered. However, a breach of the Code will not of itself lead to exclusion of the confession. There must be a causal link between the breach and the unreliability of any confession that might have been made. Thus, if denial of access to legal advice is relied upon, it will be difficult to establish a causal link if the defendant is an experienced criminal who says that he was fully aware of his rights. On the other hand, a young, inexperienced defendant may find it easier to establish the unreliability principle in such circumstances.

It should be noted that, in contrast to oppression, the unreliability ground need not necessarily involve any misconduct on the part of the police.

Example 1

R v Harvey [1988] Crim LR 241: D and her lesbian lover were questioned about a murder. D had a low IQ and was an alcoholic. D's lover, in the presence of D, confessed. D then made a confession exonerating her lover. The lover subsequently died and D was tried for murder, the prosecution relying on her confession. The confession was excluded on the unreliability ground, the court finding that D may well have been trying to protect her lover who had initially confessed in D's presence.

Example 2

R v Trussler (Barry) [1988] Crim LR 446: D, a drug addict, was kept in custody for 18 hours. He was interviewed several times without being given any rest and was denied access to legal advice. His confession was excluded on the unreliability ground.

Example 3

R v Alladice (Colin Carlton) (1988) 87 Cr App R 380: D was denied access to legal advice and confessed to a robbery. When giving evidence, D stated that he knew of his rights and that he understood the caution. D's application to exclude his confession was correctly rejected by the trial judge. Although there had been a serious breach of the Code of Practice, there was nothing to suggest that this might render any confession made by D unreliable.

The discretion to exclude a confession

If the prosecution fails to discharge the burden of proof imposed by the Police and Criminal Evidence Act 1984, s 76, exclusion of a confession is mandatory. The court also has a general discretion to exclude prosecution evidence under s 78 on the basis that the admission of the evidence will have an adverse effect on the fairness of the proceedings (see **9.2.5**). Again, breaches of the Code of Practice may be the basis of an application under s 78.

In *R v Canale (Ramon Michael)* [1990] 2 All ER 187, the defendant denied making certain statements attributed to him by the police. The interviewing officers had failed to make a contemporaneous note of two of the interviews and had therefore failed to give the defendant a chance to comment on the accuracy of the record of these interviews. The evidence was excluded under s 78 on the basis that its admission would be unfair to the defendant. The court had been deprived of the assistance of contemporaneous notes and had thereby lost the most cogent evidence that would have been available to resolve the conflict of evidence between the parties. As with s 76, a breach of the Code will not lead to automatic exclusion of the confession. If *Canale* had not challenged the accuracy of the officer's evidence, it is difficult to see how the absence of contemporaneous notes could have led to a successful application to exclude under s 78.

The discretion to exclude a confession has also been used where the police have misrepresented the strength of the evidence available to them and have thereby effectively tricked the defendant into confession (*R v Mason* [1988] 1 WLR 139).

The procedure for challenging the admissibility of a confession

In the Crown Court, the admissibility of a confession will be determined by the judge, in the absence of the jury, at a 'trial within a trial' sometimes referred to as a *voir dire*. If the prosecution is seeking to adduce the confession, the interviewing officer will give evidence as to how the confession was obtained and the defendant will be given the opportunity of relating his version of events. The judge will then rule on admissibility. If it is ruled to be inadmissible, the confession will not be put to the jury. If it is ruled to be admissible, the interviewing officer will give evidence of it to the jury. It is open to the defence to attack the cogency of the confession in order to persuade the jury to attach no weight to it.

In the magistrates' court, a ruling as to the admissibility of the confession can be sought when the interviewing officer gives evidence (*R v Liverpool Juvenile Court, ex p R* [1988] QB 1). If the application is made under s 76, the magistrates must hold a 'trial within a trial'. There is no such obligation if the application is made under s 78. If submissions are made under both s 76 and s 78, then both applications should be examined at the same 'trial within a trial' (*Halawa v Federation Against Copyright Theft* [1995] 1 Cr App R 21). Alternatively, the question of admissibility can be left to the close of the prosecution case (if no defence evidence is required to challenge the admissibility of the confession) or to the end of the trial (before the defence closing speech). Whatever the procedure adopted, it is inevitable that the magistrates will know that a confession has been made. Furthermore, if the defendant makes allegations of police misconduct in challenging the confession, this may expose him to cross-examination on his previous convictions.

Evidence obtained in consequence of an inadmissible confession

The fact that a confession is excluded under s 76 shall not affect the admissibility in evidence of any facts discovered as a result of the confession. However, the prosecution may not call evidence that such facts were discovered as a result of a statement made by the defendant.

Example

Martin is charged with murder. As a result of statements made by him, the police are able to recover both the murder weapon and the body. If the confession is ruled inadmissible, the jury will hear evidence as to where and when these items were discovered. If his confession is ruled admissible, the jury will, in addition, hear that the defendant was able to say exactly where these items could be found.

If a confession is relevant as showing that the accused speaks, writes or expresses himself in a particular way, so much of the confession as is necessary to show that he does so will be admissible (s 76(4)–(6), s 76(A)(4)–(6)).

Admissions by agents

Section 118(1) admissions by agents preserves:

Any rule of law under which in criminal proceedings –
(a)   an admission made by an agent of a defendant is admissible against the defendant as evidence of any matter stated, or
(b)   a statement made by a person to whom a defendant refers to a person for information is admissible against the defendant as evidence of any matter stated.

Admissions made by the defendant's agents are only admissible if it is proved that the admissions were made on the defendant's authority. For cases involving defence solicitors and counsel as agents, see *R v Evans* [1981] Crim LR 699; *R v Hutchinson* (1985) 82 Cr App R 51; *R v Turner* (1975) 61 Cr App R 67.

Common enterprise

Section 118(1) common enterprise preserves:

> Any rule of law which in criminal proceedings a statement made by a party to a common enterprise is admissible against another party to the enterprise as evidence of any matter stated.

Where two or more persons are engaged in a common enterprise, the acts and declarations of one in pursuance of the common enterprise are admissible against the other.

Expert evidence

Section 118(1) expert evidence preserves:

> Any rule of law under which in criminal proceedings an expert witness may draw on the body of expertise relevant to his field.

9.6.2.4   The 'safety valve' – the discretion

The 'safety valve' provision in s 114(1)(d) marks a significant relaxation of the hearsay rule. It makes admissible a statement given otherwise than in testimony as evidence of any matter stated if the court is satisfied that, despite the difficulties there may be in challenging the evidence, it would not be contrary to the interests of justice for it to be admissible.

In deciding whether a statement should be admitted under s 114(1)(d) the court must, by s 114(2), have regard to the following factors (and to any others it considers relevant):

(a)   how much probative value of the statement (assuming it to be true) in relation to a matter in issue in the proceedings, or how valuable it is for the understanding of other evidence in the case;

(b)   what other evidence has been, or can be, given on the matter or evidence mentioned in paragraph (a);

(c)   how important the matter or evidence mentioned in paragraph (a) is in the context of the case as a whole;

(d)   the circumstances in which the statement was made;

(e)   how reliable the maker of the statement appears to be;

(f)   how reliable the evidence of the making of the statement appears to be;

(g)   whether oral evidence of the matter stated can be given and, if not, why it cannot;

(h)   the amount of difficulty involved in challenging the statement;

(i)   the extent to which that difficulty would be likely to prejudice the party facing it.

Thus, the court must take into account all these factors in deciding whether to admit the evidence.

The court must begin by considering the statement itself in the circumstances of the case (and assuming the statement to be true), what is its probative value and its significance to the case. Insignificant evidence of little probative value should be excluded. However, the greater the probative value, the more carefully it must be considered. If the statement has the necessary significance and probative value, the court must consider the circumstances of the making of the statement and its reliability.

If the circumstances or the statement itself clearly indicate that the statement is, or may be, unreliable, then the court should not admit it. But, in the absence of clear indications, the court is not obliged to conduct a detailed inquiry (or hold a trial within a trial, in the Crown Court) to determine whether there is the possibility of such indications. It may be preferable for the court then to admit the evidence, and if later evidence shows it to be, or may be, unreliable, to exclude the evidence or direct the jury to do so.

Finally, once the court has considered the probative value and reliability of the statement, it must consider whether the evidence can be given, alternatively, as oral evidence (and, therefore, subject to cross-examination). It must then consider the amount of difficulty the opposing party would have in challenging the statement and the prejudice in doing so. The means of doing so might include the cross-examination of other witnesses, putting the credibility of the maker in issue, or calling evidence to challenge the statement. However, the court must consider how practical these means are in the particular case.

The Law Commission (Law Com No 245, para 8.140) gave some examples of when it would be in the interests of justice that the statement be admitted.

Example 1

D is prosecuted for indecent assault on a child. The child is too young to testify, but she initially described her assailant as 'a coloured boy' [sic]. The defence is identity and the defendant is white.

Example 2

D is prosecuted for the murder of his girlfriend. He denies that it was he who killed her. Fixing the time of the murder is an essential part of proving that D must have done it. An eight-year-old child tells the police that he saw the victim leaving her home at a time after the prosecution says that she was dead. By the time the case comes to trial the child can remember nothing about when he saw the victim.

Example 3

D is charged with assault. X, who is not charged, admits to a friend that he, X, committed the assault. D and X are similar in appearance. X's confession is inadmissible hearsay.

It should be remembered that, by definition, the witness in question under s 114(1)(d) is available. Otherwise, save in the context of incompetence, or loss of memory, the case should be dealt with under s 116. Further, a witness statement has not been given to the police or other investigating agency, for otherwise the case would be dealt with under s 117.

9.6.2.5 Previous inconsistent statements

Inconsistent statements are admissible pursuant to s 119 of CJA 2003. If the witness denies making the previous statement it can be proved under ss 3, 4 and 5 of the Criminal Procedure Act 1865. If the previous statement is admitted as an exhibit, it must not accompany the jury when they retire to consider their verdict unless the court considers it appropriate, or all the parties to the proceedings agree that the jury should have the document with them.

9.6.2.6 Other previous statements

Under s 120 of CJA 2003, other statements made by a witness in proceedings will be admissible as to the truth of their contents in the following circumstances:

(a) Where a previous statement is used to rebut a suggestion of recent fabrication.

(b) Where a previous statement is used by a witness to refresh his memory (see **9.3.2.2**) provided that the witness has been cross-examined on that statement and as a consequence is received in evidence in the proceedings.

(c) Where a witness indicates that to the best of his belief he made the statement to be relied upon and that to the best of his belief it states the truth. This is relevant to only three situations:

(i) where the statement identifies or describes a person, object or place;

(ii) where the statement was made by the witness when the matters stated were fresh in his memory but he does not remember them, and cannot reasonably be expected to remember them well enough to give oral evidence of them in the proceedings;

(iii) where the statement constitutes evidence of recent complaint. For evidence of recent complaint to be admitted all the criteria in s 120(7) of CJA 2003 must be met.

If the previous statement is admitted as an exhibit, it must not accompany the jury when they retire to consider their verdict unless the court considers it appropriate, or all the parties to the proceedings agree that the jury should have the document with them.

9.6.2.7 Multiple hearsay

Section 121 of CJA 2003 permits the admission of multiple hearsay where business documents or inconsistent statements or other previous statements are concerned. Furthermore, multiple hearsay is also admissible when either all parties to the proceedings agree to the admission or the court considers that it is in the interests of justice to do so.

9.6.2.8 Safeguards

Capability to make a statement

Under s 123 of CJA 2003 the court, when considering admitting a statement under s 116 (witness unavailable to give evidence), s 119 (inconsistent statements) and s 120 (other previous statements of witnesses), is empowered to examine the capability of the person concerned to have made the statement that is in issue. A person has the required capability if he is capable of understanding the questions put to him and giving answers that can be understood. The court can in appropriate cases receive expert evidence.

Matters regarding credibility

Section 124 of CJA 2003 allows for the admission of evidence casting doubt on the credibility of a hearsay statement if such evidence would have been admissible had the maker of the statement given oral evidence of the facts stated. Evidence of previous inconsistent statements is similarly admissible.

Stopping the case where the evidence is unconvincing

In a Crown Court case if the case against the defendant is based wholly or partly on a hearsay statement, the judge can stop the case at any time after the close of the prosecution case if the evidence provided by the statement is so unconvincing that, considering its importance to the case against the defendant, his conviction for the offence would be unsafe. The court may either acquit the defendant or order a retrial under s 125 of CJA 2003.

General discretion to exclude hearsay statements

Under s 126 of CJA 2003 the court may refuse to admit hearsay evidence if satisfied that the case for excluding the statement, taking account of the danger that to admit it would result in an undue waste of time, substantially outweighs the case for admitting it, taking account of the evidence. This does not affect the court's discretion under s 78 of the Police and Criminal Evidence Act 1984 or at common law to exclude unfair or prejudicial evidence.

Directions to the jury

In the Crown Court a further safeguard is to be found in the direction the judge must give the jury. If the statement is read or hearsay relied upon it will be necessary to warn the jury to bear in mind, when deciding whether they can rely on it, that they have not had the benefit of hearing the evidence of the maker tested in cross-examination (see *Scott (Richard) v R* (1989) 89 Cr App R 153; *R v Curry* (1998) *The Times*, 23 March; *R v Kennedy and Burrell* [1994] Crim LR 37; *R v Kennedy* [1992] Crim LR 37). In the magistrates' court the defence advocate should address the court on these matters in his closing speech.

9.6.2.9   The Human Rights Act 1998

Article 6 of the European Convention on Human Rights protects the right of a defendant to a fair trial. In particular Article 6(3)(d) confers the right on a defendant to examine or have examined witnesses against him, and to obtain the attendance and examination of witnesses on his behalf under the same conditions as witnesses against him. The Convention looks at the fairness of the trial, not necessarily the detailed content of rules of evidence, which is primarily for domestic law to determine (see *Doorson v Netherlands* (1996) 22 EHRR 33 and *R v Khan (Sultan)* [1996] 3 All ER 289). The hearsay provisions of the Criminal Justice Act 2003 are intended, and believed, to be ECHR compliant. In particular, the Joint Committee on Human Rights (Second report, Session 2002–2003, para 24 et seq) was of the view that the compatibility of the new provisions may turn on a court's assessment of the adequacy of the safeguards to prevent a conviction being based, wholly or mainly, on unsafe or unfair use of hearsay evidence.

9.6.2.10   Other statutory provisions

Section 114(1)(a) of CJA 2003 preserves the other statutory exceptions to the hearsay rule that are not repealed by the new law. In some cases there may be overlap between the preserved statutory provision and the terms of either s 116, (where a witness is unavailable), and s 117 (business and other documents). Of particular importance are the provisions of s 9 of the Criminal Justice Act 1967 and s 68 and Sch 2 to the Criminal Procedure and Investigations Act 1996.

Criminal Procedure and Investigations Act 1996, s 68 and Sch 2, paras 1 and 2

68.   Schedule 2 to this Act (which relates to the use at the trial of written statements and depositions admitted in evidence in committal proceedings) shall have effect.

SCHEDULE 2

STATEMENTS AND DEPOSITIONS

Statements

1.   (1)   Sub-paragraph (2) applies if—

(a)   a written statement has been admitted in evidence in proceedings before a magistrates' court inquiring into an offence as examining justices,

(b)   in those proceedings a person has been committed for trial,

(c)   for the purposes of section 5A of the Magistrates' Courts Act 1980 the statement complied with section 5B of that Act prior to the committal for trial,

(d)   the statement purports to be signed by a justice of the peace, and

(e)   sub-paragraph (3) does not prevent sub-paragraph (2) applying.

(2)   Where this sub-paragraph applies the statement may without further proof be read as evidence on the trial of the accused, whether for the offence for which he was committed for trial or for any other offence arising out of the same transaction or set of circumstances.

(3)   Sub-paragraph (2) does not apply if—

(a)   it is proved that the statement was not signed by the justice by whom it purports to have been signed,

(b)   the court of trial at its discretion orders that sub-paragraph (2) shall not apply, or

(c)   a party to the proceedings objects to sub-paragraph (2) applying.

(4)   If a party to the proceedings objects to sub-paragraph (2) applying the court of trial may order that the objection shall have no effect if the court considers it to be in the interests of justice so to order.

Depositions

2.   (1)   Sub-paragraph (2) applies if—

(a)   in pursuance of section 97A of the Magistrates' Courts Act 1980 (summons or warrant to have evidence taken as a deposition etc) a person has had his evidence taken as a deposition for the purposes of proceedings before a magistrates' court inquiring into an offence as examining justices,

(b)   the deposition has been admitted in evidence in those proceedings,

(c)   in those proceedings a person has been committed for trial,

(d)   for the purposes of section 5A of the Magistrates' Courts Act 1980 the deposition complied with section 5C of that Act prior to the committal for trial,

(e)   the deposition purports to be signed by the justice before whom it purports to have been taken, and

(f)   sub-paragraph (3) does not prevent sub-paragraph (2) applying.

(2)   Where this sub-paragraph applies the deposition may without further proof be read as evidence on the trial of the accused, whether for the offence for which he was committed for trial or for any other offence arising out of the same transaction or set of circumstances.

(3)   Sub-paragraph (2) does not apply if—

(a)   it is proved that the deposition was not signed by the justice by whom it purports to have been signed,

(b)   the court of trial at its discretion orders that sub-paragraph (2) shall not apply, or

(c)   a party to the proceedings objects to sub-paragraph (2) applying.

(4)   If a party to the proceedings objects to sub-paragraph (2) applying the court of trial may order that the objection shall have no effect if the court considers it to be in the interests of justice so to order.

Written statements and depositions which have been admitted as evidence in committal proceedings can be read at the trial in the Crown Court. The prosecution will have tendered these written statements and depositions. This provision allows for written statements or depositions to be admitted at the Crown Court trial where all parties agree.

It is not, however, limited to cases where the parties agree. If the court considers it to be in the interests of justice, the court may order that the written statement or deposition be read at the trial.

Criminal Justice Act 1967, s 9(1), (2)

(1)   In any criminal proceedings, other than committal proceedings, a written statement by any person shall, if such of the conditions mentioned in the next following subsection as are applicable are satisfied, be admissible as evidence to the like extent as oral evidence to the like effect by that person.

(2)   The said conditions are—

(a)   the statement purports to be signed by the person who made it;

(b)   the statement contains a declaration by that person to the effect that it is true to the best of his knowledge and belief and that he made the statement knowing that, if it were tendered in evidence, he would be liable to prosecution if he willfully stated in it anything which he knew to be false or did not believe to be true;

(c)   before the hearing at which the statement is tendered in evidence, a copy of the statement is served, by or on behalf of the party proposing to tender it, on each of the parties to the proceedings; and

(d)   none of the other parties or their solicitors, within seven days from the service of the copy of the statement, serves a notice on the party so proposing objecting to the statement being tendered in evidence under this section.

An example of the correct form of a s 9 statement is included at **Appendix 2(M)**.

In practice, the use of s 9 statements should largely be confined to evidence that is not in dispute. If the other side wishes to challenge the admissibility of the contents of the statement or cross-examine the maker of the statement, they should object.

9.6.2.11   Making the application

The Criminal Procedure Rules 2005, Pt 34 deals with the procedure of adducing hearsay evidence in the Crown Court and the magistrates' court.

If the prosecution seeks to adduce hearsay evidence, it must give notice in the prescribed form:

(a)   in the magistrates' court, at the same time as the prosecutor complies or purports to comply with disclosure under s 3 of the Criminal Procedure and Investigations Act 1996; or

(b)   in the Crown Court, not more than 14 days after the committal of the defendant or, where a person is sent for trial under s 51 of the Crime and Disorder Act 1998, not more than 14 days after the service of copies of the documents on which the charge or charges are based (CrimPR, r 34.3).

If the defendant seeks to adduce hearsay evidence, he must give notice of hearsay evidence not more than 14 days after the prosecutor has complied with or purported to comply with s 3 of the Criminal Procedure and Investigations Act 1996 (CrimPR, r 34.3). A copy of the prescribed form appears at **Appendix 2(X)**.

On receipt of the notice of hearsay evidence, a party may oppose the application by giving notice in the prescribed form to the court and all other parties not more than 14 days after receiving the notice of hearsay evidence (CrimPR, r 34.5). A copy of the prescribed form appears at **Appendix 2(Y)**.

The court may allow the application to be made orally or in a different format to the prescribed form. It may also shorten or extend the time limits (even where they have expired (CrimPR, r 34.7)).

Notice may also be given by fax or by e-mail with the consent of the recipient (CrimPR, r 34.6). Different rules govern the introduction of hearsay evidence in the Court of Appeal (see CrimPR, r 68.20).

9.7 The defendant

This paragraph deals with rules of evidence which are of particular application to the defendant.

9.7.1 Competence and compellability

9.7.1.1 The defendant as a prosecution witness

A defendant is not competent as a prosecution witness. Thus, if two defendants are jointly charged the prosecution cannot call one as a witness against the other unless he has pleaded guilty or is tried separately from the other defendant (*R v Richardson* (1967) 51 Cr App R 381). This means that at Stage A of the trial (see **9.1.1**) a defendant cannot be called to give evidence unless he pleads guilty or is tried separately.

9.7.1.2 The defendant as a defence witness

A defendant is a competent defence witness but is not compellable (Criminal Evidence Act 1898, s 1(1)).

If a defendant does give evidence then he must be called before any other witnesses for the defence, unless the court 'otherwise directs' (Police and Criminal Evidence Act 1984, s 79).

If a defendant gives evidence in his own defence and in so doing implicates a codefendant then this is admissible evidence against that co-defendant.

If the defendant does not give evidence he is likely to be subject to the provisions of s 35 of the Criminal Justice and Public Order Act 1994.

9.7.1.3 Section 35 — failure of defendant to give evidence

(1)   At the trial of any person for an offence, subsections (2) and (3) below apply unless—

    (a)   the accused's guilt is not in issue; or

    (b)   it appears to the court that the physical or mental condition of the accused makes it undesirable for him to give evidence; ...

(2)   Where this subsection applies, the court shall, at the conclusion of the evidence for the prosecution, satisfy itself (in the case of proceedings on indictment, in the presence of the jury) that the accused is aware that the stage has been reached at which evidence can be given for the defence and that he can, if he wishes, give evidence and that, if he chooses not to give evidence, or having been sworn, without good cause refuses to answer any question, it will be permissible for the court or jury to draw such inferences as appear proper

from his failure to give evidence or his refusal, without good cause, to answer any question.

   (3)   Where this subsection applies, the court or jury, in determining whether the accused is guilty of the offence charged, may draw such inferences as appear proper from the failure of the accused to give evidence or his refusal, without good cause, to answer any question.

Thus, if the prosecution evidence has raised issues which call for an explanation from the defendant and he fails to give evidence, a court will be entitled to infer guilt from that failure.

In *R v Cowan (Donald); R v Gayle (Ricky); R v Ricciardi (Carmine)* [1995] 4 All ER 939, the Court of Appeal considered how the judge should direct the jury. It was essential that it should be made clear to the jury that:

(a)   the burden of proof remained on the prosecution throughout;

(b)   the defendant was entitled to remain silent;

(c)   before drawing an adverse inference from the defendant's silence, they had to be satisfied that there was a case to answer on the prosecution evidence;

(d)   an adverse inference from failure to give evidence cannot on its own prove guilt;

(e)   no adverse inference could be drawn unless the only sensible explanation for the defendant's silence was that he had no answer to the case against him, or none that could have stood up to cross-examination.

The procedure to be adopted in relation to s 35 is found in the *Practice Direction (Criminal Proceedings: Consolidation)* [2002] 3 All ER 904, para 44, *Defendant's right to give or not to give evidence).*

9.7.1.4 The defendant's spouse as a prosecution witness

A spouse is competent to give evidence for the prosecution. The spouse is not compellable except in certain specified cases (eg, where the offence involved an assault on that spouse or it was an assault or sexual offence on a person under 16) (Police and Criminal Evidence Act 1984, s 80).

This rule does not apply to a witness who has been, but is no longer, married to the defendant (s 80(5)).

9.7.1.5 The defendant's spouse as a defence witness

The defendant's spouse is always competent to give evidence on behalf of the defendant and a co-defendant.

The defendant's spouse is compellable to give evidence for the defendant.

9.8 Evidence of bad character

The Criminal Justice Act 2003 introduced a new statutory scheme for the admissibility of bad character evidence relating to non-defendants and defendants.

The Criminal Justice Act 2003 adopts a different approach to non-defendants' and defendants' bad character. Non-defendants are given protection against their bad character being exposed unless it is evidence with important explanatory value, or evidence going to a matter in issue or the parties agree to the evidence being admissible. A diagram illustrating the law governing the bad character of non-defendants appears at **Appendix 1(V)**.

The Criminal Justice Act 2003 has an inclusionary approach, rather than an exclusionary approach, to bad character of a defendant. A defendant's bad character evidence is admissible if it is relevant to an important matter in issue, subject to the court's discretion to exclude. A diagram illustrating the law governing the bad character of defendants appears at **Appendix 1(U)**.

9.8.1   Definition of bad character

Section 98 defines 'bad character' as evidence of, or of a disposition towards, misconduct. Misconduct means the commission of an offence or other 'reprehensible conduct' (s 112).

The definition of bad character is wide enough to apply to conduct arising out of a conviction, or conduct where there has been an acquittal (*R v Z* [2000] 2 AC 483) and a person who has been charged with another offence, and a trial is pending, the use of the evidence relating to that charge in current proceedings.

Whether a particular kind of behaviour would be regarded as 'reprehensible conduct' should be looked at objectively. The types of conduct that could come within this definition include: racism; bullying; a bad disciplinary record at work for misconduct and minor pilfering from employers. The term 'reprehensible conduct' avoids arguments about whether or not conduct alleged against a person amounted to an offence where this has not resulted in a charge or conviction.

The definition of 'bad character' is the same for defendants and non-defendants.

9.8.1.1   Exceptions to bad character

The definition of bad character in s 98 is subject to two exceptions in relation to two categories of evidence. The exceptions are:

(a)   evidence which has to do with the alleged facts of the offence with which the defendant is charged (s 98(a)); and

(b)   evidence of misconduct in connection with the investigation or prosecution of that offence (s 98(b)).

Under s 98(b), evidence of misconduct in connection with the investigation or prosecution of the charge would cover conduct such as: evidence of resisting arrest by running away because it may imply an acknowledgement of guilt; allegations of intimidation of witnesses; the defendant absconded during the course of the current proceedings; and the defendant breaching bail conditions.

The key test of whether evidence is admissible where the two exceptions apply is relevance. If the evidence goes to an issue in the case and tends to prove one of the elements of the offence then it is relevant and admissible.

9.8.1.2   Abolition of common law rules

Section 99(1) abolishes the common law rules governing the admissibility of evidence of bad character.

The following rules are expressly preserved:

(a)   Any rule of law under which in criminal proceedings evidence of reputation is admissible for the purpose of proving *good* character, but only so far as it allows the court to treat such evidence as proving the matter concerned (s 99(2) and s 118(1)).

(b)   Section 41 of the Youth Justice and Criminal Evidence Act 1999, which restricts evidence or cross-examination about the complainant's sexual history in trials for sexual offences (s 112(3)(b)). This means that in a trial for a sexual offence, to adduce evidence of a complainant's previous sexual behaviour that is also 'bad character' evidence, both tests will have to be satisfied.

9.8.2 Bad character of non-defendants

9.8.2.1 The statutory framework

Section 100 governs the admissibility of the evidence of bad character of non-defendants. Courts will be required to ensure that evidence of 'bad character' of a non-defendant witness meets the statutory criteria for admissibility. Other than evidence admitted by agreement, the leave of the court must be obtained (s 100(4)).

'Non-defendants' are not defined in CJA 2003 but the term could include victims, whether or not they give evidence; the deceased in cases of homicide; witnesses; police officers who have been involved in the case; and third parties who are not witnesses in the case and defence witnesses.

Section 100(1) provides the three gateways by which evidence of bad character can be admitted in the case of a non-defendant:

> (1)   In criminal proceedings evidence of the bad character of a person other than the defendant is admissible if and only if:
>   (a)   it is important explanatory evidence,
>   (b)   it has substantial probative value in relation to a matter which—
>   (i)   is a matter in issue in the proceedings, and
>   (ii)   is of substantial importance in the context of the case as a whole, or
>   (c)   all parties to the proceedings agree to the evidence being admissible.

Gateway 1 – Important explanatory evidence

> For the purposes of s 100(1)(a) evidence is important explanatory evidence if—
>   (a)   without it, the court or jury would find it impossible or difficult properly to understand other evidence in the case, and
>   (b)   its value for understanding the case as a whole is substantial. (s 101(2))

The term 'important explanatory evidence' imports the concept of background evidence. Background evidence must be such that the court would find it impossible or difficult to understand other evidence in the case. Moreover, the explanatory evidence must give the court some substantial assistance in understanding the case as a whole. The word 'substantial' is not defined in the Act but this is likely to mean 'more than minor or trivial' (see the Law Commission Paper No 273, para 7.17 and *R v Egan* [1992] 4 AER 470). If the evidence is more than minor or more than trivial it will be admissible if it assists the court to understand the case as a whole.

Gateway 2 – Evidence going to a matter in issue

In order to adduce evidence under s 100(1)(b), the court must be satisfied that the evidence is of 'substantial probative value'.

In assessing the probative value of evidence for the purposes of s 100(1)(b) the court must have regard to the following factors under s 100(3):

(a)   the nature and number of the events, or other things, to which the evidence relates;

(b)   when those events or things are alleged to have happened or existed;

(c)   the nature and extent of the similarities and the dissimilarities between each of the alleged instances of misconduct where the evidence is evidence of a person's misconduct, and it is suggested that the evidence has probative value by reason of similarity between that misconduct and other alleged misconduct;

(d)   the extent to which the evidence shows or tends to show that the same person was responsible each time where the evidence is evidence of a person's misconduct, and it is suggested that that person is also responsible for the misconduct charged and the identity of the person responsible for the misconduct charged is disputed;

(e)   any other factors the court considers relevant.

The relationship between the first two factors (nature and number of events and when those events or things are alleged to have taken place) and the probative value are relatively straightforward. These factors will be the most relevant and frequently applied when determining defence applications to adduce the bad character of prosecution witnesses.

The credibility of a prosecution witness may have substantial probative value in relation to a matter in the proceedings and is of substantial importance in the context of the case as a whole. Recent convictions for dishonesty are more likely than one old conviction for dangerous driving to be of substantial probative value where the credibility of a prosecution witness is of substantial importance in the context of the case as a whole, for example, in a case of theft where the defence alleges the witness gave the items to the defendant or taking without consent and the defendant alleges that the witness allowed the defendant to take the car.

It is important that previous convictions between non-defendants and defendants are treated in the same way, ie, that convictions, which show a propensity to be untruthful, should apply equally between witnesses and defendants (but bearing in mind the different provisions set out in CJA 2003).

There is some overlap between the third and the fourth factors. The third factor may be relevant when the defendant alleges that another person is responsible for the offence(s) with which he is charged and he seeks to rely on 'similar fact' evidence.

Example

John is charged with assault outside a nightclub. He claims that he acted in self-defence against an unprovoked attack by Sean, the main prosecution witness and alleged victim. The fact that Sean has convictions for assault in highly similar circumstances is a matter to which the court must have regard. The court must also have regard to the lack of similarities, for example, of incidents of minor scuffles at football matches involving Sean.

It will also need to be considered where the prosecution needs to prove the role of an accomplice, for example, where a burglar has a known modus operandi and those hallmarks are also evident in the burglary with which the defendant is charged, and the accomplice has not been charged.

The fourth factor will be applicable where the defendant wishes to show that another person was responsible by adducing evidence of that person's previous misconduct or conviction. There will usually be some evidence to link the two (or more) offences together and to show that the same person committed both offences.

Example

Lindsey is charged with thefts of money from her workplace. She wishes to allege that the thefts (the occurrence of which is not disputed) were committed by a fellow employee Kate, who is a witness against Lindsey. Lindsey wishes to adduce evidence that Kate was dismissed from her last job because of theft in the workplace. The court must have regard to the extent to which the bad character evidence shows, or tends to show, that Kate may have committed the thefts with which Lindsey is charged.

Gateway 3 – All parties agree to the evidence being admissible

This is self-explanatory.

9.8.2.2   Procedure

Where the prosecution is aware that a prosecution witness has previous convictions or cautions, that information should be disclosed to the defence as disclosure under the Criminal Procedure and Investigations Act 1996. All previous convictions, except minor traffic offences, must be disclosed irrespective of their age or whether they are regarded as spent under s 7(2) Rehabilitation of Offenders Act 1974.

The CPS is also under a duty to disclose to the defence information about police officers who are witnesses that might undermine the prosecution case or that might reasonably assist a defence. It does not matter whether the officers are called as witnesses, their statements are read to the court or their statements are unused material.

The effect of s 100 means that witnesses will be protected from wide-ranging and humiliating attacks on their credit and ensures that only relevant evidence is admissible. Leave of the court is required before the evidence can be admissible.

9.8.2.3   Making the application

The Criminal Procedure Rules 2005, Pt 35 deals with the procedure of adducing a non-defendant's bad character in the Crown Court and the magistrates' court.

A party who seeks to introduce evidence of a non-defendant witness or who wants to cross-examine a witness with a view to eliciting that evidence must apply in a prescribed form, and the application must be received by the relevant court and all other parties to the proceedings no more than 14 days after the prosecutor has complied or purported to comply with disclosure under s 3 of the Criminal Procedure and Investigations Act 1996, or as soon as reasonably practicable where the application concerns a witness for the defendant (CrimPR, r 35.2).

A copy of the prescribed form appears at **Appendix 2(Z)**.

On receipt of the form, a party may oppose the application by giving notice in writing to the appropriate officer of the court and all other parties not more than 14 days after receiving the application (CrimPR, r 35.3).

The court may allow the application to be made orally or in a different format to the prescribed form. It may also shorten or extend the time limits (even where they have expired) if it is in the interests of justice to do so (CrimPR, r 35.8).

Applications may also be made by fax or by e-mail with the consent of the recipient (CrimPR, r 35.8). Different time limits apply for proceedings in the Court of Appeal (see The Criminal Appeal (Amendment No 2) Rules 2004).

Section 100 not only applies to a defendant wanting to adduce bad character of a prosecution witness; it also applies to the prosecution wanting to adduce bad character evidence of a defence witness. It is likely that the prosecution will not know the names of defence witnesses until they give evidence at trial, in which case the Criminal Procedure Rules allow for the prosecution to make the application at that time (CrimPR, r 35.2).

9.8.3 Bad character of the defendant

The Criminal Justice Act 2003 introduced a new approach towards the admission of a defendant's bad character that starts from the position that evidence that is relevant to the case should be admissible.

9.8.3.1 The statutory framework

Section 101 of CJA 2003 is the main provision permitting the admissibility of evidence of a defendant's bad character. There are seven gateways, set out in s 101(1)(a)–(g). There is a staged approach to the admissibility of bad character evidence.

First, a defendant's bad character is not admissible unless one of the conditions in subsection (1) applies.

Second, if the evidence does fall within s 101(1)(a)–(c), (e) and (f), the evidence is admissible, and where the evidence falls with s 101(d) or (g) it is admissible unless, on application by a defendant, it has such an adverse effect on the fairness of the proceedings that the court ought not to admit it.

Section 101 provides:

    (1)   In criminal proceedings evidence of the defendant's bad character is admissible if, but only if—

        (a)   all parties to the proceedings agree to the evidence being admissible,

        (b)   the evidence is adduced by the defendant himself or is given in answer to a question asked by him in cross-examination and intended to elicit it,

        (c)   it is important explanatory evidence,

        (d)   it is relevant to an important matter in issue between the defendant and the prosecution,

        (e)   it has substantial probative value in relation to an important matter in issue between the defendant and a co-defendant,

        (f)   it is evidence to correct a false impression given by the defendant, or

        (g)   the defendant has made an attack on another person's character.

    (2)   Sections 102 to 106 contain provisions supplementing subsection (1).

    (3)   The court must not admit evidence under subsection (1)(d) or (g) if, on an application by the defendant to exclude it, it appears to the court that the admission of the evidence would have such an adverse effect on the fairness of the proceedings that the court ought not to admit it.

    (4)   On an application to exclude evidence under subsection (3) the court must have regard to, in particular, the length of time between the matters to which that evidence relates and the matters which form the subject of the offence charged.

Sections 102 and 106 expand on five of the seven gateways where evidence of the defendant's bad character is admissible. Section 101(a) and (b) are not further defined in the Act.

Gateway 1 – Agreement of the parties (s 101(a))

Clearly, it makes no sense in excluding evidence, if all parties agree that it should be admitted. Therefore in these circumstances the evidence of bad character is admissible.

Gateway 2 – Waiver by the defendant (s 101(b))

The defendant's bad character is admissible if it is adduced by him, or is given in answer to a question asked by him in cross-examination and intended to elicit it. This allows a defendant to adduce his own bad character if it is felt that it would be helpful to do so. There may be circumstances where a defendant chooses to do this. Examples may include: where a defendant raises an alibi that he was in prison at the time and where his bad character is relatively innocuous in the context of the trial, that he might prefer to put it in evidence rather than leave it to the jury to speculate about it.

The points to note about s 101(b) are:

(a) there is no statutory discretion to exclude evidence;

(b) a defendant may lead evidence of his bad character, if he chooses, and whether or not the co-defendant agrees;

(c) evidence is inadmissible if the defendant did not intend to elicit the evidence, such as an unsolicited disclosure by a witness of a defendant's bad character or evidence of bad character elicited in cross-examination due to a carelessly framed question.

Gateway 3 – Important explanatory evidence (s 101(c))

Bad character evidence is admissible if it is important explanatory evidence. Section 102 defines 'important explanatory evidence' as if without the evidence, the court or jury would find it impossible or difficult properly to understand other evidence in the case, and its value for understanding the case as a whole is substantial. This is the same definition as important explanatory evidence in s 100(2) when dealing with a non-defendant's bad character (see **9.8.2.1**).

If the evidence is more than minor or more than trivial it will be admissible if it assists the court to understand the case as a whole. Examples of background evidence might include the existence of a pre-existing relationship between the victim and the defendant and evidence revealing a motive for the offence (see *R v Underwood* [1999] Crim LR 227).

Bad character evidence that is comprehensible without additional explanatory evidence is inadmissible. In *R v Dolan* [2003] 1 Cr App R 281 the defendant was charged with murder – probably by shaking his infant son. The prosecution adduced evidence of his violence during the course of a previous relationship towards inanimate objects. The Court of Appeal quashed the conviction because the evidence should not have been admitted. It could not be said that the case was incomplete or incomprehensible without the admission of the evidence.

The prosecution does not require leave before evidence can be admitted but notice will have to be given by the prosecution to adduce such evidence. However, there may be arguments on whether the evidence meets the threshold test.

Gateway 4 – Relevant to an important matter in issue between the defendant and the prosecution (s 101(1)(d))

The intention behind this is that evidence of previous misconduct that has relevance to an issue in the case should be admitted to give courts the fullest possible relevant information for them to determine guilt or innocence.

Facts in issue are those necessary by law to establish the offence or defence to the charge. Relevant means evidence that tends, as a matter of logic, to make the fact in issue more or less likely. Facts relevant to an issue are facts that tend, either directly or indirectly, to prove or disprove a fact in issue (eg, a fact in issue, propensity to commit offences or credibility).

Section 101(1)(d) depends only on relevance to 'an important matter in issue' (meaning, according to s 112, 'a matter of substantial importance in the context of the case as a whole'). 'Substantial' means no more than minor or trivial. If the evidence is relevant to an issue in the case, it passes the threshold for admissibility. It is important to note that nothing requires the evidence to have any 'substantial probative value'.

Section 101 has to be read in conjunction with s 103. In deciding what is a matter in issue, s 103(1) provides that a matter in issue includes:

(a)   the question whether a defendant has a propensity to commit crimes of the kind with which he is charged, except where his having such a propensity makes it no more likely that he is guilty of the offence;

(b)   the question whether a defendant has a propensity to be untruthful, except where it is not suggested that the defendant's case is untruthful in any respect.

Propensity to commit crimes

As s 103(1)(a) highlights, this includes evidence that shows that a defendant has a propensity to commit offences 'of the kind with which he is charged'. This means that if a defendant is on trial for grievous bodily harm, a history of violent behaviour could be admissible to show the defendant's propensity to use violence.

Section 103(1) means that the evidence of bad character can be adduced as proof of guilt.

The proviso to s 103(1)(a) 'except where his having such a propensity makes it no more likely that he is guilty of the offence' means where there is no dispute about the facts of the case and the question is whether those facts constitute an offence, eg, on a charge of possession of drugs whether a particular drug was controlled or not.

Example

Colin is charged with assaulting his wife. He has a history of violence, both in relation to his wife, and others. He claims that on one occasion in issue, she received her injuries falling down the stairs. In this case, Colin's previous convictions for violence are admissible (subject to the discretion to exclude) to show that his propensity to commit offences of the kind with which he is charged, and subject to the facts, any acquittals would also be admissible too (as the definition of bad character also includes acquittals).

Where propensity to commit offences is in issue, s 103(2) provides that his propensity may be established, without prejudice to any other way of doing so, by evidence that the defendant has been convicted of an offence of the same description as the one with which he is charged or an offence of the same category as prescribed by the Secretary of State.

Offences of the same description are offences where the statement of offence in a written charge or indictment is in the same terms (s103(4)(a)). It is not necessary for the earlier conviction to be described in identical terms. What matters is whether the facts of the earlier conviction would be sufficient to support an offence charged in the same terms, for example, on a charge of burglary, a previous conviction for theft committed on premises whilst the defendant was a trespasser, would be in the same terms as the burglary.

Therefore s 103 is not limited just to the same offences (eg, charged with rape and has a previous conviction for rape) but also includes offences of the same kind (eg, charged with assault by penetration and has a previous conviction for sexual touching).

Under s 103(4)(b), the Secretary of State may prescribe categories of offences that are of the 'same type' for use as an indicator that a defendant has a propensity to commit offences of a certain type. The Secretary of State has prescribed two categories, theft offences and sexual offences on persons under 16 (The Criminal Justice Act 2003 (Categories of Offences) Order 2004).

The Order means that where a defendant has previous convictions for an offence in one of the categories, theft or sexual offences on persons under 16, then an offence charged in the same category creates a strong presumption that the previous conviction should be admitted. However, the defence will still be able to argue that such evidence should not be admitted because it would be unfair to do so.

The common theme of the offences listed in the theft category is that they all relate directly to stealing property that belongs to others. The category of sexual offences on persons under 16 covers offences which involve sexual touching, penetration and activity, and which were committed in relation to children and young people under the legal age of consent.

The reason for only these two categories initially is that they cover areas of offending that cause the public particular concern, and where there is a strong risk of re-offending.

The absence of categories for other types of offending will not prevent previous convictions from being admitted if they demonstrate a propensity to commit offences of the same kind. Evidence of such convictions will be admissible under the main provisions of CJA 2003, provided those convictions are relevant and probative. The categories of offences only support CJA 2003's main provisions. For example, a person charged with rape of a child may have a history of sexual offences (such as child pornography or grooming), even though those previous convictions would not appear within the same category as the offence charged.

Propensity to be untruthful

The other matter in issue between the defendant and the prosecution identified is whether the defendant has a propensity to be untruthful (in other words, is not to be regarded as a credible witness) except where it is not suggested that the defendant's case is untruthful in any respect (s 103(1)(b)).

In the majority of not guilty trials, whether the defendant is telling the truth or whether the defence is true is itself an issue in the case. Under s 103(1)(b), propensity becomes admissible to prove untruthfulness, provided that the prosecution contends that the defendant's case is untruthful in some respect. This is intended to enable the admission of a limited range of evidence such as convictions for perjury or other dishonesty offences, for example deception as opposed to the wider range of evidence where the defendant puts his character in issue by, eg, attacking another person's character.

The types of previous convictions, which may show a propensity to be untruthful, would include convictions for perjury, perverting the course of justice (depending on the facts of the case), theft, deception and other dishonesty offences. Therefore, those previous convictions which are not generally to be treated as relevant to a general propensity to be untruthful are those convictions not involving any element of theft, dishonesty or deception.

Whether a conviction shows a propensity to be untruthful should apply equally to non-defendants as well as defendants. For example, where the prosecution seek routinely to adduce a defendant's conviction for theft on the basis that it says something important about a defendant's propensity to be untruthful, then this should also apply to a prosecution witness who has a conviction for theft. Against this must be considered the different standards in CJA 2003 itself in relation to the bad character evidence of defendants (relevant to an important matter in issue) and the higher threshold test of non-defendants (substantial probative value in relation to a matter which is of substantial importance in the context of the case as a whole).

If the defendant's explanation is so similar to that advanced by him on a previous occasion, then it is unlikely to be true.

Example 1

Dennis is accused of robbing a mini-cab driver at knifepoint but claims that he entered the cab only after the robbery had taken place. Where this was an almost identical defence to the one he had raised in another and very similar robbery trial, this will be admissible (subject to the discretion to exclude).

Example 2

Anna is stopped at 2 am driving a car that has been reported stolen. She tells the police that the car belongs to a friend and that she has been given permission to borrow the vehicle. It is discovered Anna has three recent previous convictions for taking without consent. There is a statutory defence to taking without consent if the court is satisfied that the accused acted in the belief that he had lawful authority, or that the owner would have consented if he or she had known of the circumstances of the taking. Under s 103(1)(b) (propensity to be untruthful), Anna's previous convictions would clearly be relevant to whether her version of events is true, and so evidence of her bad character would be admissible.

Bad character will not be admissible under s 103(1)(b) where it is not suggested that the defendant's case is untruthful in any respect, for example, where the defendant and prosecution are agreed on the facts and the question is whether all the elements of the offence have been made out.

A defendant will always be in jeopardy where he has given a previous unsuccessful defence (pleaded not guilty and was convicted). Therefore it is important for the prosecution and defence to obtain as much information about the defendant's bad character as possible, such as details of the offence, whether it was a plea of guilty or a conviction following a not guilty trial and what was the nature of the defence.

Safeguards

There is a safeguard under s 103(3) to the admission of evidence of propensity to commit a crime. Evidence of propensity should not be admitted if due to the length of time since the conviction, or for any other reason, the court is satisfied it would be unjust to admit it.

Example

Daniel, aged 50 years, is charged with burglary (he smashed a shop window and took an item on display). It would be very unlikely that the court would admit evidence of Daniel's only previous conviction (a residential burglary), which happened 30 years previously.

The term 'any other reason' is not defined, but it is wide enough to include the nature and extent of the similarities and the dissimilarities between each of the instances of misconduct.

The effect of s 103(3) means that the court will not allow previous misconduct as evidence of propensity to commit a crime if it is unjust to do so. This is not defined in CJA 2003 but it means that the court would regard it as unjust if the admission of the bad character evidence has such an adverse effect on the fairness of the proceedings that the court ought not to admit it (the test in s 101(3)).

Although s 103(3) only applies to a propensity to commit a crime, evidence of a propensity to be untruthful is subject to s 101(3).

Gateway 5 – Matter in issue between the defendant and a co-defendant (s 101(1)(e))

Evidence of a defendant's bad character is admissible if it has substantial probative value in relation to an important matter in issue between the defendant and the co-defendant. Once this threshold is met there is no power in CJA 2003 for the evidence to be excluded.

The power to admit bad character evidence in respect of an issue between the defendant and a co-defendant under s 101(1)(e) is restricted to evidence either adduced by the co-defendant, or which the co-defendant needs to elicit in cross-examination. Only a co-defendant and not the prosecution can adduce evidence of a defendant's bad character under this section (s 104(2)).

The test for admissibility is probative value in relation to an important matter in issue. As previously mentioned, the requirement of substantial is likely to be interpreted only as more than merely trivial.

Section 101(1)(e) includes cases where the defence not only undermines the co-defendant's defence but is also inconsistent with that being run by the co-defendant (*Murdoch v Taylor* [1965] AC 574). It would be applicable in a 'cut-throat' defence where two defendants are charged and their defence is that the other was responsible.

In considering matters in issue between the defendant and a co-defendant, where defendant 1 seeks to adduce defendant 2's bad character on the ground that defendant 2 has a propensity to be untruthful, the evidence is only admissible if the nature and conduct of defendant 2's defence is such as to undermine that of defendant 1, ie, where the question of 2's truthfulness is truly relevant to the case for defendant 1 (s 104(1)).

Gateway 6 – Evidence to correct a false impression (s 101(f))

The defendant gives a false impression if he is responsible for making an express or implied assertion which is apt to give the court a false or misleading impression about him (s 105(1)(a)).

Section 105(2) defines the circumstances when a defendant is to be treated as being 'responsible' for such an assertion. This includes assertions the defendant makes during the proceedings (not necessarily whilst giving evidence) (s 105(2)(a)), when being questioned after caution (s 105(2)(b)(i)), and on being charged (s 105(2)(b)(ii)).

The defendant can also be responsible for assertions made by other people. An assertion can be made by a witness who is called by the defendant (s 105(2)(c)), a witness being cross-examined who makes such an assertion where the court is satisfied that it was the defendant's intention to elicit such a response from the witness or the question was likely to do so (s 105(2)(d)), and an assertion is made by any person out of court and the defendant adduces evidence of it in the proceedings (s 105(2)(e)).

Therefore if the court is satisfied that the defendant is responsible for giving a false impression, then the evidence of his bad character will be admissible. However, a defendant is not responsible for an assertion if he either withdraws or disassociates himself from the assertion (s 105(3)). The Criminal Justice Act 2003 does not elaborate on how this must be done. Presumably once the court decides that the defendant is responsible for the assertion he, or those he instructs, should make it known to the court and the prosecution that he withdraws or disassociates himself from it. The court may give a warning to a defendant of the consequences of not withdrawing or disassociating himself from the assertion but such a warning is not obligatory.

Where the assertion is made in interview and the prosecution seek to adduce the evidence of bad character on this ground, and the defendant has not withdrawn or disassociated himself from it, then the defendant should do so in his notice opposing the prosecution's application to adduce bad character evidence.

Warnings may be particularly important in summary proceedings where the defendant is unrepresented. In such a case, the clerk and the prosecutor should give a warning to the defendant in the absence of the magistrates. Prosecutors should therefore ask for an adjournment so this can be done.

The defendant will also be responsible for the giving of a false impression by his conduct in the proceedings (other than the giving of evidence) (s 105(4)). Conduct includes appearance or dress. An example might be a defendant who attends trial dressed as a priest: he may not assert verbally that he is of good character but if he is of bad character this conduct could constitute the giving of a false impression.

Evidence (ie, evidence which has probative value) that becomes admissible can only go as far as it is necessary to correct the false impression given (s 105(6)). In correcting the impression only the prosecution may introduce evidence of the defendant's bad character (s 105(7)).

Gateway 7 – Attack on another person's bad character (s 101(1)(g))

Under s 101(1)(g) a defendant's bad character will become admissible when there has been an attack on another person's character. This can happen in one of three ways:

(a)   the defendant adduces evidence attacking the other person's character (s 106(1)(a));

(b)   he (or his legal representative appointed under s 38(4) of the Youth Justice and Criminal Evidence Act 1999 to cross-examine a witness in his interests) asks questions in cross-examination that are intended to elicit such evidence or are likely to do so (s 106(1)(b)); or

(c)   the defendant imputes the other person's character when questioned under caution or on being charged or officially informed he may be prosecuted (s 106(1)(c)). This means that it will be important that the police include such an attack in the record of the tape recorded interview.

Evidence attacking the other person's character is defined as evidence to the effect that the other person has committed an offence or has behaved, or is disposed to behave, in a reprehensible way (s 106(2)). For the meaning of 'behaving in a reprehensible way' see **9.8.1**.

Bad character evidence will be admissible against a defendant who has made an attack upon any other person's character, whether or not a defendant chooses to give evidence. It is not necessary that the person attacked should be a witness in the proceedings, or a deceased victim, or a person whose hearsay statement is admitted in evidence, or even that the individual should be named. For example, an attack on another person's character will include the defendant alleging that an unknown person or an associate he refuses to name committed the crime.

Where the court determines that an attack has taken place, evidence of the defendant's bad character becomes admissible (but only by the prosecution, s 106(3)).

Section 101(1)(g) is subject to the court's discretion to exclude bad character, on application by a defendant, on the ground that it would have such an adverse effect on the fairness of the proceedings that the court ought not to admit it (s 101(3)).

There is no requirement in CJA 2003 that the attack on the other person's character should be untrue or unfounded. This is an important rule because it prevents the court from becoming embroiled in deciding collateral issues of the truth or otherwise of the defendant's allegations. However, where it can be shown that those allegations are true, then the court may exercise its discretion and exclude the evidence of bad character on the basis that it is fair to do so.

The CJA 2003 does not specify that the evidence should only go to credit, but bad character evidence may also be relevant to the issue of guilt. The Explanatory Notes to the Act provide:

> It is expected that judges will explain the purpose for which the evidence is being put forward and direct the jury about the sort of weight that can be placed on it.

9.8.3.2   Applications by defence to exclude bad character evidence (s 101(3))

In relation to s 101(1)(d) (evidence of bad character relevant to an important matter in issue between the defendant and the prosecution) and s 101(g) (the defendant has made an attack on another person's character), the court must not admit such evidence if it appears that its admission would have such an adverse effect on the fairness of the proceedings that it ought not to admit it. In applying the test the court is directed to take account, in particular, of the amount of time that has elapsed since the previous events and the current charge.

The test in s 101(3) is designed to reflect the existing position set out in s 78 of the Police and Criminal Evidence Act 1984 (see **9.2.5**), under which the court has a discretion to exclude otherwise admissible evidence when the admission of the evidence would have such an adverse affect on the fairness of the proceedings.

The CJA 2003 does not specify any factors (apart from s 101(4)) that the court should take into account. However, other factors that the court may consider could include:

(a)   the nature of the defence or possible defence, such as mistake, innocent association, accident etc;

(b)   similarities or dissimilarities of the previous misconduct and the offence charged;

(c)   the nature and number of the events of previous misconduct, although one previous conviction can be sufficient to show propensity to commit a crime and to be untruthful; and

(d)   other evidence against the defendant showing that he committed the offence. The stronger the evidence against a defendant the less likely that the court would exclude it.

The test to be applied under s 101(3) is stricter than that under s 78 of the Police and Criminal Evidence Act 1984; under s 78 the court *may* refuse to admit the evidence, whereas under s 101(3) the court *must not* admit such evidence if it would have such an adverse effect on the fairness of the proceedings. For guidance on how the discretion under s 101(3) should be exercised, see *R v Hanson, Gilmore and Parkstone* (2005) *The Times*, 24 March.

The court can only exclude evidence of bad character on the application of the defendant and not of its own motion after the prosecution has served notice on the defendant and the court that it intends to adduce the defendant's bad character evidence.

Therefore where evidence is admissible under s 101(1)(d) or (g), the prosecution should always serve a notice of intention to adduce bad character evidence unless it is highly likely that the court would not admit the evidence because of the adverse effect on the fairness of the proceedings.

If the prosecution gives notice to the defence to adduce such evidence, it is likely that the defence will in almost every case apply to exclude it.

Does s 78 apply to the other circumstances set out in s 101(1)?

The issue is whether the defence can rely on s 78 of the Police and Criminal Evidence Act 1984 in relation to the other circumstances in s 101(1), namely subsections (c) and (f). Clearly s 78 does not apply to subsections (1)(a) and (b) where all parties agree and the defendant adduces evidence of his own character, or evidence under subsection (1)(e) of substantial probative value to an important matter in issue between the defendant and co-defendant because this can only be adduced by a co-defendant and not by the prosecution.

The argument in favour of the continued application of s 78 to s 101(c) and (f) is s 112(3)(c) which provides that: 'Nothing in this Chapter affects the exclusion of evidence . . . on the grounds other than the fact that it is evidence of a person's bad character'.

In addition, the Explanatory Notes to the Act suggest that s 78 applies and this was the Government's position during the passage of the Bill through Parliament. However, there are arguments against s 78 applying to those circumstances. Part 11, Chapter 1, which deals with bad character, makes no specific reference to s 78. Part 11, Chapter 2, which relates to hearsay evidence, does at s 126(2).

The starting point under the Act when dealing with a defendant's bad character is that such evidence is admissible if one of the seven gateways set out in s 101(1) are met. Although there is a leave requirement for non-defendant's bad character to be adduced, no such leave is required as a pre-requisite in relation to defendants. This demonstrates that the admissibility is to be considered the norm rather than the exception.

The circumstances where the defence can seek the exclusion of evidence in s 101(1) are restricted; only under circumstances set out in (d) and (g) is the defence entitled to seek exclusion of bad character. If Parliament intended that s 78 should apply to the other circumstances it would have so stated in s 101(3).

It is submitted that s 78 may apply to circumstances set out in s 101(1)(c) and (f), although in practice s 78 will have a very limited application. Given the definition of important explanatory evidence in subsection (1)(c) and evidence in subsection (1)(f) can only be given to the extent that it is necessary to correct the false impression, then s 78 is likely only to apply in rare or extreme cases.

9.8.4 Practice and procedure

Evidence of a defendant's bad character will play a major part in the investigation and prosecution of cases. It is likely to form an essential part of the evidence against a defendant because bad character is now not only relevant to credit but also relevant to the issue of guilt.

The police will obtain details of a defendant's bad character including previous convictions, such as the facts of the previous convictions, the nature of any defences used in the previous cases, and whether the defendant pleaded guilty or was found guilty. This information will be passed on to the CPS.

9.8.4.1 Proving bad character

If the defence do not agree the details of the bad character, then this will need to be proved in the normal way, such as, by a certificate of conviction, relying on s 74 of the Police and Criminal Evidence Act 1984, or calling witnesses proving the bad character.

9.8.4.2 Making the application to adduce bad character

The Criminal Procedure Rules 2005, Pt 35 deals with the procedure of adducing bad character evidence in the Crown Court and magistrates' court. The procedure, time limits and forms are the same for both courts.

If the prosecution proposes to adduce evidence of a defendant's bad character under s 101, or proposes to cross-examine a witness with a view to eliciting such evidence, they must serve notice on the defendant in the prescribed form (s 111(2)).

A copy of the notice appears at **Appendix 2(ZA)**. Once the notice is served and so long as the evidence falls within one of the circumstances of s 101, then it is admissible unless, on the application by the defendant under s 101(1)(d) or (g), the court excludes such evidence on the grounds of fairness.

This notice must be served at the same time as the prosecutor complies or purports to comply with disclosure (CrimPR, r 35.4(2)).

Once the prosecution has served the notice, the defendant has to apply to exclude the evidence of bad character not more than seven days after receiving notice (CrimPR, r 35.6). A copy of the prescribed form appears as **Appendix 2(ZB)**.

A co-defendant who wants to adduce evidence of a defendant's bad character must give notice within 14 days after the prosecutor complies with or purports to comply with disclosure under s 3 of the Criminal Procedure and Investigations Act 1996 (CrimPR, r 35.5). The defendant has seven days after the receipt of the notice to apply to exclude such evidence (CrimPR, r 35.6). The only basis on which a defendant may exclude such evidence is that the evidence does not satisfy the test, namely that it is of substantial probative value to an important matter in issue. The court has no power to exclude the evidence on the ground of fairness.

The defendant has power to waive his entitlement to notice if he informs the court and the party who would have given notice (CrimPR, r 35.9).

The court may allow an oral notice or application and extend or shorten any time-limit even if it has expired, if it is in the interests of justice to do so. This allows the prosecution to apply to adduce the evidence of bad character where, for example, the defendant gives a false impression in court or where he attacks a prosecution witness in court (CrimPR, r 35.8).

Any notice or application may be sent by fax or e-mail with the consent of the recipient (Crim PR, r 35.7).

There are different time limits that apply to proceedings in the Court of Appeal (see The Criminal Appeal (Amendment No 2) Rules 2004).

The Criminal Procedure Rules 2005 permit notices and applications to adduce bad character evidence to be made prior to trial, but they may, and likely will, be dealt with at the trial. The defence may seek to persuade the magistrates to disqualify themselves because they may be prejudiced having become aware that the defendant has previous misconduct. Such an application is unlikely to be successful. The arguments against this defence application include: the court must be made aware of 'bad character' evidence in the course of such applications to make sense of them; magistrates are judges of both fact and law and case law. *R v Sang* [1980] AC 402 has established that as magistrates have always been responsible for determining issues of admissibility, they must know what evidence it is proposed to adduce; and that CJA 2003 has as its starting point an inclusionary approach to the evidence of bad character.

9.8.4.3   Stopping contaminated cases

Section 107 deals with circumstances in which bad character evidence has been admitted but it later emerges that the evidence is contaminated, that is, has been affected by an agreement with other witnesses or by hearing the views or evidence of other witnesses so that it is false or misleading.

Section 107 provides that a court may stop a case where evidence of bad character has been adduced under any of the paragraphs 101(c)–(g) and it later appears that the evidence has been contaminated, such that any resulting conviction would be unsafe. The power applies to a trial before a jury (s 107(1)) or where a jury is required to decide whether a person, who is deemed unfit to plead, did the act or omission charged under the Criminal Procedure (Insanity) Act 1964 (s 107(3)). Section 107(4) makes it clear that the section does not affect any existing court powers in relation to ordering an acquittal or discharging a jury.

There exist common law powers for a judge to withdraw a case from the jury at any time following the close of the prosecution case, such as no case to answer. Section 107 supplements those powers by conferring a duty on the judge to stop the case if the contamination is such that, considering the importance of the evidence to the case, a conviction would be unsafe (s 107(1)(b)). This is intended to be an onerous test. If the judge were to consider that a direction to the jury along the lines in *R v H* [1995] 2 AC 596, that if they are not satisfied that the evidence can be relied as free of contamination then they cannot rely on it against the defendant, would be sufficient to deal with any potential difficulties, then the case should not be withdrawn from the jury.

The reason why s 107 applies only to trials by judge and jury is the fact that fact-finders other than juries will be sufficiently disciplined to evaluate the evidence correctly and to disregard the evidence if it is contaminated, and reach a finding on the basis of any other evidence that remains.

Having stopped the case the judge may consider that there is still sufficient uncontaminated evidence against the defendant to merit his retrial or may consider that the prosecution case has been so weakened that the defendant should be acquitted (s 107(1)(b)(ii)). If the judge orders an acquittal then the defendant is also to be acquitted of any other offence for which he could have been convicted, if the judge is satisfied that the contamination would affect a conviction for that offence in the same way (s 107(2)).

Evidence is contaminated where it is false or misleading in any respect, or is different from what it would otherwise have been (s 107(5)(b)).

9.8.4.4 Offences committed by a defendant when a child

Section 108 provides that the admissibility of offences committed by a defendant when a child will depend on two factors. First, that the previous conviction and the present charge are offences triable only on indictment, and secondly, that the court has to be satisfied that it is in the interests of justice to admit such evidence.

9.8.4.5 Assumption of the truth

It is a general practice of the courts to assume that the relevance of the evidence or its probative value in relation to its admission is true solely for the purpose of determining the admissibility issue. Section 109(1) places this practice on a statutory basis.

However, the court need not assume that the evidence is true if it appears to the court, on the basis of the material before it, or of any evidence it hears, that no court or jury could reasonably find it to be true (s 109(2)).

9.8.4.6 Court's duty to give reasons

Where a court rules that evidence is evidence of a person's bad character or makes a ruling under ss 100 and 101, or where the judge stops the case due to a ruling of contamination, the court must state its reasons in open court. Where the ruling relates to the magistrates' court, the ruling and the reasons for it must be entered into the court's register (s 110).

9.9 Spent convictions

The Rehabilitation of Offenders Act 1974 provides that after a prescribed period of time certain convictions are spent. This means that the convicted person is to be treated as never having been convicted of the spent offence.

The rehabilitation periods vary with the sentence:

Absolute discharge	6 months
Conditional discharge	1 year or period of order if longer

Attendance centre order	1 year after expiry of order
Fine or community sentence	5 years
Custodial sentence of up to 6 months	7 years
Custodial sentence of between 6 and 30 months	10 years

A conviction for an offence which was punished by a custodial sentence exceeding 30 months cannot become spent.

The Act does not apply to evidence admitted in criminal proceedings. Instead, the matter is governed by *Practice Direction (Criminal Proceedings: Consolidation)* [2002] 3 All ER 904, para 6, *Spent Convictions*. This provides that a spent conviction should be referred to only if it is in the interests of justice to do so. If a defendant has convictions which are not spent, it will usually be unnecessary to refer to spent convictions. If a defendant has previous convictions which are spent, he may, with the leave of the court, be entitled to put himself forward as a person of previous good character (*R v Bailey* [1989] Crim LR 723).

9.10 Further reading

Textbooks dealing with the general principles of criminal evidence include:

Peter Murphy, *Murphy on Evidence* (Oxford University Press, 2003)

Richard May and Steven Powles, *Criminal Evidence* (Sweet & Maxwell, 2004)

Chapter 10

Sentencing

10.1 Introduction

This chapter deals with the law, practice and procedure of sentencing of offenders who are aged 18 or older. Offenders under the age of 18 are dealt with in the youth court.

The purposes of sentencing are identified as:

(a) the punishment of offenders;

(b) the reduction of crime (including its reduction by deterrence);

(c) the reform and rehabilitation of offenders;

(d) the protection of the public;

(e) the making of reparation by offenders to persons affected by their offences (Criminal Justice Act 2003, s 142).

A large part of a solicitor's time is taken up with the sentencing process, either following a guilty plea by his client or on conviction at a summary trial. Unless the solicitor has higher rights of audience, he will have limited rights of audience in the Crown Court on sentencing matters (see **1.4.2**), and in any event must brief counsel if counsel is appearing in the Crown Court on any matter that will be relevant to sentence if the client pleads guilty or is convicted by a jury.

This chapter examines:

(a) the powers of the court;

(b) procedure on sentencing; and

(c) mitigation.

10.2 The powers of the court

10.2.1 The Sentencing Guidelines Council (CJA 2003, ss 167–168, s 170 and ss 172–173)

The Sentencing Guidelines Council (SGC), created by the Criminal Justice Act (CJA) 2003, is chaired by the Lord Chief Justice and comprises others appointed by the Lord Chancellor after consultation with the Home Secretary and the Lord Chief Justice. The purpose of the SGC is to continue and develop the work previously done by the Court of Appeal, through guideline judgments, and the Magistrates' Association. The SGC produces sentencing guidelines that the criminal courts are obliged to consider when sentencing a defendant. The court will have to state reasons if it departs from SGC guidance. The SGC has issued guidelines in relation to reduction of sentence for a guilty plea, the assessment of seriousness and the new sentences implemented under the CJA 2003. In due course it will issue guidelines with regard to the allocation of cases between courts and for specific types of offences.

The SGC guidelines are available at www.sentencing-guildelines.gov.uk.

10.2.2   Sentencing Advisory Panel (CJA 2003, s 169 and s 171)

The Sentencing Advisory Panel, created by the Crime and Disorder Act 1998, can propose that the SGC issues new or revised sentencing or allocation guidelines, and must be informed of all such proposals to issue or amend guidelines that have been initiated by the Secretary of State or the Council itself. The Panel will continue to consult on such proposals, and formulate and communicate its views to the Council.

10.2.3   The seriousness of the offence

The CJA 2003 provides a structured approach to sentencing. Can the offence be dealt with by a fine or discharge? If not, is the offence serious enough for a community sentence? If not, is the offence so serious that neither a fine alone nor a community sentence can be justified?

In deciding the seriousness of the offence, the court may take into account:

(a)   the present offence (see **10.2.3.1** below);

(b)   any associated offences (as defined at **10.2.3.2** below);

(c)   previous convictions (see **10.2.3.3** below);

(d)   offending while on bail (see **10.2.3.4** below);

(e)   racial or religious aggravation (see **10.2.3.5** below); and

(f)   sexual orientation and diability (see **10.2.3.6** below).

The court will then consider any offender mitigation and information from the Probation Service before reaching a provisional sentence in the case.

A diagram illustrating the CJA 2003 sentencing scheme appears at **Appendix 1(N)**.

10.2.3.1   The present offence

In assessing seriousness the court must consider the offender's culpability and any harm that was caused, or might foreseeably have been caused (CJA 2003, s 143(1)). The SGC guideline on the assessment of seriousness states that harm must always be judged in the light of culpability: 'The culpability of the offender in the particular circumstances of an individual case should be the initial factor in determining the seriousness of the offence.'

There are four levels of culpability: intention, recklessness, knowledge, and negligence. The provisions have been widely drafted to include not only offences where harm is actually caused to individuals or the community, but offences where no harm is suffered but a risk of harm is present.

10.2.3.2   Associated offences

An associated offence is one in which the defendant has been convicted in the same proceedings or sentenced at the same time, or an offence which the defendant has asked the court to take into consideration when passing sentence (see **10.3.2.3** below for offences taken into consideration) (Powers of Criminal Courts (Sentencing) Act (PCC(S)A) 2000, s 161).

Example

Courtney is convicted of three offences of theft. In applying the seriousness test, the court will look at the most serious offence first. If the offence was so serious that neither a fine nor a community sentence can be justified for the offence then a custodial sentence can be imposed. The seriousness test is satisfied. If one offence alone is not serious enough for a custodial sentence then the court may look at all three offences together in deciding whether the seriousness test is satisfied in relation to the imposition of a custodial sentence.

10.2.3.3 Previous convictions

Each previous conviction must, provided the court considers such consideration to be reasonable, be treated as an aggravating factor (CJA 2003, s 143(2)). Previous convictions relate to those convictions recorded by a court in the United Kingdom, service offences, or, in cases where the court considers it appropriate, convictions by a court outside of the United Kingdom. In deciding whether it is reasonable to treat the previous offence as aggravating, the court should have particular regard to the nature of the offence and its relevance to the current offence, and the time elapsed since the original offence.

10.2.3.4 Offending whilst on bail

The court must treat an offence committed on bail as an aggravating factor (CJA 2003, s 143(3)).

10.2.3.5 Racial or religious aggravation

If an offence is 'racially or religiously aggravated', the court must treat that fact as an aggravating factor and must state in open court that the offence was so aggravated (CJA 2003, s 145).

The Crime and Disorder Act 1998, s 28(1), provides that an offence is racially or religiously aggravated if:

(a)   at the time of committing the offence, or immediately before or after doing so, the offender demonstrates towards the victim of the offence hostility based on the victim's membership (or presumed membership) of a racial or religious group; or

(b)   the offence is motivated (wholly or partly) by hostility towards members of a racial or religious group based on their membership of that group.

'Membership' includes association with members of that group.

'Racial group' means a group of persons defined by reference to race, colour, nationality, (including citizenship) or ethnic or national origins (s 28(4)). 'Religious group' means a group of persons defined by reference to religious belief or lack of religious belief (s 28(5)).

Section 145 of the CJA 2003 will not apply if the defendant has been charged with one of the racially aggravated offences under ss 29–32 of the Crime and Disorder Act 1998 (assault, criminal damage, public order offences and harassment).

The approach to be adopted in deciding to what degree the offence should be treated as aggravated, is to be found in *R v Kelly and Donnelly* [2001] Crim LR 41.

10.2.3.6 Offences aggravated by reference to disability or sexual orientation

Offences that are motivated by hostility in relation to a person's disability or sexual orientation are to be treated as aggravated (CJA 2003, s 146). This section would also apply if hostility was demonstrated toward the victim based on disability or sexual orientation. A court is required to state when sentencing that it has treated the above factors as aggravating features of the case.

10.2.4 Effect of guilty plea

In determining what sentence to pass, the court must take into account, in relation to an offender who has pleaded guilty, the stage in the proceedings at which he indicated his intention to plead guilty and the circumstances in which the indication was given (CJA 2003, s 144).

The SGC guideline on reduction in sentence for guilty pleas emphasises that a reduction in sentence is appropriate because it speeds up the case, saves costs, and saves victims and witnesses having to give evidence. The guideline recommends that the court applies a sliding scale of reduction, usually between one-tenth and one-third, to the provisional sentence, one-third being applied when the guilty plea is entered at the first available opportunity, a quarter when entered after the trial date has been set, and one-tenth when entered on the day of the trial.

10.2.5 Absolute or conditional discharge (PCC(S)A 2000, ss 12–15)

In order to impose either an absolute or a conditional discharge, the court must be satisfied that, having regard to the circumstances and nature of the offence, and the character of the defendant, punishment is inexpedient. A conditional discharge may be imposed, for example, where a person of previous good character commits a petty theft. The court may feel that a court appearance with the attendant publicity is punishment enough. An absolute discharge is sometimes imposed where the court feels that the defendant, although technically guilty of an offence, is morally blameless.

A person can be conditionally discharged for a period not exceeding three years. If he commits any offence during that time, he may be sentenced afresh for the original offence.

10.2.6 Fines (PCC(S)A 2000, ss 126–129 and ss 135–142)

Where the Crown Court or magistrates' court decides that a fine is the appropriate sentence for an offence, the PCC(S)A 2000, s 128 provides that:

(1) Before fixing the amount of any fine ... a court shall inquire into the financial circumstances of the offender.

(2) The amount of any fine fixed by a court shall be such as, in the opinion of the court, reflects the seriousness of the offence.

(3) In fixing the amount of any fine ... a court shall take into account the circumstances of the case including, among other things, the financial circumstances of the offender so far as they are known, or appear, to the court.

(4) Subsection (3) above applies whether taking into account the financial circumstances of the offender has the effect of increasing or reducing the amount of the fine.

10.2.6.1 Financial circumstances order

The court has power to order an defendant to provide details of his financial circumstances before passing sentence. Such an order is known as a financial circumstances order. Section 162 of the CJA 2003 sets out the preconditions and consequences of failure to comply.

10.2.6.2 The Crown Court's power to fine

Section 163 of the CJA 2003 allows a Crown Court in certain circumstances to impose a fine instead of, or as well as, dealing with a defendant in any other way.

10.2.7 Community sentences (CJA 2003, ss 147–151, ss 177–180, ss 196–223)

A court must not pass a community sentence unless it is of the opinion that the offence, or a combination of the offence and one or more of the offences associated with it, was serious enough to warrant such a sentence (CJA 2003, s 148).

A community sentence is a sentence composed of one or more of the following community orders:

(a)   an unpaid work requirement;

(b)   an activity requirement;

(c)   a programme requirement;

(d)   a prohibited activity requirement;

(e)   a curfew requirement;

(f)   an exclusion requirement;

(g)   a residence requirement;

(h)   a mental health treatment requirement;

(i)   a drug rehabilitation requirement;

(j)   an alcohol treatment requirement

(k)   a supervision requirement;

(l)   an attendance centre requirement (for offenders below 25 years of age).

The specific requirements of these orders are set out at **10.2.7.5** below. Each order can last for up to three years.

Thus a community sentence is a single sentence to which requirements can be attached in order to meet the seriousness of the offence and address the needs of the individual offender. In effect, the list of requirements is a menu from which selections can be made to suit each case. More than one requirement can be imposed, but the overall sentence must be proportionate to the seriousness of the offence or offences.

The SGC, in its guidelines on new sentences under the CJA 2003, proposes that there be three flexible sentencing ranges within the community sentence band: low, medium and high. Once the court has decided that the offences are within the community sentence band, it needs to consider which requirements to include.

In deciding which requirements to impose the court must ensure that:

(a)   any restriction of liberty is commensurate with the seriousness of the offence or offences;

(b)   the requirements are the most suitable for the offender; and

(c)   where there are two or more requirements, they are compatible with each other.

The court should then look again at the seriousness of the offence and decide whether the offence is just over the community threshold (low); or obviously well within the community band (medium); or just falls below the custody threshold, or has crossed the custody threshold but a community penalty is more appropriate (high).

In deciding on the nature and severity of the requirements to be included in a community sentence the court should be guided by:

(a)   the assessment of offence seriousness (low, medium, or high);

(b)   the purposes of sentencing that the court wishes to achieve (punishment, deterrence, rehabilitation, public protection and rehabilitation);

(c)   the risk of re-offending;

(d)   the ability of the offender to comply; and

(e)   the availability of requirements in the local area.

The resulting restriction on liberty must be a proportionate response to the offence that was committed.

10.2.7.1   Persistent petty offenders (CJA 2003, s 151)

The CJA 2003 makes special provision for those persistent petty offenders who repeatedly commit minor offences, for which they are fined and for which a community sentence would not otherwise be possible.

Where an offender, on three or more occasions, is convicted of an offence for which only a fine and/or compensation is imposed, and a community sentence would not otherwise be available because the test of seriousness is not satisfied, a community sentence may be imposed if the court decides it is in the interests of justice to make such an order.

Before imposing a community sentence on such a petty offender, the court should have regard to the circumstances of the earlier offences, their relationship to current offending, and the time that elapsed since the offender's earlier convictions.

The persistent petty offender provisions are not in force at the time of writing.

10.2.7.2   Remands in custody (CJA 2003, s 149)

The court is under a duty, in deciding what restrictions on liberty are to be imposed by a community sentence, to have regard to any period of a remand in custody in respect of that offence, or any other offence the charge for which was founded on the same facts or evidence.

10.2.7.3   All community sentences (CJA 2003, ss 217 and 220)

Courts must ensure, as far as practicable, that the requirements imposed in a community sentence avoid conflict with the offender's religious beliefs, any interference with times when the defendant would normally work, attend school or any other educational establishment, or with the requirements of any other order to which the defendant may be subject.

All community sentences require the defendant to keep in contact with his supervising officer as directed, and to notify them of any change of address.

10.2.7.4   Responsible officers (CJA 2003, ss 197–198)

Where a community sentence is imposed there may be one or more responsible officers. These are the people who will be making the arrangements for the requirements imposed by the order to be undertaken, promote the defendant's compliance with those requirements and be responsible for taking steps to enforce the requirements.

Normally the responsible officer will be a probation officer, but he may be, as in the case of a curfew order (see **10.2.7.5** below), an individual employed by a contractor providing a service (for example, the electronic monitoring of offenders).

10.2.7.5 Community orders

Unpaid work requirement (CJA 2003, ss 200–201)

An unpaid work requirement is, as its name suggests, a requirement for the defendant to perform unpaid work for the community, on the instructions of the responsible officer.

Before imposing an unpaid work requirement the court should obtain a report on the defendant's suitability for such a requirement. A court may dispense with a report if it decides that such a report is unnecessary.

The aggregate number of hours of unpaid work must not be less than 40, nor more than 300. Work should normally be completed within 12 months, but the requirement will continue until all the work has been done or the order revoked.

Activity requirement (CJA 2003, s 201)

This requires a defendant to present himself at a specified place and participate in specified activities. The activities may consist of, or include, activities the purpose of which is reparation, and can involve contact between the defendant and the victims of his offence, provided that such victims consent.

Before imposing an activity requirement the court should obtain a report on the offender's suitability for such a requirement. A court may dispense with such a report if it decides that a report is unnecessary. However, it must consult a probation officer and be satisfied that it is feasible to secure compliance with the requirement.

The aggregate number of days of an activity order must not exceed is 60.

Programme requirement (CJA 2003, s 202)

The programme requirement requires the defendant to participate in a programme of activity, which has been accredited by a body established by the Home Secretary, specified in the order at a specified place and on specified days.

A court cannot include a programme requirement in an order unless the accredited programme has been recommended to the court by a probation officer.

The programme requirement is particularly suitable for addressing behavioural causes of offending – sex offending, anger management and other similar programmes. The CJA 2003 does not provide any limits on the length of attendance. The order will specify the number of days and the place, but detailed operation (for example, as to when to attend) is left to the responsible officer.

Care will need to be taken that the totality of the requirement is one which is not disproportionate given the characteristics of the offence and the offender (for example, age), and, of course, that the requirements of either the requirement or the responsible officer do not infringe s 21 of the CJA 2003 (requirement to avoid conflict with religious beliefs, interference with work or education).

Prohibited activity requirement (CJA 2003, s 203)

This requires the offender to refrain from participating in specified activities named in the order on any day or days so specified, or during a period so specified. The court may not include a prohibited activity requirement in an order unless it has consulted a probation officer. The requirements that may be included in a prohibited activity requirement are not limited by legislation and may include the prohibition of activities that would otherwise be lawful.

The scope for specifying prohibited activities is endless, but must be viewed in the context also of curfew orders and exclusion orders (see below). Prohibited activities are wider than curfew and exclusion orders. Examples might include driving motor vehicles, attending football matches generally, or drinking alcohol. Again, care needs to be taken to ensure that any prohibitions (which are, by definition, restrictions on liberty) are reasonable, relate to offence seriousness and do not have a disproportionate effect on the personal life of the defendant. The factors in CJA 2003, s 217 should also be borne in mind.

Curfew requirement (CJA 2003, s 204)

The curfew requirement requires a defendant to remain at a specified place for between two and 12 hours in any 24-hour period. The order may specify different periods of curfew on different days, and different places for different days.

Before imposing a curfew requirement a court must obtain and consider information about the premises, the effect on any third party and the attitude of persons likely to be affected by the enforced presence of the defendant.

A curfew requirement may operate for a period of up to six months. It must usually be monitored electronically.

As with all of these requirements, restrictions on liberty of this type must be necessary and proportionate.

Exclusion requirement (CJA 2003, s 205)

This directs a defendant not to enter any place or an area specified in the order. The order can provide for the prohibition to operate only during specified periods, and may specify different places for different periods or days during the order. 'Place' in this context includes not only specific locations but extends to include 'an area'. The term 'area' is not defined but could include, say, a district of a town, city or village – a city centre, village green, or the area around a nightclub or football ground (all examples given in the Explanatory Notes to the Criminal Justice Bill 2003). Whether it could legally include a large city or county is more arguable, The larger the 'area' defined, the harder it will be for the requirement to be justified in law as a necessary and proportionate restriction on the liberty of the defendant. There will be a need for a clear definition, both to provide clarity for the offender and to give the necessary exactitude to provide a means to determine whether there has been a breach.

An exclusion requirement must not exceed two years. It is usually monitored electronically.

Residence requirement (CJA 2003, s 206)

As its name suggests, this requirement directs the defendant to reside at a place specified in the order for a specified period. The order cannot specify a hostel or other institution unless a probation officer has recommended it. It may also permit the defendant to live at an alternative address, with the approval of his responsible officer, thus providing flexibility in the requirement and obviating the need for variation orders. The order of the court must state specifically that this is to apply, although it will not need to specify the alternative address or addresses.

Before imposing a residence requirement, a court is obliged to consider the home circumstances of the defendant.

Mental health treatment requirement (CJA 2003, ss 207–208)

A mental health treatment requirement requires the defendant to submit to treatment by a medical practitioner or a chartered psychologist, with a view to treating the offender's mental condition. The medical practitioner or psychologist must be named in the order.

The treatment may be as a resident patient in a hospital or care home (but not in a high security psychiatric unit), as a non-resident patient in a hospital or care home, or under the direction of a registered medical practitioner and/or chartered psychologist.

This requirement cannot be imposed unless the court is satisfied on the evidence of an approved medical practitioner that the condition of the offender is susceptible to treatment, and that it is not so serious as to warrant the making of a hospital or guardianship order under the Mental Health Act 1983.

The defendant must express a willingness to comply with this requirement.

The responsible officer will supervise the defendant only to the extent necessary for revoking or amending the order.

Drug rehabilitation requirement (CJA 2003, ss 209–211)

This requirement provides that during a specified period (the treatment and testing period) the defendant must submit to treatment under the direction of a specified person with a view to reducing or eliminating his drug dependency, and must provide samples to ascertain whether he has any drug in his body. The requirement for treatment can be either as a resident, or as a non-resident.

A court cannot include a drug rehabilitation requirement unless it is satisfied that the offender is dependent on, or has a propensity to misuse, drugs and his dependency/propensity is susceptible to treatment. The treatment and testing period must be a minimum of six months and a maximum of three years. A court can impose this requirement only if a probation officer recommends it.

The court can review the drug rehabilitation requirements at regular intervals. The defendant must attend these reviews. At these hearings the court will be given a written report on the defendant's progress, and the report will include test results and the views of the treatment provider as to the treatment and testing of the defendant.

The court will have power to amend the order so far as it relates to the drug rehabilitation requirement. It cannot reduce the period of the order to less than six months. The defendant must consent to any amendments.

If during the review the defendant fails to express a willingness to comply with the requirements as amended, the court may revoke the order and re-sentence the defendant in some other way.

Where the court is satisfied that the defendant is progressing satisfactorily, the order may be amended so as to provide for subsequent reviews to be held without the need for a formal hearing or the defendant attending.

Alcohol treatment requirement (CJA 2003, s 212)

The alcohol treatment requirement provides a means by which courts can specifically respond to those defendants who are dependent on alcohol, and whose dependency requires and may be susceptible to treatment. The alcohol treatment requirement does not have to be made in respect of an offence directly related to alcohol misuse, although a court is likely to make such an order if it is of the opinion that alcohol plays a part in the offending behaviour.

Like a drug treatment requirement, the alcohol treatment can be delivered to the defendant as a resident or non-resident of an institution, under the direction of a person having the necessary qualifications and experience. The order must specify that person.

The defendant is required to express his willingness to comply with the requirement. The period of treatment cannot be less than six months.

Supervision requirement (CJA 2003, s 213)

Under the terms of a supervision requirement the offender must, during the relevant period, attend appointments with the responsible officer (or any other person specified) at times and places determined by that officer. The purpose of the supervision requirement is to promote the defendant's rehabilitation.

Attendance centre requirement (CJA 2003, s 214 and s 221)

For an attendance centre requirement the defendant must be under 25 years of age. It requires the defendant to attend at a centre for between 12 and 36 hours. Attendance is limited to one attendance per day and for not more than three hours at a time.

Before imposing the order, the court must be satisfied that the attendance centre is reasonably accessible to the defendant, having regard to the means of access available to him and any other relevant circumstances.

The Home Secretary is empowered to provide attendance centres and to make arrangements with local authorities and police authorities regarding the premises to be used.

Electronic monitoring requirement (CJA 2003, s 215)

When the court imposes a community sentence with a curfew or exclusion requirement, it must normally impose an electronic monitoring requirement.

When facilities are available, the court may also impose electronic monitoring in respect of other community requirements.

10.2.7.6 Breach, revocation, amendment and subsequent conviction (CJA 2003, s 179 and Sch 8)

Breach

An offender will receive only a single warning from the responsible officer about his failure to comply with a requirement (including misconduct); on a second failure, breach proceedings will be commenced. However, if the failure is significant, breach proceedings can be commenced immediately.

A warning must describe the circumstances of the failure, state that the failure is unacceptable, and inform the offender that if, within 12 months, he further breaches the order breach proceedings will be commenced.

Breach – magistrates' court orders

Once before the court for breach, if it is proved that the offender has failed without reasonable excuse to comply with any of the requirements of the order, the court can:

(a)   revoke the order and re-sentence for the original offence(s); or

(b)   amend the order to make requirements more onerous; or

(c)   where the community sentence was made in respect of a non-imprisonable offence and the court is satisfied that the offender has wilfully and persistently failed to comply with the requirements, deal with the offender by imposing a term of imprisonment for a term not exceeding six months (Criminal Justice Act 2003 (Sentencing) (Transitory Provisions) Order 2005, SI 2005/643).

Breach – Crown Court orders

Orders made by the Crown Court will be dealt with by the Crown Court unless the order included a direction that failure to comply with the order was to be dealt with by the magistrates' court. This power recognises that in many instances the Crown Court will be content for the magistrates' court to decide whether a breach should be committed to the Crown Court for re-sentencing (with the offender remanded either on bail, or in custody), or whether it can be dealt with by the magistrates' court in one of the three ways specified above.

The Crown Court can deal with the offender in any one of the three ways specified above in relation to magistrates' court orders.

In dealing with an offender for breach requirements, the magistrates' court and the Crown Court must take into account the extent to which the offender has complied with the order.

Revocation

The offender or responsible officer may make an application for the order to be revoked in the interests of justice. A court may then either revoke the order, or revoke the order and deal with the offender in some other way for the original offence(s).

Circumstances in which a community order may be revoked include the offender making good progress, or responding satisfactorily to supervision or treatment.

If the offender is re-sentenced the court must take into account the extent to which the offender has complied with any of the requirements of the order.

Orders made by the Crown Court will be dealt with by the Crown Court, unless the order included a requirement that revocation of the order was to be dealt with by the magistrates' court.

Amendment

A court may amend an order where the offender proposes to change, or has changed, residence from one petty sessions area to another. A responsible officer may also apply for a community sentence to be amended by cancelling requirements, or replacing any of the requirements with another requirement.

An amendment with regard to a requirement for mental health treatment, drug rehabilitation or alcohol treatment cannot be made unless the offender consents to the amendment.

Orders made by the Crown Court will be dealt with by the Crown Court, unless the order included a direction that amendment of the order was to be dealt with by the magistrates' court.

Subsequent conviction

An offender convicted of an offence during the currency of a community sentence may have his order revoked if it appears in the interests of justice to do so. On revoking an order the court can re-sentence for the original offence. In dealing with the offender the court must take into account the extent to which he has complied with any of the requirements of the order.

The Crown Court can deal with a community sentence made either by a magistrates' court, or by a Crown Court. However, where the offender subject to a Crown Court community sentence is convicted of an offence by the magistrates' court, the magistrates' court must commit the offender for sentence to the Crown Court in custody, or release him on bail until he can be brought before the Crown Court.

10.2.8 Custodial sentences

Offenders aged 18–21 are sent to young offender institutions. Offenders aged 21 or above are sent to prison.

Where the court intends to impose a sentence of imprisonment for the first time, or impose detention in a young offender institution, the offender must be legally represented at the time of sentence, unless he has been given the opportunity to apply for representation and has failed to do so (PCC(S)A 2000, s 83(1)).

10.2.8.1 Qualification for a discretionary custodial sentence (CJA 2003, s 152)

The court cannot impose a discretionary custodial sentence unless one of the following applies.

The seriousness test

The court must not pass a custodial sentence unless it is of the opinion that the offence, or the combination of the offence and one or more offences associated with it, was so serious that neither a fine alone nor a community sentence can be justified for the offence.

Refusal of a community sentence

A custodial sentence may be imposed if the defendant refuses to consent to a community sentence where his consent is required.

10.2.8.2 Aggravating and mitigating factors

In applying the seriousness test, the court must also have regard to any aggravating and mitigating factors about the offence and (in the case of violent and sexual offences) the offender (PCC(S)A 2000, s 81(4)).

10.2.8.3 Criteria for deciding length of term of imprisonment (CJA 2003, s 153)

The sentence must be for the shortest term (not exceeding the permitted maximum) that in the opinion of the court is commensurate with the seriousness of the offence, or the combination of the offence and one or more offences associated with it.

Any aggravating or mitigating factors will also be taken into account in determining length of sentence (PCC(S)A 2000, s 81(4)).

A person aged 21 or over may be sentenced to imprisonment:

(a)   by the Crown Court up to the maximum fixed by statute;

(b)   by a magistrates' court for up to six months, unless statute fixes a lower maximum.

Magistrates may, however, impose consecutive sentences up to a maximum of 12 months in aggregate when dealing with two or more either way offences (Magistrates' Courts Act 1980, s 31, s 133(2)).

The maximum sentence in a young offender institution for a person aged between 18 and 21 is the same as for imprisonment.

Once s 154 of the CJA 2003 is brought into effect, magistrates' courts will have the power to impose a sentence of no more than 51 weeks in respect of any one offence, and a maximum for more than one offence of 65 weeks. The CJA 2003 confers on the Home Secretary the power to amend these limits to maxima of 18 months and 24 months respectively. At the same time it limits the circumstances when a magistrates' court may commit an offender to the Crown Court for sentence. Implementation of the increased sentencing powers is not expected until 2006/2007.

10.2.8.4   Custody plus (CJA 2003, ss 181–182 and s 187)

This new custodial sentence for sentences under 12 months' imprisonment has become known as 'custody plus'. It consists of a short period in prison of up to three months, with a significant period of supervision on release into the community. Implementation of custody plus is not expected until 2006/2007.

10.2.8.5   Intermittent custody (CJA 2003, ss 183–187)

Intermittent custody allows the offender to serve the custodial element of a sentence in blocks either during the week, or at weekends. Between the blocks of custody the offender will be released on licence to enable him to maintain community links, employment and caring responsibilities. The court can add requirements that the offender must comply with whilst on licence in the community. Failure to comply with any requirement will result in the offender being returned to custody.

Intermittent custody is currently being piloted in a number of areas. Full implementation is not expected until the outcomes of the pilots have been considered.

10.2.8.6   Suspended sentence of imprisonment (CJA 2003, ss 189–194)

A suspended sentence is a sentence of imprisonment for all purposes, and the threshold for a custodial sentence applies. A court cannot impose a community sentence (see **10.2.7** above) at the same time.

The CJA 2003 amends the provisions in relation to the suspending of sentences of imprisonment. However, the suspended sentence provisions are based on the availability of custody plus (see **10.2.8.4**) and the increased sentencing powers in the magistrates' courts (see **10.2.8.3**). These are not being implemented yet, and consequently transitional provisions have been introduced by the the Criminal Justice Act 2003 (Sentencing) (Transitory Provisions) Order 2005 (SI 2005/643).

Elements of a suspended sentence

The suspended sentence consists of three elements:

(a)   *The term of imprisonment.* The Crown Court may suspend a term of imprisonment of at least 14 days but not more than 12 months. The magistrates' courts may suspend a term of imprisonment subject to their maximum (see **10.2.8.3**). It is not possible to suspend detention in a young offender institution.

(b)   *The operational period.* The operational period is the period during which the offender can be re-sentenced should he commit a further offence in that period. The operational period must be for at least six months and not more than two years.

(c)   *The supervision period.* The supervision period must not exceed the operational period of the suspended sentence and must be for at least six months. During the supervision period the court may order the offender to comply with one or more requirements to be carried out in the community. The list of requirements is the same as that for a community sentence (see **10.2.7.5**). The court can provide for the order to be reviewed. A responsible officer will report to the court on the offender's progress. The offender must attend the review hearings and the court has power to amend the requirements. The offender must express his willingness to comply with amendments. The court cannot amend the operational period.

The sentence of imprisonment does not take effect unless, during the operational period, the offender either fails to comply with a requirement in the order, or commits another offence, and a court having the power to do so orders the sentence to have effect.

Breach of the suspended sentence (CJA 2003, s 193 and Sch 12)

Failure to comply with a requirement, or commission of a further offence, even if non-imprisonable, can constitute a breach and place the offender at risk of having the suspended sentence activated.

An offender will receive only a single warning about failure to comply with a requirement under a suspended sentence. This is similar to breaches of community sentences (see **10.2.7.6** above). If there is a failure to comply without reasonable excuse within 12 months following such a warning, proceedings must be commenced by the issue of a summons or warrant of arrest.

If the offender is found to be in breach of a requirement or by conviction for an offence then, in respect of an order imposed by a magistrates' court, the offender may be dealt with by any Crown Court or any magistrates' court before which he appears. In respect of a Crown Court order, only the Crown Court may deal with him.

The court must deal with the offender in one of the following ways:

(a)   order the prison sentence originally suspended to take affect unaltered;

(b)   order the sentence to take effect by substituting a shorter prison sentence;

(c)   amend the order by imposing more onerous requirements;

(d)   amend the order by extending the operational period, or by extending the supervision period.

The court must make an order under (a) or (b) above unless it considers that it would be unjust to do so in view of all the circumstances, including the extent to which the offender has complied with any community requirements and the facts of the subsequent offence. If it is of the opinion that it must make an order under (c) or (d) then it must announce its reasons for doing so.

The SGC guideline on new sentences under the CJA 2003 states that there is a presumption that in response to either type of breach the court will activate the suspended sentence (either with the original term, or with a reduced term), unless the court takes the view that this would, in all the circumstances, be unjust. The SGC guideline provides that it is expected that any activated suspended sentence will be consecutive to the sentence imposed for the new offence.

The CJA 2003 allows the court to consider other factors, such as the time that has elapsed since passing the original sentence and any change in the offender's circumstances, before deciding whether to amend the order or activate the suspended sentence.

10.2.8.7 Dangerous offenders (CJA 2003, ss 224–236)

The CJA 2003 introduces new sentences for those who are deemed to be dangerous offenders and have committed specified violent or sexual offences. The court will be able to order extended sentences and extended periods may be imposed. The majority of these sentences will be available only to the Crown Court as they relate to indefinite custodial terms and terms of 12 months or more. Detailed consideration of these provisions is beyond the scope of this book.

10.2.8.8 Release on licence (CJA 2003, ss 237–268)

The rules governing the early release of prisoners are beyond the scope of this book.

10.2.9 Motoring penalties

10.2.9.1 Endorsement of driving licences (RTOA 1988, s 44)

Dangerous driving, careless driving and aggravated vehicle-taking all carry obligatory endorsement of the driving licence with particulars of the conviction. The licence must also be endorsed with the appropriate number of penalty points, unless at the same time the defendant is disqualified from driving.

Where a licence is ordered to be endorsed, particulars of the endorsement are recorded on the licence, and are also recorded centrally at the Driver and Vehicle Licensing Agency (DVLA) at Swansea.

Where the defendant is convicted of two or more endorsable offences committed on the same occasion, the court will endorse the highest number of points unless it thinks fit to order otherwise (Road Traffic Offenders Act (RTOA) 1988, s 28(4)). In such circumstances, the court must state its reasons in open court.

Example

Peter is convicted of speeding (3 to 6 penalty points) and using a vehicle with defective brakes (3 penalty points), both offences being committed on the same occasion. The court takes the view that the speeding offence merits 6 points. Only 6 points will go on his driving licence unless the court thinks fit to order otherwise. The court may endorse points for both offences if it is satisfied that Peter has been driving with defective brakes for a number of months.

10.2.9.2 Disqualification for the offence itself (RTOA 1988, s 34)

Obligatory disqualification

A number of offences, including dangerous driving and aggravated vehicle-taking, carry obligatory disqualification. Where an offence carries obligatory disqualification, the court must generally order the defendant to be disqualified from driving for at least 12 months.

Discretionary disqualification

Where an offence carries discretionary disqualification for committing the offence itself, the court may order the defendant to be disqualified for such period as it thinks fit. Careless driving, taking a conveyance and theft of a motor vehicle carry discretionary disqualification.

Interim disqualification

Section 26 of the RTOA 1988 enables a magistrates' court, when committing a defendant to the Crown Court under certain statutory provisions for sentencing, deferring sentence or adjourning for sentence, to impose an interim period of disqualification from driving for an offence involving obligatory or discretionary disqualification. This can last until the case is concluded.

Disqualification under PCC(S)A 2000, s 146

Where a defendant is convicted of any offence, the court may order him to be disqualified from driving for such period as it thinks fit. That no vehicle was used in the commission of the offence is irrelevant. The disqualification may be in addition to dealing with him in any other way, or may be instead of any other sentence.

Disqualification under PCC(S)A 2000, s 147

Where a defendant is convicted on indictment of an offence carrying imprisonment of two years or more, or is committed for sentence, under s 38 or s 38A of the Magistrates' Courts Act 1980 to be sentenced for such an offence, the Crown Court may disqualify him for such period as it thinks fit if satisfied that a motor vehicle was used in committing the offence. This applies even if the offence is not endorsable and even if the defendant disqualified had not himself used the vehicle (ie, it was used by an accomplice).

10.2.9.3 Disqualification under the penalty points system (RTOA 1988, s 35 and Pt II)

A defendant will be liable to disqualification for at least six months if the penalty points to be taken into account number 12 or more.

Where the defendant is convicted of an offence which carries obligatory endorsement, the penalty points to be taken into account are:

(a) any points attributed to the offence of which he is convicted, disregarding any offence in respect of which an order for disqualification for committing the offence itself is made (see **10.2.9.2** above); *plus*

(b) any points previously endorsed on his licence in respect of offences committed within the three years immediately preceding the commission of the most recent offence.

Note that any penalty points endorsed on the defendant's licence prior to a previous disqualification under the points system must be ignored. Only a disqualification for accumulating 12 or more penalty points has the effect of 'wiping the slate clean', ie removing all existing penalty points from the licence; all other disqualifications leave them undisturbed.

Example 1

Raj is convicted of careless driving. The offence was committed on 1 April 2003. He has the following endorsement on his licence: careless driving committed on 31 March 2001, 5 points.

If Raj is disqualified for the offence itself, his licence will not be endorsed with any penalty points. If he is not disqualified for the offence itself, between 3 and 9 points will be awarded. If the number of points awarded are 7 or more, Raj is liable to be disqualified under the points system.

Example 2

Sameira is convicted of careless driving. The offence was committed on 1 June 2004. She has the following endorsements on her licence:

Offence	Date of Offence	Sentence
Speeding	1 October 2004	4 points
Speeding	1 March 2004	(disqualified for 6 months under penalty points system)
Careless driving	1 July 2003	8 points
Speeding	1 July 2002	3 points

If Sameira is disqualified for the current offence of careless driving itself, her licence will not be endorsed with any penalty points. If she is not disqualified for the offence itself, she will be awarded 3 to 9 points. The only relevant points on the licence to date which are to be taken into account are the 4 points awarded on 1 October 2004. Although all the other points were awarded for offences committed within three years of the date of commission of the current offence, they are not taken into account as Sameira was disqualified for these under the penalty points system. Therefore, if the number of points awarded for the current offence of careless driving is 8 or more, Sameira is liable to be disqualified under the points system.

The disqualification under the points system must be for a minimum period. If the defendant has no previous disqualification of 56 days imposed within three years of the commission of the most recent offence for which penalty points are to be taken into account, then the period is six months. If there is one such disqualification in the three years, the period is a minimum of one year. If there are two or more such disqualifications imposed within three years of the most recent offence, then the minimum period is two years. Disqualifications under the RTOA 1988, s 26, the PCC(S)A 2000, s 147, and those imposed for theft of a motor vehicle or taking a conveyance without the consent of the owner are not to be taken into account.

The Road Traffic (New Drivers) Act 1995 provides a 'probationary period' for a newly qualified driver of two years, beginning with the day on which he becomes a newly qualified driver. If such drivers accumulate 6 or more penalty points during that period, the court notifies the DVLA. The DVLA then issues a notice of revocation of the driving licence and requires the surrender of the existing driving licence, if still in the driver's possession. The driver is invited to apply for a provisional licence. A full driving licence may not be granted until the driver has passed another driving test.

10.2.9.4   Relationship between disqualification for the offence itself and disqualification under the penalty points system

It is not possible to be disqualified under both provisions for the one offence.

When considering the proper sentence for an offence carrying discretionary disqualification, the court should first consider whether this is warranted. In doing so, it will have regard to the defendant's full driving record. If it considers that a mandatory period of disqualification under the RTOA 1988, s 35 (disqualification under the penalty points system) would be the best disposal, the court can exercise its discretion not to disqualify for the offence itself under RTOA 1988, s 34 and to impose an appropriate number of points to bring the defendant within s 35 (*Jones v DPP* [2001] RTR 80).

When the court disqualifies for the offence, it is obliged to take into account other offences which were committed, and to take into account and attribute points to those offences with a view to disqulaification under s 35. So disqualification can arise under both provisions when the defendant is being dealt with for more than one offence.

10.2.9.5   Avoiding disqualification or endorsement

Obligatory disqualification or obligatory endorsement arising out of the offence itself

Obligatory penalties can be avoided if the defendant can show the existence of 'special reasons'. Special reasons may avoid endorsement or disqualification, or secure a reduced period. There is no statutory definition of special reasons. A special reason is one that is:

(a)   a mitigating circumstance;

(b)   which does not constitute a defence to the charge;

(c)   connected with the commission of the offence not personal to the offender; and

(d)   which the court ought properly to take into account when considering sentence (*R v Crossan* [1939] NI 106; *Whittall v Kirby* [1946] 2 All ER 552; *R v Wickins* (1958) 42 Cr App R 236).

Therefore, the fact that the defendant was driving dangerously because of an emergency may constitute a special reason. The fact that the defendant would lose his job if disqualified is not a special reason: it is personal to the offender and is not connected with the commission of the offence itself.

It is possible for the court to find the reasons special enough to avoid obligatory disqualification but not special enough to avoid obligatory endorsement. If that is the case, the court will endorse the defendant's driving licence with penalty points. If the defendant already has sufficient penalty points on his driving licence, he may find himself liable to be disqualified under the penalty points system.

Example

Elaine is charged with driving with excess alcohol, which carries an obligatory disqualification. She argues special reasons. The court finds the reasons special enough to avoid obligatory disqualification but not special enough to avoid obligatory endorsement. Elaine already has 9 points on her licence, and so is liable to be disqualified under the penalty points system as 3–11 points must be endorsed on her driving licence for the offence.

The defendant must prove special reasons exist on the balance of probabilities. If the court finds special reasons, they must be stated in open court (and in magistrates' courts, recorded in the court register) (RTOA 1998, s 47(1)).

Discretionary disqualification for the offence itself

Whenever the court has a discretion to disqualify, mitigating factors can be put to the court with a view to avoiding disqualification or reducing the period. Mitigating factors are any factors which are relevant to the offence before the court. They can be connected with the circumstances of the offence itself, or be personal to the offender. Therefore, unlike special reasons, factors such as loss of job on disqualification can be taken into account.

Disqualification under the points system

If the court is satisfied that there are mitigating circumstances, it may decide not to disqualify under the points system, or to reduce the period. All circumstances can be taken into account (both those connected with the offence and those personal to the offender) except:

(a)   the triviality of the present offence;

(b)   hardship (unless it is exceptional);

(c)   mitigating circumstances taken into account to avoid disqualification (or reduce the period) under the points system within the preceding three years (RTOA 1988, s 35(4)).

Example 1

Himesh is liable to disqualification under the points system. He puts forward the fact that if disqualified he will lose his job. This can be taken into account only if the court is satisfied that loss of his job would constitute exceptional hardship.

Example 2

Joan is liable to disqualification under the points system. She avoided a points disqualification 18 months ago on the basis that disqualification would cause exceptional hardship due to the fact that she lives in an isolated area, with no public transport, and suffers from arthritis, making walking difficult. She cannot put forward these factors again at the current hearing.

The defendant must prove mitigating circumstances exist on the balance of probabilities. If the court finds mitigating circumstances, they must be stated in open court (and in the magistrates' court recorded in the court register) (RTOA 1988, s 47(1)).

10.2.10 Ancillary orders

A court has power to make the following ancillary orders.

10.2.10.1 Compensation orders (PCC(S)A 2000, ss 130–134)

The defendant can be ordered to pay compensation to the victim of an offence. Compensation cannot normally be ordered in respect of motoring offences. Magistrates can make an order of up to £5,000 per offence. There is no limit in the Crown Court, but the court must have regard to the defendant's means.

10.2.10.2 Forfeiture orders (PCC(S)A 2000, ss 143–145)

A court may order forfeiture of any property which was in the defendant's possession or control at the time of apprehension, if the property was used for committing or facilitating any offence, or was intended by him to be so used or was in his unlawful possession.

An order for the forfeiture and destruction of a controlled drug is made under s 27 of the Misuse of Drugs Act 1971.

10.2.10.3   Confiscation orders (Crime and Disorder Act 1998, s 3)

A magistrates' court has the power to make a confiscation order in respect of the proceeds of crime if it commits a defendant to the Crown Court for sentence under s 3 or s 4 of the PCC(S)A 2000. The Crown Court may make a confiscation order in respect of the proceeds of crime (Proceeds of Crime Act 2002). This is subject to detailed conditions beyond the scope of this book.

10.2.10.4   Prosecution costs (Prosecution of Offences Act 1985, s 18)

If the defendant is convicted of any offence, the court may order the defendant to pay to the prosecution such costs as are just and reasonable, and must specify the amount.

10.2.10.5   Defence costs (Access to Justice Act 1999, s 17; Criminal Defence Service (Recovery of Defence Costs Orders) Regulations 2001, SI 2001/856)

A defendant who is not represented under a representation order and who is acquitted should normally be awarded costs from central funds (Prosecution of Offences Act 1985, s 16). There are exceptions. For example, a defendant who by his conduct has brought suspicion upon himself, and who has misled the prosecution into thinking that the case against him is stronger than it is, may find that costs are not awarded in his favour. (See further *Practice Direction (Crime: Costs)* [1991] 1 WLR 498, as amended by *Practice Direction (Costs in Criminal Proceedings) (No 2)* [2000] 1 Cr App R 60.)

At the conclusion of a case in the Crown Court the judge has the power to order a defendant who is represented under a representation order to pay some or all the costs of his defence (a recovery of defence costs order (RDCO)).

The judge has to consider making an RDCO at the end of the case and after all other financial orders and penalties that may be made. An RCDO should be made against every defendant who is convicted and has the means to pay. However, the order is not dependent on the defendant being convicted, although an order against an acquitted defendant would be exceptional. The order can be for any amount up to the full costs incurred in representing the defendant, and can include costs incurred in other courts.

An RDCO may not be made against a defendant who:

(a)   only appears in the magistrates' court;

(b)   has been committed for sentence to the Crown Court;

(c)   is appealing against sentence in the Crown Court;

(d)   has been acquitted other than in exceptional circumstances.

The defendant must complete Form B (see **Appendix 2(O)**) and return it to the Crown Court at least four days before the first hearing at the Crown Court. The Crown Court will then refer the financial resources of the defendant to the Legal Services Commission, who will prepare a report for the judge outlining the income and capital available to the defendant. The report will also be made available to the defence. The judge will then consider the report at the conclusion of the case and determine whether to make an RDCO. The judge may require the solicitor representing the defendant to provide an estimate of the costs likely to be incurred in the proceedings. If it later turns out that the actual costs incurred were less than the amount of the RDCO, the balance must be repaid.

In deciding how much should be paid under an RDCO the judge will take into account the resources of the defendant together with the resources of his partner. The resources of other people who have been making funds available to the defendant can also be considered. Generally an order will not be made against the first £3,000 of any capital available. The defendant's main dwelling may be treated as capital for the purposes of an RDCO, but the first £100,000 of any equity (ie, the market value less any outstanding mortgages) in that property will be disregarded. In most cases, RDCOs will be made on the basis of capital rather than income. Income will be taken into account only if the defendant's gross annual income exceeds £24,000.

The Crown Court has the power to make an order freezing the defendant's assets where it is appropriate to do so in support of the RDCO provisions. An RDCO may provide for payment to be made forthwith, or by instalments. Payments are made to the Legal Services Commission. The Legal Service Commission may enforce an order as if it was a civil debt.

10.2.11 Deferment of sentence (CJA 2003, s 278 and Sch 23)

A court may defer sentence for up to six months so that it can have regard to the conduct of the defendant after conviction, or to any change in his circumstances. This is a useful provision and can be used, for example, where the defendant claims that a recent change in circumstances in his life will mean that he is unlikely to offend again. If he has the offer of a job, or is about to be married, the court may decide to defer sentence for a period of up to six months to see how the defendant reacts to the change in his circumstances. If the reaction is favourable, a custodial sentence should not normally be imposed at the end of the period of deferment.

The court can impose requirements on the defendant, and the matters to which the court can have regard when it sentences include the extent to which he has complied with any requirements imposed on the deferment.

A court may defer sentence only if:

(a)   the defendant consents:

(b)   the defendant undertakes to comply with the requirements as to his conduct during the period of deferment that the court considers it appropriate to impose; and

(c)   the court is satisfied, having regard to the nature of the offence and the character of the defendant, that it is in the interests of justice to do so.

The SGC guideline on new offences under the CJA 2003 states that a deferred sentence should be used predominantly for a small group of cases close to a significant threshold (ie, custody or community sentence) where, should the defendant be prepared to adapt his behaviour in a way specified by the court, the court may be prepared to impose a lesser sentence.

The provisions in the CJA 2003 do not specify a range of requirements that can be imposed, except that a residence requirement may be imposed. The general provision is that the court can impose any requirements as to the defendant's conduct during the period of the deferment that the court considers it appropriate to impose. The SGC guideline states that any requirements should be specific and measureable so that the defendant knows exactly what is required and the court can assess compliance. The restriction on liberty should be limited to ensure that the defendant has a reasonable expectation of being able to comply whilst mainataining his social responsibilities. Progress and compliance with the requirements will continue to act as a mitigating factor for the court to take into consideration.

The court can appoint a probation officer or any other person as a supervisor to monitor the defendant's compliance with the order. Persons other than probation staff must consent to act as supervisor. The duties of the supervisor include providing information to the court in relation to the defendant's compliance or otherwise.

The defendant must consent to undertake the requirements. Failure to comply with any of the requirements may result in the defendant being brought back to court. A defendant may be summoned to appear back before the court, or a warrant for his arrest may be issued.

A deferment of sentence is an adjournment of the proceedings, and therefore the court's powers remain the same as if the offence had just been committed. These powers include committal to the Crown Court for sentence where appropriate.

The court can defer sentence only once. Deferment cannot exceed six months, nor can a sentence be further deferred.

10.2.12   Committal to the Crown Court for sentence

10.2.12.1   Powers of Criminal Courts (Sentencing) Act 2000, s 3

A magistrates' court may commit an offender of 18 years of age or above to the Crown Court for sentence if:

(a)   it has convicted him of an offence triable either way; and either

(b)   the offence (or the combination of the offence and one or more associated offences) was so serious that greater punishment should be inflicted for the offence than the court has power to impose; or

(c)   in the case of a violent or sexual offence, a prison sentence for a term longer than the court has power to impose is necessary to protect the public from serious harm from him.

The Crown Court may then deal with the defendant as if he had been convicted on indictment.

At plea before venue, the defendant is asked to indicate a plea. If the defendant indicates a guilty plea, the magistrates may still commit the defendant to the Crown Court for sentence if they consider their sentencing powers inadequate.

Example 1

Kevin is charged with assault occasioning actual bodily harm. He indicates a guilty plea. The plea before venue procedure comes to an end and the magistrates proceed to sentence.

When the prosecution summarise the facts, the magistrates learn that the defendant attacked a bus driver who sustained extensive injuries. Kevin may be committed to the Crown Court for sentence.

Example 2

Sheila is charged with theft. She indicates a guilty plea. The plea before venue procedure comes to an end and the magistrates proceed to sentence.

The prosecutor hands into the court a list of Sheila's previous convictions. She has numerous previous convictions for dishonesty offences. This may now be a suitable case for committal for sentence to the Crown Court.

In *R v Warley Magistrates' Court, ex p DPP; R v Staines Magistrates' Court, ex p DPP; R v North East Suffolk Magistrates' Court, ex p DPP; R v Lowestoft Justices, ex p DPP* [1998] 2 Cr App R 307, the Divisional Court considered the plea before venue procedure and committal for sentence. In deciding whether the powers of punishment were adequate, the magistrates should take into account the sentencing discount granted on a guilty plea. Where it was obvious that the gravity of the offence required punishment that would exceed the magistrates' powers, they should commit to the Crown Court without seeking any pre-sentence report or hearing mitigation. The defence should, however, be allowed to make a brief submission in opposition to this course of action, and the prosecution should be allowed to reply.

If the defendant indicates a not guilty plea, the magistrates hear representations from the prosecution and the defence as to mode of trial. If the offence is so serious that the magistrates do not have sufficient sentencing powers, this will usually be revealed at the mode of trial enquiry and the magistrates will commit to the Crown Court for trial. A decision to commit for sentence is likely to be based on factors which were unknown at the mode of trial enquiry.

Example 3

Andrew indicates a not guilty plea, the magistrates accept jurisdiction, and Andrew consents to summary trial. Having been convicted he asks for 16 other offences to be taken into consideration (TIC) (see 10.3.2.3). The TICs were not known at the mode of trial enquiry. Andrew may be committed to the Crown Court for sentencing.

Example 4

Having indicated a not guilty plea, Paul is convicted by the magistrates. At the mode of trial enquiry, it appeared that the offence involved unoccupied premises. It later transpires that part of the premises consisted of a dwelling and the victim was frightened by Paul. This may now be a suitable case for committal for sentence to the Crown Court.

10.2.12.2   Powers of Criminal Courts (Sentencing) Act 2000, s 4

This provision deals with the situation where the magistrates' court has committed a defendant for trial for some offences, but has to deal with him for other, related either way offences. In this context, one offence is related to another if they can both be tried on the same indictment. If the defendant committed for trial has indicated an intention to plead guilty to those related offences, he must, by virtue of the mode of trial procedure, be treated as if he has pleaded guilty to them (see **4.4**). Section 4 gives the magistrates power to commit the defendant to the Crown Court for sentence for the related offences, even if they do not meet the requirements laid down in s 3, ie, that the offence is so serious that the magistrates' powers of punishment are inadequate, or (in the case of a violent or sexual offence) that a longer sentence than they have power to impose is necessary to protect the public from serious harm from him.

Example

Imogen is charged with aggravated vehicle-taking and theft of a radio cassette player from the same vehicle.

At plea before venue, she indicates a plea of not guilty to the theft charge and the magistrates proceed to mode of trial. The magistrates accept jurisdiction and Imogen elects trial by jury.

> She indicates a guilty plea to the aggravated vehicle-taking charge which means that the magistrates will proceed to sentence.
>
> Instead of sentencing her, the magistrates can commit Imogen for sentence for the aggravated vehicle-taking charge under s 4, even though it does not meet the requirements for committal for sentence under s 3.

The powers of the Crown Court to sentence the defendant for the offence committed under s 4 depend on whether it convicts him of the original offence, ie the theft offence in the above example. If it convicts him of the original offence then the Crown Court will have the power to impose any sentence which it would have power to impose if the defendant had been convicted on indictment. If not, the Crown Court's powers to deal with the defendant in respect of offences for which he has been committed for sentence are limited to those of the magistrates.

10.2.12.3 Committal for sentence – bail or custody

In most cases where a plea of guilty is made at the plea before venue, it will be unusual to alter the position as regards bail or custody. When a defendant who has been on bail pleads guilty at the plea before venue, the practice should normally be to continue bail, even if it is anticipated that a custodial sentence will be imposed at the Crown Court, unless there are good reasons for remanding the defendant in custody. If the defendant is in custody then, after entering a plea of guilty at the plea before venue, it will be unusual, if the reasons for remanding in custody remain unchanged, to alter the position (*R v Rafferty* [1999] 1 Cr App R 235).

10.3 Sentencing procedure

10.3.1 Reports to be obtained before sentence

Following a guilty plea or conviction of the defendant, it will often be necessary for the court to adjourn for reports to be prepared to assist the court in sentencing.

10.3.1.1 Mentally disordered offenders

Unless the court is of the opinion that a report is unnecessary, it must obtain and consider a medical report on the offender before passing a custodial sentence, other than one fixed by law (CJA 2003, s157). A sentence will not be invalidated by failure to obtain and consider such a report, but in such instances any appeal court should obtain such a report itself.

10.3.1.2 Pre-sentence reports

Sections 156, 158 and 159 of the CJA 2003 lay down the requirements for the obtaining and purpose of pre-sentence reports, including the disclosure of the same.

Pre-sentence reports are ordered by the court and made by a probation officer. The purpose of the report is to assist the court in deciding the most suitable method of dealing with the offender, addressing issues of risk of harm and likelihood of re-offending. If a custodial sentence is being considered by the court, the report should contain detailed information about how the offender might be punished in the community.

Pre-sentence reports will often be ordered before:

(a)   imposing any custodial sentence, unless the offence (or an associated offence) is triable only on indictment and the court is of the opinion that it is unnecessary;

(b)   making a community sentence.

A court need not obtain a pre-sentence report if it considers that it is unnecessary to do so. There will be cases, for example, when a custodial sentence is inevitable irrespective of the content of a pre-sentence report. A court may feel that a report is therefore not necessary.

There are two pre-sentence report formats: a standard delivery pre-sentence report and a fast delivery pre-sentence report. The key difference between the two formats is the level and quantity of information that they provide and, consequently, the speed with which they can be produced. The ordering of a standard pre-sentence report will result in the case being adjourned for a few weeks for a full report. However, some community sentence requirements may not necessitate the preparation of such a full report and the court may order a fast delivery pre-sentence report. The fast delivery pre-sentence report will normally involve the case being put back in the court list for only a couple of hours or so, thereby enabling the court to sentence the defendant on the same day as the ordering of the report. Copies of a pre-sentence report should be given by the court to the offender or his solicitor, and to the prosecutor.

10.3.2   Procedure

Magistrates' court sentencing procedures are illustrated in a flowchart at **Appendix 1(O)**.

Unless the defendant pleaded not guilty and sentencing follows immediately after trial, the prosecution will summarise the facts of the case.

10.3.2.1   Victim impact statement

This statement, which will be referred to by the prosecutor, gives a victim of crime a formal opportunity to say how the crime has affected him. It may identify a need for protection or support and can be taken into account when sentencing. (See *Practice Direction (Criminal Proceedings: Consolidation)* [2002] 3 All ER 904, para 28, 'Personal statements of victims'.)

10.3.2.2   'Newton hearing'

Although the defendant pleads guilty, he may still dispute some prosecution allegations. If the dispute is substantial the court must either accept the defence account, and sentence accordingly, or give the parties the opportunity of calling evidence so that the dispute may be resolved (*R v Newton (Robert John)* (1983) 77 Cr App R 13). If evidence is called this is known as a *Newton* hearing.

Example

Fred pleads guilty to s 47 actual bodily harm. The prosecution allege that he was the aggressor and launched an unprovoked attack. Fred says that he attacked the other man only after being subjected to racial abuse. The difference would have a major effect on the sentence the court would impose, and so the court must either hold a *Newton* hearing, or accept Fred's account as true.

The prosecution will present details of the defendant's background and a record of his previous convictions to the court. When considering the seriousness of the offence, the court can take into account any previous convictions of the offender, or any failure of his to respond to previous sentences. If the offence was committed whilst on bail, the court must treat that as an aggravating factor.

10.3.2.3   Offences taken into consideration

The prosecution will give details of other offences to be taken into consideration (TICs). In addition to the offence or offences charged, the defendant may have committed a number of other crimes. It is likely to be in the defendant's interest that all matters outstanding against him should be dealt with at the same time. The defendant can ask a court to take other offences into consideration on sentence. These should be offences of a similar or less serious nature. When sentencing the defendant, the court has the power to sentence only in respect of the offences of which he is convicted. The effect of asking for other offences to be taken into consideration is that the court is entitled to take them into account when passing sentence. If the defendant qualifies for a custodial sentence (see **10.2.8**), a number of TICs may increase the length of the sentence. In practice, the overall effect on the sentence is unlikely to be great, particularly when the offence charged is the most serious one.

If an offence is taken into consideration the defendant cannot subsequently be prosecuted for it. It is not a conviction, but compensation can be awarded to the victim of a 'TIC' offence.

The practice involved in asking for other offences to be taken into consideration is that the defendant will be given a form by the police giving details of the various offences. He will sign the form and will be asked to admit before the court that he wishes the other offences to be taken into consideration on sentence. An example of a 'TIC' form appears at **Appendix 2(R)**.

10.3.2.4   Pre-sentence report and financial circumstances statement

If a pre-sentence report has been ordered (see **10.3.1.2**), it will now be made available to the court. In a magistrates' court, the defence will also have to produce a financial circumstances statement. This will be used by the court if a financial penalty is being considered.

The defence plea in mitigation is presented to the court (see **10.4**).

10.3.2.5   Duties to outline sentence and its effects to defendants

Section 174 of the CJA 2003 provides that a court must state in open court, and in ordinary language and general terms, the reasons for deciding on the sentence passed. The court must explain to the offender the effects of the sentence and the effects of not complying with court orders that may form part of that sentence. The court must outline the effects of failing to pay any fine ordered and any powers of the court to review a sentence that has been passed. In passing a custodial or community sentence the court must state that the criteria for such sentences have been met, and why. Aggravating and mitigating factors, including a guilty plea, must be mentioned during sentence.

In order to greater promote the use of and adherence to sentencing guidelines, the court must state its reasons for deciding on a sentence that is of a different kind to, or outside the range of, the guideline sentence.

The duties imposed by s 174 require assistance from advocates. Advocates should have regard to *Attorney-General's Reference (No 7 of 1997)* [1998] 1 Cr App R (S) 268, for guidance as to prosecuting advocates' duty of assistance to the court. It is now the duty of prosecuting advocates not only to be able to refer judges to key sentencing authorities, but also to be able to provide the judge with a copy (*Attorney-General's Reference (No 52 of 2003)* (2003) *The Times*, 12 December, CA).

10.4   The plea in mitigation

10.4.1   The purpose of the plea in mitigation

The role of the defence solicitor in presenting a plea in mitigation to the court is either to reduce the severity of the sentence to be passed, or, in appropriate cases, to persuade the court that punishment, as such, would be inexpedient and that a sentence which will help the defendant should be passed. The objective of the plea in mitigation is to ensure that a sentence is passed by the court which is appropriate both to the circumstances of the offence and to the circumstances of the defendant. The aim is to obtain the most lenient punishment which can reasonably be imposed.

10.4.2   Assessing the likely sentence

A common fault of young solicitor advocates is to 'talk up' a sentence. In other words, the advocate has not made any attempt to assess the likely range of penalties to be imposed for the offence and addresses the court on potential penalties which may be wholly inappropriate. The starting point for any plea in mitigation is to attempt to make a realistic assessment of the likely range of sentences which will be in the mind of the court.

A useful starting point in the magistrates' court is to consult the Magistrates' Association Sentencing Guidelines and any relevant guidelines issued by the SGC. If more than one offence is being dealt with, it is also necessary to bear in mind that the overall sentence should be kept in proportion to the 'totality' of the offending behaviour. This simply means that care should be taken in sentencing for several minor offences to avoid an overall sentence that would be more appropriate to a much more serious crime.

Extracts from the Magistrates' Association Sentencing Guidelines appear in **Appendix 3**. Care must be exercised in using the Guidelines as they were issued before the CJA 2003 came into force.

10.4.3   The plea in mitigation

When making a plea in mitigation, the advocate should address the court on the circumstances of the offence, the circumstances of the offender and the sentence he is seeking to persuade the magistrates to impose. An effective plea in mitigation will try to 'sell' a particular sentence by reference to the mitigating factors available. Whatever the advocate says about the offence and the offender should be designed to persuade the magistrates to impose a particular sentence.

The court may have ordered a pre-sentence report (see **10.3.1.2**). The advocate should note any comments contained in the report about the offence, the defendant's background and any recommendation on sentence.

The court may hear character witnesses, or receive letters or references on the defendant's behalf.

When the defendant wishes to avoid obligatory disqualification or endorsement for a driving offence (see **10.2.9**), he will give evidence on oath of special reasons or mitigating circumstances.

The following are matters commonly dealt with by the advocate in his plea in mitigation.

10.4.3.1 The offence

Aggravating features

The advocate should identify any aggravating features which would normally encourage a court to take the view that a sentence at the higher end of the scale would be appropriate, and see if it is possible to disassociate the defendant's case from those features.

It may therefore be necessary for the advocate to explain the circumstances of the previous offences and the effect of the sentences imposed.

Mitigating features

The advocate should identify whether there are any mitigating factors which should be brought to the attention of the court to reduce the seriousness of the offence. For example, if the offence is an offence against the person, provocation can be relevant mitigation.

10.4.3.2 The offender

The Magistrates' Association Sentencing Guidelines set out some examples of offender mitigation, but there are frequently others to be considered in individual cases.

Age

The younger the offender, the more likely a court will be to pass a sentence designed to help him rather than punish him. Equally, a defendant of advanced age may receive more sympathetic treatment than would otherwise be the case.

Health (physical or mental)

One of the most common explanations given to a court for criminal conduct is that the defendant was under the effects of drink or drugs. As a basic rule, the voluntary ingestion of drink or drugs will not be good mitigation. If, on the other hand, there is evidence that the defendant is an alcoholic or a drug addict, this may point towards the need for a sentence which will overcome these problems, as opposed to the imposition of a punitive penalty.

Co-operation with the police

If a defendant has assisted the police with their enquiries by naming others involved in the crime, or by revealing the whereabouts of stolen property which is subsequently recovered, this may be effective mitigation.

The fact that the defendant confessed when being questioned by the police can also be presented in a favourable light as the defendant has not wasted time during the investigation process.

Voluntary compensation

A defendant who voluntarily makes good the damage which has been caused, or who makes voluntary payments of compensation, may get credit from the court for this. The motive behind the reparation is obviously important. It is far easier for a wealthy person to make voluntary payments of compensation than for a person of limited means. The court will therefore look not only at whether reparation has been made, but also at the reasons for it.

Remorse

Evidence of remorse is undoubtedly effective mitigation in many cases. The fact that an advocate apologises to the court on behalf of his client is unlikely to have any great effect. The court is likely to be more impressed with tangible signs of remorse, for example the defendant taking positive steps to tackle the problems which led him to commit the offence.

Other offender mitigation

The defendant's advocate will explain to the court the defendant's reasons for committing the offence. If the offence is one involving dishonesty, the fact that the defendant was in serious financial difficulty can be put forward, although it must be appreciated that a mere plea 'that the defendant found it difficult to live on benefit' is unlikely to meet with any sympathy. A stressful home background which has driven the defendant to committing an offence can validly be put forward.

The advocate should explain why the defendant committed the offence in a way that puts the offence in the context of the defendant's life generally. The court will want to try to understand the defendant and why he committed the offence.

If the defendant has been convicted following a plea of not guilty, it will not usually be appropriate then to explain to the court why the defendant committed the offence.

A person of previous good character should be given credit for this fact. The defendant should be given some credit if he has no previous convictions for the kind of offence of which he has been convicted. For example, the advocate might say in mitigation that, although the defendant has a record for dishonesty offences, he has no history of violence so that, in relation to the assault, he should be treated as a person of good character. The defendant should also be given some credit if there has been a substantial gap between the present offence and the last one, indicating that the offender has made a genuine attempt to 'go straight'.

The defendant's present situation is of great importance. The court will be looking for evidence of the defendant's stability, a regular home and job, and people who will be supportive of the defendant. The advocate will need to compare the defendant's present situation with the time the offence was committed.

The mere fact that the defendant or his family will be upset by the imposition of a custodial sentence is unlikely to have any effect on the court. If, however, it can be shown that there are exceptional circumstances, the effect of imprisonment can, in appropriate cases, be effective mitigation. If the defendant's partner is seriously ill, for example, a court may decide not to impose an immediate custodial sentence. This, of course, will depend on the nature of the offence. It must be appreciated that some offences are so serious that custody is inevitable.

If conviction will result in dismissal from employment, this factor may be taken into account by the court, although if the offence is related to the defendant's employment it will be less effective mitigation.

In driving offences, the loss of licence will inevitably lead to hardship, and this can be taken into account to avoid discretionary disqualification for the offence but not to avoid disqualification under the points system unless such hardship is exceptional.

When a fine is a possibility, the advocate will need to obtain considerable detail about the defendant's financial position (eg, income after tax, outgoings out of income, any capital) in order to help the court fix the fine at a proper level. In the magistrates' court, the defence will have to produce a completed means enquiry form. The advocate will also need to take the defendant's instructions on how much time the defendant will need to pay any fine imposed and the level of weekly instalments he could meet.

10.4.3.3 Sentence

The CJA 2003, s 144 requires a court to take into account in deciding the sentence to pass on an offender who has pleaded guilty:

(a)   the stage in the proceedings for the offence at which the offender indicated his intention to plead guilty; and

(b)   the circumstances in which the indication was given.

The object of this provision is to save court time and spare, for example, victims of crime the anxiety of giving evidence. Section 144 may result in a discount being given on any of the punitive elements of a sentence. The guilty plea reduction has no impact on sentencing decisions in relation to ancillary orders. For detailed guidance see the SGC Guideline: Reduction in Sentence for a Guilty Plea.

The possible sentencing options should be addressed, and the advocate should identify the advantages of the sentence he is arguing for and any detrimental effects of those he is arguing against.

The advocate should also deal with any ancillary orders, for example compensation, forfeiture and costs, which the prosecution may have applied for (see **10.2.10**).

The mitigating factors which are set out above are not exhaustive but are some of those most commonly used.

10.5 Further reading

Archbold: Criminal Pleading, Evidence and Practice (Sweet & Maxwell, 2005)

Blackstone's Criminal Practice (Oxford University Press, 2005)

Sprack, J, *Emmins on Criminal Procedure* (Oxford University Press, 2002)

Wallis and Halnan, *Wilkinson's Road Traffic Offences* (Sweet & Maxwell, 2003)

Chapter 11

Appeals

11.1 Appeals from the magistrates' court and youth court

A flowchart summarising appeals from the magistrates' court and youth court appears at **Appendix 1(P)**.

11.1.1 Appeals to the Crown Court

The defendant may appeal against conviction or sentence, but if he pleaded guilty he may only appeal against sentence unless he claims his plea was equivocal (Magistrates' Courts Act 1980, s 108).

If the Crown Court is satisfied that the plea was equivocal, it will remit the case to the magistrates' court with a direction that a plea of not guilty be entered.

Notice of appeal must be given both to the justices' clerk and the prosecution within 21 days of sentence. The Crown Court has power to grant leave to appeal out of time, but this is rarely exercised. An example of a notice of appeal appears at **Appendix 2(T)**.

Appeals against conviction and/or sentence will be heard by a Crown Court judge or a recorder sitting with between two and four magistrates. The appeal will take the form of a re-hearing. If the appeal is against conviction, all of the evidence will be heard again. If the appeal is against sentence, the prosecution will outline the facts of the case to the court who will decide what the appropriate sentence is.

On an appeal to the Crown Court, the court may:

(a) confirm, reverse or vary the magistrates' decision; or

(b) remit the matter (eg, on an equivocal plea) with its opinion thereon to the magistrates; or

(c) make such other order in the matter as the court thinks just and by such order exercise any power which the magistrates might have exercised. This means, for example, that orders for costs and compensation can be made.

The Crown Court may issue any sentence, which may be heavier or lighter than that of the magistrates, provided the sentence is one which the magistrates' court had power to issue. It is important, therefore, to point out to a defendant who wishes to appeal to the Crown Court that his sentence could be increased up to the maximum sentencing powers of the magistrates' court which originally dealt with the case.

11.1.2 Appeals to the High Court (Queen's Bench Division) by case stated

Either the defence or the prosecution may appeal from the decision of a magistrates' court to the High Court (Queen's Bench Division). The right of appeal is available where the magistrates' decision is wrong in law or was given in excess of the magistrates' jurisdiction (Magistrates' Courts Act 1980, s 111). The High Court may affirm, reverse or vary the decision of the magistrates or remit the case to the magistrates' court with its opinion. The procedure for the appeal is not a re-hearing. The appeal will be decided after hearing arguments on points of law put forward by the parties.

11.2   Appeals from the Crown Court

A flowchart summarising appeals from the Crown Court following a trial on indictment appears at **Appendix 1(Q)**.

A defendant may appeal against conviction to the Court of Appeal only with leave of the Court of Appeal or where the trial judge has issued a certificate of fitness for appeal. This applies whether the appeal is on a question of fact, a question of law or a mixed question of fact and law (Criminal Appeals Act 1995, s 1).

The test for granting leave to appeal is whether the court feels that the conviction is unsafe. In practice, this comes down to the question of whether there is a real danger that the defendant might have been prejudiced.

As a result of the decision in *Condron and Another v United Kingdom* (see **2.9.6**) where the procedure at trial is held to be in violation of art 6 of the European Convention on Human Rights (right to a fair trial), a conviction will be deemed unsafe.

A defendant may appeal his sentence with leave of the Court of Appeal. The Court of Appeal cannot increase the sentence but may either confirm or reduce it.

The prosecution cannot appeal to the Court of Appeal against the acquittal of a defendant or against the sentence imposed on the defendant. However, if it appears to the Attorney-General that the sentencing of a person in the Crown Court has been unduly lenient he may, with the leave of the Court of Appeal, refer the case to the Court of Appeal to review the sentencing of that person. On such a referral, the Court of Appeal may quash any sentence passed on the defendant and, in place of it, pass such sentence as it thinks appropriate for the case and in accordance with the powers which the Crown Court had in dealing with that person.

11.3   New prosecution right of appeal against termination rulings

Part 9 of CJA 2003 creates two new categories of prosecution appeal to the Court of Appeal:

(a)   a general right of appeal against certain (termination or de facto termination) rulings made by a judge during trial; and

(b)   other rulings in respect to evidence.

These provisions only apply to trials on indictment. There are important procedural differences between the two categories. The provisions in respect to appeals against evidentiary rulings are not in force at the time of writing.

The first set of appeal provisions in s 58, previously titled 'termination rulings' in the Bill, refer to those rulings that have the effect of stopping the case such as a stay of the indictment (for abuse of process) or a successful submission of no case to answer.

The second set of provisions in s 62 refers to more routine evidentiary rulings defined by s 63(2) as those which significantly weaken the prosecution case. The exclusion of a confession under ss 76 or 78 of the Police and Criminal Evidence Act 1984 may remove evidence which is central to the prosecution case from the trial and will amount to an evidentiary ruling provided it relates to a qualifying offence.

No appeal under Pt 9 can be made in respect of decisions to discharge a jury or in relation to matters which may be appealed under other legislation.

Leave is required before a ruling can be appealed and the Court of Appeal can only reverse a ruling where it is satisfied that the ruling was wrong in law, involved an error of law or principle or was not reasonable (s 67).

A more detailed consideration of the topic is beyond the scope of this book.

11.4 Further reading

See, for example:

Archbold: Criminal Pleading, Evidence and Practice (Sweet & Maxwell, 2005)

Blackstone's Criminal Practice (Oxford University Press, 2005)

John Sprack, *Emmins on Criminal Procedure* (Oxford University Press, 2005)

APPENDICES

Appendix 1

Procedural Charts and Diagrams

(A)   An overview of criminal procedure

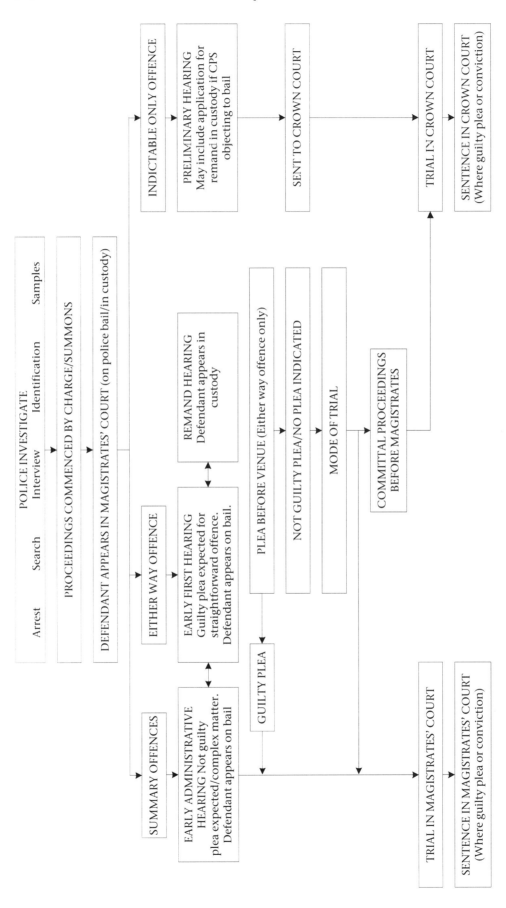

(B)   Police ranks

SUPERINTENDENT

CHIEF INSPECTOR*

INSPECTOR

SERGEANT

CONSTABLE

* Not a significant rank under PACE 1984

(C)   Police station procedure

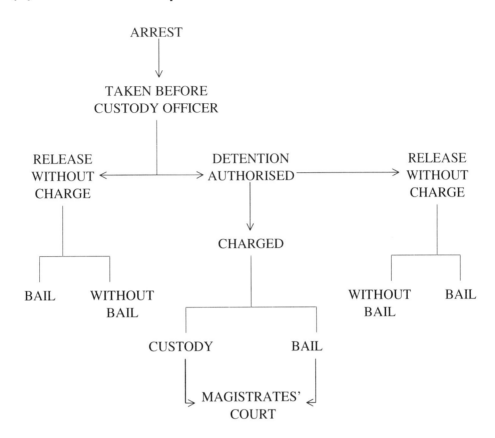

(D) The detention process

Hours

0.00   *Arrival at the police station.* Detention clock begins (but see s 41 for exceptional cases involving arrest outside England and Wales).

0.10   *Detention authorised.* Insufficient evidence to charge detention necessary to secure or preserve evidence or obtain such evidence by questioning the suspect (s 37(2)). Review clock begins.

6.10   Latest time for *first review of detention.* Carried out by inspector. Suspect, or solicitor if available, must be given chance to make representations (s 40). Must be noted in custody record.

15.10   Latest time for *second review of detention.* Must be noted in custody record. Thereafter at 9-hourly intervals (s 40).

24.00   *Suspect to be released (with or without bail) or charged* unless superintendent has reasonable grounds for believing:

     (a)   detention grounds in s 37(2) still exist; and

     (b)   offence for which suspect arrested is an arrestable offence; and

     (c)   investigation conducted diligently and expeditiously.

     Authorisation cannot be granted before second review or after 24 hours (s 42).

36.00   *Superintendent's authority expires.* Suspect to be released (with or without bail) or charged unless extension of warrant of further detention obtained from magistrates' court. A warrant of further detention is only available if the offence is a serious arrestable offence and the grounds in s 43 are satisfied.

72.00   *Maximum period warrant can authorise expires.* Suspect to be released (with or without bail) or charged unless extension of warrant obtained from magistrates (s 43).

96.00   *Absolute maximum period of detention.* Suspect to be released (with or without bail) or charged.

(E)   Commencement of criminal proceedings

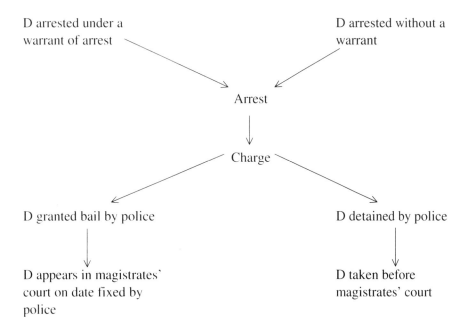

OR

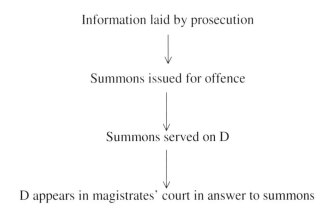

(F) Contested bail application procedure

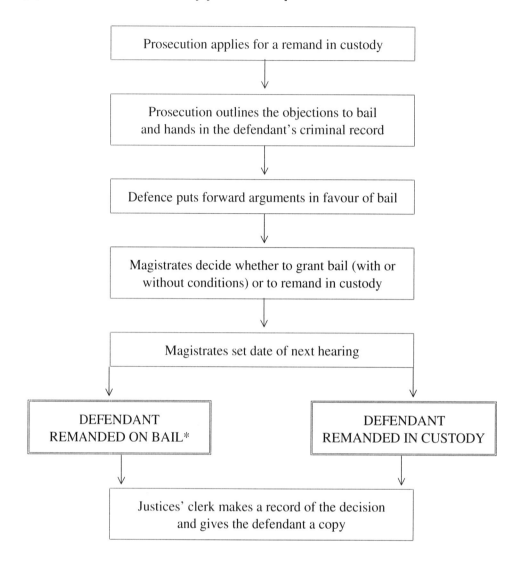

* *Note*: If the magistrates require a surety, the surety will have to enter into his/her recognisance before the defendant is released.

(G) Witness unavailable (CJA 2003, s 116)

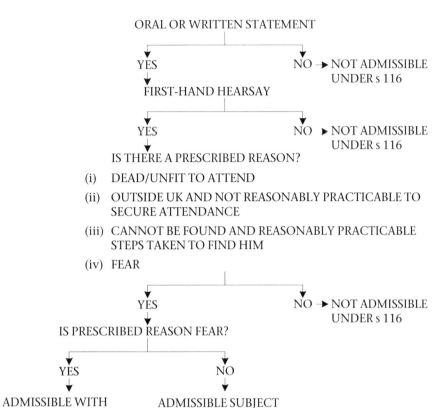

ORAL OR WRITTEN STATEMENT

YES   NO → NOT ADMISSIBLE
                      UNDER s 116

FIRST-HAND HEARSAY

YES   NO ▸ NOT ADMISSIBLE
                      UNDER s 116

IS THERE A PRESCRIBED REASON?

(i)   DEAD/UNFIT TO ATTEND

(ii)   OUTSIDE UK AND NOT REASONABLY PRACTICABLE TO
       SECURE ATTENDANCE

(iii) CANNOT BE FOUND AND REASONABLY PRACTICABLE
       STEPS TAKEN TO FIND HIM

(iv)   FEAR

YES   NO → NOT ADMISSIBLE
                      UNDER s 116

IS PRESCRIBED REASON FEAR?

YES   NO

ADMISSIBLE WITH   ADMISSIBLE SUBJECT
LEAVE   TO A GENERAL
(court admits the   DISCRETION TO
statement if in the   EXCLUDE (s 126)
interests of justice
(s 116(4))

(H) Documentary hearsay (CJA 2003, s 117)

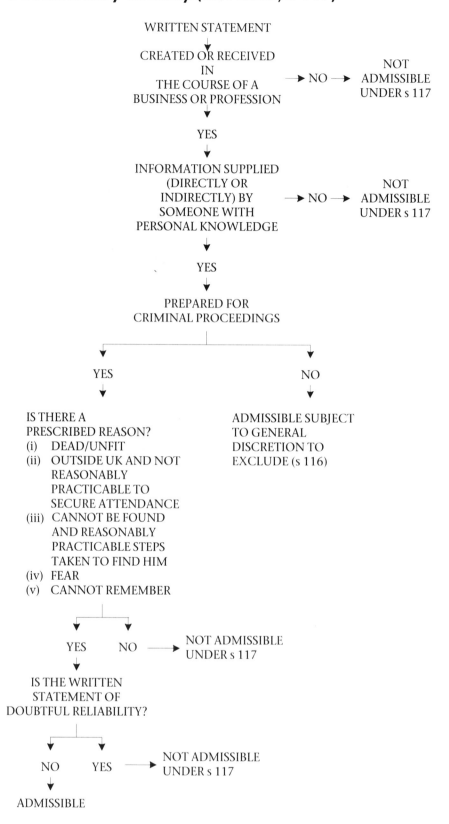

(I)   Magistrates' court procedure: Not guilty plea

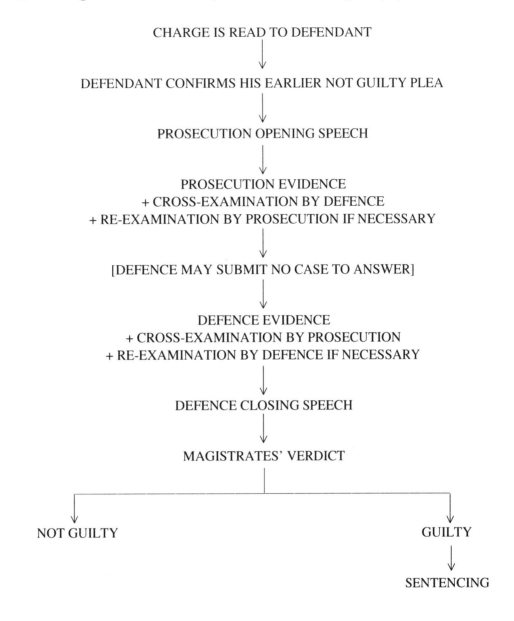

CHARGE IS READ TO DEFENDANT

↓

DEFENDANT CONFIRMS HIS EARLIER NOT GUILTY PLEA

↓

PROSECUTION OPENING SPEECH

↓

PROSECUTION EVIDENCE
+ CROSS-EXAMINATION BY DEFENCE
+ RE-EXAMINATION BY PROSECUTION IF NECESSARY

↓

[DEFENCE MAY SUBMIT NO CASE TO ANSWER]

↓

DEFENCE EVIDENCE
+ CROSS-EXAMINATION BY PROSECUTION
+ RE-EXAMINATION BY DEFENCE IF NECESSARY

↓

DEFENCE CLOSING SPEECH

↓

MAGISTRATES' VERDICT

NOT GUILTY   GUILTY

↓

SENTENCING

(J)   Plea before venue and mode of trial procedure

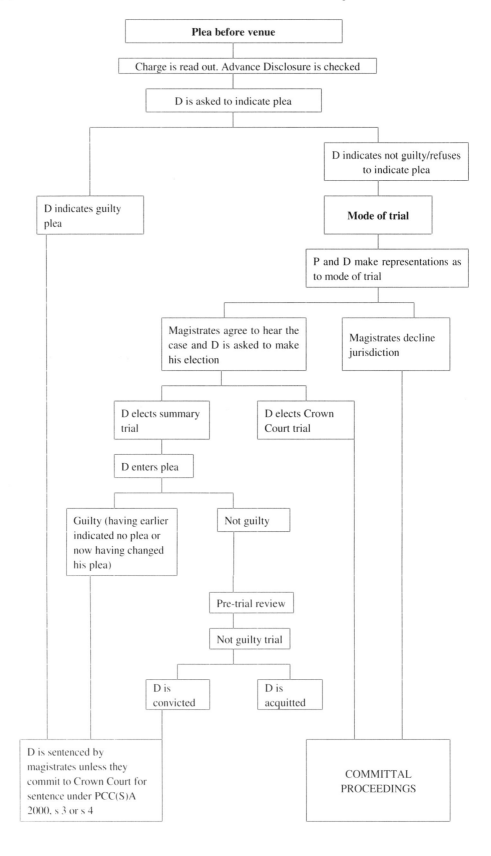

(K) Committal without consideration of the evidence (MCA 1980, s 6(2))

DEFENDANT PRESENT (NO PLEA TAKEN)

↓

CHARGE READ TO DEFENDANT

↓

JUSTICES' CLERK CHECKS ALL EVIDENCE
SERVED ON DEFENDANT'S SOLICITOR
(MCA 1980, s 5B STATEMENTS)

↓

DEFENCE RAISES NO OBJECTIONS TO EVIDENCE

↓

DEFENDANT COMMITTED

↓

WRITTEN EVIDENCE WARNING
(CPIA 1996, s 68)

↓

REPRESENTATION ORDER
(EXTEND TO COVER CROWN COURT)

↓

BAIL

(L)   Committal with consideration of the evidence (MCA 1980, s 6(1))

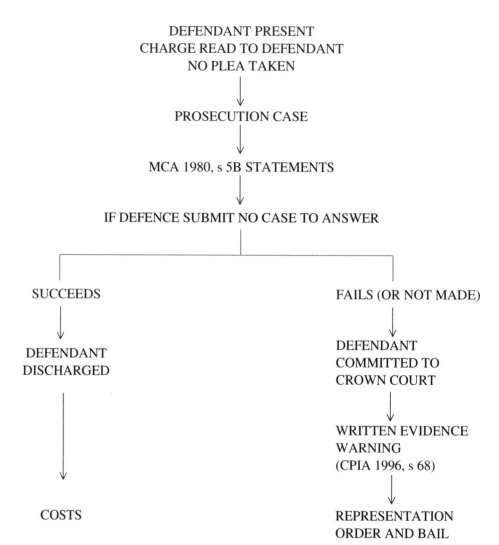

(M) Crown Court procedure: Not guilty plea

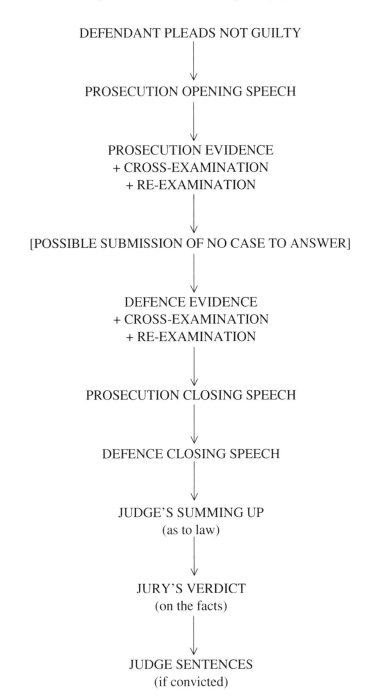

DEFENDANT PLEADS NOT GUILTY

↓

PROSECUTION OPENING SPEECH

↓

PROSECUTION EVIDENCE
+ CROSS-EXAMINATION
+ RE-EXAMINATION

↓

[POSSIBLE SUBMISSION OF NO CASE TO ANSWER]

↓

DEFENCE EVIDENCE
+ CROSS-EXAMINATION
+ RE-EXAMINATION

↓

PROSECUTION CLOSING SPEECH

↓

DEFENCE CLOSING SPEECH

↓

JUDGE'S SUMMING UP
(as to law)

↓

JURY'S VERDICT
(on the facts)

↓

JUDGE SENTENCES
(if convicted)

(N)   The Criminal Justice Act 2003: Sentencing scheme for adult offenders

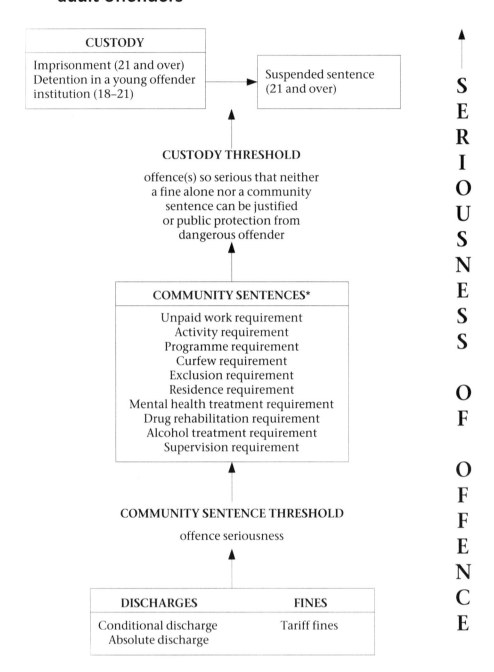

* Selection of particular requirements necessitates justification in terms
of both 'suitability' for the offender and restrictions on liberty
commensurate with the 'seriousness of offence'.

(O) Magistrates' court and Crown Court sentencing procedures

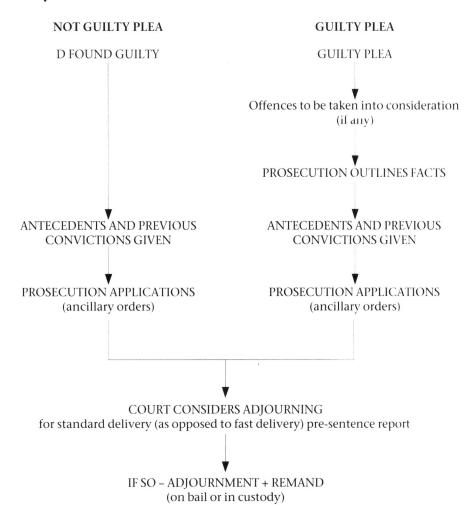

NOT GUILTY PLEA

D FOUND GUILTY

GUILTY PLEA

GUILTY PLEA

Offences to be taken into consideration
(if any)

PROSECUTION OUTLINES FACTS

ANTECEDENTS AND PREVIOUS
CONVICTIONS GIVEN

ANTECEDENTS AND PREVIOUS
CONVICTIONS GIVEN

PROSECUTION APPLICATIONS
(ancillary orders)

PROSECUTION APPLICATIONS
(ancillary orders)

COURT CONSIDERS ADJOURNING
for standard delivery (as opposed to fast delivery) pre-sentence report

IF SO – ADJOURNMENT + REMAND
(on bail or in custody)

IF NOT

MITIGATION

SENTENCE

(P)   Summary trials: Appeals

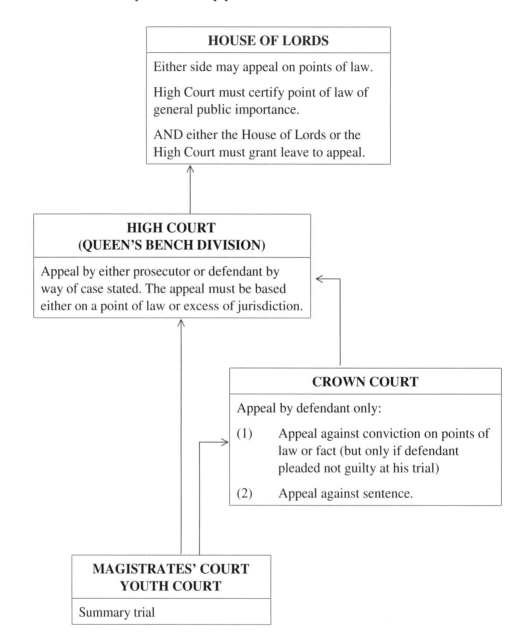

(Q) Trial on indictment: Appeals

HOUSE OF LORDS
Appeal on points of law only
Court of Appeal must certify point of law of general public importance; AND Court of Appeal or House of Lords must grant leave to appeal.
Either side may appeal.
(Attorney-General's references may reach House of Lords.)
(Attorney-General's references on sentence may also reach House of Lords.)

↑

COURT OF APPEAL (CRIMINAL DIVISION)
Appeal by defendant only
(1) against conviction – on a point of law or fact or mixed law and fact – leave required (unless trial judge has issued certificate of fitness for appeal).
(2) against sentence – leave required (unless trial judge has issued certificate of fitness for appeal).
[Following an acquittal in the Crown Court, the Attorney-General may refer a point of law for clarification to Court of Appeal – but this does not affect the acquittal (Criminal Justice Act 1972, s 36).]
Where the Attorney-General believes that the trial judge has imposed a sentence which is unduly lenient (in certain serious offences) he may refer the case to the Court of Appeal where the sentence can be replaced by one the Court of Appeal considers to be more appropriate (Criminal Justice Act 1988, ss 35, 36).

↑

CROWN COURT
Trial on indictment before judge and jury

(R)   Committal proceedings to Crown Court trial

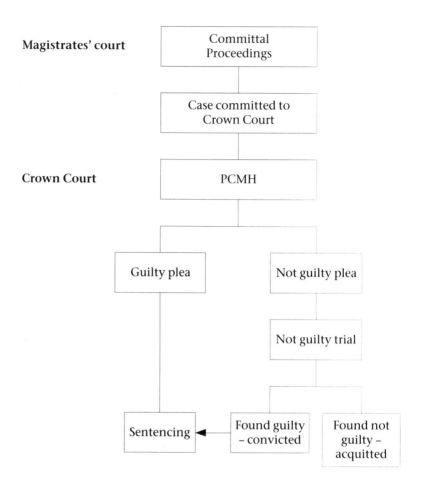

(S)   Sending for trial to Crown Court

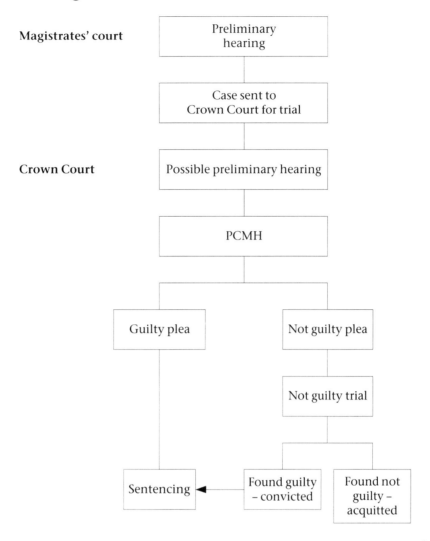

(T)   Summary trial: Summary offence

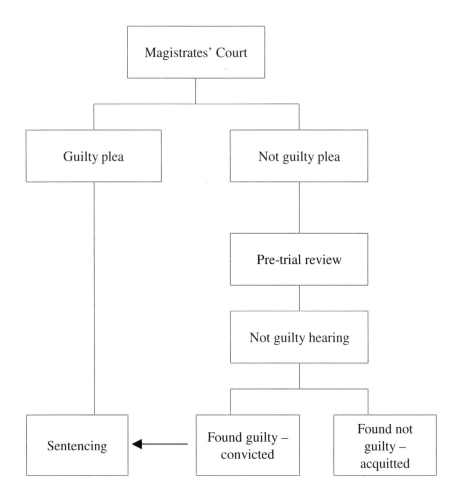

(U) Bad character: Defendant (CJA 2003, s 101)

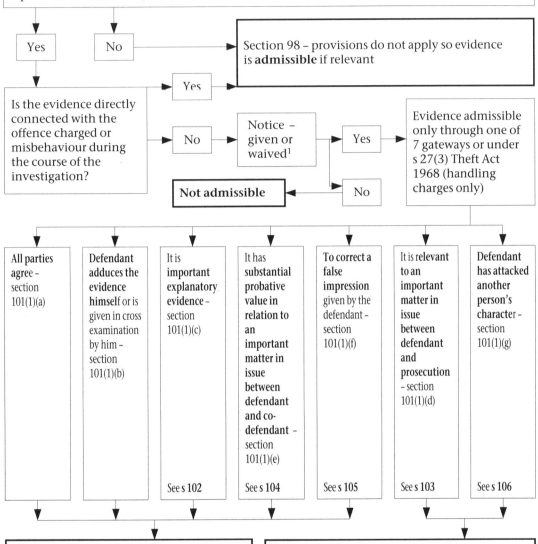

Is the evidence of, or of a disposition towards, misconduct (commission of an offence or other reprehensible behaviour)?

Yes

No

Section 98 – provisions do not apply so evidence is **admissible** if relevant

Is the evidence directly connected with the offence charged or misbehaviour during the course of the investigation?

Yes

No

Notice – given or waived[1]

Yes

No

Not admissible

Evidence admissible only through one of 7 gateways or under s 27(3) Theft Act 1968 (handling charges only)

All parties agree – section 101(1)(a)

Defendant adduces the evidence **himself** or is given in cross examination by him – section 101(1)(b)

It is important explanatory evidence – section 101(1)(c)

See s 102

It has substantial probative value in relation to an important matter in issue between defendant and co-defendant – section 101(1)(e)

See s 104

To correct a false impression given by the defendant – section 101(1)(f)

See s 105

It is relevant to an important matter in issue between defendant and prosecution – section 101(1)(d)

See s 103

Defendant has attacked another person's character – section 101(1)(g)

See s 106

Automatically **admissible**.[2] Court must record reasons where it makes a ruling

Admissible but court must not admit evidence if, on an application by the defendant to exclude it, it appears to the court that the admission of the evidence would have such an adverse effect on the fairness of the proceedings – section 101(3).

Considerations may include:
- Strength of the other evidence on the matter in issue (the more tenuous the evidence, the more likely the admission of that evidence will be prejudicial)
- The strength of the evidence of bad character (when it is disputed by the defendant)

Court must record reasons where it makes a ruling

[1] *Crim PR, rule 35.9*
[2] *It is unclear whether s 78 PACE 1984 and common law discretion to exclude apply – where evidence is adduced by a defendant (eg, under s 101(1)(e)) s 78 cannot apply as it is not prosecution evidence*

(V) Bad character: Non-defendant (CJA 2003, s 100)

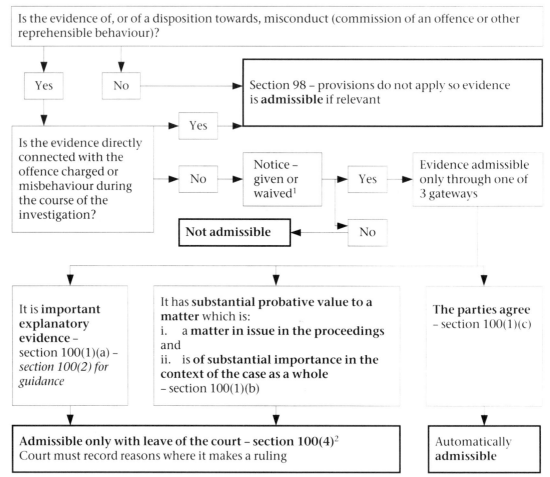

[1]CrimPR, 35.9

[2]It is suggested that the requirement for leave does not introduce a further element of discretion, it merely ensures the court checks that the criteria are met.

Notice – CrimPR, Part 35

Non-defendants
- Notice to introduce in a prescribed form
  - Not more than 14 days after initial disclosure, or
  - As soon as reasonably practicable, where the application concerns a non-defendant who is to be invited to give (or has given) evidence for a defendant
- Notice to exclude in writing not more than 14 days after receipt of notice

Defendants
- Notice by prosecutor in prescribed form with initial disclosure
- Notice by co-accused in prescribed form not more than 14 days after initial disclosure
- Notice to exclude not more than 7 days after receipt of notice

But – in either case
- Requirements for notice may be waived by the defendant
- Court may shorten notice periods or allow application in different form or orally if it is in the interest of justice to do so

Reasons – Section 110 CJA 2003

The court must give reasons which must be recorded in the register of
- a ruling on whether an item of evidence is evidence of a person's bad character
- a ruling on whether an item of such evidence is admissible under section 100 or 101 (including any ruling on an application under section 101(3))

Appendix 2

Documents

(A) Custody record

BLANKSHIRE POLICE
CUSTODY RECORD

Station: WEYFORD	EM No:		Custody No: WE 17963 9

1. Reasons for Arrest: TAKING A CONVEYANCE – s12(1) THEFT ACT 1968, THEFT OF £750 – s1(1) THEFT ACT 1968

2. † Comment made by person if present when facts of arrest explained
Yes ☐   No ☑   If "Yes" record on Log of Events

3. Place of Arrest: 123 SOMERSET AVENUE, WEYFORD

4.

	Time	Date
Arrested at:	20.45	30/7/00
Arrived at Station:	21.00	30/7/00
Relevant Time:	21.00	30/7/00

Condition on Arrival: ......
Relevant time not applicable ☐ ✓ if appropriate

5. DETENTION DECISION   *Delete as appropriate
A. Detention authorised*:
B. Detention not authorised*
Signature: John Platt
Name: JOHN PLATT
Time: 21.10   Date: 30 / 7 / 00

REASON FOR DETENTION:
(i)   To charge .... ☐
&/or (ii) Other authority (state authority) .... ☐
&/or (iii) Other secure or preserve evidence .... ☐
&/or (iv) To obtain evidence by questioning .... ☑
Record grounds for detention – MUST complete for (iii) and (iv).
ARRESTED IN POSSESSION OF PROPERTY STOLEN FROM MOTOR VEHICLE, DETENTION NECESSARY TO OBTAIN EVIDENCE BY QUESTIONING

Person present when grounds recorded: Yes ☑ : No ☐ ×
Person informed of grounds: Yes ☑ : No ☐ ×
x : If 'No', in either case, record reason(s) in Log of Events

6. † Comment made by person when informed of detention
Yes ☐   No ☑   If "Yes" record on Log of Events

7. Drugs Referral Information leaflet issued:
Time: ......   Date: ...... / ...... / ......

OFFICER OPENING CUSTODY RECORD
Signature: John Platt
Name: JOHN PLATT
Rank/No: SGT 3456
Time: 21.10   Date: 30 / 7 / 00

11.97

8. PERSONAL DETAILS
Surname: EVERETT
Forename(s): RONALD EDWIN
Address: 123 SOMERSET AVENUE, WEYFORD, BLANKSHIRE
Telephone No: 01730 400902 Post Code: WE2 1AE
Occupation: LABOURER
Age: 43   Date of Birth: 25/6/57
Height: 1M 80   Sex: Male/Female
Ethnic Origin: GB
Place of Birth: GB

9. Arresting Officer: ALAN BROWN
Rank: DC   No: 2907   Stn: WEYFORD

10. Officer in the case: ALAN BROWN
Rank: DC   No: 2907   Stn: WEYFORD

11. DETAINED PERSON'S RIGHTS
An extract from a notice setting out my rights has been read to me and I have been given a copy. I have also been provided with a written notice setting out my entitlements while in custody.
Signature: Everett
Time: 21.10   Date: 30 / 7 / 00

LEGAL ADVICE REQUESTED
I want to speak to a solicitor as soon as practicable:
Signature: Everett
Time: 21.10   Date: 30 / 7 / 00

LEGAL ADVICE DECLINED
I have been informed that I may speak to a solicitor IN PERSON or ON THE TELEPHONE:
Signature: ......
Time: ......   Date: ...... / ...... / ......
I DO NOT WANT TO SPEAK TO A SOLICITOR at this time:
Signature: ......
Time: ......   Date: ...... / ...... / ......
† Reasons, if given, for not wanting legal advice:

Notification of named person: Requested Yes ☐ : No ☑
Nominated person: ......
Detainees signature: ......

12. APPROPRIATE ADULT / **INTERPRETER**
Yes ☐ : No ☑   Yes ☐ : No ☑
Notices served, rights and grounds for detention explained in presence of Appropriate Adult/Interpreter.
Signature of A/Adult: ......
Time: ......   Date: ...... / ...... / ......
Signature of Interpreter: ......
Time: ......   Date: ...... / ...... / ......

13. FOREIGN NATIONALS
Embassy/Consulate informed: Yes ☐ : Not Applicable ☑
(Record details in Log of Events)
Force Immigration Dept informed: Yes ☐ : Record on 7K

RECORD OF RIGHTS

| Surname | EVERETT | Custody Record No. | WE | 17963 | 9 |

Interpreter present   Yes ☐ No ☑   Detained person informed of rights   Yes ☑ No ☐
(If No, record reason on detention log)

"You have the right to have someone informed that you have been detained. You have the right to consult privately with an independent solicitor either in person, in writing or on the telephone. Independent legal advice is available from the duty solicitor free of charge. You also have the right to consult a copy of the Codes of Practice covering police powers and procedures. You may do any of these things now, but if you do not you may still do so at any time whilst detained at the police station."

Solicitor requested   Yes ☑ No ☐
(If No, remind the person of the right to speak to a solicitor, in person, or on the telephone)

Solicitor requested   Yes ☑ No ☐
(If No, ask for and if applicable, record reason)

Name of solicitor requested   MR. ANDREW CRAWFORD

Reason, if given, for not
wanting legal advice

Notification of named person requested   Yes ☐ No ☑

Details of nominated person (if appropriate)

Name

Address

Telephone number

Details of appropriate adult (if appropriate)

Name

Address

Telephone number

An extract from a notice setting out a detained person's rights has been read to me and I have been given a copy. I have been provided with a written notice setting out a detained person's entitlements while in custody.

I ~~do~~/do not .... want a person informed.

I understand that my right to speak to a solicitor includes the right to speak on the telephone.

I do ~~/do not want to speak~~ to a solicitor at this time.

Signature   Everett   Time 21.10   Date 30/7/00

DETENTION LOG

Surname: EVERETT   Custody Record No. WE | 17963 | 9

Date	Time		Signed
30/7/00	21.10	Detention authorised for questioning. Everett informed of rights. Requested access to solicitor but no notification to a third party.	JPlatt
30/7/00	21.15	Search of Everett. Wallet marked 'A' containing £10 retained.	JPlatt
30/7/00	21.20	Telephoned Mr. Andrew Crawford, Solicitor at Everett's request. Consultation on telephone between Everett and solicitor. Mr. Crawford asked note to be made that travelling to station to see Everett.	JPlatt
30/7/00	21.30	Everett taken cup of tea and placed in cell.	JPlatt
30/7/00	21.45	Mr. Crawford, Solicitor arrived to see Everett. Everett taken from cell to interview room by PC Smith. Private consultation with solicitor.	JPlatt
30/7/00	22.30	Everett transferred to custody of Inspector Kingston for identification parade.	Platt
30/7/00	23.05	Everett transferred to my custody by Inspector Kingston who confirmed all provisions of Identification Code complied with.	JPlatt
30/7/00	23.15	Everett transferred to custody of DC Brown. Taken to interview room. Interviewed by DC Brown in presence of WDC Carpenter and Mr Crawford, Solicitor.	JPlatt
30/7/00	23.45	Everett returned to my custody by DC Brown who stated to me that all provisions of Detention Code complied with.	JPlatt
30/7/00	23.55	Sufficient evidence to charge Everett. Everett placed in cell by PC Smith while papers prepared.	JPlatt
31/7/00	00.20	Everett charged. Copy charge supplied.	JPlatt
31/7/00	00.25	Authorised Everett to be kept in custody on grounds I believed that he would not answer bail. Informed Everett and Mr. Crawford accordingly.	Platt
31/7/00	00.55	Everett returned to his cell by PC Smith. Given snack and cup of tea.	Platt
31/7/00	01.00	Visited. Everett awake. Detention reviewed. No representations. Ground for detention unchanged.	JPlatt

DETENTION LOG

Surname | EVERETT | Custody Record No. | WE | 17963 | 9

Date	Time		Signed
31/7/00	02.00	Visited. Asleep.	J Platt
31/7/00	03.00	Visited. Asleep.	J Platt
31/7/00	04.00	Visited. Asleep.	J Platt
31/7/00	05.00	Visited. Asleep.	J Platt
31/7/00	06.00	Visited. Asleep.	J Platt
31/7/00	07.00	Everett given breakfast.	J Platt
31/7/00	08.30	Transferred to custody of Group 4 Security to take to Weyford Magistrates' Court.	J Platt

(B)   Volunteer's notice

BLANKSHIRE POLICE

**PERSON ATTENDING VOLUNTARILY AT POLICE STATION
AND NOT UNDER ARREST**

You can speak to a solicitor at the police station at any time, day or night. It will cost you nothing.

If you do not know a solicitor, or you cannot contact your own solicitor, ask for the duty solicitor. He or she is nothing to do with the police. Or you can ask to see a list of local solicitors.

You can talk to the solicitor in private on the telephone, and the solicitor may come and see you at the police station.

If the police want to question you, you can ask for the solicitor to be there. If there is a delay ask the police to contact the solicitor again. You can ask the police to wait for the solicitor to be at the interview.

The Law Society   **The Criminal Defence Service**

(C)   Notice to detained person

BLANKSHIRE POLICE

Notice to Detained Person

> The section in capital letters is to be read to the detained person by the custody officer before giving the notice to the detained person.

YOU HAVE THE RIGHT TO:

(1)   SPEAK TO AN INDEPENDENT SOLICITOR FREE OF CHARGE
(2)   HAVE SOMEONE TOLD THAT YOU HAVE BEEN ARRESTED
(3)   CONSULT THE CODES OF PRACTICE COVERING POLICE POWERS AND PROCEDURES.

YOU MAY DO ANY OF THESE THINGS NOW, BUT IF YOU DO NOT, YOU MAY STILL DO SO ANY TIME WHILST DETAINED AT THE POLICE STATION.

If you are asked questions about a suspected offence, you do not have to say anything. But it may harm your defence if you do not mention when questioned something which you later rely on in court. Anything you do say may be given in evidence.

Free Legal Advice

You can speak to a solicitor at the police station at any time, day or night. It will cost you nothing.

Access to legal advice can only be delayed in certain circumstances (see Annex B of Code of Practice C).

If you do not know a solicitor, or you cannot contact your own solicitor, ask for the duty solicitor. He or she is nothing to do with the police. Or you can ask to see a list of local solicitors.

You can talk to the solicitor in private on the telephone, and the solicitor may come to see you at the police station.

If the police want to question you, you can ask for the solicitor to be there.

If there is a delay, ask the police to contact the solicitor again. Normally, the police must not question you until you have spoken to the solicitor. However, there are certain circumstances in which the police may question you without a solicitor being present (see paragraph 6.6 of Code of Practice C).

If you want to see a solicitor, tell the custody officer at once. You can ask for legal advice at any time during your detention. Even if you tell the police you do not want a solicitor at first, you can change your mind at any time.

Your right to legal advice does not entitle you to delay procedures under the Road Traffic Act 1988 which require the provision of breath, blood and urine specimens.

THE LAW SOCIETY   The Criminal Defence Service

The right to have someone informed of your detention.

You may on request have one person known to you, or who is likely to take an interest in your welfare, informed at public expense as soon as practicable of your whereabouts. If the person you name cannot be contacted you may choose up to two alternatives. If they too cannot be contacted the custody officer has discretion to allow further attempts until the information can be conveyed. This right can only be delayed in exceptional circumstances (see Annex B of Code of Practice C).

The right to consult the Codes of Practice.

The Codes of Practice will be made available to you on request. These Codes govern police procedures. The right to consult the Codes of Practice does not entitle you to delay unreasonably any necessary investigative and administrative action, neither does it allow procedures under the Road Traffic Act of 1988 requiring the provision of breath, blood or urine specimens to be delayed.

The right to a copy of the Custody Record.

A record of your detention will be kept by the custody officer. When you leave police detention or are taken before a court, you and your legal representative or the appropriate adult shall be supplied on request with a copy of the custody record as soon as practicable. This entitlement lasts for 12 months after your release from police detention.

(D) Notice of entitlements

BLANKSHIRE POLICE

NOTICE OF ENTITLEMENTS

This notice summarises provisions contained in Codes C and D of the Codes of Practice regarding your entitlements whilst in custody. The letters and numbers in brackets relate to the appropriate Code and paragraph references. If you require more detailed information please ask to consult the Codes.

All detainees should read parts A and B of the notice. Part C explains provisions which apply to juveniles and persons suffering from a mental disorder or are mentally vulnerable and Part D explains additional provisions which apply to citizens of independent commonwealth countries and nationals of foreign countries.

PART A – GENERAL ENTITLEMENTS

Whilst in custody you are entitled to the following:–

1. **Visits and contact with outside persons**
    In addition to your rights to have someone informed of your arrest, and legal advice, you may receive visits, at the custody officer's discretion. Unless certain conditions apply you may also make one telephone call, and be supplied with writing materials ('C'5.4 and 5.6).

2. **Reasonable Standards of Physical Comfort**
    Where practicable you should have your own cell ('C'8.1), which is clean, heated, ventilated and lit ('C'8.2). Bedding should be clean and serviceable ('C'8.3).

3. **Adequate Food and Drink**
    Three meals per day. Drinks with and, upon reasonable request, between meals ('C' 8.6).

4. **Access to Toilets and Washing Facilities** ('C' 8.4).

5. **Replacement Clothing**
    If your own clothes are taken from you, you must be given replacements that are clean and comfortable ('C'8.5).

6. **Medical Attention**
    You may ask to see the police surgeon (or other doctor at your own expense) for a medical examination, or if you require medication. You may also be allowed to take or apply your own medication at appropriate times, but in the case of controlled drugs the police surgeon will supervise you when doing so ('C'9.8– 'C'9.12).

7. **Exercise**
    Where practicable, brief outdoor exercise every day ('C'8.7).

8. **If in 'Police Detention' to make representations when your detention is reviewed**
    When the grounds for your detention are periodically reviewed, you have a statutory right to say why you think you should be released, unless you are unfit to do so because of your condition or behaviour ('C'15.3 and 15.3B).

PART B – CONDUCT OF INTERVIEWS

1. Interview rooms should be adequately heated, lit and ventilated ('C'12.4).

2. Persons being interviewed should not be required to stand ('C'12.6).

3. In any 24 hour period you must be allowed at least 8 hours rest, normally at night 'C'12.2).

4. Breaks should be made at recognised meal times, and short breaks for refreshments should normally be made at intervals of approximately two hours ('C'12.8).

5. Interviewing officers should identify themselves by name and rank (or by warrant number in terrorism cases) ('C'12.7).

PART C – APPROPRIATE ADULTS

If you are under 17 years of age or suffering from a mental disorder or are mentally vulnerable, you should be assisted by an 'appropriate adult' as explained in Code C, paragraph 1.7. A solicitor present at the station in a professional capacity may not be the appropriate adult ('C' Note 1F). The appropriate adult will be present when you are:

1. informed of and served with notices explaining the rights of detained persons, and when informed of the grounds for detention ('C'3.17);

2. interviewed (except in urgent cases), or provide or sign a written statement ('C'11.12);

3. intimately searched ('C' Annex A, paragraph 5);

4. cautioned ('C'10.12);

5. given information, asked to sign documentation, or asked to give consent regarding any identification procedure ('D'2.12–2.14); or

6. charged ('C'16.1); or

7. when the grounds for detention are periodically reviewed ('C'15.3).

PART D – FOREIGN NATIONALS/COMMONWEALTH CITIZENS

If you are a citizen of a foreign or commonwealth country, you are entitled to the following:

1. To communicate at any time with your High Commission, Embassy or Consulate, and have them told of your whereabouts and the grounds for your detention ('C'7.1).

2. To private visits from a consular officer to talk, or to arrange for legal advice ('C'7.3).

(E)   Record of tape-recorded interview

BLANKSHIRE POLICE

RECORD OF TAPE RECORDED INTERVIEW

Name of person interviewed __Ronald E. Everrett__   at   __Weyford__   Police Station

Date of interview __30.7.0-__   Time commenced __22.30__   Time concluded __22.45__

Interviewing Officer(s) __DC 2907 Brown__   Tape Reference __9_/WPS/1697__

Other Person(s) Present __Donald Crawford Solicitor__   Exhibit Number __AB/2__

This record consisting of __2__ pages is the exhibit referred to in the statement made and signed by me. The interviewee has been cautioned by me and informed that at the end of the interview a notice will be given to him/her about what will happen to the tapes

Signature   _Alan Brown_

Signature of officer preparing record   _____
(if different from above)

Tape Times		
50		Introductions. Caution.
		You have been positively identified as the man who took away a Jaguar
		from New Street this afternoon. What do you have to say?
	R	He's wrong. It wasn't me.
	2907	Well, he's certain about it. There was £750 stolen from that car and
		in your flat there is very nearly £750 in cash. How do you
		account for that?
	R	I've saved it. We're trying to buy a house.
30	2907	And the leather jacket is just a coincidence?
	R	I've told you. I don't know anything about any of it - lots of people
		have leather jackets.
00	2907	Was your wife with you this afternoon?
	R	Yes.
	2907	She remembers it differently from you.
	R	How do you mean?
	2907	She told us all about it - that you and she took the car and stole
		the money.
	R	You're lying.
	2907	No. It's written down. Want to think again?
	R	We didn't do it.
	2907	So she's lying

CONTINUATION OF RECORD OF TAPED INTERVIEW OF _____ Ronald E. Everett _____ PAGE

Tape Times	
R	[No reply]
2907	Well
R	We didn't do it. It's nothing to do with us. That's final.

Signature of officer preparing record   *Alan Brown*

(F)   Written statement under caution

BLANKSHIRE POLICE

STATEMENT

Commenced: 12.15
Finished: 12.45

WEYFORD Division
G Station

23 August 200-

I make this statement of my own free will. I understand that I need not say anything unless I wish to do so but that it may harm my defence if I do not mention now something which I later rely on in court. I also understand that anything I do say may be given in evidence.

(Signed)   *June South*

I had run out of food this morning and as a friend was coming to tea this evening I had to go to the shops. I took the children on the bus into Weyford. I went to Tescos. The kids played in the shop and made a lot of noise. I decided to buy some salmon for tea. I picked out as well some toothpaste for everyone, and some bread and margarine and other things. I paid for everything in the basket but did not pay for the salmon and toothpaste. I must have put the other things into my bag by mistake as I meant to pay for them because I had enough money. I was stopped outside the shop by a store detective and taken back inside. I never meant to steal anything.

(Signed)   *June South*

Statement and signatures witnessed by A. Butchers DC 1007

(G)   Solicitor's record of attendance at police station

POLICE STATION ATTENDANCE FORM	
UFN:	Book no:
Date:	Own/Duty
CLIENTS DETAILS	
Name:	Address:
Date of birth:	
Tel:	
Referral from third party: Yes/No	
Name:	Tel:
Address:	Relationship to client:
ARREST DETAILS	
Police station:	Custody no: Arrest/Voluntary
Tel:	Officer in case:
Time & Date of arrest:	Relevant time:
Allegation (Including date):	

	F/E				F/E	
Time of first call:			Time of request for attendance:			
Time of first contact with client:			Time of attendance:			
Time between call & contact: mins			Time between request & attendance: mins			
Delay in contact/attendance: Yes/No			If yes, reason:			

Access to client delayed: Yes/No	Extent of delay: hours
Reason:	
Representation made: Yes/No	
Appropriate adult required: Yes/No	Name:
Address:	Relationship to client:
	Police contacted AA: Yes/No
Tel:	Client advised on AA's role: Yes/No
Attendance required because of interview/ID parade/complaint: Yes/No	
If no attendance, reason:	
If attendance, sufficient benefit test met: Yes/No	

NAME:
UFN:

TELEPHONE CALLS						
Date	Time	R/A	Person spoken to	F/E	Instructions / Advice / Action	Duration

INFORMATION FROM POLICE	
Inspected custody record: Yes/No	

Search of client: Yes/No Tick if intimate	**Client's consent given:** Yes/No
Legal authority & reason:	
Evidence obtained:	

Search of premises: Yes/No	**Address**
Legal authority & reason S.32/S.18	
Evidence obtained:	

Samples taken: Yes/No	**Client's consent given:** Yes/No
Type: Intimate/non-intimate	**Refusal implications explained:** Yes/No
Legal authority & reason:	

Previous questioning/interview: Yes/No	
Details:	
Previous attendance at police station: Yes/No	**Was legal advice received:** Yes/No **Was it sought:** Yes/No

Client fit for interview: Yes/No	**FME called/attended:** Yes/No

Co-accused: Yes/No

Name	Solicitor	Known to client?	In custody?	Conflict?

Significant statement or silence: Yes/No	**Advised client to comment on this in** · **interview:** Yes/No

Consultation with officer	**Name:**

CONSULTATION WITH CLIENT

Previous convictions/cautions: Yes/No	
Details	

Outstanding criminal cases/on bail: Yes/No	
Details	

Health problems: Yes/No	
Details (including nature & effect of illness, & medication taken):	
FME called: Yes/No	Note in custody record: Yes/No

Other vulnerabilities (e.g. language): Yes/No	
Details	

Injuries: Yes/No	
Details (including description & cause):	
Witness to injuries: Yes/No	Name:
FME called: Yes/No	Affects fitness for IV: Yes/No
Note on custody record: Yes/No	Photographs required: Yes/No

Searches made/samples taken: Yes/No	Consent given: Yes/No

Witness(es):   Yes/No
Name & Address:
Alibi: Yes/No
Where & when:
Name & Address of alibi witness:

Advised client on implications from silence under   s34: Yes/No   s36: Yes/No   s37: Yes/No
Advised client to answer questions/remain silent/issued prepared statement
Reasons:
In interview, client answered questions/remained silent/issued statement/mixed

Complaint against police: Yes/No	Advised client on procedure for
Make complaint prior to release: Yes/No	complaint: Yes/No

Note: attach clients instructions on substance of allegations and issues in dispute.
Include instructions on role of co-suspects; and anything said by them.
Keep full note of any interview.

IDENTIFICATION PROCEDURES

Obtained original description provided by each witness: Yes/No	
Advised client on methods of identification & procedure: Yes/No	
Advised client of right of refusal & implications thereof: Yes/No	
Advised client to consent to:	
Client consented to:	Representation made:
Date of ID procedure:	Place: Type:
Result:	

Witness	Identified?	Witness remarks
1.	Yes/No	
2.	Yes/No	
3.	Yes/No	
4.	Yes/No	

Make full note separately of procedure used and checks made

ATTENDANCE DETAILS

Date of attendance	Outcome (enter bail to return/place: date: time)	Fee earner attending
1.		
2.		
3.		
4.		

OUTCOME

No further action: Yes/No	
Caution/warning/reprimand: Yes/No	Advised client of implications: Yes/No
Charge: Yes/No	
Advised client on implications of reply to charge & inference from silence: Yes/No	
Advise to client: reply to charge/remain silent	
Reasons:	
Time of charge:	Reply:
Advised client on prints, photos & DNA: Yes/No	

Bail refused: Yes/No	Representations made: Yes/No
Procedure for future application explained: Yes/No	Prospects of success: low/medium/high
Bail granted: Yes/No	Explained consequences of FTA: Yes/No
Conditions:	Explained consequences of breach: Yes/No

Charge (including date):			
Court:	Venue:	Date:	Time:

File allocated to		

Costs form completed: Yes/No

(H) Charge sheet

```
Police Station   WEYFORD            Custody No       WGG/0-/33
Station Code     WFF
Charged Persons Surname   DOE        Title            MR
          Forenames      JOHN
Place of Birth  GUILDFORD           Date of Birth    01/02/34

Address      NO FIXED ABODE
             WOODBRIDGE MEADOWS
             WEYFORD WE1 1AA
```

```
You are charged with the offence/s shown below.
You do not have to say anything. But it may harm your defence if you do not
mention anything now something which you later rely on in court.
Anything you do say may be given in evidence.
```

```
                                                Page 1 of 1

No: 1          Crime No: WG/0-/1234             Local Code: C203

ON MONDAY 15TH MAY 200- AT WEYFORD IN THE COUNTY OF BLANKSHIRE STOLE AN
AIRMAIL LETTER OF A VALUE UNKNOWN BELONGING TO CHARLES BLAKE


CONTRARY TO SECTION 1(1) OF THE THEFT ACT 1968
```

```
Reply to charges
          None

Charged Persons Signature  JDoe
```

```
Person Charging Name                    Charged 17/6/0-
Signature _____                         Time 10.30 am
Officer Charging Name
Signature _____   PS/333/DICKSON        Date ___
Officer In Case     INSP/N/MEAD
```

CHARGE RECORD

DETAINEE COPY

```
Police Station    WEYFORD          Custody No      WGG/0-/33
Station Code      WFF
Charged Persons Surname   DOE       Title           MR
              Forenames   JOHN
Place of Birth  GUILDFORD           Date of Birth   01/02/34
Address      NO FIXED ABODE
             WOODBRIDGE MEADOWS
             WEYFORD WE1 1AA
```

You are charged with the offence/s shown on the charge sheet.

You do not have to say anything. But it may harm your defence if you do not mention anything now something which you later rely on in court. Anything you do say may be given in evidence.

YOU ARE REQUIRED TO ATTEND COURT

at WEYFORD MAGS CT

on 20/06/0-   at 10 00 a.m.

If you fail without reasonable cause to surrender to the Court at the appointed place and time, you commit an offence for which you may be fined, imprisoned or both.

LEGAL AID

IF YOU REQUIRE LEGAL REPRESENTATION AT COURT AND CANNOT AFFORD A SOLICITOR YOU MAY BE ENTITLED TO LEGAL AID. IF YOU WISH TO APPLY FOR LEGAL AID A SPECIAL FORM IS OBTAINABLE FROM ANY POLICE STATION, MAGISTRATES CLERKS OFFICE, OR A SOLICITOR DEALING IN CRIMINAL LEGAL AID CASES.

YOU SHOULD MAKE YOUR APPLICATION IMMEDIATELY

THE COURT WILL NOT AUTOMATICALLY ADJOURN THE CASE WHEN THERE HAS BEEN A DELAY IN APPLYING FOR LEGAL AID.

PRODUCTION OF DRIVING LICENCE

If the offence with which you have been charged is one for which your driving licence may be endorsed (and the Inspector or Sergeant on duty at the station will advise you) you are required to have your driving licence at Court when you appear. If you are convicted you may be required to produce the licence.
FAILURE TO PRODUCE IT IS AN OFFENCE AND THE LICENCE IS AUTOMATICALLY SUSPENDED UNTIL IT IS PRODUCED.

(Section 101(4), Road Traffic Act, 1988).

```
Custody Officer    PS/333/DICKSON
Signature          _____
```

(I)   Summons

In Blankshire

Petty Sessional Division of Weyford

To: James Baker..the Defendant

      of   18 Dorset Avenue   Date of Birth: 20.8.1958

              Weyford   Unemployed

              Blankshire   being the last known or usual place of above

              BE1 8BT

THE INFORMATION of Barry Williams Sgt 891 of Blankshire Constabulary this day laid before me that you the Defendant, on 20th August 200–, at Station Road, Weyford in the said County drove a Ford Contrary to s. 2 Road Traffic Act 1988

Barry Williams

YOU THE DEFENDANT ARE THEREFORE HEREBY SUMMONED to appear on 1st November 200–, at 10.00 before the Magistrates' Court sitting at The Law Courts, The Civic Centre, Weyford, Blankshire to answer the said information.

DATED this 25th September 200–

Paul French

Justice of the Peace

LEGAL AID:— If you require details you should immediately communicate with the Clerk to the Justices at the address on the notice herewith.

CERTIFICATE OF SERVICE
(Magistrates' Courts Rules, 1981, Rule 67(2))

Defendant _____ JAMES   BAKER _____

I HEREBY CERTIFY that I this day served the within-named defendant with a document of which this is a true copy, in the manner shown a (a) below.

(a)   By sending it by post to him in a prepaid recorded delivery letter posted by me on   5 - 10 - 200 — at the WEYFORD   Post Office situated at   HIGH STREET, WEYFORD addressed as overleaf being his last known place of abode.

(b)   Delivering to him personally.

(c)   By leaving it for him with a person at the address overleaf, being the defendant's last known place of abode.

(d)   By sending it by post in a prepaid recorded delivery letter posted by me on
       at the   Post Office situated at

       to the registered office of the defendant company.

Dated this   5ᵗʰ   day of OCTOBER   20 0 —

_____ Signature
                J.C. Water

(J)   Application for the right to representation in criminal proceedings: Magistrates' court or Crown Court (Form A)

Application for the Right to
Representation in Criminal Proceedings:
Magistrates' Court or Crown Court

Form A

I apply for the right to representation for the purposes of proceedings before the   Crown Court ☐   Magistrates' court ☑   Youth court ☐

1. Personal details

1a	Surname	PRESCOTT
1b	Forename(s)	JAKE
1c	Title *Mr, Mrs, Miss, Ms, or another*	MR
1d	Date of birth	17.06.1983

1e Home address

10 AGRARIA ROAD
WEYFORD
WE2 7AF

1f Present address
If different from above

2. Case details

2a What charges have been brought against you? *Describe briefly what it is that you are accused of doing. For example, theft of £10 worth of CDs, or assault on a neighbour.*

ROBBERY OF A GAMEBOY ADVANCE MACHINE FROM A 14 YEAR OLD BOY IN A PEDESTRIAN SUBWAY DURING THE HOURS OF DARKNESS.

2b Are there any co-defendants in this matter?

No ☐   Yes ☑ If **Yes**, give their names

NOEL ALEXANDER

2c Give reasons why you and your co-defendants cannot be represented by the same solicitors

THERE IS A CONFLICT OF INTEREST. HE CLAIMS THAT I TOOK PART IN THE ROBBERY AND FORCED HIM TO PARTICIPATE. I DENY BEING PRESENT.

3. The Court Proceedings

3a   I am due to appear before

The NEWTOWN	magistrates' court ☑ youth court ☐
Date 21.01.200—	at 10 am / ~~pm~~

or

3b   I appeared before

The	magistrates' court ☐ youth court ☐
Date	at am / pm

and

Tick whichever applies

My case has been sent to the Crown Court for trial under Section 51 of the Crime and Disorder Act 1998	
My case has been transferred to the Crown Court for trial	
I was convicted and committed for sentence to the Crown Court	
I was convicted and/or sentenced and I wish to appeal against the conviction/sentence	

4. Outstanding matters

If there are any other **outstanding** criminal charges or cases against you, give details including the court where you are due to appear

N/A

5. Reasons for wanting representation

To avoid the possiblity of your application being delayed, or publicly funded representation being refused because the court does not have enough information about the case, you must complete the rest of this form.

When deciding whether to grant publicly funded representation, the court will need to know why it is in the interests of justice for you to be represented.

If you need help in completing the form you should speak to a solicitor.

	Details	Reason(s) for grant or refusal *For court use only*
5a It is likely that I will lose my liberty *You should consider seeing a solicitor before answering this question*	I HAVE PREVIOUS CONVICTIONS FOR OFFENCES OF VIOLENCE AND DISHONESTY. THE VICTIM WAS A SCHOOLBOY, ALONE IN A PEDESTRIAN SUBWAY DURING THE HOURS OF DARKNESS	

5. Reasons for wanting representation *continued*

Details

5b I am currently subject to a sentence that is suspended or non-custodial that if breached may allow the court to deal with me for the original offence
Please give details

> PROBATION ORDER FOR THEFT, IMPOSED BY WESTVILLE MAGISTRATES' COURT FOR 2 YEARS ON _____ .

5c It is likely that I will lose my livelihood

> breach of patient doc relationship.
> breach of trust.

5d It is likely that I will suffer serious damage to my reputation

5e A substantial question of law is involved
You will need the help of a solicitor to answer this question

> *Please give authorities to be quoted with law reports' references* CASE INVOLVES:
> • DISPUTED IDENTIFICATION (TURNBULL GUIDELINES APPLY)
> • CHALLENGING ADMISSIBILITY OF CONFESSION (ss 76 + 78 PACE)
> • ADVERSE INFERENCES (s 34 CJPO ACT 1996)

5f I shall be unable to understand the court proceedings or state my own case because:
  i)   My understanding of English is inadequate
  ii) I suffer from a disability

5g Witnesses have to be traced and/or interviewed on my behalf
State the circumstances

> AT THE TIME OF THE ALLEGED OFFENCE, I WAS IN AN AMUSEMENT ARCADE. AS WELL AS A FRIEND WHO WAS WITH ME, THERE MAY BE OTHER WITNESSES WHO SAW ME THERE.

5h The case involves expert cross examination of a prosecution witness
Give brief details

> THE POLICE OFFICER WHO INTERVIEWED ME AS TO BREACHES OF PACE AND THE CODES, THE VICTIM AS TO MISTAKEN IDENTIFICATION, MY CO-ACCUSED AS TO IMPLICATING ME.

5. Reasons for wanting representation *continued*

Details

5i   It is in someone else's interests that I am represented

IT IS NOT APPROPRIATE THAT A SCHOOLBOY BE CROSS-EXAMINED IN PERSON BY ONE OF HIS ALLEGED ATTACKERS.

5j   Any other reasons
Give full particulars

I INTEND TO PLEAD NOT GUILTY AND THE TRIAL WILL TAKE PLACE AT NEWTOWN CROWN COURT.

6. Legal representation

a)   If you do not give the name of a solicitor, the court will select a solicitor for you.

b)   You must tell the solicitor that you have named him.

c)   If you have been charged together with another person or persons, the court may assign a solicitor other than the solicitor of your choice.

The solictor I wish to act for me is:

JOHN SMITH

Give the firm's name and address (if known)

COLLARDS SOLICITORS, 14 THE HIGH STREET, NEWTOWN NA17 2BA

Declaration to be completed on behalf of the solicitor named above

i)   I certify that the named solicitor above has a crime franchise contract or a general criminal contract, or an individual case contract.

ii)   I understand that only firms with a general criminal contract or individual case contract may provide representation in the magistrates' court.

Signed_____   Date_____

7. Declaration

> If you knowingly make a statement which is false, knowingly withhold information, you may be prosecuted.
>
> If convicted, you may be sent to prison for up to three months or be fined or both (*section 21 Access to Justice Act 1999*)

I apply for representation for the charge(s) that are currently before the court.

I understand that should my case proceed to the Crown Court or any higher court, the court may order that I pay for some or all of the costs of representation incurred in the proceedings by way of a Recovery of Defence Costs Order.

I understand that should my case proceed to the Crown Court or any higher court, I will have to furnish details of my means to the court and/or the Legal Services Commission.

Signed _Jake Prescott_   Date _14·01·0–_

For Court use only

Any additional factors considered when determining the application, including any information given orally

Decision on Interests of Justice Test

I have considered all available details of all the charges and it /it is not in the interests of justice that representation be granted for the following reasons:

Signed _____ Appropriate officer

Date | | | | | | |

To be completed where the right to representataion extends to the Crown Court

Statement of Means Form B given to the defendant on *(date)*_____

Indicate type of case:

Indictable only   Yes ☐   No ☐

Section 51 offence   Yes ☐   No ☐

Either-way offence and
elected/not suitable for summary trial   Yes ☐   No ☐

First date of hearing at the Crown Court   _____

(K)   Representation order: Magistrates' court

WEYFORD MAGISTRATES' COURT

Court Code: 2936
Reference: LA/2936/00/1341
Date of Hearing: –

REPRESENTATION ORDER (MAGISTRATES' COURT)

In accordance with the Access to Justice 1999 the Court now grants representation
to   for the following purpose:

Delete (1) to (4) as necessary.

(1)   Proceedings before a Magistrates' Court in connection with

(2)   Appealing to Crown Court against a decision of the Magistrates' Court on

(3)   Resisting an appeal to the Crown Court against a decision of the Magistrate
      Court

(4)   Proceedings for (both a Magistrates' Court and *) the Crown Court in
      connection with   including in the event of his
      being convicted or sentenced in those proceedings, advice and assistance in
      regard to the making of an appeal to the Criminal Division of the Court of
      Appeal.

The representation granted shall consist of the following:—

Magistrates' Court proceedings*—

Solicitor
Solicitor and Junior Counsel

Crown Court proceedings*—

Solicitor
Solicitor and Junior Counsel
Solicitor and Queen's Counsel (only available where the offence charged is
murder)
Solicitor, Junior Counsel and Queen's Counsel (only available where prosecution
brought by Serious Fraud Office)

including advice on the preparation of the case for the proceedings.

The Solicitor/Counsel assigned is
of

The assisted person has been committed to   prison/released on bail and
may be communicated with at

................................(signed)   ....(dated)

* Delete as necessary

(L)   Record of decision to grant or withhold bail and certificate as to hearing on application for bail

WEYFORD MAGISTRATES' COURT

Date 31/7/2000   Accused RONALD EDWIN EVERETT   Date of birth 25/6/1943

Alleged offence(s) TAKING A CONVEYANCE , THEFT

BAIL

The accused is granted bail (subject to the conditions set out below) with a duty to surrender to the custody of

☑ WEYFORD   Magistrates'/~~Youth~~ Court at Weyford
on Monday -day the 14ᵗʰ August   at 9.45   am/~~pm~~

☐ the Crown Court at Guildford/   at 10am on   or on such a day and at such a time and place as may be notified to the accused by the appropriate officer of that court

N.B. If you fail to surrender to bail or to comply with bail conditions you may be arrested and taken into custody.

Failure to surrender to bail is an offence punishable with imprisonment and/or a fine.

Conditions to be complied with

Before release

☑ To provide   1   suret(y)~~(ies)~~ in the sum of £ 500   ~~(each)~~   ☐ To surrender passport to police

☐ To provide a security in the sum of £   to be deposited with the court

After release

☐ To live and sleep each night at   ☐ To abide by the rules of the hostel

☐ To remain indoors at   between the hours of

☐ To report to Weyford   Police Station each Wednesday and   between   1900 — 2100 hours
Saturday

☐ Not to go

except to see solicitor by prior written appointment or to attend court

☐ To make himself available as and when required to enable pre-sentence/medical report to be prepared

☐ Not to contact directly or indirectly

☐

☐

The reasons for imposing conditions are to ensure that the accused:-

☑ surrenders to custody   ☐ does not commit an offence while on bail

☐ does not interfere with witnesses or obstruct the course of justice

☐ is available to enable enquiries or a report to be made   ☐ goes to see his solicitor (legal representative)

CUSTODY

The court withholds bail, having found the exception(s) to the right to bail specified in the first column of the schedule hereto (and applying the exception(s) for the reasons specified in the second column)

☐ The accused is remanded in custody for appearance before WEYFORD
Magistrates'/Youth Court at Weyford   at 10 am on

☐ The accused is committed in custody for appearance before the Crown Court at Weyford
on   at 10 am or on such a day and at such a time and place as may be notified to the accused by the appropriate officer of that court

☐ The accused has consented to the hearing and determination in his absence of future applications for remand in custody and the notice overleaf applies

SCHEDULE

EXCEPTIONS TO THE RIGHT TO BAIL - SCHED. 1	REASONS FOR APPLYING EXCEPTIONS (pt I, paras 2, 2A)
Indictable/either-way cases (Part I, para 2A)	☐ Nature and seriousness of offence and likely conclusion
☐ Alleged offence committed while on bail	☐ Character, antecedents and lack of community ties
Imprisonable (Part I, paras 2(a)-(c), 5, 7)	☐ Accused's record under previous grants of bail
☐ Belief would fail to surrender	☐ Strength of evidence against accused
☐ Belief would commit offence while on bail	☐
☐ Belief would interfere with witnesses or obstruct the course of justice	☐
☐ Insufficient information for bail decision	
☐ Otherwise impracticable to complete enquiries or make report	**CERTIFICATE OF FULL ARGUMENT**
All cases (Pt I, paras 3, 4, 6; Pt II, paras 3, 4, 5)	I hereby certify that at the hearing today the court heard full argument on application for bail by or on behalf of accused and
☐ Serving a custodial sentence	☐ that the court has not previously heard full argument in these proceedings (except at the last hearing)
☐ For accused's (protection) (welfare) (youths only)	☐ that the following new considerations/change in circumstances apply
☐ Arrested for absconding or breaching bail conditions	
Non-imprisonable (Part II, para 2)	
☐ Previous failure to answer bail and belief would fail to surrender to custody	Signed Ian Gallagher Clerk of the Court
	present during the proceedings

Solicitor	FEB 2000

(M) Witness statement

BLANKSHIRE POLICE

Statement or Section	WEYFORD	**Division**	G
		Date	23rd August 200–

Statement of (name of witness)   IAN GOVERN
       (In full - Block Letters)

Date and place of birth   25.8.1954   Cardiff

This statement, (consisting of   1   pages each signed by me), is true to the best of my knowledge and belief and I make it knowing that, if it is tendered in evidence, I shall be liable to prosecution if I wilfully stated in it anything which I know to be false or do not believe to be true.

     Dated the   23rd   day of   August   20 0–

                     Signature ...*Ian Govern*...................................

.... being unable to read the above statement I ....

of ....read it to him before he signed it.

     Dated the   day of   20

I am the manager of Tesco Supermarket, Oxford Street, Weyford. At about 11.15 a.m. on Monday 23rd August I was called to my office by Mr. Astor Teck who is employed as a security officer by Tesco Limited. A woman I now know to be Mrs. June South was in the office with her three children. In my presence Mr. Teck went through the cash receipt and checked it against the items in Mrs South's shopping bag. Five items appeared not to have been paid for, two 7 oz tins of John West Salmon and three large tubes of Gibbs S.R. Toothpaste. These I identified as coming from this store by the price ticket on them. The goods were recovered from Mrs. South No one has authority to take items from this store without payment.

Signature ...*Ian Govern*..............................

Taken by ...*A Butchers ℞ 1007*.............

                                                (continued overleaf)

Address   2A, The Parade, Weyford
           Blankshire   WE9 6BB
Telephone Number   W 686872   Occupation Retail Manager

Dates to avoid:
18-12-0- - 8-1-0

(N) Notice to accused: Right to object to written statement or deposition

FORM 14A

Notice to accused: right to object to written statement or deposition being read out at trial without further proof (CPI Act 1996, s 68, Sch 2, paragraphs 1(3)(c) and 2(3)(c): MC Rules 1981, r 4B (as inserted by MC (Amendment) Rules 1997)

To AB, of

If you are committed for trial, the Crown Court may try you in respect of the charge or charges on which you are committed or in respect of any other charge arising out of the same transaction or set of circumstances which may, with leave of the Court, be put to you.

[Written statements] [and] [depositions] have been made by the witness named below and copies of their [statements] [and] [depositions] are enclosed. Each of these [statements] [and] [depositions] will be read out at the trial without oral evidence being given by the witness who has made the [statement] [or] [deposition] unless you want that witness to give oral evidence and to be cross-examined on such oral evidence. If you want any of these witnesses to give oral evidence, and be cross-examined if necessary, you should inform the Crown Court and me in writing within 14 days of being committed for trial. If you do not do so you will lose your right to prevent the [statement] [or] [deposition] being read out without any oral evidence being given by the witness in question and to require the attendance of that witness unless the Court gives you leave to do so, but that will not prevent the prosecutor from exercising his discretion to call that witness to give oral evidence, and be cross-examined, at the trial if the prosecutor so wishes.

[* [Pre-paid] reply forms [and pre-paid envelopes] are enclosed and if you object to any [statement] [or] [deposition] being read out at the trial without oral evidence being given by the witness who made it you must let the Crown Court and myself know within 14 days of being committed for trial, and at the same time indicate which of these witnesses you want to give oral evidence at the trial.

If you have a solicitor acting for you in your case you should hand this notice and the [statements] [and] [depositions] to him at once, so that he may deal with them].

Names of witnesses whose [statements] [and] [depositions] are enclosed:–

Address any reply to:–

(Signed) ....

[On behalf of the Prosecutor]

* Omit if documents are sent to accused's solicitor.

(O) Statement of means for right to representation in criminal proceedings in the Crown Court (Form B)

Statement of Means for Right to Representation in Criminal Proceedings in the Crown Court

Form B

Reference

Now that you have been granted publicly funded representation in the Crown Court you must complete this form and return it to the court at least **4 days** before your first hearing at the Crown Court. If you do not comply, the judge may make a Court Order against you requiring you to pay for all costs incurred in your defence.

If you or your partner are receiving one of the following benefits, you are only required to complete Parts I and 2A of this form:
- Income-based Job Seeker's Allowance
- Income Support
- Working Families' Tax Credit
- Disabled Person's Tax Credit

If you indicate one of the above, and no further enquiries are made of you or your partner, only this information will go before the judge to consider whether to make a Recovery of Defence Costs Order.

A partner is a person with whom the applicant lives as a couple and includes a person with whom the person concerned is not currently living but from whom he or she is not living separate and apart.

You should inform the Court if your circumstances change once you have completed this form and returned it to the Crown Court.

See the Declaration at the end of this form for enquiries that can be made about the information you provide.

Part I - Personal details

Ia	Surname	PRESCOTT
Ib	Surname at birth *If different*	
Ic	Title *Mr/Mrs/Miss/Ms/other*	MR
Id	Date of birth	17·06·198—
Ie	Forename(s)	JAKE
If	Home address *Including postcode*	10 HERARIA ROAD WEYFORD WE2 7AF
Ig	Address where we can contact you *If different from above*	

Ih Marital status
Tick as appropriate

Single ☑   Cohabiting ☐   Widowed ☐

Married ☐   Married but separated ☐   Divorced ☐

Part 2 - Financial position

Part A - Benefits

If you or your partner receive Income-based Job Seeker's Allowance, Income Support, Working Families' Tax Credit or Disabled Person's Tax Credit, please provide the following details:

(i) The address of the Social Security Office or Jobcentre or Tax Credit Office that is dealing with you or your partner's claim

> 1 HIGH STREET
> NEWTOWN
> NE 19 2BX

(ii) National Insurance number of the person claiming benefit.

> NA 37 81 26 X

This is required so that we can verify your, or your partner's, claim with the Benefits Agency or Inland Revenue

(iii) Name of Benefit

> JOB SEEKER'S ALLOWANCE

(iv) Name of recipient of Benefit

> JAKE PRESCOTT

(v) Date of birth of recipient of Benefit

> 17 . 06 . 198—

Please go to the end of the form and sign the Declarations if you have completed this section.

Part B - Income from work

In this section you are asked to give details of the money you receive.

You should answer these questions with annual amounts. Where you are paid monthly, multiply the amount by 12 or where you are paid weekly, multiply the amount by 52.

	You	Your partner	Additional details	Court use
1 Provide details of gross earnings, including bonuses, overtime or commission				
Do you or your partner receive benefits from work that are not money? *For example: luncheon vouchers, company car, free health insurance etc. Please specify*	Yes ☐ No ☐	Yes ☐ No ☐		
Employer's name and address				
2 Are you or your partner, self-employed / in partnership?	Yes ☐ No ☐	Yes ☐ No ☐		
Indicate nature of work for you and/or your partner			(i) Turnover (ii) Business expenses (not taken out for personal use) (iii) Net profit (Turnover minus business expenses) (iv) Period of trading	
Indicate you and/or your partner's role in company				

Part B - Income (continued)

		You		Your partner		Additional details	Court use
3	Part-time work : gross earnings including bonuses, commission and overtime						
	Employer's name and address						
4	Are you or your partner a shareholder in a private limited company, or are you or your partner a company director?	Yes ☐	No ☐	Yes ☐	No ☐	Provide details for you and/or your partner.	
5	Is anybody else, including a company or other body, supporting either you or your partner financially or making resources available to either of you?	Yes ☐	No ☐	Yes ☐	No ☐	Examples of non-financial support may include the following: Do you live in someone else's house or drive someone else's car? Indicate the nature of the support and what period this support covered. Provide details of connection to individual or company, and name the individual or company.	
6	Do you receive any other income not mentioned in any of the above questions?	Yes ☐	No ☐	Yes ☐	No ☐	Indicate the nature of this income. For example, an allowance or income from trust. Indicate how often this income is received.	
7	Do you receive any income from state benefits? *Give details of benefit received, how much and how often*	Yes ☐	No ☐	Yes ☐	No ☐		

Part C - Capital and Savings

Please provide details of all your capital and savings.

	You		Your partner		Additional details	Court use
1 **Main dwelling** Do you and/or your partner own the house/property that you treat as your main dwelling?	Yes ☐	No ☐	Yes ☐	No ☐	If **Yes**, please provide the following details: i) What is the out-standing mortgage on your property? ii) What is its current market value? iii) What share do you own in this property and if not shared with your partner, who do you own this property with? iv) What type of property is this? *For example, flat* v) How many bed-rooms does this property have?	
2 **Other property** Do you and/or your partner own any other property?	Yes ☐	No ☐	Yes ☐	No ☐	If **Yes**, provide the following details: i) What is the out-standing mortgage on this property? ii) What is its current market value? iii) What share do you own in this property and if not with your partner, who do you own this property with? iv) What type of property is this? *For example, flat* v) How many bed-rooms does this property have?	

Part C - Capital and Savings (continued)

		You		Your partner		Additional details	Court use
3	Savings *Please provide details of savings, including money in the bank, building society, or at home or in current accounts, National Savings Certificates, ISA's.*					If you have savings certificates, provide details of the issue and how many units you have	
4	Do you and/or your partner own any stocks or shares? *Include Unit Trusts, PEPs or ISAs.*	Yes ☐	No ☐	Yes ☐	No ☐	If **Yes**, please provide details of the company and name of the fund if appropriate. Also provide the present value and the amount of the yearly dividend	
5	Do you and/or your partner have any rights under a trust fund?	Yes ☐	No ☐	Yes ☐	No ☐	If **Yes**, what are the details of the fund and what rights do you have?	
6	Articles of value *Please provide details of any articles of value that you and/or your partner own, and their approximate value.*					Include antiques, jewellery, art etc.	
7	Do you or your partner have any other capital assets that you have not indicated above?	Yes ☐	No ☐	Yes ☐	No ☐	If **Yes**, please provide details of the same	

Part D - Financial commitments

		You		Your partner		Additional details	Court use
I	Do you have any dependants who live with you?	Yes ☐	No ☐	Yes ☐	No ☐	If **Yes**, please provide details of how many, their relationship and their ages.	
2	Do you and/or your partner have any financial orders that this court should know about?	Yes ☐	No ☐	Yes ☐	No ☐	If **Yes**, please indicate the nature of the order(s) and the amount(s).	
3	How much do you and/or your partner pay in housing costs?					Provide details of rent or mortgage on your main dwelling. Indicate the period that this amount covers.	

Part E - Further information

		You		Your partner		Additional details	Court use
I	Has any other person been paying towards your legal costs and expenses in these or any other proceedings prior to your grant of representation?	Yes ☐	No ☐			If **Yes**, please provide details of the amount and from whom this support came. Indicate their relationship.	
2	Are any of your and/ or your partner's assets subject to a mareva injunction or freezing order?	Yes ☐	No ☐	Yes ☐	No ☐	If **Yes**, please provide details of the nature of the assets, the value of the order and whose order or injunction it is.	

Part E - Further information

	You	Your partner	Additional details	Court use
3 Do you and/or your partner have interests in any business abroad?	Yes ☐ No ☐	Yes ☐ No ☐	If **Yes**, please provide details of the nature of the business, its name and address and your and/or your partner's interest in it.	
4 Are you and/or your partner currently bankrupt or subject to bankruptcy proceedings or subject to an Individual Voluntary Arrangement?	Yes ☐ No ☐	Yes ☐ No ☐	If **Yes**, please provide full details	

Is there any other information that you feel is relevant to the Court or the Legal Services Commission which should be taken into account when considering your means?

Please provide details where relevant.

Declaration

1. I declare that to the best of my knowledge and belief, I have given a complete and correct statement of my income and/or savings and/or capital and those of my partner.

2. I understand I may be required to provide evidence to support the information I have supplied on this form.

3. I authorise such enquiries as are considered necessary to enable the Court or the Legal Services Commission to ascertain mine and/or my partner's income, outgoings, savings, business interests.

4. I consent to the disclosure of any information by other parties that may assist in their enquiries.

5. I authorise the Court or the Legal Services Commission to make such enquiries to the Benefits Agency, Tax Credit Office or Inland Revenue as they feel necessary and I consent to the disclosure of information to confirm that I am in receipt of such benefits as I have stated.

6. I understand that the Court and the Legal Services Commission can provide a report on my financial position to the trial judge and my representative, with a view to a Recovery of Defence Costs Order being made for up to the full amount of the costs incurred in defending me in the proceedings, in this and any other court.

7. I understand that if I knowingly make a statement which is false or knowingly withhold information I may be prosecuted. If convicted of such an offence I may be sent to prison for up to three months or fined or both (section 21 Access to Justice Act 1999).

8. I understand that I must co-operate fully and immediately with any enquiry into my financial circumstances by the Court or Legal Services Commission, and that if the information I have provided is not correct or complete, then an Order may be made against me requiring me to pay all costs incurred in defending me in the proceedings, in this and any other court.

Signature	*Jake Prescott*	Date	14 -01 -0-

Full name in Block Capitals	JAKE PRESCOTT

Declaration and authority by person receiving the benefit

This additional declaration should be signed by the person receiving the benefit if they are not the person applying for publicly funded representation.

I consent to the Court or Legal Services Commission disclosing information about me to the Department of Social Security and making such enquiries as may be necessary to check the information provided in this application. The Department of Social Security may carry out such processing as is necessary to check this information remains correct and may inform the Court or Legal Services Commission of any relevant changes.

Signature		Date	

(P) Plea and case management hearing in the Crown Court form and guidance notes

PLEA AND CASE MANAGEMENT HEARING IN THE CROWN COURT

Date of hearing: Judge:

P			represented by:		☐
D1		in custody/on bail	represented by:		☐
D2		in custody/on bail	represented by:		☐
D3		in custody/on bail	represented by:		☐
D4		in custody/on bail	represented by:		☐
D5		in custody/on bail	represented by:		☐

Tick right hand column if the advocate is instructed for trial

No. of case in Crown Court: URN:

	D1	D2	D3	D4	D5
Has the defendant been advised about credit for pleading guilty?	☐	☐	☐	☐	☐
Has the defendant been warned that if he is on bail and fails to attend, the proceedings may continue in his absence?	☐	☐	☐	☐	☐
Is the Crown Court Case Details form up-to-date?	P ☐ ☐	☐	☐	☐	☐

Matters likely to be applicable to all trials

1) TRIAL JUDGE
Should the future management of the case be under the supervision of the trial or a nominated judge?   **YES/NO**

2) RESOLVING THE CASE WITHOUT A TRIAL   **Not applicable ☐**

	D1	D2	D3	D4	D5
a. **Might the case against a defendant be resolved by a plea of guilty to some counts on the indictment or to a lesser offence?**	☐	☐	☐	☐	☐
b. **If so, how?**					
c. **Is the prosecution prepared to resolve the case in this way?**	☐	☐	☐	☐	☐
d. **If no, does the court take the provisional view that the case should be resolved in this way?**	☐	☐	☐	☐	☐
e. *If yes, the court orders:*					

3) GUILTY PLEA   **Not applicable ☐**

	D1	D2	D3	D4	D5
a. **Is there a written basis of plea?**	☐	☐	☐	☐	☐
b. **Is the basis of plea acceptable to the prosecution?**	☐	☐	☐	☐	☐
a. Is the basis of plea acceptable to the court?	☐	☐	☐	☐	☐

b. If not acceptable, section 25 (Newton Hearing) will also apply.
c. *The defendant(s) will be sentenced on:*
d. *The prosecution to serve any further material relevant to sentence by:*
e. *The pre-sentence report, if required, to be received by the Crown Court and made available to the defence and the prosecution by:*
f. *The defence to serve any material which it wishes the court to consider when sentencing the defendant by:*

1

g. **Will "derogatory assertions" be made in mitigation?** ☐ ☐ ☐ ☐ ☐

h. *If yes, the court orders:*

i. **Are there any other matters which should be dealt with at the same time as these proceedings (other offences/TICs)?** ☐ ☐ ☐ ☐ ☐

j. **If yes, give brief details:**

k. *If there are other matters, the court orders:*

l. *Further orders (e.g. orders re medical or psychiatric reports or confiscation proceedings):*

4) NOT GUILTY - TRIAL DATE   Not applicable ☐
a. **If the defendant is in custody and if the provisions regarding custody time limits apply, when does the custody time limit (or any extension thereof) expire?**
   D1:   ; D2:   ; D3:   ; D4:   ; D5:   .
b. **Set out other reasons why the trial should take place earlier or later than it might otherwise?**

c. *If the defendant is in custody and the date of the trial is outside the custody time limit period, the court makes the following orders:*

d. **What is the estimated length of the prosecution, defence cases?**
   Prosecution   Defence
e. *The trial will take place on: and the length of it will be:*

5) READINESS FOR TRIAL
The parties' case progression officers to inform the Crown Court case progression officer in writing that the case is ready for trial, that it will proceed as a trial on the date in 4e and will take no more/less time than the period in 4e, by:

6) EVIDENCE - WITNESSES
a. **Have the parties completed Annex A?**   **YES/NO**
b. If yes, does the court approve Annex A?   YES/NO
c. *If the list of witnesses to be called orally is not agreed or approved, agreement (which is subject to the court's approval) must be reached and notified to the court by:*
d. *Absent agreement, the prosecution shall seek further directions by:*

7) EVIDENCE - DEFENDANTS' INTERVIEWS   Not applicable ☐
                                                P D1 D2 D3 D4 D5
a. **Should the interviews be edited before the trial?** ☐ ☐ ☐ ☐ ☐ ☐

b. *Proposals for the editing of interviews shall be drafted by: and served by:*
c. *The other parties shall respond by:*
d. *The agreed interviews shall be filed with the Court by:*
e. *Absent agreement, the party(ies) named in b) shall seek further directions by:*

8) DEFENCE STATEMENT
                                                D1 D2 D3 D4 D5
a. **Has a defence statement been served?**   ☐ ☐ ☐ ☐ ☐

b. **Is there an issue as to its adequacy?**   ☐ ☐ ☐ ☐ ☐
c. *The court gives a warning to:*   ☐ ☐ ☐ ☐ ☐
d. *The court orders:*

2

9) PROSECUTION ADDITIONAL EVIDENCE   **Not applicable** ☐
a.   *Any additional evidence to be served by*:

b.   **Which topic/issue will the additional evidence relate to?**

10) FURTHER PROSECUTION DISCLOSURE   **Not applicable** ☐
a.   *The prosecution to complete any further disclosure by:*
b.   **Is the defence alleging that the prosecution has not complied with its**   D1 ☐ D2 ☐ D3 ☐ D4 ☐ D5 ☐
     obligation to disclose material?
c.   *If yes, the court orders:*

11) EVIDENCE - ADMISSIONS/SCHEDULES
a.   **Have the parties considered which admissions/schedules can be agreed:**   **YES/NO**
b.   *If yes and if the court agrees that the proposed admissions/schedules are sufficient, they shall be drafted by:*
c.   *and sent to the other parties by:*
d.   *The other parties shall respond by:*
e.   *The agreed admissions/schedules shall be filed with the court by:*
f.   *Absent agreement, the named party in b) shall seek further directions by:*
g.   *If the answer to question a. is no or if the court does not approve the proposed admissions/schedules, the court orders:*

Matters which may apply to any trial

12) EVIDENCE - EXHIBITS
a.   **Have the parties completed and agreed Annex B?**   **YES/NO**
b.   *If Annex B is not agreed, agreement must be reached and notified to the court by:*
c.   *In the absence of agreement, the prosecution shall seek further directions by:*
d.   *If, in the view of the court, any exhibits should be presented in a particular way in order to be more easily understood by the jury, the court orders:*

e.   *Further orders:*

13) EVIDENCE - VIDEO EVIDENCE   **Not applicable** ☐
a.   **Has the prosecution delivered to the defence the transcript of video**   D1 ☐ D2 ☐ D3 ☐ D4 ☐ D5 ☐
     witness evidence upon which it proposes to rely?
b.   *If no, the prosecution to do so by:*
c.   *The defence shall submit any editing proposals by:*
d.   *The prosecution shall respond by:*
e.   *The agreed transcripts and edited video shall be filed with the court by:*
f.   *Absent agreement, the prosecution shall seek further directions by:*

14) EVIDENCE - CCTV EVIDENCE   **Not applicable** ☐
a.   **Has any unedited CCTV evidence been made available in full to**   P ☐ D1 ☐ D2 ☐ D3 ☐ D4 ☐ D5 ☐
     the other parties?
b.   *If yes, copy of proposed composite/edited film/stills to be served by:*
c.   *The other parties to respond by:*
d.   *Absent agreement, the party seeking to rely on the evidence shall seek directions by:*

15) EVIDENCE - EXPERT EVIDENCE   **Not applicable** ☐
a.   **Expert evidence is likely to be called by:**   P ☐ D1 ☐ D2 ☐ D3 ☐ D4 ☐ D5 ☐

3

b.   **To prove/disprove:** P:
     D1/2/3/4/5:

c.   Does the court approve of the need for the identified expert evidence?   ☐   ☐   ☐   ☐   ☐   ☐
d.   If no, why?

e.   *In any event the evidence to be served by:*

f.   **Should the expert evidence be presented in a particular way in**   ☐   ☐   ☐   ☐   ☐   ☐
     order to be more easily understood by the jury?
g.   *If yes, the court orders:*

h.   **Would it be helpful if the experts consulted together and if possible**   ☐   ☐   ☐   ☐   ☐   ☐
     agreed a written note of points of agreement or disagreement with
     a summary of reasons?
i.   *If yes, and if the parties agree, the court orders:*

16) ELECTRONIC EQUIPMENT – COMPATIBILITY   Not applicable ☐
    a.   **Does the trial courtroom have the appropriate equipment to allow**   P   D1   D2   D3   D4   D5
         the presentation of electronic evidence (CCTV, live link, audio   ☐   ☐   ☐   ☐   ☐   ☐
         recordings, DVD etc)?
    b.   *If no, the court orders:*

17) EVIDENCE - SPECIAL MEASURES AND LIVE LINK   Not applicable ☐
    a.   **Any outstanding issues about special measures or live links?**   D1   D2   D3   D4   D5
                                                                                  ☐   ☐   ☐   ☐   ☐
    b.   If yes, the court orders:

18) MISCELLANEOUS ORDERS RE. WITNESSES AND DEFENDANT   Not applicable ☐
    a.   **Does any witness or defendant need an interpreter or have special**   P   D1   D2   D3   D4   D5
         needs for which arrangements should be made?   ☐   ☐   ☐   ☐   ☐   ☐
    b.   *If yes, the court orders:*

    c.   **Are any special arrangements needed for a child defendant?**   ☐   ☐   ☐   ☐   ☐   ☐
    d.   *If yes, the court orders:*

    e.   **Will a defendant be unrepresented at trial?**   ☐   ☐   ☐   ☐   ☐   ☐
    f.   *If yes, the court orders:*

19) HEARSAY / BAD CHARACTER EVIDENCE   Not applicable ☐
    a.   **Further applications regarding hearsay evidence or bad character**   P   D1   D2   D3   D4   D5
         evidence are to be made by: ☐   ☐   ☐   ☐   ☐   ☐
    b.   *The court orders:*

20) PRODUCTION OF MATERIAL FROM THIRD PARTIES   Not applicable ☐
    a.   **Applications for production of material (e.g. social services,**   P   D1   D2   D3   D4   D5
         hospital, banking records) from third parties to be made by: ☐   ☐   ☐   ☐   ☐   ☐
    b.   *The court orders:*

21) PRE-TRIAL RESOLUTION OF ISSUES   Not applicable ☐

4

a. **What are the legal or factual issues which should be resolved before the trial:**

b. *If the issues are not capable of being resolved at the plea and case management hearing, the necessary hearing will take place on   and will last:*

c. **Do the parties wish to call witnesses to give evidence orally to enable the court to resolve the issues?**

P	D1	D2	D3	D4	D5
☐	☐	☐	☐	☐	☐

d. *If yes, and if the court approves, the court makes the following orders:*

e. *Skeleton arguments to be submitted by: P by: D1/2/3/4/5 by:*

22) PUBLIC INTEREST IMMUNITY: ON NOTICE APPLICATIONS   **Not applicable** ☐

a. **What is the nature of the prosecution's application on notice for public interest immunity?**

b. *The court orders:*

23) FURTHER ORDERS CONCERNING THE CONDUCT OF THE TRIAL

a. *Prosecution case summary/opening, if necessary, to be served by:*

b. *To ensure that the trial does not take more time than the period in 4e., the court orders:*

24) ANY FURTHER MISCELLANEOUS ORDERS - INCLUDING ORDERS RE. LITIGATION SUPPORT

25) NEWTON HEARING   **Not applicable** ☐

a. *The Newton hearing will take place on: and the length of it will be:*

b. *The issues to be resolved are:*

c. *The prosecution to serve any further material by: and the defence by:*

d. *The following witnesses will be called to give evidence orally:*

e. *Further orders (including any orders re. hearsay/bad character):*

<u>Judge's signature:</u>

ANNEX A

Witnesses upon whom the prosecution intends to rely and who will give evidence orally

Name of witness	Page No	Type of witness	Required by:						Order of calling
			P ☐	D1 ☐	D2 ☐	D3 ☐	D4 ☐	D5 ☐	
			P ☐	D1 ☐	D2 ☐	D3 ☐	D4 ☐	D5 ☐	
			P ☐	D1 ☐	D2 ☐	D3 ☐	D4 ☐	D5 ☐	
			P ☐	D1 ☐	D2 ☐	D3 ☐	D4 ☐	D5 ☐	
			P ☐	D1 ☐	D2 ☐	D3 ☐	D4 ☐	D5 ☐	
			P ☐	D1 ☐	D2 ☐	D3 ☐	D4 ☐	D5 ☐	
			P ☐	D1 ☐	D2 ☐	D3 ☐	D4 ☐	D5 ☐	
			P ☐	D1 ☐	D2 ☐	D3 ☐	D4 ☐	D5 ☐	
			P ☐	D1 ☐	D2 ☐	D3 ☐	D4 ☐	D5 ☐	
			P ☐	D1 ☐	D2 ☐	D3 ☐	D4 ☐	D5 ☐	
			P ☐	D1 ☐	D2 ☐	D3 ☐	D4 ☐	D5 ☐	
			P ☐	D1 ☐	D2 ☐	D3 ☐	D4 ☐	D5 ☐	
			P ☐	D1 ☐	D2 ☐	D3 ☐	D4 ☐	D5 ☐	
			P ☐	D1 ☐	D2 ☐	D3 ☐	D4 ☐	D5 ☐	
			P ☐	D1 ☐	D2 ☐	D3 ☐	D4 ☐	D5 ☐	
			P ☐	D1 ☐	D2 ☐	D3 ☐	D4 ☐	D5 ☐	
			P ☐	D1 ☐	D2 ☐	D3 ☐	D4 ☐	D5 ☐	
			P ☐	D1 ☐	D2 ☐	D3 ☐	D4 ☐	D5 ☐	
			P ☐	D1 ☐	D2 ☐	D3 ☐	D4 ☐	D5 ☐	
			P ☐	D1 ☐	D2 ☐	D3 ☐	D4 ☐	D5 ☐	

ANNEX B

Exhibits which the prosecution intends to make available to the jury at the start of the trial

Exhibit reference	Page No	Exhibit reference	Page No.	Exhibit reference	Page No.

Use continuation sheets as necessary

6

PLEA AND CASE MANAGEMENT HEARING IN THE CROWN COURT

GUIDANCE NOTES

General notes

These notes accompany the plea and case management hearing ('PCM7U') form. The Consolidated Criminal Practice Direction provides:

IV.4 1.8   Active case management at the PCMH should reduce the number of ineffective and cracked trials and delays during the trial to resolve legal issues. The effectiveness of a PCMH hearing in a contested case depends in large measure upon preparation by all concerned and upon the presence of the trial advocate or an advocate who is able to make decisions and give the court the assistance which the trial advocate could be expected to give. Resident Judges in setting the listing policy should ensure that list officers fix cases as far as possible to enable the trial advocate to conduct the PCMH and the trial.

IV.41.9   In Class 1 and Class 2 cases, and in all cases involving a serious sexual offence against a child, the PCMH must be conducted by a High Court judge; by a circuit judge or by a recorder to whom the case has been assigned in accordance with paragraph IV.33 (allocation of business within the Crown Court); or by a judge authorised by the Presiding Judges to conduct such hearings. In the event of a guilty plea before such an authorised judge, the case will be adjourned for sentencing by a High Court judge or by a circuit judge or recorder to whom the case has been assigned.

Use of the PCMH form: pilot schemes

IV.4 1.10 The pilot courts will be the Central Criminal Court, Preston Crown Court and Nottingham Crown Court. In pilot courts the PCMH form as set out in annex E will be used in accordance with the guidance notes.

Use of the PCMH form: general

IV.4 1.11 In other courts the Resident Judge should exercise discretion as to the manner in which the form is used taking account of the views of the local criminal justice agencies and of practitioners. In the event of the Resident Judge deciding to use the form in a manner that is not agreed to by either the local criminal justice agencies or the practitioners, the Resident Judge should consult the Presiding Judge of his circuit before doing so.

Further pre-trial hearings after the PCMH

IV. 41.12 Additional pre-trial hearings should be held only if needed for some compelling reason. Where necessary the power to give, vary or revoke a direction without a hearing should be used. Paragraph 5 of the PCMH form enables the Court to require the parties' case progression officers to inform the Crown Court case progression officer that the case is ready for trial, that it will proceed as a trial on the date fixed and will take no more or less time than that previously ordered.

The parties must complete only one copy of the form and make it available to the judge at or before the hearing (if there are more than five defendants, a further form should be filled in only so far as necessary). The answers to the questions in bold must be filled in before the hearing. The proposed italicised orders should be filled in before the hearing, if possible. Tick the "Not applicable" box if no part of the section is relevant. Local practice will determine how the form should be completed and by whom and whether electronically or not. The directions must be easily understood by, and made available to, the case progression officers. Time limits should normally be expressed by reference to a particular date rather than by the number of days allowed, to make the task of the case progression officers easier.

The court may make rulings which have binding effect (subject to being discharged or varied) under section 40 of the Criminal Procedure and Investigations Act 1996 as to:

"(a)   any question as to the admissibility of evidence;

(b)   any other question of law relating to the case concerned."

The extent to which courts exercise the power to make these rulings at this hearing is a matter for the court, after considering representations.

Except where otherwise required, a direction to "serve" material means serve on the other party(ies) and file with the Crown Court.

Where a direction requires a party to respond to a proposal (e.g. a proposed edited interview) the party responding will be expected to suggest a counter-proposal.

Notes relevant to specific sections

1)   TRIAL OR NOMINATED JUDGE

If the case is due to last for more than 4 weeks or if there are issues of law to be considered or if the prosecution intends to make a public interest immunity application, then the future management of the case should normally be under the supervision of the trial judge or a nominated judge.

Where it is deemed appropriate for the management of the case to be under the supervision of the trial judge or a nominated judge the court should normally continue with the plea and case management hearing and then direct that the case be considered by the Resident Judge.

2)   RESOLVING THE CASE WITHOUT A TRIAL

2e.   The court should normally grant the prosecution a very short adjournment to resolve the issue.

3)   GUILTY PLEA

If there is an issue about whether the defendant is fit to plead the court should be informed for the court to make appropriate orders.

3i.   Where the defence intend to make a "derogatory assertion" against a person's character in the course of mitigation advance notice of that intention enables the prosecution to decide whether to challenge the assertion and enables the sentencing court to consider whether to make an order restricting the publication of the assertion under sections *58-61* of the Criminal Procedure and Investigations Act 1996 ("CPIA 1996").

3l.   If the defendant is facing charges in other courts give brief details of offence, court and court number.

4)   NOT GUILTY – TRIAL DATE

4b.   These reasons could include the health, vulnerability or availability of a witness or of the defendant or the fact that the defendant falls within the definition of a persistent young offender.

4c. The court should, if possible, deal with the extension of a custody time limit at this stage rather than adjourn any application to a subsequent date. Regulation 7 of the Prosecution of Offences (Custody Time Limits) Regulations 1987 permits the defendant to waive the requirements of notice and gives the court authority to waive them.

4e. It will often not be possible to fill in these answers until the balance of the form has been considered.

6) EVIDENCE – WITNESSES

The parties shall before the hearing agree or try to agree which witnesses are properly required to give oral evidence, on which day of the trial and in which order the witnesses will be called.

The parties must use their best endeavours to reduce the amount of oral evidence to a minimum, in particular by reducing the number of witnesses who give similar evidence, or by the deletion of challenged passages the omission of which will not materially affect the case for the party calling that witness, or by the use of admissions which make the calling of the witness in person unnecessary.

The parties will be expected to be able to justify to the court what they have agreed.

7) EVIDENCE – DEFENDANTS' INTERVIEWS

In order to assist editing of defendants' interviews it will be helpful if the prosecution can supply interviews to the defence in an electronic form.

In the absence of agreement before the trial, the party responsible for the editing shall have available at the trial the interviews in electronic form so that the necessary editing can be done during the trial.

See also the provisions of paragraph IV 43 of the Consolidated Criminal Practice Direction in relation to interviews.

8) DEFENCE STATEMENT

The defence is required to serve a defence statement by section 5 of the CPIA 1996. The defence statement will have to comply with new section 6A as inserted by section 33 of the Criminal Justice Act 2003. If the defendant has not provided a defence statement, the court should be told what are the issues in his case.

8b. See s. 11 of the CPIA 1996 as substituted by section 39 of the Criminal Justice Act 2003.

8c. The judge will have to consider whether to give a warning under section 6E of the CPIA 1996, as substituted by section 36 of the Criminal Justice Act 2003.

9) PROSECUTION ADDITIONAL EVIDENCE

The court may wish to order that any evidence served after the due date may not be introduced without the court's permission. If so, insert that in the box.

10) FURTHER PROSECUTION DISCLOSURE

10b. Section 8 of the CPJ[A 1996 provides for an application to be made by the defence for an order obliging the prosecution to disclose material where the accused has reasonable cause to believe that the prosecution has not complied with its obligation to disclose.

11) EVIDENCE ADMISSIONS / SCHEDULES

11a. See section 10 of the Criminal Justice Act 1967.

12) EVIDENCE – EXHIBITS

Exhibits should be presented so that they can be easily understood by the jury, for example by the jury being given edited or summarized versions of documents, by the use of schedules, electronic presentation of material, or by the use of graphics.

13) EVIDENCE – VIDEO EVIDENCE

Transcripts are costly and time consuming to obtain. It is the video which is the evidence, not the transcript. Therefore a transcript should normally only be obtained when there is to be a trial and a need for a transcript is identified.

14) EVIDENCE – CCTV EVIDENCE

14b. Consideration should be given to requiring the videos to be copied on to a DVD.

15) EVIDENCE – EXPERT EVIDENCE

15c. If the court does approve the need for the instruction of an expert on behalf of a publicly funded defendant, the court may wish to explain why, so that the Legal Services Commission can be informed accordingly. If the court does not approve the need for the expert evidence, the court may wish to note the reasons. If the court does give reasons, those reasons must be notified to the Legal Services Commission if all application is being made for public funding of the expert's fees.

15f. In order that expert evidence can be easily understood by the jury the court may order, for example, that the jury be given a copy of the report, or an edited or summarized version thereof, or may direct the use of schedules or graphics.

15i. The words "if the parties agree" have been included because such an order, in the absence of agreement, may raise issues of costs and of privilege, which the Criminal Procedure Rule Committee has not yet addressed.

It must be borne in mind that the costs of an expert may not be met by the Legal Services Commission.

18) MISCELLANEOUS ORDERS RE. WITNESSES AND DEFENDANT

18a. In the event of an interpreter being required, set out the relevant language and, where applicable, the dialect. The Court should establish in each case who is responsible for providing the interpreter.

18c. If the defendant is a child the parties and the court should consider what provisions are required so that, in accordance with Part IV.39 of the Consolidated Criminal Practice Direction, the defendant is not exposed to avoidable intimidation, humiliation or distress.

18e. If the defendant will not be represented at trial there are orders which may have to be made prohibiting him from cross-examining certain witnesses (see Youth Justice and Criminal Evidence Act 1999, Chapter II).

20) PRODUCTION OF MATERIAL FROM THIRD PARTIES

Note the Attorney General's 2005 Guidelines on disclosure of information in criminal proceedings.

21) PRE-TRIAL RESOLUTION OF ISSUES

The parties shall, before the hearing, agree or try to agree what legal issues are likely to be raised (joinder, severance, admissibility of evidence, abuse of process, issues of substantive law etc) and at what stage they should properly be resolved and will be expected to be able to justify to the court what they have agreed. Although paragraph IV 36.1 of the Consolidated Criminal Practice Direction provides that written notice of an application to stay an indictment on the grounds of abuse of process must be given not later than 14 days before the date fixed or warned for trial, this issue should be considered at the PCMH.

22) PUBLIC INTEREST IMMUNITY: ON NOTICE APPLICATIONS

If the prosecution does not make an application for public interest immunity until later, the court and the defence must be informed as soon thereafter as practicable.

24) ANY FURTHER MISCELLANEOUS ORDERS – INCLUDING ORDERS RE. LITIGATION SUPPORT

Note the Guide to the Award of Costs in Criminal Proceedings on www.jsboard.co.uk.

25) NEWTON HEARING

The parties must agree or try to agree which witnesses are properly required to give oral evidence, in which order the witnesses will be called and what special arrangements need to be made to facilitate the giving of evidence. The parties must use their best endeavours to reduce the amount of oral evidence to a minimum, in particular by reducing the number of witnesses who give similar evidence, or by the deletion of challenged passages the omission of which will not materially affect the case for the party calling that witness, or by the use of admissions which makes the calling of the witness in person unnecessary. The court will decide which witnesses should be called to give oral evidence.

(Q) Brief to counsel

IN THE CROWN COURT

AT GUILDFLEET

REPRESENTATION ORDER

Case No.0–/1732

REGINA

v

ALAN TRIP

BRIEF TO COUNSEL ON BEHALF OF THE DEFENDANT
TO APPEAR AT THE PDH ON 7 NOVEMBER 200– AT 10.30 AND AT
THE TRIAL ON A DATE TO BE FIXED

Counsel has copies of the following –

1. Statements of Alan Trip (including comments on prosecution statements)
2. Bundle of prosecution witness statements
3. Custody record of Alan Trip
4. List of Alan Trip's previous convictions
5. Representation Order
6. Indictment
7. Bail notice
8. Primary disclosure by the prosecution under the Criminal Procedure and Investigations Act 1996 ('the 1996 Act')
9. 'Defence statement' under the 1996 Act

INTRODUCTION

Counsel is instructed on behalf of Alan Trip of 1 Oakwell Terrace, Guildfleet. The defendant is on bail and charged with theft of a gold ring to the value of £225, the property of Cedric Mane, contrary to s 1 Theft Act 1968. The defendant will plead not guilty. He was committed under s 6(2), Magistrates' Courts Act 1980 to Guildfleet Crown Court for trial by Guildfleet Magistrates on 30th September 200–. All prosecution witnesses should attend the trial to give oral evidence. There are no defence witnesses other than the defendant.

The prosecution and defence have complied with the disclosure provisions of the 1996 Act. The prosecution has confirmed in writing that there is no material which might undermine the prosecution case; instructing solicitors have set out in the 'defence statement' the general nature of the defence and the matters on which the defence takes issue with the prosecution and the reasons for doing so.

THE PROSECUTION CASE

The prosecution case is that the defendant took the ring from 6 Marchant Crescent, Guildfleet, a property belonging to Mr. Mane, on 3rd May 200–. The defendant was a lodger at 6 Marchant Crescent from 2nd January 200– to 3rd May 200–. On the morning of 3rd May, following a row with Mr. Mane, the defendant was asked to leave. Mr. Mane will say that he left the ring on the coffee table in the lounge when he left for work on 3rd May at approximately 8.30 a.m. At this time the defendant was still packing his bags prior to leaving. When Mr. Mane returned home from work at 5.30 p.m. both the defendant and the ring had gone. There was no sign of a forcible entry into the property and nothing else had been taken. Peter Plant, a friend of Mr. Mane's will say that the defendant offered him a gold ring for £50 in the Cat and Lion Public House, Guildfleet, on the evening of 3rd May. Plant allegedly refused the offer but informed Mr. Mane on hearing of the theft. The defendant was arrested on 6th May. Counsel will note from the custody record that he did not, on arrival at the police station, ask for a solicitor. The defendant was interrogated by D.C. Blakeway and D.C. Hind and made both oral and written confessions of guilt.

THE DEFENCE CASE

The defendant denies all knowledge of the ring. He claims that Mr. Mane is making allegations of theft against him to 'get even' following their row. The defendant admits talking to Peter Plant in the Cat and Lion Public House but denies offering him a ring. Whilst the defendant cannot put forward any real motive for Plant lying, he suspects that Mane has some 'hold' over Plant and is forcing him to give false testimony. There is no dispute that the defendant confessed his guilt but he claims that he did so only after being denied access to a solicitor and being threatened with physical violence.

EVIDENCE

Counsel's attention is particularly drawn to the following points of evidence:-

The confession – the admissibility of the defendant's confession should be challenged under s.76 and s.78 Police and Criminal Evidence Act 1984. The threats of violence, if accepted by the judge, may constitute oppression and Counsel will be aware of a number of recently reported cases in which denial of access to a solicitor has led to exclusion of a confession under s.78. Although the defendant did not request a solicitor on arrival at the police station he claims that he did so prior to being interrogated. Under the Code of Practice dealing with detention and interrogation the defendant is entitled to request a solicitor at any time. The custody record is silent on the issue and it would appear that the police will deny all knowledge of the request.

The defendant's previous convictions – Counsel will note that the defendant has six previous convictions for theft. In view of the allegations being made against Mr. Mane and the police (if the confession is admitted) it would seem likely that the prosecution will seek to adduce evidence under the Criminal Justice Act 2003. Instructing solicitors have explained this to Mr. Trip.

MITIGATION

Instructing solicitors have considered the question of a plea in mitigation if the defendant is convicted. Mr. Trip is a single man, aged 23, and has been unemployed since leaving school at 16. Counsel will note that the present offence was allegedly committed three months into the operational period of a suspended sentence imposed for theft. If the defendant is convicted, a custodial sentence would seem to be inevitable.

Counsel is requested to advise in conference, attend the PCMH, represent the defendant at the trial on a plea of not guilty and, if necessary, to make a plea in mitigation and advise on the prospects of an appeal.

(R)   'TIC' Form

BLANKSHIRE POLICE

WEYFORD	STATION
G	DIVISION
23/8/0–	DATE

OTHER OFFENCES

To: ......Jayne Jones...............

charged with)   Theft ....
indicated)

for (hearing)   at ...Weyford Magistrates' Court... on ....27th August 200–
     (trial   )

MEMORANDUM FOR THE INFORMATION OF THE ACCUSED

(1)   The list on the back hereof gives particulars of _____ FIVE _____
other offences with which you are charged.

   In the event of you(r) **being found guilty** / **convicted** of any offence of which you are **charged** /
indicted it will be open to you, before **the court makes an order** / **sentence is passed,** to admit all or
any of the other offences, and you may thereupon ask that any of these other offences which you have admitted
may be taken into consideration in any **order the court may make** / **sentence the court may pass upon you.**

(2)   Please sign the receipt below, and retain for your own information the copy of this document.

(3)   If you wish now to volunteer any statement concerning any of these other offences, or to ask
for any further information in respect thereto, you may do so in writing, either in the space at the foot of this
document or in a separate letter. Or, if you prefer, you may ask for a Police Officer to take any statement you
may wish to give.

FORM OF RECEIPT TO BE SIGNED BY THE ACCUSED

I have received a copy of this document.

Signed   ....
Date   ....
In the presence of   ....

SPACE FOR ANY STATEMENT THE ACCUSED MAY WISH TO VOLUNTEER

Signed   ....
Date   ....
In the presence of   ....

CHARGES OUTSTANDING AGAINST _____ Jane Jones

No.	Crime Ref.	Place of Offence	Date of Offence	Details of Offence	Name and Address of Victim	Remarks
1		Weyford	6.6.0–	Stole a packet of frozen peas valued a £1.77 Contrary to s.1(1) Theft Act 1968	Tesco Ltd. 88 High Street, Weyford	
2		Weyford	6.6.0–	Stole a tube of toothpaste valued at £0.70 Contrary to s.1(1) Theft Act 1968	Boots Ltd 84 High Street, Weyford	
3		Weyford	6.6.0–	Stole some writing paper valued at £1.50 Contrary to s.1(1) Theft Act 1968	W.H. Smith Ltd 86 High Street, Weyford	
4		Weyford	10.7.0–	Stole coffee, butter, sardines, and chocolate valued at £5.50 Contrary to s.1(1) Theft Act 1968	Tesco Ltd 88 High Street, Weyford	
5		Weyford	24.7.0–	Stole toothpaste, baked beans and tea valued at £2.10 Contrary to s.1(1) Theft Act 1968	Keymarkets Ltd 98 High Street, Weyford	

A. Butchers DC 1007

(S)   Notice of appeal

MAGISTRATES' COURT

NOTICE OF APPEAL TO CROWN COURT, AGAINST CONVICTION

To the Justices' Clerk of the Magistrates' Court sitting at Weyford

AND TO the Crown Prosecution Services, Weyford Branch Office, 9 Guildfleet Road, Weyford, Blankshire WE7 5XX

TAKE NOTICE THAT I, Barry Jones of 42 Murdstone Close Weyford, Blankshire WE4 2AF

intend to appeal to the Crown Court at Weyford against my conviction on 11 November 200– by Weyford Magistrates' Court for the offence of driving a Ford Escort motor car Reg. No L207 LBP on Hamilton Avenue, Weyford without due care and attention Contrary to Section 3 Road Traffic Act 1988.

The basis of my appeal is that the magistrates' decision was wrong and contrary to the evidence. I am not guilty of the offence.

Dated 18 November 200–   **Signed** *Barry Jones*

Case Reference Number WE 24105

(T)   Defence statement (CPIA 1996, s 5(5))

Crown Court Case No. 2456/200_

To the Prosecutor: Crown Prosecution Service, 2 Crown Buildings, Castleton CA2 8BT

To the Court: Castleton Crown Court

NAME OF ACCUSED: Jake Prescott   **URN:** SH/42/200_

Charge: Robbery   **Date of next hearing:** 10 February 200_

Name and address of solicitors for the accused: Collaws Solicitors, 14 High
                                                       Street, Newtown NT17 2BA

Date: 30 January 200_

If called upon to establish a defence, the following statement is served in accordance with the provisions of the Criminal Procedure and Investigations Act 1996.

1.   **The nature of the accused's Defence is:** alibi

2.   **The accused takes issue with the prosecution in relation to the following matters:**

      (i)   the allegation that the accused was in the Newtown Shopping Precinct at approximately 17.00 hours on 12 December 200_

      (ii)   the allegation that the accused was in the Market Street subway at approximately 17.00 on 12 December 200_

      (iii) the allegation that the accused threatened the complainant, Michael Shields

      (iv)   the allegation that the accused robbed the complainant, Michael Shields, of a Gameboy Advance games machine.

3.   **The accused takes issue with the prosecution about these matters for the following reasons:** the allegations are untrue.

4.   **The accused will give the following evidence of alibi:** that at about 17.00 on 12 December 2000_ the accused was at the Newtown Amusement Arcade. The accused will call a witness in support of this alibi. The name of the witness is Peter Storey (date of birth 20 August 1968). The address of the witness is 61 Poplar Avenue, Newtown NE19 5BA.

      I was at home in bed

5.   **The accused will raise the following points of law:**

      (i)   The identification evidence of the complainant Michael Shields. The use of the confrontation identification procedure was contrary to the identification Code of Practice. The accused will seek to exclude such evidence under s 78 PACE 1984.

      (ii)   The confession: 'He's just a boy, you will not make it stick.' The correct procedure contained in the Detention Code of Practice for the recording of comments outside the context of an interview was not followed. The accused, though he denies making such a confession, will seek to exclude such evidence under s 78 PACE 1984.

      (iii) The confession contained in the police record of tape recorded interview, the accused will allege that such a confession is inadmissible under s 76 PACE 1984 and s 78 PACE 1984.

6. The accused requests the following disclosure of material which might undermine the prosecution case or which might assist the defence disclosed by this statement:

7.

(a) Has a sensitive materials schedule been prepared?

(b) Has the prosecutor been informed separately of the existence of material deemed to be too sensitive to be included in the schedule?

(c) Has the prosecutor been informed separately of information about any prosecution witnesses previous convictions (including spent convictions) or disciplinary issues involving police officers relating to this matter?

(d) If the answer to (a), (b) or (c) above is yes, has the prosecutor decided that he is not under a duty to disclose:

 (i) any material in (a) above?

 (ii) any material in (b) above?

 (iii) any material in (c) above?

(e) If the answer to answer (a), (b) or (c) above is yes, has an application been made to the court to order non-disclosure of any such material?

The defence reserves the right to amend the above statement on the receipt of further evidence.

Signed ....

Dated ....

don't need to put into exam.

(U) Crown Court: Case progression, preliminary hearing form

CROWN COURT

CASE PROGRESSION

PRELIMINARY HEARING

Date of hearing: /   /   Judge:

Prosecution advocate:		
D1	[bail][custody] represented by:	
D2	[bail][custody] represented by:	
D3	[bail][custody] represented by:	
D4	[bail][custody] represented by:	
D5	[bail][custody] represented by:	

No. of case in Crown Court: [   ]   URN: [   ]

Has the defendant been advised about credit for pleading guilty?

D1	D2	D3	D4	D5

Has the defendant been warned that if he is on bail and fails to attend, the proceedings may continue in his absence?

1) TRIAL JUDGE

Should the future management of the case be under the supervision of the trial judge or a nominated judge?   YES/NO

2) PLEA

a.   **Is it likely that the case can be concluded by the defendant pleading guilty?**

D1	D2	D3	D4	D5

b.   If yes and if the defendant cannot be sentenced at the preliminary hearing, go to 3) and/or 4) as appropriate

3) LIKELY GUILTY PLEA

a.   *The defendant will be sentenced on: /   /   or at the plea and case management hearing*

b.   *The directions made by the magistrates' court when the case was sent shall apply subject to the following amendments:*

c.   *The pre-sentence report (if required) to be received by the Crown Court and made available to the defence and the prosecution by:*

d.   *The defence to serve any material which it wishes the court to consider when sentencing by:*

e.   **Does the defence intend to make "derogatory assertions" against a person's character in the course of mitigation?**

D1	D2	D3	D4	D5

f.   *If yes, the court orders:*

g.   **Are there any other matters against a defendant which should be dealt with at the same time as the proceedings in this case (other offences/TIC's)?**

D1	D2	D3	D4	D5

h.   **If yes, give brief details:**

i.   *If there are other matters, the court orders:*

j.   *Further orders (e.g. orders re medical, psychiatric reports, confiscation proceedings or Newton hearings):*

4)   DIRECTIONS FOR PLEA AND CASE MANAGEMENT HEARING
   a.   *The directions made by the Magistrates' Court when the case was sent shall apply subject to the following amendments:*

   b.   *Further orders:*

5)   EXPERT EVIDENCE
   a.   **Is this a case in which the parties will rely on expert evidence?**

P	D1	D2	D3	D4	D5

   b.   *If yes, the court orders:*

6)   TRIAL
   a.   **Can the date of the trial or the period during which the trial will take place be fixed now?**   YES/NO

   b.   *If yes, the trial will take place on:*
        or within the period of :
        and it is estimated that it will last:

(V) Magistrates' court: Case progression, cases committed for trial

**MAGISTRATES' COURT
CASE PROGRESSION**

**CASE SENT TO THE CROWN COURT UNDER SECTION 51 OF THE
CRIME AND DISORDER ACT 1998**

Sent to Crown Court at [   ] on [/ /]

Prosecution advocate:		
D1	[bail][custody] represented by:	
D2	[bail][custody] represented by:	
D3	[bail][custody] represented by:	
D4	[bail][custody] represented by:	
D5	[bail][custody] represented by:	

No. of case in Magistrates' Court: [   ]   URN: [   ]

	D1	D2	D3	D4	D5
Has the defendant been advised about credit for pleading guilty?					
Is the defendant likely to plead guilty?					
Has the defendant been warned that if he is on bail and fails to attend, the proceedings may continue in his absence?					

1.   PRELIMINARY HEARING & PLEA AND CASE MANAGEMENT HEARING

a.   *If this is a case for which a preliminary hearing in the Crown Court is necessary the preliminary hearing will take place on:*   / /

b.   *The plea and case management hearing will take place on:*   / /

c.   *If a defendant is likely to plead guilty, and a pre-sentence report would be appropriate, the court orders:*

	D1	D2	D3	D4	D5
d. **If a defendant is likely to plead guilty, are there any other matters which should be dealt with at the same time as these proceedings (other offences/TICs)?**					

e.   **If yes, give brief details:**

f.   *If there are other matters, the court orders:*

g.   *Further orders (e.g. orders re medical or psychiatric reports):*

2.   FURTHER DIRECTIONS

a.   The prosecution to serve copies of the documents containing the evidence on which the charge or charges are based ("the prosecution case papers") together with a draft indictment within 50 days where the defendant is in custody and within 70 days in other cases.

b.   The indictment to be preferred within 28 days of the service of the prosecution case papers.

c. Any notice of application by the defence to dismiss the charges shall be made within 14 days of the service of the prosecution case papers.

d. If the defence wish a prosecution witness to be called to give evidence in person at the trial, the defence shall so notify the prosecution and the Crown Court within 7 days of receiving the prosecution case papers.

e. Following receipt of the notification referred to in d., the police to notify the prosecution and the Crown Court of the dates when the witness is unavailable to give evidence and the reasons therefor so that the information is available for the plea and case management hearing.

f. The prosecution to comply with its initial duty of disclosure at the same time as service of the prosecution case papers.

g. The defence to serve the defence statement, including alibi details if appropriate, within 14 days of the date on which the prosecution complied, or purported to comply, with its initial duty of disclosure.

h. The prosecution to serve any application for special measures within 28 days of the service of the prosecution case papers.

i. The defence to serve any response to the application for special measures within 14 days of service of the application.

j. The prosecution to serve any notice of intention to introduce hearsay evidence within 14 days of the service of the prosecution case papers.

k. The defence to serve any notice opposing the prosecution notice under j. within 14 days of receipt of that notice.

l. The defence to serve any notice of intention to introduce hearsay evidence within 14 days of the date on which the prosecution complied, or purported to comply, with its initial duty of disclosure.

m. The prosecution to serve any notice opposing the defence notice under l. within 14 days of receipt of that notice.

n. The defence to serve any application to introduce the bad character of a prosecution witness within 14 days of the date on which the prosecution complied, or purported to comply, with its initial duty of disclosure.

o. The prosecution to serve any notice opposing the defence application under n. to introduce the bad character of a prosecution witness within 14 days of receipt of the application.

p. The prosecution to serve any notice to introduce the defendant's bad character within 14 days of the service of the prosecution case papers.

q. The defence to serve any application to exclude evidence of the defendant's bad character within 7 days of receipt of the prosecution notice under p.

r. *Any further orders relating to bad character:*

s. The parties shall, within 14 days, give to the Crown Court case progression officer responsible for this case all the relevant information to enable the Crown Court Case Details form to be completed.

t. *Further orders:*

....
....
....

(W) Magistrates' court: Case progression, cases to be tried in the magistrates' court

MAGISTRATES' COURT
CASE PROGRESSION

CASE COMMITTED FOR TRIAL TO THE CROWN COURT UNDER SECTION 6 OF THE MAGISTRATES' COURTS ACT 1980

Committed to Crown Court at [   ] on [/ /]

Prosecution advocate:	
D1	[bail][custody] represented by:
D2	[bail][custody] represented by:
D3	[bail][custody] represented by:
D4	[bail][custody] represented by:
D5	[bail][custody] represented by:

No. of case in Magistrates' Court: [   ] URN: [   ]

	D1	D2	D3	D4	D5
Has the defendant been advised about credit for pleading guilty?					
Has the defendant been warned that if he is on bail and fails to attend, the proceedings may continue in his absence?					

1. PLEA AND CASE MANAGEMENT HEARING

The plea and case management hearing will take place on:

2. DIRECTIONS

a.   The indictment to be preferred within 28 days and the draft indictment, if not already served, to be served forthwith.

b.   If the defence wish a prosecution witness to be called to give evidence in person at the trial, the defence shall so notify the prosecution and the Crown Court within 14 days.

c.   Following receipt of the notification referred to in b., the police to notify the prosecution and the Crown Court of the dates when the witness is unavailable to give evidence and the reasons therefor so that the information is available at the plea and case management hearing.

d.   The prosecution to comply with its initial duty of disclosure (if not already done) within 14 days.

e.   The defence to serve the defence statement, including alibi details if appropriate, within 14 days of the date on which the prosecution complied, or purported to comply, with its initial duty of disclosure.

f.   The prosecution to serve any application for special measures within 28 days.

g.   The defence to serve any response to the application for special measures within 14 days of service of the application.

h.   The prosecution to serve any notice of intention to introduce hearsay evidence within 14 days.

i.   The defence to serve any notice opposing the prosecution notice under h., within 14 days of receipt of that notice.

j.   The defence to serve any notice of intention to introduce hearsay evidence within 14 days of the date on which the prosecution complied, or purported to comply, with its initial duty of disclosure.

k.   The prosecution to serve any notice opposing the defence notice under j. within 14 days of receipt of that notice.

l.   The defence to serve any application to introduce the bad character of a prosecution witness within 14 days of the date on which the prosecution complied, or purported to comply, with its initial duty of disclosure.

m.   The prosecution to serve any notice opposing the defence application under l. to introduce the bad character of a prosecution witness within 14 days of receipt of the application.

n.   The prosecution to serve any notice to introduce the defendant's bad character within 14 days of the service of the prosecution case papers.

o.   The defence to serve any application to exclude evidence of the defendant's bad character within 7 days of receipt of the prosecution notice under n.

p.   The parties shall, within 14 days, give to the Crown Court case progression officer responsible for this case all the relevant information to enable the Crown Court Case Details form to be completed.

q.   *Further orders*:

       ....
       ....
       ....

Annex E

MAGISTRATES' COURT
CASE PROGRESSION

CASE TO BE TRIED IN THE MAGISTRATES' COURT

Date of hearing: /   /

The court will fix the trial date at (or shortly after) the hearing at which the defendant pleads not guilty. The directions below apply from that hearing unless they are modified or deleted by the court.

DEFENDANT

Name of defendant_____Age___Date of Birth_____
Address_____
_____
In custody /on bail Contact telephone number (if defendant agrees)_____

CASE

No. of case in Magistrates' Court: [_____]   URN: [_____]
Charges:_____
_____
_____
_____

LEGAL REPRESENTATION

Prosecution Reviewing Lawyer: _____Address:_____
_____
Tel.:_____   Fax: _____
Email: _____   DX _____

Defence Solicitor: _____Solicitors Firm & Address:_____
_____
Tel.:_____   Fax: _____
Email: _____   DX _____

CASE PROGRESSION OFFICERS

Magistrates' Court	Prosecution	Defence
Name:	Name:	Name:
Address:	Address:	Address:
Tel:	Tel:	Tel:
Fax:	Fax:	Fax:
Email:	Email:	Email:
DX:	DX:	DX:

Has the defendant been advised about credit for pleading guilty? YES/NO

Has the defendant been warned that if he is on bail and fails to attend, the proceedings may continue in his absence? YES/NO

TRIAL DATE *The trial will take place on:*   *and is expected to last for:*

DIRECTIONS

Special measures

a.   The prosecution to serve any application for special measures within **14 days**

b.   The defence to serve any response to the application for special measures within **14 days** of service of the prosecution application.

Prosecution case and disclosure

c.   To the extent it has not done so, the prosecution must serve copies of the documents containing the evidence on which the charge or charges are based, including witness statements and any documentary exhibits, tapes of interview, video tapes and CCTV tapes within **[28] days**.

d.   To the extent it has not done so, the prosecution must comply with its initial duty of disclosure within **[28] days**.

Hearsay evidence

e.   The prosecution to serve any notice of intention to introduce hearsay evidence at the same time as it complies, or purports to comply with its initial duty of disclosure.

f.   The defence to serve any notice opposing the prosecution's notice under e., within **14 days** of receipt of the notice.

g.   The defence to serve any notice of intention to introduce hearsay evidence within **14 days** of the date on which the prosecution complied, or purported to comply, with its initial duty of disclosure.

h.   The prosecution to serve any notice opposing the defence's notice under g. within **14 days** of receipt of the application.

Bad character evidence

i.   The defence to serve any application to introduce the bad character of a prosecution witness within **14 days** of the date on which the prosecution complied, or purported to comply, with its initial duty of disclosure.

j.   The prosecution to serve any notice opposing the defence application to introduce the bad character of a prosecution witness under i. within **14 days** of receipt of the application.

k.   The prosecution to serve any notice to introduce the defendant's bad character at the same time as it complies, or purports to comply with its initial duty of disclosure.

l.   The defence to serve any application to exclude evidence of the defendant's bad character within **7 days** of receipt of the prosecution application under k.

m.   *Any further orders relating to bad character:*

Defence statement

n.   If a defence statement is to be given, the defence must serve it within **14 days** of the prosecution complying or purporting to comply with its initial duty of disclosure.

Witness statements

o.   If the defence wish a prosecution witness to give evidence in person at the trial, the defence shall so notify the prosecution within **7** days of receiving the prosecution case under c.

p.   The defence must serve any statements of defence witnesses who the defence propose not to give evidence in person at the trial within **[14] days** of receiving the prosecution case under c.

q.   If a party requires a witness whose statement has been served under p. to give evidence in person at the trial, the party shall so notify the prosecution within **7** days of service of the statement.

Further disclosure

r.   The prosecution to complete any further disclosure at least **[14]** days before the trial.

Written admissions

s.   The parties must file any written admissions made under section 10 of the Criminal Justice Act 1967 within **[56] days**.

Expert evidence

t.   If either party intends to rely on expert evidence, the directions below apply.

Point of law

u.   If any point of law is to be taken by a party and a skeleton argument would be helpful, it must be served together with authorities at least **[21] days** prior to the trial.

v.   The other party must serve a skeleton argument in reply together with authorities at least **[7] days** prior to the trial.

Trial readiness

w.   The parties must certify readiness for trial, by filing a certificate of readiness if appropriate, at least **[7] days** prior to the trial.

x.   *Any other orders:*

Further case management

y.   *A further case management hearing will take place on:*

EXPERT EVIDENCE

a.   A party seeking to rely on expert evidence must serve the expert's report within **[28] days**.

b.   A party served with expert evidence must indicate whether the expert is required to attend at the trial, and either serve their own expert evidence in response or indicate that they are not intending to rely on expert evidence within **[28] days** of receipt of the other party's expert evidence.

c.   A meeting of experts to agree non-contentious matters and identify issues, if appropriate and if the parties agree, must take place within **[28] days** of service of both parties' expert evidence.

d.   The parties must notify the court within **[14] days** of an experts' meeting whether the length of the trial is affected by the outcome of the meeting.

(X)   Notice of intention to admit hearsay evidence

HEARSAY EVIDENCE
(CRIMINAL PROCEDURE RULES, PART 34)

**Notice of intention to introduce hearsay evidence
under s.114, Criminal Justice Act 2003**
(Criminal Procedure Rules, rr 34.2, 68.20(1))

This form shall be used to give notice of intention to introduce hearsay evidence on one or more of the grounds set out in s. 114(1), Criminal Justice Act 2003.

Details of party giving notice

Surname	State the name and address of the party giving notice of hearsay evidence. (If in custody give address where detained.)
Forenames	
Address	

Case Details

The .. .. Court at.. .. ..
Case Reference Number.. .. ..

Name of judge:

Date the trial or proceedings is due to start/or started:

Name of prosecuting agency (if relevant)
Name of defendant(s):

Charges:

Enter the name of the Court and the case no.

Give brief details of the charges to which this notice applies.

To the named recipient(s) of this notice:

I hereby give you notice of my intention to introduce hearsay evidence, details of which are set out below, in these proceedings.

- page 1 -

Grounds for introducing the hearsay evidence

On which of the following grounds do you intend to introduce the hearsay evidence?

(a) ☐ Any statutory provision makes it admissible;   Tick as appropriate

(b) ☐ Any rule of law preserved by s 118, Criminal Justice Act 2003 makes it admissible;

(c) ☐ All parties to the proceedings agree to it being admissible; or

Specify which provision of the CJA 2003 or other statute, or which rule of law preserved by s.118 CJA 2003 you rely on to introduce the evidence.

(d) ☐ It is in the interests of justice for it to be admissible.

Where box (d) above is ticked, you must specify which of the factors set out in s. 114(2), CJA 2003 are relevant and explain how they are relevant.

Further details of grounds:

Details of hearsay evidence

The details of the hearsay evidence are as follows:

Give brief details of the evidence that you want to introduce as hearsay evidence.

A complete copy of that evidence must be attached to this notice, if it has not already been served on the other parties.

Extension of time

Are you applying for an extension of time within which to give this notice?   *YES/NO

*delete as appropriate

If yes, state your reasons:

Signed:
Dated:

- page 2 -

(Y)   Notice of opposition to the introduction of hearsay evidence

---

**Notice of opposition to the introduction of hearsay evidence
under s. 114 Criminal Justice Act 2003**
(Criminal Procedure Rules, rr 34.3, 34.5, 68.20(1))

This form shall be used to give notice of opposition to the introduction of hearsay evidence, as specified in a notice of hearsay evidence given under rule 34(2).

Details of party opposing the introduction of hearsay evidence

Surname	State the name and address of the party giving notice of their opposition to the introduction of hearsay evidence. (If in custody give address where detained.)
Forenames	
Address	
Date that you were given notice that hearsay evidence will be introduced in these proceedings:	

Case Details

The .. .. Court at.. .. .. Case Reference Number..	Enter the name of the Court and the case no.
Name of judge:	
Date the trial or proceedings is due to start/or started:	
Name of prosecuting agency (if relevant) Name of defendant(s):	
Charges:	Give brief details of the charges to which this notice applies.

Details of the hearsay evidence that you want to exclude

Give a brief description of the hearsay evidence that you want to exclude from the proceedings. Specify whether you object to all or part of that evidence.

Grounds for excluding the evidence

Set out the grounds for excluding the hearsay evidence that you object to.

Any relevant skeleton argument or case law that might bear on the issue may be attached to this notice.

Extension of time

Are you applying for an extension of time within which to give this notice?   *YES/NO

*delete as appropriate

If yes, state your reasons:

Signed:
Dated:

(Z) Application for leave to adduce non-defendant's bad character

EVIDENCE OF BAD CHARACTER
(CRIMINAL PROCEDURE RULES, PART 35)

Application for leave to adduce non-defendant's bad character under s.100 Criminal Justice Act 2003 *(Criminal Procedure Rules, rr 35.2, 68.21)*	
Details required	*Notes*
1. Details of applicant Name: Address: Name of prosecuting agency (if relevant)	
2. Case details Case reference numbers: Date the trial or proceedings is due to start/or started: Name of defendant(s): Charges:	*Give brief details of those charges to which this application applies.*
3. Details of this application Please provide the following details (a) the particulars of the bad character evidence including how it is to be adduced or elicited in the proceedings (including the name of the relevant non-defendant and all other relevant witnesses); and (b) the grounds for the admission of evidence of a non-defendant's bad character under section 100 of CJA 2003.	*s.100 Criminal Justice Act 2003* *Please attach any relevant documentation.*
4. Extension of time Are you applying for an extension of time for service? (yes/no) If so please provide details.	
Signed: Dated	

[Note: Formerly set out in the Schedule to the Magistrates' Courts (Amendment) Rules 2004 (SI 2004/2993) relating to rule 72A of the Magistrates' Courts Rules 1981 and form BC1 of the Crown Court (Amendment No.3) Rules 2004 (SI 2004/2991) relating to rule 23D of the Crown Court Rules 1982 and form 21 of the Criminal Appeal (Amendment No.2) Rules 2004 (SI 2004/2992) relating to rule 9D of the Criminal Appeal Rules 1968].

(ZA) Notice of intention to adduce the defendant's bad character

<table>
<tr><td colspan="2">Notice of intention to adduce bad character evidence
under s.101 Criminal Justice Act 2003

(Criminal Procedure Rules, rr 35.4(1), 68.21)</td></tr>
<tr><td>Details required</td><td>Notes</td></tr>
<tr><td>1. Details of party giving notice

Name:
Address:
Name of prosecuting agency (if relevant)</td><td></td></tr>
<tr><td>2. Case details

Case reference numbers:
Date the trial or proceedings is due to start/or started:
Name of defendant(s):
Charges:</td><td>Give brief details of those charges to which this application applies.</td></tr>
<tr><td>3. Details of this Notice

To the named defendant:
You are hereby given notice that bad character evidence, particulars of which are detailed below, is to be adduced or elicited in these proceedings.
The particulars of that bad character evidence are as follows:</td><td>In this section include:
a) a description of the bad character evidence and how it is to be adduced or elicited in the proceedings (including the names of any relevant witnesses); and
b) the grounds for the admission of evidence of the defendant's bad character under section 101 of the Criminal Justice Act 2003. Please attach any relevant documentation.</td></tr>
<tr><td>4. Extension of time

Are you applying for an extension of time for service? (yes/no).
If yes, state your reasons.</td><td></td></tr>
<tr><td>Signed:
Dated:</td><td></td></tr>
</table>

[Note: Formerly set out in the Schedule to the Magistrates' Courts (Amendment) Rules 2004 (SI 2004/2993) relating to rule 72A of the Magistrates' Courts Rules 1981 and form BC2 of the Crown Court (Amendment No.3) Rules 2004 (SI 2004/2991) relating to rule 23D of the Crown Court Rules 1982 and form 22 of the Criminal Appeal (Amendment No.2) Rules 2004 (SI 2004/2992) relating to rule 9D of the Criminal Appeal Rules 1968].

(ZB) Application to exclude evidence of the defendant's bad character

Application to exclude evidence of the defendant's bad character under ss 101, 108(2) Criminal Justice Act 2003

(Criminal Procedure Rules, rr 35.6, 68.21)

Details required	*Notes*
1. Details of the defendant Name: Address: Date of Birth: If you are in custody, please give your Prison Index No. and address where detained:	
2. Case details Case reference numbers: Date the trial or proceedings is due to start/or started: Charges: Date that you were served with the notice of the intention to adduce bad character evidence in these proceedings:	
3. Details of the application This section must include the following information: (a) why the admission of the bad character evidence would have such an adverse effect on the fairness of the proceedings that the court should not admit it.	*Note that an application to exclude this evidence under section 101(3) of the Criminal Justice Act 2003 can only be made if you have been notified of a party's intention to adduce this evidence under subsection 101(1)(d) (it is relevant to an important matter in issue between the defendant and the prosecution) or subsection 101(1)(g) (that the defendant has made an attack on another person's character).*
(b) details as to the length of time between the matters to which the bad character evidence relates and the matters which form the subject of the offence charged.	*Section 101(4) of the 2003 Act.*
(c) if you are applying for the exclusion of this evidence on grounds other than section 101(3) of CJA 2003, please set out such objections.	

- page 1 -

4. Extension of time	
Are you applying for an extension of time for service (yes/no) If so, state your reasons	
Signed: Date:	

- page 2 -

[Note: Formerly set out in the Schedule to the Magistrates' Courts (Amendment) Rules 2004 (SI 2004/2993) relating to rule 72A of the Magistrates' Courts Rules 1981 and form BC3 of the Crown Court (Amendment No.3) Rules 2004 (SI 2004/2991) relating to rule 23D of the Crown Court Rules 1982 and form 23 of the Criminal Appeal (Amendment No.2) Rules 2004 (SI 2004/2992) relating to rule 9D of the Criminal Appeal Rules 1968].

Appendix 3

Magistrates' Association Sentencing Guidelines

Introduction

These Sentencing Guidelines cover offences with which magistrates deal regularly and frequently in the adult criminal courts. They provide a sentencing structure which sets out how to:

- establish the seriousness of each case
- determine the most appropriate way of dealing with it.

The Sentencing Guidelines provide a method for considering individual cases and a guideline from which discussion should properly flow; but they are not a tariff and should never be used as such. **The guideline sentences are based on a first-time offender pleading not guilty.**

Using the sentencing structure

The sentencing structure used for these Guidelines was established by the Criminal Justice Act 1991. This reaffirms the principle of 'just deserts' so that any penalty must reflect the seriousness of the offence for which it is imposed and the personal circumstances of the offender. Magistrates must always start the sentencing process by taking full account of all the circumstances of the offence and making a judicial assessment of the seriousness category into which it falls. It is important that the court makes clear the factual basis on which the sentence is based.

In every case, the Criminal Justice Act 1991 requires sentencers to consider:

- Is discharge or a fine appropriate?
- Is the offence serious enough for a community penalty?
- Is it so serious that only custody is appropriate?

If the last, in either way cases, justices will also need to consider if magistrates' courts' powers are sufficient.

The format of the Sentencing Guidelines

---

1. | **CONSIDER THE SERIOUSNESS OF THE OFFENCE**

Magistrates must always make an assessment of seriousness following the structure of the Criminal Justice Act 1991. **The guideline sentences are based on a first-time offender pleading not guilty**.

Where this guideline is discharge or fine, a suggested starting point guideline fine is also given. Refer to the guidance on pages 85–87 and 101–102.

Where the starting point guideline is a community penalty, refer to the guidance on pages 91 and 92.

Where the starting point guideline is custody, think in terms of weeks and credit as appropriate for a timely guilty plea.

For some either way offences the guideline is 'are your sentencing powers sufficient?'. This indicates that magistrates should be considering whether the seriousness of the offence is such that six months (or 12 months in the case of two or more offences) is insufficient, so that the case must be committed to the Crown Court (consult the legal adviser with regard to Crown Court sentencing and guideline cases). If the case is retained in the magistrates' court a substantial custodial sentence is likely to be necessary.

It should be noted that if magistrates consider (say) nine months to be the appropriate sentence, to be reduced for a timely guilty plea to six months, then the case falls within their powers and must be retained. Subject to offender mitigation, six months would appear to be the appropriate sentence. However, if sentence is passed on this basis the court should specifically say so in its reasons.

---

2. | **CONSIDER AGGRAVATING AND MITIGATING FACTORS**

Make sure that all aggravating and mitigating factors are considered. The lists in the Sentencing Guidelines are neither exhaustive nor a substitute for the personal judgment of magistrates. **Factors which do not appear in the Guidelines may be important in individual cases**.

If the offence was racially or religiously aggravated, the court must treat that fact as an aggravating factor under statute (s.153 of the Powers of Criminal Courts (Sentencing) Act 2000). Refer to page 98 for further guidance.

If the offence was committed while the offender was on bail, the court must treat that as an aggravating factor under statute (s.151 Powers of Criminal Courts (Sentencing) Act 2000).

Consider previous convictions, or any failure to respond to previous sentences, in assessing seriousness. Courts should identify any convictions relevant for this purpose and then consider to what extent they affect the seriousness of the present offence.

3.

> ## TAKE A PRELIMINARY VIEW OF SERIOUSNESS, THEN CONSIDER OFFENDER MITIGATION

When an initial assessment of the seriousness of the offence has been formed, consider the offender.

The Guidelines set out some examples of offender mitigation but there are frequently others to be considered in individual cases. Any offender mitigation that the court accepts must lead to some downward revision of the provisional assessment of seriousness, although this revision may be minor. **Remember, however, that the guideline sentences are based on a first-time offender pleading not guilty.**

A previous criminal record may deprive the defendant of being able to say that he is a person of good character.

4.

> ## CONSIDER YOUR SENTENCE

The law requires the court to consider reducing the sentence for a timely guilty plea. Credit for a timely guilty plea may result in a sentencing reduction of up to one-third but the precise amount of credit will depend upon the facts of each case and a last minute plea of guilty may attract only a minimal reduction.

Credit may be given in respect of the amount of a fine or periods of community service or custody. Periods of mandatory disqualification or mandatory penalty points cannot be reduced for a guilty plea.

5.

> ## DECIDE YOUR SENTENCE

Remember that magistrates have a duty to consider the award of compensation in all appropriate cases, and to give reasons if compensation is not awarded. See pages 89–90, Section Three.

Agree the form of words that the Chairman will use when announcing sentence.

Assault – actual bodily harm	Offences Against the Person Act 1861 s.47 Triable either way – see Mode of Trial Guidelines Penalty: Level 5 and/or 6 months

CONSIDER THE SERIOUSNESS OF THE OFFENCE
(INCLUDING THE IMPACT ON THE VICTIM)

IS DISCHARGE OR FINE APPROPRIATE?

IS IT SERIOUS ENOUGH FOR A COMMUNITY PENALTY?

GUIDELINE: → *IS IT SO SERIOUS THAT ONLY CUSTODY IS APPROPRIATE?*

ARE YOUR SENTENCING POWERS SUFFICIENT?

THIS IS A GUIDELINE FOR A FIRST-TIME OFFENDER PLEADING NOT GUILTY

 ## CONSIDER AGGRAVATING AND MITIGATING FACTORS AND THE WEIGHT TO ATTACH TO EACH

for example
  Abuse of trust (domestic setting)
  Deliberate kicking or biting
  Extensive injuries (may be psychological)
  Headbutting
  Group action
  Offender in position of authority
  On hospital/medical or school premises
  Premeditated
  Victim particularly vulnerable
  Victim serving the public
  Weapon
  This list is not exhaustive
	for example
	  Minor injury
	  Provocation
	  Single blow
	  This list is not exhaustive

If offender is on bail, this offence is more serious
If offender has previous convictions, their relevance and any failure to respond to previous sentences should be considered – they may increase the seriousness. The court should make it clear, when passing sentence, that this was the approach adopted.

TAKE A PRELIMINARY VIEW OF SERIOUSNESS, THEN CONSIDER OFFENDER MITIGATION

for example
  Age, health (physical or mental)
  Co-operation with police
  Evidence of genuine remorse
  Voluntary compensation

CONSIDER YOUR SENTENCE

Compare it with the suggested guideline level of sentence and reconsider your reasons carefully if you have chosen a sentence at a different level. Consider a reduction for a timely guilty plea.

DECIDE YOUR SENTENCE
NB. COMPENSATION – Give reasons if not awarding compensation

Burglary (dwelling)	Theft Act 1968 s.9 Triable either way – see Mode of Trial Guidelines Penalty: Level 5 and/or 6 months

CONSIDER THE SERIOUSNESS OF THE OFFENCE
(INCLUDING THE IMPACT ON THE VICTIM)

IS DISCHARGE OR FINE APPROPRIATE?

IS IT SERIOUS ENOUGH FOR A COMMUNITY PENALTY?

IS IT SO SERIOUS THAT ONLY CUSTODY IS APPROPRIATE?

GUIDELINE: →   **ARE YOUR SENTENCING POWERS SUFFICIENT?**

THIS IS A GUIDELINE FOR A FIRST-TIME OFFENDER PLEADING NOT GUILTY

 CONSIDER AGGRAVATING AND MITIGATING FACTORS AND THE WEIGHT TO ATTACH TO EACH

for example	for example
Force used or threatened	First offence of its type AND low value property stolen AND no significant damage or disturbance AND no injury or violence
Group enterprise	
High value (in economic or sentimental terms) property stolen	
More than minor trauma caused	Minor part played
Professional planning/organisation/ execution	Theft from attached garage
Significant damage or vandalism	Vacant property
Victim injured	*ONLY if one or more of the above factors are present AND none of the aggravating factors listed are present should you consider NOT committing for sentence.*
Victim present at the time	
Vulnerable victim	
IF ANY of the above factors are present you should commit for sentence.	

If racially or religiously aggravated, or offender is on bail, this offence is more serious
If offender has previous convictions, their relevance and any failure to respond to previous sentences should be considered – they may increase the seriousness. The court should make it clear, when passing sentence, that this was the approach adopted.

TAKE A PRELIMINARY VIEW OF SERIOUSNESS, THEN CONSIDER WHETHER THE CASE SHOULD BE COMMITTED FOR SENTENCE, THEN CONSIDER OFFENDER MITIGATION

for example
  Age, health (physical or mental)
  Co-operation with police
  Evidence of genuine remorse
  Voluntary compensation

CONSIDER COMMITTAL OR YOUR SENTENCE

Compare it with the suggested guideline level of sentence and reconsider your reasons carefully if you have chosen a sentence at a different level.
Consider a reduction for a timely guilty plea.

DECIDE YOUR SENTENCE
NB. COMPENSATION – Give reasons if not awarding compensation

Theft Act 1968 s.9 Triable either way – see Mode of Trial Guidelines Penalty: Level 5 and/or 6 months	Burglary (non-dwelling)

CONSIDER THE SERIOUSNESS OF THE OFFENCE
(INCLUDING THE IMPACT ON THE VICTIM)

IS DISCHARGE OR FINE APPROPRIATE?
GUIDELINE: →   IS IT SERIOUS ENOUGH FOR A COMMUNITY PENALTY?
IS IT SO SERIOUS THAT ONLY CUSTODY IS APPROPRIATE?
ARE YOUR SENTENCING POWERS SUFFICIENT?

THIS IS A GUIDELINE FOR A FIRST-TIME OFFENDER PLEADING NOT GUILTY

 ## CONSIDER AGGRAVATING AND MITIGATING FACTORS AND THE WEIGHT TO ATTACH TO EACH

for example	for example
Forcible entry Group offence Harm to business Occupants frightened Professional operation Repeat victimisation School or medical premises Soiling, ransacking, damage *This list is not exhaustive*	Low value Nobody frightened No damage or disturbance *This list is not exhaustive*

If racially or religiously aggravated, or offender is on bail, this offence is more serious
If offender has previous convictions, their relevance and any failure to respond to previous sentences should be considered – they may increase the seriousness. The court should make it clear, when passing sentence, that this was the approach adopted.

TAKE A PRELIMINARY VIEW OF SERIOUSNESS, THEN CONSIDER OFFENDER MITIGATION

for example
> Age, health (physical or mental)
> Co-operation with police
> Evidence of genuine remorse
> Voluntary compensation

CONSIDER YOUR SENTENCE

Compare it with the suggested guideline level of sentence and reconsider your reasons carefully if you have chosen a sentence at a different level. Consider a reduction for a timely guilty plea.

DECIDE YOUR SENTENCE
NB. COMPENSATION – Give reasons if not awarding compensation

Common assault	Criminal Justice Act 1988 s.39 Triable only summarily Penalty: Level 5 and/or 6 months

CONSIDER THE SERIOUSNESS OF THE OFFENCE
(INCLUDING THE IMPACT ON THE VICTIM)

IS DISCHARGE OR FINE APPROPRIATE?

GUIDELINE: →   *IS IT SERIOUS ENOUGH FOR A COMMUNITY PENALTY?*

IS IT SO SERIOUS THAT ONLY CUSTODY IS APPROPRIATE?

THIS IS A GUIDELINE FOR A FIRST-TIME OFFENDER PLEADING NOT GUILTY

 ## CONSIDER AGGRAVATING AND MITIGATING FACTORS
AND THE WEIGHT TO ATTACH TO EACH

for example	for example
Abuse of trust (domestic setting)	Impulsive
Group action	Minor injury
Injury	Provocation
Offender in position of authority	Single blow
On hospital/medical or school premises	*This list is not exhaustive*
Premeditated	
Spitting	
Victim particularly vulnerable	
Victim serving the public	
Weapon	
This list is not exhaustive	

If offender is on bail, this offence is more serious
If offender has previous convictions, their relevance and any failure to respond to previous
sentences should be considered – they may increase the seriousness. The court should make
it clear, when passing sentence, that this was the approach adopted.

TAKE A PRELIMINARY VIEW OF SERIOUSNESS, THEN
CONSIDER OFFENDER MITIGATION

for example
  Age, health (physical or mental)
  Co-operation with police
  Evidence of genuine remorse
  Voluntary compensation

CONSIDER YOUR SENTENCE

Compare it with the suggested guideline level of sentence and reconsider
your reasons carefully if you have chosen a sentence at a different level.
Consider a reduction for a timely guilty plea.

DECIDE YOUR SENTENCE
NB. COMPENSATION – Give reasons if not awarding compensation

Handling stolen goods	Theft Act 1968 s.22 Triable either way – see Mode of Trial Guidelines Penalty: Level 5 and/or 6 months

CONSIDER THE SERIOUSNESS OF THE OFFENCE
(INCLUDING THE IMPACT ON THE VICTIM)

IS DISCHARGE OR FINE APPROPRIATE?
GUIDELINE: → **IS IT SERIOUS ENOUGH FOR A COMMUNITY PENALTY?**
IS IT SO SERIOUS THAT ONLY CUSTODY IS APPROPRIATE?
ARE YOUR SENTENCING POWERS SUFFICIENT?

THIS IS A GUIDELINE FOR A FIRST-TIME OFFENDER PLEADING NOT GUILTY

 ## CONSIDER AGGRAVATING AND MITIGATING FACTORS AND THE WEIGHT TO ATTACH TO EACH

for example	for example
High level of profit accruing to handler High value (including sentimental) of goods Provision by handler of regular outlet for stolen goods Proximity of the handler to the primary offence Seriousness of the primary offence Sophistication The particular facts, eg the goods handled were the proceeds of a domestic burglary Threats of violence or abuse of power by handler in order to obtain goods *This list is not exhaustive*	Isolated offence Little or no benefit accruing to handler Low monetary value of goods *This list is not exhaustive*

If offender is on bail, this offence is more serious
If offender has previous convictions, their relevance and any failure to respond to previous sentences should be considered – they may increase the seriousness. The court should make it clear, when passing sentence, that this was the approach adopted.

TAKE A PRELIMINARY VIEW OF SERIOUSNESS, THEN CONSIDER OFFENDER MITIGATION

for example
Age, health (physical or mental)
Co-operation with police
Evidence of genuine remorse
Voluntary compensation

CONSIDER YOUR SENTENCE

Compare it with the suggested guideline level of sentence and reconsider your reasons carefully if you have chosen a sentence at a different level.
Consider a reduction for a timely guilty plea.

DECIDE YOUR SENTENCE
NB. COMPENSATION – Give reasons if not awarding compensation

| Theft Act 1968 s.15
Triable either way – see Mode of Trial Guidelines
Penalty: Level 5 and/or 6 months | **Obtaining by deception** |

CONSIDER THE SERIOUSNESS OF THE OFFENCE
(INCLUDING THE IMPACT ON THE VICTIM)

IS DISCHARGE OR FINE APPROPRIATE?

GUIDELINE: →   IS IT SERIOUS ENOUGH FOR A COMMUNITY PENALTY?

IS IT SO SERIOUS THAT ONLY CUSTODY IS APPROPRIATE?

ARE YOUR SENTENCING POWERS SUFFICIENT?

THIS IS A GUIDELINE FOR A FIRST-TIME OFFENDER PLEADING NOT GUILTY

 ## CONSIDER AGGRAVATING AND MITIGATING FACTORS AND THE WEIGHT TO ATTACH TO EACH

| **for example**
Committed over lengthy period
Large sums or valuable goods
Two or more involved
Use of stolen credit/debit card, cheque
    books, or giros
Victim particularly vulnerable
This list is not exhaustive | **for example**
Impulsive action
Short period
Small sum
This list is not exhaustive |

If offender is on bail, this offence is more serious
If offender has previous convictions, their relevance and any failure to respond to previous
sentences should be considered – they may increase the seriousness. The court should make
it clear, when passing sentence, that this was the approach adopted.

TAKE A PRELIMINARY VIEW OF SERIOUSNESS, THEN CONSIDER OFFENDER MITIGATION

for example
    Age, health (physical or mental)
    Co-operation with police
    Evidence of genuine remorse
    Voluntary compensation

CONSIDER YOUR SENTENCE

Compare it with the suggested guideline level of sentence and reconsider
your reasons carefully if you have chosen a sentence at a different level.
Consider a reduction for a timely guilty plea.

DECIDE YOUR SENTENCE
NB. COMPENSATION – Give reasons if not awarding compensation

Racially or religiously aggravated assault – actual bodily harm	Offences Against the Person Act 1861 s.47 Crime and Disorder Act 1998 s.29 Anti-Terrorism, Crime and Security Act 2001 Triable either way – see Mode of Trial Guidelines Penalty: Level 5 and/or 6 months

CONSIDER THE SERIOUSNESS OF THE OFFENCE
(INCLUDING THE IMPACT ON THE VICTIM)

IS DISCHARGE OR FINE APPROPRIATE?

IS IT SERIOUS ENOUGH FOR A COMMUNITY PENALTY?

IS IT SO SERIOUS THAT ONLY CUSTODY IS APPROPRIATE?

GUIDELINE: →   **ARE YOUR SENTENCING POWERS SUFFICIENT?**

THIS IS A GUIDELINE FOR A FIRST-TIME OFFENDER PLEADING NOT GUILTY

 ## CONSIDER AGGRAVATING AND MITIGATING FACTORS AND THE WEIGHT TO ATTACH TO EACH

for example	for example
Deliberate kicking or biting Extensive injuries (may be psychological) Group action Headbutting **Motivation** for the offence was racial or religious Offender in position of authority On hospital/medical or school premises Premeditated Setting out to humiliate the victim Victim particularly vulnerable Victim serving the public Weapon *This list is not exhaustive*	Minor injury Provocation Single blow *This list is not exhaustive*

If offender is on bail, this offence is more serious
If offender has previous convictions, their relevance and any failure to respond to previous sentences should be considered – they may increase the seriousness. The court should make it clear, when passing sentence, that this was the approach adopted.

TAKE A PRELIMINARY VIEW OF SERIOUSNESS, THEN CONSIDER WHETHER THE CASE SHOULD BE COMMITTED FOR SENTENCE, THEN CONSIDER OFFENDER MITIGATION

for example
    Age, health (physical or mental)
    Co-operation with police
    Evidence of genuine remorse
    Voluntary compensation

CONSIDER COMMITTAL OR YOUR SENTENCE

Compare it with the suggested guideline level of sentence and reconsider your reasons carefully if you have chosen a sentence at a different level. Consider a reduction for a timely guilty plea.

DECIDE YOUR SENTENCE
NB. COMPENSATION – Give reasons if not awarding compensation

Criminal Justice Act 1988 s.39 Crime and Disorder Act 1998 s.29 Anti-Terrorism, Crime and Security Act 2001 Triable either way – see Mode of Trial Guidelines Penalty: Level 5 and/or 6 months	**Racially or religiously aggravated common assault**

CONSIDER THE SERIOUSNESS OF THE OFFENCE
(INCLUDING THE IMPACT ON THE VICTIM)

IS DISCHARGE OR FINE APPROPRIATE?

IS IT SERIOUS ENOUGH FOR A COMMUNITY PENALTY?

GUIDELINE: **→** ***IS IT SO SERIOUS THAT ONLY CUSTODY IS APPROPRIATE?***

ARE YOUR SENTENCING POWERS SUFFICIENT?

THIS IS A GUIDELINE FOR A FIRST-TIME OFFENDER PLEADING NOT GUILTY

 ## CONSIDER AGGRAVATING AND MITIGATING FACTORS AND THE WEIGHT TO ATTACH TO EACH

for example	for example
Group action Injury **Motivation** for the offence was racial or religious Offender in position of authority On hospital/medical or school premises Premeditated Setting out to humiliate the victim Victim particularly vulnerable Victim serving the public Weapon *This list is not exhaustive*	Impulsive Minor injury Provocation Single blow *This list is not exhaustive*

If offender is on bail, this offence is more serious
If offender has previous convictions, their relevance and any failure to respond to previous sentences should be considered – they may increase the seriousness. The court should make it clear, when passing sentence, that this was the approach adopted.

TAKE A PRELIMINARY VIEW OF SERIOUSNESS, THEN CONSIDER OFFENDER MITIGATION

for example
> Age, health (physical or mental)
> Co-operation with police
> Evidence of genuine remorse
> Voluntary compensation

CONSIDER YOUR SENTENCE

Compare it with the suggested guideline level of sentence and reconsider your reasons carefully if you have chosen a sentence at a different level. Consider a reduction for a timely guilty plea.

DECIDE YOUR SENTENCE
NB. COMPENSATION – Give reasons if not awarding compensation

Racially or religiously aggravated wounding – grievous bodily harm	Offences Against the Person Act 1861 s.20 Crime and Disorder Act 1998 s.29 Anti-Terrorism, Crime and Security Act 2001 Triable either way – see Mode of Trial Guidelines Penalty: Level 5 and/or 6 months

CONSIDER THE SERIOUSNESS OF THE OFFENCE
(INCLUDING THE IMPACT ON THE VICTIM)

IS DISCHARGE OR FINE APPROPRIATE?

IS IT SERIOUS ENOUGH FOR A COMMUNITY PENALTY?

IS IT SO SERIOUS THAT ONLY CUSTODY IS APPROPRIATE?

GUIDELINE: →   ***ARE YOUR SENTENCING POWERS SUFFICIENT?***

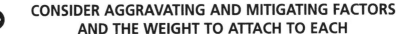 THIS IS A GUIDELINE FOR A FIRST-TIME OFFENDER PLEADING NOT GUILTY

⊕ CONSIDER AGGRAVATING AND MITIGATING FACTORS   ⊖
AND THE WEIGHT TO ATTACH TO EACH

for example	for example
Deliberate kicking/biting Extensive injuries Group action **Motivation** for the offence was racial or religious Offender in position of authority On hospital/medical or school premises Premeditated Setting out to humiliate the victim Victim particularly vulnerable Victim serving the public Weapon *This list is not exhaustive*	Minor wound Provocation *This list is not exhaustive*

If offender is on bail, this offence is more serious
If offender has previous convictions, their relevance and any failure to respond to previous sentences should be considered – they may increase the seriousness. The court should make it clear, when passing sentence, that this was the approach adopted.

TAKE A PRELIMINARY VIEW OF SERIOUSNESS, THEN CONSIDER WHETHER THE CASE SHOULD BE COMMITTED FOR SENTENCE, THEN CONSIDER OFFENDER MITIGATION

for example
  Age, health (physical or mental)
  Co-operation with police
  Evidence of genuine remorse
  Voluntary compensation

CONSIDER COMMITTAL OR YOUR SENTENCE

Compare it with the suggested guideline level of sentence and reconsider your reasons carefully if you have chosen a sentence at a different level. Consider a reduction for a timely guilty plea.

DECIDE YOUR SENTENCE
NB. COMPENSATION – Give reasons if not awarding compensation

Theft	Theft Act 1968 s.1 Triable either way – see Mode of Trial Guidelines Penalty: Level 5 and/or 6 months May disqualify where committed with reference to the theft or taking of a vehicle

CONSIDER THE SERIOUSNESS OF THE OFFENCE
(INCLUDING THE IMPACT ON THE VICTIM)

IS DISCHARGE OR FINE APPROPRIATE?

GUIDELINE: → ***IS IT SERIOUS ENOUGH FOR A COMMUNITY PENALTY?***

IS IT SO SERIOUS THAT ONLY CUSTODY IS APPROPRIATE?

ARE YOUR SENTENCING POWERS SUFFICIENT?

THIS IS A GUIDELINE FOR A FIRST-TIME OFFENDER PLEADING NOT GUILTY

 ## CONSIDER AGGRAVATING AND MITIGATING FACTORS AND THE WEIGHT TO ATTACH TO EACH

for example	for example
High value Planned Sophisticated Adult involving children Organised team Related damage Vulnerable victim *This list is not exhaustive*	Impulsive action Low value *This list is not exhaustive*

If racially or religiously aggravated, or offender is on bail, this offence is more serious
If offender has previous convictions, their relevance and any failure to respond to previous
sentences should be considered – they may increase the seriousness. The court should make
it clear, when passing sentence, that this was the approach adopted.

TAKE A PRELIMINARY VIEW OF SERIOUSNESS, THEN CONSIDER OFFENDER MITIGATION

for example
 Age, health (physical or mental)
 Co-operation with police
 Evidence of genuine remorse
 Voluntary compensation

CONSIDER YOUR SENTENCE

Compare it with the suggested guideline level of sentence and reconsider
your reasons carefully if you have chosen a sentence at a different level.
Consider a reduction for a timely guilty plea.

DECIDE YOUR SENTENCE
NB. COMPENSATION – Give reasons if not awarding compensation

Theft Act 1968 s.1 Triable either way – see Mode of Trial Guidelines Penalty: Level 5 and/or 6 months	Theft in breach of trust

CONSIDER THE SERIOUSNESS OF THE OFFENCE
(INCLUDING THE IMPACT ON THE VICTIM)

IS DISCHARGE OR FINE APPROPRIATE?

IS IT SERIOUS ENOUGH FOR A COMMUNITY PENALTY?

GUIDELINE: → *IS IT SO SERIOUS THAT ONLY CUSTODY IS APPROPRIATE?*

ARE YOUR SENTENCING POWERS SUFFICIENT?

THIS IS A GUIDELINE FOR A FIRST-TIME OFFENDER PLEADING NOT GUILTY

 ## CONSIDER AGGRAVATING AND MITIGATING FACTORS AND THE WEIGHT TO ATTACH TO EACH

for example	for example
Casting suspicion on others	Impulsive action
Committed over a period	Low value
High value	Previous inconsistent attitude by employer
Organised team	Single item
Planned	Unsupported junior
Senior employee	*This list is not exhaustive*
Sophisticated	
Vulnerable victim	
This list is not exhaustive	

If racially or religiously aggravated, or offender is on bail, this offence is more serious
If offender has previous convictions, their relevance and any failure to respond to previous sentences should be considered – they may increase the seriousness. The court should make it clear, when passing sentence, that this was the approach adopted.

TAKE A PRELIMINARY VIEW OF SERIOUSNESS, THEN CONSIDER OFFENDER MITIGATION

for example
    Age, health (physical or mental)
    Co-operation with police
    Evidence of genuine remorse
    Voluntary compensation

CONSIDER YOUR SENTENCE

Compare it with the suggested guideline level of sentence and reconsider your reasons carefully if you have chosen a sentence at a different level.
Consider a reduction for a timely guilty plea.

DECIDE YOUR SENTENCE
NB. COMPENSATION – Give reasons if not awarding compensation

Wounding – grievous bodily harm	Offences Against the Person Act 1861 s.20 Triable either way – see Mode of Trial Guidelines Penalty: Level 5 and/or 6 months

CONSIDER THE SERIOUSNESS OF THE OFFENCE
(INCLUDING THE IMPACT ON THE VICTIM)

IS DISCHARGE OR FINE APPROPRIATE?

IS IT SERIOUS ENOUGH FOR A COMMUNITY PENALTY?

IS IT SO SERIOUS THAT ONLY CUSTODY IS APPROPRIATE?

GUIDELINE: →   ***ARE YOUR SENTENCING POWERS SUFFICIENT?***

THIS IS A GUIDELINE FOR A FIRST-TIME OFFENDER PLEADING NOT GUILTY

 ## CONSIDER AGGRAVATING AND MITIGATING FACTORS AND THE WEIGHT TO ATTACH TO EACH

for example	for example
Abuse of trust (domestic setting) Deliberate kicking/biting Extensive injuries Group action Offender in position of authority On hospital/medical or school premises Premeditated Prolonged assault Victim particularly vulnerable Victim serving the public Weapon *This list is not exhaustive*	Minor wound Provocation *This list is not exhaustive*

If offender is on bail, this offence is more serious
If offender has previous convictions, their relevance and any failure to respond to previous sentences should be considered – they may increase the seriousness. The court should make it clear, when passing sentence, that this was the approach adopted.

TAKE A PRELIMINARY VIEW OF SERIOUSNESS, THEN CONSIDER WHETHER THE CASE SHOULD BE COMMITTED FOR SENTENCE, THEN CONSIDER OFFENDER MITIGATION

for example
  Age, health (physical or mental)
  Co-operation with police
  Evidence of genuine remorse
  Voluntary compensation

CONSIDER COMMITTAL OR YOUR SENTENCE

Compare it with the suggested guideline level of sentence and reconsider your reasons carefully if you have chosen a sentence at a different level. Consider a reduction for a timely guilty plea.

DECIDE YOUR SENTENCE
NB. COMPENSATION – Give reasons if not awarding compensation

Stating the reasons for sentence

1.   We are dealing with an offence of:

    ....

2.   We have considered the impact on the victim which was ....

    ....

3.   We have taken into account these features which make the offence more serious:

    ....

    ....

4.   We have taken into account these features which make the offence less serious:

    ....

    ....

5.   (*where relevant*) We have taken into account that the offence was:
        racially and/or religiously aggravated
        committed on bail

6.   We have taken into account your previous record, specifically the offences of.........................
    .... and your failure to respond to the sentences imposed.

7.   We have taken into account what we have heard in your favour about the offence and
    about you:

    ....

    ....

8.   We have taken into account the fact that you pleaded guilty [at an early stage] [but not
    until ....] and we have reduced the sentence by [state how much].

9.   And, as a result, we have decided that the most appropriate sentence for you is:

    ....

10.   (*where relevant*) We have decided not to award compensation in this case because:

    ....

Appendix 4

Police Station Advice: Advising on Silence

Criminal Practitioners' Newsletter, Special Edition, No 54, October 2003

© The Law Society

The legal position

Changes to the silence provisions

[handwritten annotation: Criminal Justice & Public Order Act.]

Sections 34, 36 and 37 of CJPOA 1994 have been amended by s 59 of the Youth Justice and Criminal Evidence Act 1999 so that inferences cannot be drawn where the accused was at a police station or other authorised place of detention at the time of failure to mention a relevant fact (or failure to account), and he or she had not been allowed an opportunity to consult a solicitor prior to being questioned, charged or informed that they may be prosecuted. This includes cases where the suspect has had their right of access to a solicitor delayed under the Police and Criminal Evidence Act 1984 (PACE) s 58(8) 2000 or the Terrorism Act Sch 8 para 8, but also where (exceptionally) the police can interview a suspect who has asked for legal advice before he or she has received it.[1] As a result, PACE Code of Practice C (the revised version of which came into force on 1 April 2003) now provides that in circumstances where inferences cannot be drawn as a result of these amendments, a different caution must be administered. This caution, and guidance on when it should be administered, are set out in a new Annex C to Code C.

'Silence' on its own cannot prove guilt

In this guidance the term 'silence' is used to mean failure to mention a fact subsequently relied upon by the accused in his or her defence, or failure to account for an object substance or mark etc. under CJPOA 1994 s 36, or failure to account for presence under s 37.

It is important to remember that inferences may be drawn under s 34 in circumstances where the accused did answer police questions, if the accused relies on facts at trial that he or she did not tell the police about in interview or on being charged eg, where the accused lied to police.

It remains the case, however, that silence cannot, by itself, prove guilt (CJPOA 1994 s 38), and inferences can only be drawn if the court or jury first finds that the other evidence establishes a prima facie case or is 'sufficiently compelling to call for an answer' from the accused.[2] However, this does not mean that in order for inferences to be drawn the police must disclose evidence amounting to a prima facie case prior to questioning the suspect.

Despite the inherent unfairness, the courts have consistently held that the police are **not** under a general duty to disclose evidence to the suspect at the police station.[3]

Conditions for drawing inferences

It has been held that the silence provisions of the CJPOA 1994 do not, in themselves, contravene the right to fair trial under art 6 of the European

Convention on Human Rights. The courts have given some guidance on the conditions that must be satisfied in order for inferences to be possible under s 34:[4]

1. **The silence provisions only apply in criminal proceedings.**

2. **The alleged failure to mention facts subsequently relied upon must occur before charge or on being charged.** Where there is more than one interview, inferences may be drawn from failure to mention relevant facts in one interview even if they were mentioned in a subsequent interview. Similarly, inferences may be drawn from failure to mention facts in an interview even though they were mentioned at charge, or from failure to mention facts on being charged even though no inference could be drawn from failure to mention facts in interview.[5] However, the prosecution must establish that the accused knew, or must have known, of the facts at the relevant time.[6]

3. **The suspect must have been cautioned** (Code C para 10.1 (caution at interview), Code C para 16.2 (caution at charge)). Minor variations in the wording of the caution are permissible provided that the sense of the caution is preserved. For inferences under ss 36 or 37, the accused must have been arrested and must also have been given a special warning prescribed by Code C para 10.11.

4. **The questioning must be directed to trying to discover whether or by whom the alleged offence was committed** (inferences under s 34(1((a) only). Inferences cannot be drawn if the police have already made up their mind to charge before commencing the interview.[7] However, inferences can be drawn if a court is persuaded that the police still had an open mind even if there was sufficient evidence to charge prior to the interview starting.[8]

5. **The failure of the accused must be to mention any fact relied on in his or her defence in those proceedings** (s 34 only). A defendant may be treated as relying on facts even if they do not give evidence where, for example, cross-examination of prosecution witnesses allows reliance on facts to be inferred.[9] A hypothesis proffered by the accused does not amount to a reliance on facts, and neither does a bare admission made in cross-examination, but an assertion that *something is actually the case'* (eg, an explanation given by the accused for his or her relationship with alleged co-conspirators) can amount to assertion of a fact.[10] An oral assertion of facts in interview (even though police questions are not answered), or the handing in of a written statement, can amount to the assertion of facts so that, if accepted by a court, inferences could not be drawn.[11] It was held in *R v Knight*,[12] in respect of a written statement handed to the police, that the purpose of the 'silence' legislation was to encourage early disclosure of the defence not the scrutiny and testing of the defence by police in interview. Note that inferences under ss 36 and 37 do not depend upon the facts put forward by the accused at trial since it is the mere failure or refusal to provide an account to the police that is relevant.

6. **The accused could reasonably be expected, in the circumstances existing at the time, to have mentioned the facts relied on at trial** (s 34 only).

   'Circumstances existing at the time' is to be widely interpreted, and includes:
   • what disclosure had been made to the suspect, or their lawyer, by the police
   • what information the prosecution can demonstrate the suspect knew at the time of questioning or charge

- the condition and circumstances of the suspect
- any legal advice that the suspect received.

What is reasonable is a question of fact for the court or jury. Note that there is no reasonableness requirement under ss 36 and 37.

The effect of legal advice

The fact that an accused was advised by their lawyer not to mention facts or advised not to provide an account to the police does not, of itself, prevent inferences from being drawn.[13] In *Condron v UK*[14] the European Court of Human Rights (ECtHR) made it clear that legal advice is an important safeguard in the context of Article 6 and held that the fact that an accused is advised by their lawyer to remain 'silent' must be given appropriate weight by the trial court.

This was given domestic effect by the Court of Appeal in *R v Betts and Hall*[15] in which it was held that:

> If it is a plausible explanation that the reason for not mentioning facts is that the particular appellant acted on the advice of his solicitor and not because he had no or no satisfactory answer to give then no inference can be drawn.
>
> That conclusion does not give a licence to a guilty person to shield behind the advice of his solicitor. The adequacy of the explanation advanced may well be relevant as to whether or not the advice was truly the reason for not mentioning the facts. A person, who is anxious not to answer questions because he has no or no adequate explanation to offer, gains no protection from his lawyer's advice because that advice is no more than a convenient way of disguising his true motivation for not mentioning facts.
>
> In the instant case, we were of the view that the jury had failed to appreciate on the directions given that they could only draw inferences against the appellants if they were sure that their failure to mention facts was not merely as a result of the advice, however adequate or inadequate that explanation might be, and could only do so if they were sure that the particular applicant had not at that stage any explanation to offer or none that he believed would stand up to questioning or investigation.

Betts and Hall appears to hold that legal advice to remain 'silent' will prevent inferences from being drawn provided that the court or jury is satisfied that this is a genuine reason for failure to mention the relevant facts. The fact that such advice was given will not, however, prevent inferences from being drawn if the court or jury is sure that the real reason the accused remained silent was because they had no innocent explanation to give or none that would stand up to questioning. In deciding whether legal advice was the real reason for silence the court may take account of the adequacy of the explanation put forward for remaining silent.

The effect *of Betts and Hall* is not completely clear because, of course, an accused may have a number of reasons for remaining silent one of which is the advice they received. The Judicial Studies Board Specimen Directions deal with this by advising judges to direct juries as follows:

> [Having decided that the accused relied on legal advice to remain silent, and taken into account the fact that he or she can accept or reject such advice] decide whether the defendant could reasonably have been expected to mention the facts on which he now relies. If, for example, you considered that he had or may have had an answer to give, but reasonably relied on the legal advice to remain silent, you should not draw any conclusion against him. But if, for example, you were sure that the defendant had no answer, and merely latched onto the legal advice as a convenient

shield behind which to hide, you would be entitled to draw a conclusion against him... (para 40.5)

Unfortunately, the effect of legal advice on the drawing of inferences was confused rather than clarified by the Court of Appeal decision in *R v Howell*,[16] which held that even if a court or jury were satisfied that legal advice was a genuine reason for silence, this would not prevent inferences from being drawn. The court went on to state that there *'must always be soundly based objective reasons for silence'*, but it did not set out a definitive list of what it believes to be 'objective' reasons for advice to remain silent.

Until the court is able to provide clear and consistent guidance on what it believes are relevant factors justifying advice to remain silent, solicitors should approach the issue of advising clients on silence with extreme caution and should explain to clients that the fact that they are advising them to remain silent will not necessarily prevent inferences from being drawn. Whilst solicitors must have proper regard for the decisions of the courts, if there are cogent reasons for silence solicitors must not flinch from advising accordingly, whilst ensuring that their clients are made aware of the risks of following that advice.

Advising the client

Deciding what advice to give

In deciding what advice to give solicitors will, as before, need to balance the risks of answering police questions against the risks of not answering police questions. In doing so, the following factors will be relevant (although in any particular case, some factors may be more important than others, and other factors may also be relevant):

1. **The level of disclosure**

    It has been held that the fact that the police have disclosed little or nothing of the case against the suspect, so that the solicitor cannot usefully advise the client, can be a 'good' reason for advising silence.[18] However, the fact that the police do not have a written statement from the complainant was held in *Howell* not to be a 'good' reason for advice to remain silent. Solicitors should keep a careful record of what has been disclosed by the police prior to each interview, and should ask the interviewing officer or officer in the case whether they have any information that they have not disclosed. Particular care should be taken where the police are using the tactic of 'phased disclosure', reconsidering the advice on each occasion that further disclosure is given.

2. **The nature of the case**

    Advice to remain silent is likely to be justified where the material in the hands of the police is so complex, or relates to matters so long ago, that no sensible immediate response is appropriate.[18] Advice must be reviewed if the police give the suspect the time and opportunity to consider the allegation, to review relevant documents, etc.

3. **The circumstances of the suspect**

    The courts have recognised that advice to remain silent may be appropriate where the suspect's condition is such that a response in interview would not be advisable. Relevant factors here include ill-health, mental disorder or vulnerability, confusion, intoxication, shock, etc.[19] Where possible, evidence of the condition of the suspect, from a doctor or other health care practitioner, should be obtained and, in any event, the solicitor should make a careful record of the relevant condition.

4. **The apparent strength of the police case**

    If the prosecution evidence is, or is likely to be, strong a court is likely to take the view that this is a situation calling for an explanation from the suspect. Considering the strength of the evidence will involve an assessment of the likely admissibility of the evidence concerned. In *Howell* the court held that the possibility that the complainant may withdraw the complaint was not a 'good' reason for remaining silent. Nevertheless, it may still be appropriate to advise silence in such circumstances since if the complainant does withdraw their complaint, there may be insufficient evidence for a successful prosecution. Further, the court in *Howell* stated that the fact that the lawyer believed that the suspect would be charged whatever he said in interview was also not a 'good' reason. However, it has been held in other cases that inferences should not be drawn in such circumstances.[20] The solicitor should, where relevant, ask the police in advance of an interview what their intentions are once the interview has been conducted. If they believe that the interview and/or detention is unlawful or contrary to Code C, the lawyer should make representations and request that they be noted on the custody record together with the police response.

5. **The client's instructions**

    If, having obtained instructions, the solicitor concludes that the client is guilty of the suspected offence, s/he should consider the strength of the police evidence.

    If the police evidence is strong, the solicitor should consider the potential advantages of making admissions, including any possible effect on sentence or on alternatives to prosecution eg caution, final warning or reprimand. If the police evidence is weak, or the solicitor is unclear of the strength of the police case, the solicitor should consider the advantages (and disadvantages) of remaining silent at this stage.

    Remember that if the client has admitted their guilt, the solicitor cannot go into the police interview with them in the knowledge that the client is going to assert their innocence, but it is proper for the solicitor to accompany the client in the police interview if the client does not answer questions.

    If the client has a defence, the solicitor should consider the dangers of not putting it forward in interview (especially in terms of credibility and the damage from inferences), but should also consider what strategy (eg, answering questions or making a written statement) would be most appropriate. Answering police questions may be the most persuasive evidence of the veracity of the defence, but there are risks attached to putting forward a defence in a police interview even though it is genuine.

    In deciding what advice to give it is important that solicitors remember that their principal professional obligation is to advise, and to act, in their client's best interests. This may mean advising silence even in the absence of reasons recognised by the courts as 'good' reasons.

Waiver of privilege

Consultations between solicitors and their clients are normally covered by legal professional privilege, so that an accused may not be asked, and if asked, cannot be required to state, what passed between them and their lawyer. There are special difficulties, however, in relation to advice not to answer questions because mere evidence of that advice may not be enough to prevent inferences from being drawn. The following principles can be drawn from the cases:

- If the accused simply gives evidence that he or she was advised by their solicitor to remain silent, this will not amount to waiver of privilege (but is also unlikely to be very persuasive).[21]

- If the accused, or his or her lawyer, tells the police of the reasons for the advice, or gives evidence of the basis or reasons for the advice, this is likely to amount to waiver of privilege.[22] Note that a lawyer's opening statement in a police interview can be adduced as evidence by the prosecution at trial.[23]

- Waiver of privilege is indivisible, so that if privilege is waived, the accused (and his or her lawyer if giving evidence) may be asked what else was said in consultation, and whether there were other reasons for advice to remain silent.

Normally, therefore, the solicitor should not tell the police nor state in the police interview the reason(s) for advice given to the client. Although there is no specific authority on the point, it should **not** amount to a waiver of privilege where the solicitor tells the police that they have advised their client not to answer questions, and separately informs them of facts relevant to that decision, eg, a belief on the part of the lawyer that the detention or interview is unlawful or contrary to Code C. Similarly, it should **not** amount to a waiver of privilege if the solicitor states in the police interview 'I now advise my client not to answer questions because....', **provided** that no reference is made to information obtained or advice given in privileged circumstances.

The need to keep proper records

It is essential that solicitors keep a full, clear and contemporaneous record of the information obtained, prevailing circumstances and advice given at the police station. In any particular case, the solicitor may be required to give evidence of the advice given and the reasons for it, and are open to significant judicial criticism if their records are found to be inadequate. Furthermore, since the evidence of a solicitor may be crucial in the decision whether to draw inferences, such a failure may do a considerable disservice to a client which could amount to inadequate professional service or, in an extreme case, a disciplinary offence.

A careful note, together with relevant times, should be taken of the following:

- the physical and mental state of the client
- the general conduct of the police and the 'atmosphere' in which the investigation is conducted
- what the police allege has been said by the client prior to the solicitor's attendance
- what the police assert has been said to the suspect by the police eg. a request to account for an object etc., and what reply, if any, was made
- what information is disclosed to the solicitor by the police
- what requests for information and disclosure are made to the police by the solicitor
- any request for information to be recorded in the custody record, and any representations made to the custody officer
- what information and instructions are given to the solicitor by the client
- the suspect's apparent understanding of the significance of the allegation, and the significance of his or her replies or failure to respond

- what advice the solicitor gives to the client, and the reasons for that advice
- the wording of any caution or special warning given to the client, and of any explanation of the caution or special warning
- what was said during the course of a police interview
- what was said at the time of charge/report for summons.

Strategies where the client is not answering police questions

Where the suspect is not going to answer police questions in interview, either as a result of advice given or of their own volition, the solicitor should consider and advise upon the appropriate strategy to adopt.

1. **Informing the police**

   The solicitor should normally make an opening statement at the beginning of a police interview setting out:
   - their role in the interview
   - the advice given not to answer questions (if appropriate)
   - the disclosure given to the solicitor by the police (if appropriate)
   - the circumstances in which the lawyer will intervene.

   The solicitor should inform the police that their client is not going to answer police questions, but should not normally state the reasons for any advice (see above). If, for example, the solicitor believes the detention and/or interview to be unlawful or contrary to Code C, he or she should inform the custody officer prior to the interview, and repeat it at the beginning of the interview. The interviewing officer may, following *Howell,* try to undermine the solicitor's advice by telling the suspect that they are not obliged to accept advice to remain silent. The solicitor should deal with this possibility in the following way:
   - Prior to the interview, warn the client that the interviewing officer may use this tactic, explaining the officer's aim – to make the client lose faith in the legal advice given and what the solicitor will do if the officer attempts to do so.
   - During the interview, if the officer attempts to use this tactic intervene immediately to inform the officer that (a) should the case go to trial, it will be for the court to decide on the merits of the legal advice given to the client and the client's decision, and (b) the court will draw its own conclusions as to the appropriateness of the officer's conduct.

2. **Handing in a statement**

   Handing a statement to the police setting out the relevant facts has been treated by the courts as 'mentioning' facts for the purposes of the silence provisions, and the same principle should apply to providing an account for the purposes of ss 36 and 37 CJPOA 1994.[24] This strategy should be considered where there are good reasons for informing the police of facts that are likely to relied upon by the defence at trial (or for providing an account), whilst not wanting to place the client at risk of 'cross-examination' by the police (eg, because they are nervous or because police disclosure has been limited). However, note that handing in a statement will 'fix' the suspect with the defence, and may have the effect of providing the police with sufficient evidence to charge.

   It was held in *R v Knight*[25] that handing in a statement does not 'in itself' prevent inferences from being drawn. If the defendant relies on facts at trial that were not mentioned in the statement, inferences can still be drawn from failure to mention those facts. Therefore, the statement should set out the facts that have been disclosed by the police, and cover the essential features of the defence in as much detail as possible having regard to the prosecution case as far as it is known. Care must be taken to anticipate the facts that are likely to be relied on at trial, and also to anticipate any request to account under ss 36 or 37 CJPOA 1994, and to deal with these in the statement. If there is more than one interview, the statement should be reviewed in the light of any information disclosed by the police during the course of a prior interview, or between interviews, and consideration given to handing in a supplementary statement.

A statement should normally be handed to the police at the beginning of an interview, whilst telling the police that the client does not intend to answer questions. Provided that the facts subsequently relied upon at trial are adequately covered, it should have the effect of avoiding inferences under s 34(1)(a) (or under ss 36 and 37), but will not prevent inferences under s34(1)(b). The latter could be particularly relevant if information is disclosed by the police during the interview that is not adequately covered in the statement. In these circumstances, as noted above, the solicitor should consider whether a supplementary statement should be handed to the police.

3.   **Taking a statement that is not handed to the police**

This will not prevent all inferences, but may avoid an inference that facts put forward by the defence at trial have been fabricated since the police interview.[26] If, at trial, the prosecution argue recent fabrication, the statement becomes admissible to rebut the inference. However, if the prosecution do not assert recent fabrication but, for example, seek to persuade the court or jury that an innocent person would have wanted to assert their innocence to the police, the statement will be inadmissible as a self-serving statement. Nevertheless, taking a statement that is not handed in may be an appropriate strategy where there are good reasons not to hand a statement in, and there is a real possibility that the prosecution will argue recent fabrication.

4.   **Answering some questions and not others**

This is not normally an appropriate strategy because of the adverse effects on credibility of the defence at trial. It would normally be more advisable to hand in a statement covering the relevant facts.

5.   **Refusal to be interviewed**

It is not normally appropriate to advise a client to refuse to be interviewed unless, for example, the solicitor is strongly of the view that they are not fit to be interviewed. However, clients do, on occasion, decide that they are not prepared to leave their cell for the purpose of an interview. Such a refusal may have the effect of preventing a police interview from taking place, although note Code C para 12.5 which sets out the actions that the police may take, including interviewing the suspect in their cell.

References

1   For circumstances where the police can proceed with an interview in the absence of advice that has been requested. see Code C Annex B.

2   There has been some differences of opinion on this, but see the Judicial Studies Board Specimen Directions, para 40

3   See *R v Imran and Hussein* [1997] Crim LR 754.

4   See, in particular, *R v Argent* (1997) 2 Cr App R 27, [1997] Crim LR 346.

5   *R v Dervish* [2002] 2 Cr App R 6.

6   *R v N* [1999] Crim LR 61 and *R v B (MT)* [2000] Crim LR 181.

7   *R v Pointer* [1997] Crim LR 676.

8   *R v McGuinness* [1999] Crim LR 318. *R v Elliott* [2002] EWCA Crim 931, *R v Howell* [2003] Crim LR 405.

9   *R v Bowers* [1998] Crim LR 817, *R v Ashton and others* [2002] EWCA Crim 2782.

10   *R v N* [1999] Crim LR 61, *R v Betts and Hall* [2001] Crim LR 754, *R v Milford* [2001] Crim LR 330.

11   *R v McGarry* [1998] 3 All ER 805, *R v Ashton and others* [2002] EWCA Crim 2782.

12   [2003] EWCA Crim 1977.

13   *R v Condron* [1997] 1 Cr App R 185.

14   [2000] Crim LR 679

15   [2001] 2 Cr App R 257.

16   [2003] Crim LR 405.

17   *R v Argent and R v Roble* [1997] Crim LR 449.

18   *See R v Roble and R v Howell* (n 16).

19   See *R v Howell* (n 16).

20   See, for example, *R v Pointer* (n 7).

21   See *R v Condron* (n 14), and *R v Quang Van Bui* [2001] EWCA Crim 1.

22   *R v Bowden* [1999] 4 All ER 43.

23   *R v Fitzgerald* [1998] 6 June (CA, unreported).

24   See *R v McGarry* [1999] Crim LR 316 and *R v Ali* [2001] EWCA Crim 863.

25   [2003] EWCA Crim 1977.

26   *R v Condron* (n 13].

Appendix 5

Law Commission Guidance for Bail Decision-makers and their Advisers

Note: Paragraphs 2A and 6 of Part 1 of Schedule 1 to the Bail Act 1976, referred to in the Guidance, have been repealed and replaced by new paras 2A and 6 (see **3.4.3.4**).

In June 2001, the Law Commission published Bail and the Human Rights Act 1998 (Paper No 269) accompanied by the Guidance. The Guidance has been disseminated to the judiciary and justices' clerks and is here reproduced in full.

General principles applicable to the refusal of bail

1. Any decision to refuse bail should only be taken where this can be justified both under domestic legislation, principally the Bail Act 1976 (the Act), and under the European Convention on Human Rights (the Convention), as interpreted by the European Court of Human Rights (Strasbourg jurisprudence).

2. Accordingly, a defendant should only be refused bail where this is necessary for a purpose that is recognised by Strasbourg jurisprudence applying Article 5(3) of the Convention. That is where detention is necessary to avoid a real risk that, were the defendant released,

    (1) he or she would

        (a) fail to attend trial; or

        (b) interfere with evidence or witnesses, or otherwise obstruct the course of justice; or

        (c) commit an offence while on bail; or

        (d) be at risk of harm against which he or she would be inadequately protected; or

    (2) a disturbance to public order would result.

3. Detention will only be necessary if the risk could not be adequately addressed by the imposition of appropriate bail conditions that would make detention unnecessary.

4. Any court refusing bail should give reasons that explain why detention is necessary. Those reasons should be closely related to the individual circumstances of the defendant.

The exceptions to the right to bail in English law

5. Some of the exceptions to the right to bail found in the Act correlate so closely with the above purposes recognised by the Strasbourg jurisprudence that there is no need to consider separately how they should be applied in a way that complies with the Convention. These are the exceptions in paragraph 2(a) (fail to surrender to custody) and (c) (interfere with witnesses or otherwise obstruct the course of justice) and paragraph 7 (impracticable to complete inquiries or report without keeping defendant in custody) of Part I, and paragraph 2 of Part II (also based on failure to surrender to custody), of Schedule 1 to the Act.

6. In respect of the remaining exceptions to the right to bail we offer the following guidance as an aid to compliance with the Convention.

The risk of offending on bail

7.   The decision-taker must consider whether it may properly be inferred from any previous convictions and other circumstances relating to the defendant that there is a real risk that the defendant will commit an offence if granted bail, and that the defendant therefore falls within paragraph 2(b) of Part I of Schedule 1 to the Act. Provided that a decision to withhold bail is a necessary and proportionate response to a *real risk* that, if released, the defendant would commit an offence while on bail, such a decision will comply with the Convention.

Defendant on bail at the time of the alleged offence

8.   The factor in paragraph 2A of Part I of Schedule 1 to the Act (a defendant who commits an indictable offence whilst on bail) does not, in itself, establish any Article 5(3) purpose.

9.   Consequently, a court should not base a decision to withhold bail solely on paragraph 2A. To do so would infringe Article 5 and would be unlawful under sections 3 and 6 of the Human Rights Act 1998 (HRA)

10.   That factor may, however, be relevant to a decision whether to withhold bail on the basis of another relevant exception, for example the risk that the defendant will commit an offence while on bail.

Detention for the defendant's own protection

11.   A decision to refuse bail to a defendant under the exception in paragraph 3 of Part I of Schedule 1 to the Act, that is for the defendants own protection (from self-harm or harm from others) would comply with the Convention, where

    (1)   detention is *necessary* to address a *real risk* that, if granted bail, the defendant would suffer harm, against which detention could provide protection; and

    (2)   there are exceptional circumstances in the nature of the alleged offence and/or the conditions or context in which it is alleged to have been committed.

12.   A decision of a court to order detention because of a risk of *self*-harm may be compatible with the ECHR even where the circumstances giving rise to the risk are unconnected with the alleged offence, provided that the court is satisfied that there is a real risk of self-harm, and that a proper medical examination will take place rapidly so that the court may then consider exercising its powers of detention under the Mental Health Act 1983.

Detention because of a lack of information

13.   The refusal of bail under paragraph 5 of Part I of Schedule 1 to the Act, where it has not been practicable to obtain sufficient information for the taking of a full bail decision for want of time since the institution of proceedings against the defendant, would be compatible with Article 5 provided that

    (1)   detention is for a short period, which is no longer than necessary to enable the required information to be obtained, and

    (2)   the lack of information is not due to a failure of the prosecution, the police, the court or another state body to act with 'special diligence'.

14.   There is no need in such a case for the court to be satisfied of any of the recognised purposes set out in paragraph 2 above.

15.   After the initial short period of time has passed, a lack of information that is not due to a failure of a state body to act with 'special diligence' may be taken

into account as a factor militating in favour of detention on *another* Convention compliant ground for detention.

Detention following arrest under section 7

Paragraph 6 of Part I and paragraph 5 of Part II of Schedule 1

16. The broad provisions in paragraph 6 of Part I and paragraph 5 of Part II of Schedule 1 to the Act, that a defendant arrested pursuant to section 7 need not be granted bail, should be read subject to the narrower provisions governing bail following a section 7(3) arrest, set out in section 7(5) of the Act. That provision requires that bail should again be granted unless the justice is of the opinion that the defendant is not likely to surrender to custody, or has broken or is likely to break any condition of bail. Detention on one of these grounds will comply with the Convention only where this is necessary for one or more of the recognised purposes set out above in paragraph 2.

Section 7(5) hearings

17. At the hearing of section 7(5) proceedings there is no requirement that oral evidence should be heard in every case, but account should be taken of the quality of material presented. The may range from mere assertion to documentary proof. If the material includes oral evidence, the defendant must be given an opportunity to cross-examine. Likewise, a defendant should be permitted to give relevant oral evidence if he or she wishes to do so.

Section 25 of the Criminal Justice and Public Order Act 1994

18. The expression 'exceptional circumstances' in section 25 of the Criminal Justice and Public Order Act 1994 should be construed so that it encompasses a defendant who, if released on bail, would not pose a real risk of committing a serious offence. This construction achieves the purpose of Parliament to ensure that, when making bail decisions about defendants to whom section 25 applies, decision-takers focus on the risk the defendant may pose to the public by re-offending.

19. It is possible that's some other circumstance might constitute 'exceptional circumstances'. Even if 'exceptional circumstances' do exist, bail may, nonetheless, be withheld on a Convention-compatible ground if this is deemed to be necessary in the individual case.

Conditional bail

Conditional bail as an alternative to custody

20. A defendant must be released, if need be subject to conditions, unless:
    (1) that would create a risk of the kind which can, in principle, justify pretrial detention (set out above in paragraph 2), and
    (2) that risk cannot, by imposing suitable bail conditions, be averted, or reduced to a level at which it would not justify detention.

Conditional bail as an alternative to unconditional bail

21. A court should only impose bail conditions for one of the purposes which Strasbourg jurisprudence recognises as capable of justifying detention (set out above in paragraph 2).

22. A bail condition should only be imposed where, if the defendant were to break that condition or be reasonably thought likely to do so, it may be

necessary to arrest the defendant in order to pursue the purpose for which the condition was imposed.

Reasons for imposing conditions

23. Decision-takers should state their reasons for imposing bail conditions and specify the purposes for which any conditions are imposed.

24. Decision-takers should also be alert to ensure that any bail conditions they impose do not violate the defendants other Convention rights, such as those protected by Articles 8–11 of the Convention (the right to respect for family life, freedom of thought, conscience and religion, freedom of expression and freedom of assembly and association).

Giving reasons for bail decisions

25. It is of particular importance that decision-takers or their clerks make, and retain for the file, a note of the gist of the arguments for and against the grant of bail, and the oral reasons given by the tribunal for their decision.

26. Standard forms should be completed accurately to show that a decision has been taken in a way that complies with the Convention.

Participation of the defendant

27. Strasbourg jurisprudence recognises it as sufficient participation of the defendant in bail proceedings if, where necessary, he or she participates through a legal representative. Nevertheless, a domestic court should not hear a bail application to a conclusion in the absence of a defendant where the defendant's presence is essential to fair proceedings.

Form of evidence

28. It is not necessary to hear sworn evidence in the great majority of cases. Courts should, in particular cases, consider whether fairness requires the calling of evidence on oath for the determination of the application, as a failure to call such evidence may cause a particular decision to fall foul of Article 5(4).

29. A court hearing bail proceedings should take account of the quality of the material presented. It may range from mere assertion to documentary proof. If the material includes sworn oral evidence, the defendant must be given an opportunity to cross-examine. Likewise, the defendant should be permitted to give relevant oral evidence if he or she wishes to do so.

Disclosure

30. *Ex parte Lee* recognises an ongoing duty of disclosure from the time of arrest. The Court of Appeal emphasised that at the stage before committal, there are continuing obligations on the prosecutor to make such disclosure as justice and fairness may require in the particular circumstances of the case, that is, where it could reasonably be expected to assist the defence when applying for bail. This will ensure that the defendant enjoys 'equality of arms' with the prosecution.

31. Compliance with this requirement, together with those imposed by the Attorney-General's guidelines to prosecutors, should ensure compliance with the Convention. This will apply equally to hearings pursuant to s.7(5). (see above).

32. The duty of disclosure does not require that the whole of the prosecution file be disclosed to the defence prior to the hearing. It is sufficient if disclosure is provided of the material the defendant needs in order to enjoy 'equality of

arms' with the prosecution in relation to the matter to be decided by the court.

Public hearing

33.   Where normally the hearing would be in chambers, if the defendant requests that the bail hearing be held in public, it should be held in public unless there is a good reason not to do so.

The right to challenge pre-trial detention

34.   The Convention gives a detained person the right to make further court challenges to the legality of his or her detention despite having already made one or more such challenges, where for example, with the passage of time, the circumstances which once were considered by a court to justify detention may have changed.

35.   To ensure compliance with the Convention, Part 11A of Schedule I to the Act should be applied on the basis that courts should be willing, at intervals of 28 days, to consider arguments that the passage of time constitutes, in the particular case, a change in circumstances relevant to the need to detain the defendant, so as to require the hearing of all the arguments on the question of bail. It may be, for example, that the time served on remand may have reduced the risk of the defendant absconding.

36.   If the court finds that the passage of time does amount to a relevant change of circumstances then a full bail application should follow in which all the arguments, old and new, could be put forward and taken into account.

Appendix 6
PACE Codes

Police and Criminal Evidence Act 1984

Code C

Code of practice for the detention, treatment and questioning of persons by police officers

Commencement — Transitional Arrangements

This Code applies to people in police detention after midnight on 31 July 2004, notwithstanding that their period of detention may have commenced before that time.

1 General

1.1 All persons in custody must be dealt with expeditiously, and released as soon as the need for detention no longer applies.

1.1A A custody officer must perform the functions in this Code as soon as practicable. A custody officer will not be in breach of this Code if delay is justifiable and reasonable steps are taken to prevent unnecessary delay. The custody record shall show when a delay has occurred and the reason. See *Note 1H*

1.2 This Code of Practice must be readily available at all police stations for consultation by:

• police officers

• detained persons

• members of the public.

1.3 The provisions of this Code:

• include the *Annexes*

• do not include the *Notes for Guidance*.

1.4 If an officer has any suspicion, or is told in good faith, that a person of any age may be mentally disordered or otherwise mentally vulnerable, in the absence of clear evidence to dispel that suspicion, the person shall be treated as such for the purposes of this Code. See *Note 1G*

1.5 If anyone appears to be under 17, they shall be treated as a juvenile for the purposes of this Code in the absence of clear evidence that they are older.

1.6 If a person appears to be blind, seriously visually impaired, deaf, unable to read or speak or has difficulty orally because of a speech impediment, they shall be treated as such for the purposes of this Code in the absence of clear evidence to the contrary.

1.7 'The appropriate adult' means, in the case of a:

(a) juvenile:

(i) the parent, guardian or, if the juvenile is in local authority or voluntary organisation care, or is otherwise being looked after under the Children Act 1989, a person representing that authority or organisation;

(ii) a social worker of a local authority social services department;

(iii)   failing these, some other responsible adult aged 18 or over who is not a police officer or employed by the police.

(b)   person who is mentally disordered or mentally vulnerable: See Note 1D

(i)   a relative, guardian or other person responsible for their care or custody;

(ii)   someone experienced in dealing with mentally disordered or mentally vulnerable people but who is not a police officer or employed by the police;

(iii)   failing these, some other responsible adult aged 18 or over who is not a police officer or employed by the police.

1.8   If this Code requires a person be given certain information, they do not have to be given it if at the time they are incapable of understanding what is said, are violent or may become violent or in urgent need of medical attention, but they must be given it as soon as practicable.

1.9   References to a custody officer include those performing the functions of a custody officer.

1.9A   When this Code requires the prior authority or agreement of an officer of at least inspector or superintendent rank, that authority may be given by a sergeant or chief inspector authorised to perform the functions of the higher rank under the Police and Criminal Evidence Act 1984 (PACE), section 107.

1.10   Subject to *paragraph 1.12*, this Code applies to people in custody at police stations in England and Wales, whether or not they have been arrested, and to those removed to a police station as a place of safety under the Mental Health Act 1983, sections 135 and 136. *Section 15* applies solely to people in police detention, e.g. those brought to a police station under arrest or arrested at a police station for an offence after going there voluntarily.

1.11   People in police custody include anyone detained under the Terrorism Act 2000, Schedule 8 and section 41, having been taken to a police station after being arrested under the Terrorism Act 2000, section 41. In these cases, reference to an offence in this Code includes the commission, preparation and instigation of acts of terrorism.

1.12   This Code's provisions do not apply to people in custody:

(i)   arrested on warrants issued in Scotland by officers under the Criminal Justice and Public Order Act 1994, section 136(2), or arrested or detained without warrant by officers from a police force in Scotland under section 137(2). In these cases, police powers and duties and the person's rights and entitlements whilst at a police station in England or Wales are the same as those in Scotland;

(ii)   arrested under the Immigration and Asylum Act 1999, section 142(3) in order to have their fingerprints taken;

(iii)   whose detention is authorised by an immigration officer under the Immigration Act 1971;

(iv)   who are convicted or remanded prisoners held in police cells on behalf of the Prison Service under the Imprisonment (Temporary Provisions) Act 1980;

(v)   detained for examination under the Terrorism Act 2000, Schedule 7 and to whom the Code of Practice issued under that Act, Schedule 14, paragraph 6 applies;

(vi)   detained for searches under stop and search powers except as required by Code A.

The provisions on conditions of detention and treatment in *sections 8* and *9* must be considered as the minimum standards of treatment for such detainees.

1.13   In this Code:

(a)   'designated person' means a person other than a police officer, designated under the Police Reform Act 2002, Part 4 who has specified powers and duties of police officers conferred or imposed on them;

(b)   reference to a police officer includes a designated person acting in the exercise or performance of the powers and duties conferred or imposed on them by their designation.

1.14   If a power conferred on a designated person:

(a)   allows reasonable force to be used when exercised by a police officer, a person exercising that power has the same entitlement to use force;

(b)   includes power to use force to enter any premises, that power is not exercisable by that designated person except:

(i)   in the company, and under the supervision, of a police officer;

(i)   for the purpose of:

•   saving life or limb; or

•   preventing serious damage to property.

1.15   Nothing in this Code prevents the custody officer, or other officer given custody of the detainee, from allowing civilian support staff who are not designated persons to carry out individual procedures or tasks at the police station if the law allows. However, the officer remains responsible for making sure the procedures and tasks are carried out correctly in accordance with the Codes of Practice. Any such civilian must be:

(a)   a person employed by a police authority maintaining a police force and under the control and direction of the Chief Officer of that force;

(b)   employed by a person with whom a police authority has a contract for the provision of services relating to persons arrested or otherwise in custody.

1.16   Designated persons and other civilian support staff must have regard to any relevant provisions of the Codes of Practice.

1.17   References to pocket books include any official report book issued to police officers or civilian support staff.

Notes for guidance

1A   *Although certain sections of this Code apply specifically to people in custody at police stations, those there voluntarily to assist with an investigation should be treated with no less consideration, e.g. offered refreshments at appropriate times, and enjoy an absolute right to obtain legal advice or communicate with anyone outside the police station.*

1B   *A person, including a parent or guardian, should not be an appropriate adult if they:*

•   *are*

—   *suspected of involvement in the offence*

—   *the victim*

—   *a witness*

—   *involved in the investigation*

•   *received admissions prior to attending to act as the appropriate adult.*

Note: If a juvenile's parent is estranged from the juvenile, they should not be asked to act as the appropriate adult if the juvenile expressly and specifically objects to their presence.

1C   *If a juvenile admits an offence to, or in the presence of, a social worker or member of a youth offending team other than during the time that person is acting as the juvenile's appropriate adult, another appropriate adult should be appointed in the interest of fairness.*

1D   *In the case of people who are mentally disordered or otherwise mentally vulnerable, it may be more satisfactory if the appropriate adult is someone experienced or trained in their care rather than a relative lacking such qualifications. But if the detainee prefers a relative to a better qualified stranger or objects to a particular person their wishes should, if practicable, be respected.*

1E   *A detainee should always be given an opportunity, when an appropriate adult is called to the police station, to consult privately with a solicitor in the appropriate adult's absence if they want.*

1F   *A solicitor or independent custody visitor (formerly a lay visitor) present at the police station in that capacity may not be the appropriate adult.*

1G   *'Mentally vulnerable' applies to any detainee who, because of their mental state or capacity, may not understand the significance of what is said, of questions or of their replies. 'Mental disorder' is defined in the Mental Health Act 1983, section 1(2) as 'mental illness, arrested or incomplete development of mind, psychopathic disorder and any other disorder or disability of mind'. When the custody officer has any doubt about the mental state or capacity of a detainee, that detainee should be treated as mentally vulnerable and an appropriate adult called.*

1H   *Paragraph 1.1A is intended to cover delays which may occur in processing detainees e.g. if:*

- *a large number of suspects are brought into the station simultaneously to be placed in custody;*
- *interview rooms are all being used;*
- *there are difficulties contacting an appropriate adult, solicitor or interpreter.*

1I   *The custody officer must remind the appropriate adult and detainee about the right to legal advice and record any reasons for waiving it in accordance with section 6.*

2 Custody records

2.1A   When a person is brought to a police station:

- under arrest;
- is arrested at the police station having attended there voluntarily; or
- attends a police station to answer bail

they should be brought before the custody officer as soon as practicable after their arrival at the station or, if appropriate, following arrest after attending the police station voluntarily. This applies to designated and non-designated police stations. A person is deemed to be 'at a police station' for these purposes if they are within the boundary of any building or enclosed yard which forms part of that police station.

2.1   A separate custody record must be opened as soon as practicable for each person brought to a police station under arrest or arrested at the station having gone there voluntarily or attending a police station in answer to street bail. All information recorded under this Code must be recorded as soon as practicable in the custody record unless otherwise specified. Any audio or video recording made in the custody area is not part of the custody record.

2.2   If any action requires the authority of an officer of a specified rank, subject to *paragraph 2.6A*, their name and rank must be noted in the custody record.

2.3   The custody officer is responsible for the custody record's accuracy and completeness and for making sure the record or copy of the record accompanies a detainee if they are transferred to another police station. The record shall show the:

- time and reason for transfer;
- time a person is released from detention.

2.4 A solicitor or appropriate adult must be permitted to consult a detainee's custody record as soon as practicable after their arrival at the station and at any other time whilst the person is detained. Arrangements for this access must be agreed with the custody officer and may not unreasonably interfere with the custody officer's duties.

2.4A When a detainee leaves police detention or is taken before a court they, their legal representative or appropriate adult shall be given, on request, a copy of the custody record as soon as practicable. This entitlement lasts for 12 months after release.

2.5 The detainee, appropriate adult or legal representative shall be permitted to inspect the original custody record after the detainee has left police detention provided they give reasonable notice of their request. Any such inspection shall be noted in the custody record.

2.6 Subject to *paragraph 2.6A*, all entries in custody records must be timed and signed by the maker. Records entered on computer shall be timed and contain the operator's identification.

2.6A Nothing in this Code requires the identity of officers or civilian support staff to be recorded or disclosed:

(a)   in the case of enquiries linked to the investigation of terrorism; or

(b)   if the officer or civilian support staff reasonably believe recording or disclosing their name might put them in danger.

In these cases, they shall use their warrant or other identification numbers and the name of their police station. See *Note 2A*

2.7 The fact and time of any detainee's refusal to sign a custody record, when asked in accordance with this Code, must be recorded.

Note for guidance

2A *The purpose of paragraph 2.6A(b) is to protect those involved in serious organised crime investigations or arrests of particularly violent suspects when there is reliable information that those arrested or their associates may threaten or cause harm to those involved. In cases of doubt, an officer of inspector rank or above should be consulted.*

3   Initial action

(a)   Detained persons — normal procedure

3.1 When a person is brought to a police station under arrest or arrested at the station having gone there voluntarily, the custody officer must make sure the person is told clearly about the following continuing rights which may be exercised at any stage during the period in custody:

(i)   the right to have someone informed of their arrest as in *section 5*;

(ii)   the right to consult privately with a solicitor and that free independent legal advice is available;

(iii) the right to consult these Codes of Practice. See *Note 3D*

3.2 The detainee must also be given:

- a written notice setting out:
  —   the above three rights;
  —   the arrangements for obtaining legal advice;
  —   the right to a copy of the custody record as in *paragraph 2.4A*;
  —   the caution in the terms prescribed in *section 10*.

- an additional written notice briefly setting out their entitlements while in custody, see *Notes 3A* and *3B*.

Note: The detainee shall be asked to sign the custody record to acknowledge receipt of these notices. Any refusal must be recorded on the custody record.

3.3 A citizen of an independent Commonwealth country or a national of a foreign country, including the Republic of Ireland, must be informed as soon as practicable about their rights of communication with their High Commission, Embassy or Consulate. See *section 7*

3.4 The custody officer shall:

- note on the custody record any comment the detainee makes in relation to the arresting officer's account but shall not invite comment. If the arresting officer is not physically present when the detainee is brought to a police station, the arresting officer's account must be made available to the custody officer remotely or by a third party on the arresting officer's behalf. If the custody officer authorises a person's detention the detainee must be informed of the grounds as soon as practicable and before they are questioned about any offence;

- note any comment the detainee makes in respect of the decision to detain them but shall not invite comment;

- not put specific questions to the detainee regarding their involvement in any offence, nor in respect of any comments they may make in response to the arresting officer's account or the decision to place them in detention. Such an exchange is likely to constitute an interview as in *paragraph 11.1A* and require the associated safeguards in *section 11*.

See *paragraph 11.13* in respect of unsolicited comments.

3.5 The custody officer shall:

(a) ask the detainee, whether at this time, they:

    (i) would like legal advice, see *paragraph 6.5*;

    (ii) want someone informed of their detention, see *section 5*;

(b) ask the detainee to sign the custody record to confirm their decisions in respect of (*a*);

(c) determine whether the detainee:

    (i) is, or might be, in need of medical treatment or attention, see *section 9*;

    (ii) requires:

        - an appropriate adult;

        - help to check documentation;

        - an interpreter;

(d) record the decision in respect of (*c*).

3.6 When determining these needs the custody officer is responsible for initiating an assessment to consider whether the detainee is likely to present specific risks to custody staff or themselves. Such assessments should always include a check on the Police National Computer, to be carried out as soon as practicable, to identify any risks highlighted in relation to the detainee. Although such assessments are primarily the custody officer's responsibility, it may be necessary for them to consult and involve others, e.g. the arresting officer or an appropriate health care professional, see *paragraph 9.13*. Reasons for delaying the initiation or completion of the assessment must be recorded.

3.7 Chief Officers should ensure that arrangements for proper and effective risk assessments required by *paragraph 3.6* are implemented in respect of all detainees at police stations in their area.

3.8 Risk assessments must follow a structured process which clearly defines the categories of risk to be considered and the results must be incorporated in the detainee's custody record. The custody officer is responsible for making sure those responsible for the detainee's custody are appropriately briefed about the risks. If no specific risks are identified by the assessment, that should be noted in the custody record. See *Note 3E* and *paragraph 9.14*

3.9 The custody officer is responsible for implementing the response to any specific risk assessment, e.g.:

- reducing opportunities for self harm;
- calling a health care professional;
- increasing levels of monitoring or observation.

3.10 Risk assessment is an ongoing process and assessments must always be subject to review if circumstances change.

3.11 If video cameras are installed in the custody area, notices shall be prominently displayed showing cameras are in use. Any request to have video cameras switched off shall be refused.

(b) Detained persons — special groups

3.12 If the detainee appears deaf or there is doubt about their hearing or speaking ability or ability to understand English, and the custody officer cannot establish effective communication, the custody officer must, as soon as practicable, call an interpreter for assistance in the action under *paragraphs 3.1–3.5*. See *section 13*

3.13 If the detainee is a juvenile, the custody officer must, if it is practicable, ascertain the identity of a person responsible for their welfare. That person:

- may be:
  — the parent or guardian;
  — if the juvenile is in local authority or voluntary organisation care, or is otherwise being looked after under the Children Act 1989, a person appointed by that authority or organisation to have responsibility for the juvenile's welfare;
  — any other person who has, for the time being, assumed responsibility for the juvenile's welfare.
- must be informed as soon as practicable that the juvenile has been arrested, why they have been arrested and where they are detained. This right is in addition to the juvenile's right in section 5 not to be held incommunicado. See *Note 3C*

3.14 If a juvenile known to be subject to a court order under which a person or organisation is given any degree of statutory responsibility to supervise or otherwise monitor them, reasonable steps must also be taken to notify that person or organisation (the 'responsible officer'). The responsible officer will normally be a member of a Youth Offending Team, except for a curfew order which involves electronic monitoring when the contractor providing the monitoring will normally be the responsible officer.

3.15 If the detainee is a juvenile, mentally disordered or otherwise mentally vulnerable, the custody officer must, as soon as practicable:

- inform the appropriate adult, who in the case of a juvenile may or may not be a person responsible for their welfare, as in *paragraph 3.13*, of:
  — the grounds for their detention;
  — their whereabouts.
- ask the adult to come to the police station to see the detainee.

3.16   It is imperative a mentally disordered or otherwise mentally vulnerable person, detained under the Mental Health Act 1983, section 136, be assessed as soon as possible. If that assessment is to take place at the police station, an approved social worker and a registered medical practitioner shall be called to the station as soon as possible in order to interview and examine the detainee. Once the detainee has been interviewed, examined and suitable arrangements made for their treatment or care, they can no longer be detained under section 136. A detainee must be immediately discharged from detention under section 136 if a registered medical practitioner, having examined them, concludes they are not mentally disordered within the meaning of the Act.

3.17   If the appropriate adult is:
- already at the police station, the provisions of *paragraphs 3.1* to *3.5* must be complied with in the appropriate adult's presence;
- not at the station when these provisions are complied with, they must be complied with again in the presence of the appropriate adult when they arrive.

3.18   The detainee shall be advised that:
- the duties of the appropriate adult include giving advice and assistance;
- they can consult privately with the appropriate adult at any time.

3.19   If the detainee, or appropriate adult on the detainee's behalf, asks for a solicitor to be called to give legal advice, the provisions of *section 6* apply.

3.20   If the detainee is blind, seriously visually impaired or unable to read, the custody officer shall make sure their solicitor, relative, appropriate adult or some other person likely to take an interest in them and not involved in the investigation is available to help check any documentation. When this Code requires written consent or signing the person assisting may be asked to sign instead, if the detainee prefers. This paragraph does not require an appropriate adult to be called solely to assist in checking and signing documentation for a person who is not a juvenile, or mentally disordered or otherwise mentally vulnerable (see *paragraph 3.15*).

(c) Persons attending a police station voluntarily

3.21   Anybody attending a police station voluntarily to assist with an investigation may leave at will unless arrested. If it is decided they shall not be allowed to leave, they must be informed at once that they are under arrest and brought before the custody officer, who is responsible for making sure they are notified of their rights in the same way as other detainees. If they are not arrested but are cautioned as in section 10, the person who gives the caution must, at the same time, inform them they are not under arrest, they are not obliged to remain at the station but if they remain at the station they may obtain free and independent legal advice if they want. They shall be told the right to legal advice includes the right to speak with a solicitor on the telephone and be asked if they want to do so.

3.22   If a person attending the police station voluntarily asks about their entitlement to legal advice, they shall be given a copy of the notice explaining the arrangements for obtaining legal advice. See *paragraph 3.2*

(d) Documentation

3.23   The grounds for a person's detention shall be recorded, in the person's presence if practicable.

3.24   Action taken under *paragraphs 3.12* to *3.20* shall be recorded.

(e) Persons answering street bail

3.25   When a person is answering street bail, the custody officer should link any documentation held in relation to arrest with the custody record. Any further action shall be recorded on the custody record in accordance with *paragraphs 3.23* and *3.24* above.

Notes for guidance

3A   *The notice of entitlements should:*

- *list the entitlements in this Code, including:*

  — *visits and contact with outside parties, including special provisions for Commonwealth citizens and foreign nationals;*

  — *reasonable standards of physical comfort;*

  — *adequate food and drink;*

  — *access to toilets and washing facilities, clothing, medical attention, and exercise when practicable.*

- *mention the:*

  — *provisions relating to the conduct of interviews;*

  — *circumstances in which an appropriate adult should be available to assist the detainee and their statutory rights to make representation whenever the period of their detention is reviewed.*

3B   *In addition to notices in English, translations should be available in Welsh, the main minority ethnic languages and the principal European languages, whenever they are likely to be helpful. Audio versions of the notice should also be made available.*

3C   *If the juvenile is in local authority or voluntary organisation care but living with their parents or other adults responsible for their welfare, although there is no legal obligation to inform them, they should normally be contacted, as well as the authority or organisation unless suspected of involvement in the offence concerned. Even if the juvenile is not living with their parents, consideration should be given to informing them.*

3D   *The right to consult the Codes of Practice does not entitle the person concerned to delay unreasonably any necessary investigative or administrative action whilst they do so. Examples of action which need not be delayed unreasonably include:*

- *procedures requiring the provision of breath, blood or urine specimens under the Road Traffic Act 1988 or the Transport and Works Act 1992*

- *searching detainees at the police station*

- *taking fingerprints or non-intimate samples without consent for evidential purposes.*

3E   *Home Office Circular 32/2000 provides more detailed guidance on risk assessments and identifies key risk areas which should always be considered.*

4   Detainee's property

(a) Action

4.1   The custody officer is responsible for:

(a)   ascertaining what property a detainee:

(i)   has with them when they come to the police station, whether on:

- arrest or re-detention on answering to bail;

- commitment to prison custody on the order or sentence of a court;

- lodgement at the police station with a view to their production in court from prison custody; transfer from detention at another station or hospital;

- detention under the Mental Health Act 1983, section 135 or 136;

   (ii)   might have acquired for an unlawful or harmful purpose while in custody;

  (b)   the safekeeping of any property taken from a detainee which remains at the police station.

The custody officer may search the detainee or authorise their being searched to the extent they consider necessary, provided a search of intimate parts of the body or involving the removal of more than outer clothing is only made as in *Annex A*. A search may only be carried out by an officer of the same sex as the detainee. See *Note 4A*

4.2   Detainees may retain clothing and personal effects at their own risk unless the custody officer considers they may use them to cause harm to themselves or others, interfere with evidence, damage property, effect an escape or they are needed as evidence. In this event the custody officer may withhold such articles as they consider necessary and must tell the detainee why.

4.3   Personal effects are those items a detainee may lawfully need, use or refer to while in detention but do not include cash and other items of value.

(b) Documentation

4.4   It is a matter for the custody officer to determine whether a record should be made of the property a detained person has with him or had taken from him on arrest. Any record made is not required to be kept as part of the custody record but the custody record should be noted as to where such a record exists. Whenever a record is made the detainee shall be allowed to check and sign the record of property as correct. Any refusal to sign shall be recorded.

4.5   If a detainee is not allowed to keep any article of clothing or personal effects, the reason must be recorded.

Notes for guidance

4A   *PACE, Section 54(1) and paragraph 4.1 require a detainee to be searched when it is clear the custody officer will have continuing duties in relation to that detainee or when that detainee's behaviour or offence makes an inventory appropriate. They do not require every detainee to be searched, e.g. if it is clear a person will only be detained for a short period and is not to be placed in a cell, the custody officer may decide not to search them. In such a case the custody record will be endorsed 'not searched', paragraph 4.4 will not apply, and the detainee will be invited to sign the entry. If the detainee refuses, the custody officer will be obliged to ascertain what property they have in accordance with paragraph 4.1.*

4B   *Paragraph 4.4 does not require the custody officer to record on the custody record property in the detainee's possession on arrest if, by virtue of its nature, quantity or size, it is not practicable to remove it to the police station.*

4C   *Paragraph 4.4 does not require items of clothing worn by the person be recorded unless withheld by the custody officer as in paragraph 4.2.*

5   Right not to be held incommunicado

(a) Action

5.1   Any person arrested and held in custody at a police station or other premises may, on request, have one person known to them or likely to take an interest in their welfare informed at public expense of their whereabouts as soon as practicable. If the person cannot be contacted the detainee may choose up to two alternatives. If they cannot be contacted, the person in charge of detention or the investigation has discretion to allow further attempts until the information has been conveyed. See *Notes 5C* and *5D*

5.2   The exercise of the above right in respect of each person nominated may be delayed only in accordance with *Annex B.*

5.3   The above right may be exercised each time a detainee is taken to another police station.

5.4   The detainee may receive visits at the custody officer's discretion. See *Note 5B*

5.5   If a friend, relative or person with an interest in the detainee's welfare enquires about their whereabouts, this information shall be given if the suspect agrees and *Annex B* does not apply. See *Note 5D*

5.6   The detainee shall be given writing materials, on request, and allowed to telephone one person for a reasonable time, see *Notes 5A* and *5E.* Either or both these privileges may be denied or delayed if an officer of inspector rank or above considers sending a letter or making a telephone call may result in any of the consequences in:

     (a)   *Annex B paragraphs 1* and *2* and the person is detained in connection with an arrestable or serious arrestable offence; or

     (b)   *Annex B paragraphs 8* and *9* and the person is detained under the Terrorism Act 2000, Schedule 7 or section 41

   For the purposes of this paragraph, any reference to a serious arrestable offence in *Annex B* includes an arrestable offence. However, nothing in this paragraph permits the restriction or denial of the rights in *paragraphs 5.1* and *6.1.*

5.7   Before any letter or message is sent, or telephone call made, the detainee shall be informed that what they say in any letter, call or message (other than in a communication to a solicitor) may be read or listened to and may be given in evidence. A telephone call may be terminated if it is being abused. The costs can be at public expense at the custody officer's discretion.

(b)   *Documentation*

5.8   A record must be kept of any:

     (a)   request made under this section and the action taken;

     (b)   letters, messages or telephone calls made or received or visit received;

     (c)   refusal by the detainee to have information about them given to an outside enquirer. The detainee must be asked to countersign the record accordingly and any refusal recorded.

Notes for guidance

5A   *A person may request an interpreter to interpret a telephone call or translate a letter.*

5B   *At the custody officer's discretion, visits should be allowed when possible, subject to having sufficient personnel to supervise a visit and any possible hindrance to the investigation.*

5C   *If the detainee does not know anyone to contact for advice or support or cannot contact a friend or relative, the custody officer should bear in mind any local voluntary bodies or other organisations who might be able to help. Paragraph 6.1 applies if legal advice is required.*

5D   *In some circumstances it may not be appropriate to use the telephone to disclose information under paragraphs 5.1 and 5.5.*

5E   *The telephone call at paragraph 5.6 is in addition to any communication under paragraphs 5.1 and 6.1.*

6 Right to legal advice

(a) Action

6.1 Unless *Annex B* applies, all detainees must be informed that they may at any time consult and communicate privately with a solicitor, whether in person, in writing or by telephone, and that free independent legal advice is available from the duty solicitor. See *paragraph 3.1, Note 6B* and *Note 6J*

6.2 Not Used

6.3 A poster advertising the right to legal advice must be prominently displayed in the charging area of every police station. See *Note 6H*

6.4 No police officer should, at any time, do or say anything with the intention of dissuading a detainee from obtaining legal advice.

6.5 The exercise of the right of access to legal advice may be delayed only as in *Annex B*. Whenever legal advice is requested, and unless Annex B applies, the custody officer must act without delay to secure the provision of such advice. If, on being informed or reminded of this right, the detainee declines to speak to a solicitor in person, the officer should point out that the right includes the right to speak with a solicitor on the telephone. If the detainee continues to waive this right the officer should ask them why and any reasons should be recorded on the custody record or the interview record as appropriate. Reminders of the right to legal advice must be given as in *paragraphs 3.5, 11.2, 15.4, 16.4* and *16.5* and Code D, *paragraphs 3.17(ii)* and *6.3*. Once it is clear a detainee does not want to speak to a solicitor in person or by telephone they should cease to be asked their reasons. See *Note 6K*

6.5A In the case of a juvenile, an appropriate adult should consider whether legal advice from a solicitor is required. If the juvenile indicates that they do not want legal advice, the appropriate adult has the right to ask for a solicitor to attend if this would be in the best interests of the person. However, the detained person cannot be forced to see the solicitor if he is adamant that he does not wish to do so.

6.6 A detainee who wants legal advice may not be interviewed or continue to be interviewed until they have received such advice unless:

(a) *Annex B* applies, when the restriction on drawing adverse inferences from silence in *Annex C* will apply because the detainee is not allowed an opportunity to consult a solicitor; or

(b) an officer of superintendent rank or above has reasonable grounds for believing that:

(i) the consequent delay might:

- lead to interference with, or harm to, evidence connected with an offence;
- lead to interference with, or physical harm to, other people;
- lead to serious loss of, or damage to, property;
- lead to alerting other people suspected of having committed an offence but not yet arrested for it;
- hinder the recovery of property obtained in consequence of the commission of an offence.

(ii) when a solicitor, including a duty solicitor, has been contacted and has agreed to attend, awaiting their arrival would cause unreasonable delay to the process of investigation.

Note: In these cases the restriction on drawing adverse inferences from silence in *Annex C* will apply because the detainee is not allowed an opportunity to consult a solicitor;

(c)   the solicitor the detainee has nominated or selected from a list:

(i)   cannot be contacted;

(ii)   has previously indicated they do not wish to be contacted; or

(iii)   having been contacted, has declined to attend; and

the detainee has been advised of the Duty Solicitor Scheme but has declined to ask for the duty solicitor.

In these circumstances the interview may be started or continued without further delay provided an officer of inspector rank or above has agreed to the interview proceeding.

Note: The restriction on drawing adverse inferences from silence in Annex C will not apply because the detainee is allowed an opportunity to consult the duty solicitor;

(d)   the detainee changes their mind, about wanting legal advice.

In these circumstances the interview may be started or continued without delay provided that:

(i)   the detainee agrees to do so, in writing or on tape; and

(ii)   an officer of inspector rank or above has inquired about the detainee's reasons for their change of mind and gives authority for the interview to proceed.

Confirmation of the detainee's agreement, their change of mind, the reasons for it if given and, subject to *paragraph 2.6A*, the name of the authorising officer shall be recorded in the taped or written interview record. See *Note 6I*. Note: In these circumstances the restriction on drawing adverse inferences from silence in *Annex C* will not apply because the detainee is allowed an opportunity to consult a solicitor if they wish.

6.7   If *paragraph 6.6(b)(i)* applies, once sufficient information has been obtained to avert the risk, questioning must cease until the detainee has received legal advice unless *paragraph 6.6(a), (b)(ii), (c) or (d)* applies.

6.8   A detainee who has been permitted to consult a solicitor shall be entitled on request to have the solicitor present when they are interviewed unless one of the exceptions in *paragraph 6.6* applies.

6.9   The solicitor may only be required to leave the interview if their conduct is such that the interviewer is unable properly to put questions to the suspect. See *Notes 6D* and *6E*

6.10   If the interviewer considers a solicitor is acting in such a way, they will stop the interview and consult an officer not below superintendent rank, if one is readily available, and otherwise an officer not below inspector rank not connected with the investigation. After speaking to the solicitor, the officer consulted will decide if the interview should continue in the presence of that solicitor. If they decide it should not, the suspect will be given the opportunity to consult another solicitor before the interview continues and that solicitor given an opportunity to be present at the interview. See *Note 6E*

6.11   The removal of a solicitor from an interview is a serious step and, if it occurs, the officer of superintendent rank or above who took the decision will consider if the incident should be reported to the Law Society. If the decision to remove the solicitor has been taken by an officer below superintendent rank, the facts must be reported to an officer of superintendent rank or above who will similarly consider whether a report to the Law Society would be appropriate. When the solicitor concerned is a duty solicitor, the report should be both to the Law Society and to the Legal Services Commission.

6.12   'Solicitor' in this Code means:

- a solicitor who holds a current practising certificate
- an accredited or probationary representative included on the register of representatives maintained by the Legal Services Commission.

6.12A   An accredited or probationary representative sent to provide advice by, and on behalf of, a solicitor shall be admitted to the police station for this purpose unless an officer of inspector rank or above considers such a visit will hinder the investigation and directs otherwise. Hindering the investigation does not include giving proper legal advice to a detainee as in *Note 6D*. Once admitted to the police station, *paragraphs 6.6* to *6.10* apply.

6.13   In exercising their discretion under paragraph 6.12A, the officer should take into account in particular:

- whether:
  - — the identity and status of an accredited or probationary representative have been satisfactorily established;
  - — they are of suitable character to provide legal advice, e.g. a person with a criminal record is unlikely to be suitable unless the conviction was for a minor offence and not recent.
- any other matters in any written letter of authorisation provided by the solicitor on whose behalf the person is attending the police station. See *Note 6F*

6.14   If the inspector refuses access to an accredited or probationary representative or a decision is taken that such a person should not be permitted to remain at an interview, the inspector must notify the solicitor on whose behalf the representative was acting and give them an opportunity to make alternative arrangements. The detainee must be informed and the custody record noted.

6.15   If a solicitor arrives at the station to see a particular person, that person must, unless *Annex B* applies, be so informed whether or not they are being interviewed and asked if they would like to see the solicitor. This applies even if the detainee has declined legal advice or, having requested it, subsequently agreed to be interviewed without receiving advice. The solicitor's attendance and the detainee's decision must be noted in the custody record.

(b)   Documentation

6.16   Any request for legal advice and the action taken shall be recorded.

6.17   A record shall be made in the interview record if a detainee asks for legal advice and an interview is begun either in the absence of a solicitor or their representative, or they have been required to leave an interview.

Notes for guidance

6A   *In considering if paragraph 6.6(b) applies, the officer should, if practicable, ask the solicitor for an estimate of how long it will take to come to the station and relate this to the time detention is permitted, the time of day (i.e. whether the rest period under paragraph 12.2 is imminent) and the requirements of other investigations. If the solicitor is on their way or is to set off immediately, it will not normally be appropriate to begin an interview before they arrive. If it appears necessary to begin an interview before the solicitor's arrival, they should be given an indication of how long the police would be able to wait before 6.6(b) applies so there is an opportunity to make arrangements for someone else to provide legal advice.*

6B   A detainee who asks for legal advice should be given an opportunity to consult a specific solicitor or another solicitor from that solicitor's firm or the duty solicitor. If advice is not available by these means, or they do not want to consult the duty solicitor, the detainee should be given an opportunity to choose a solicitor from a list of those willing to provide legal advice. If this solicitor is unavailable, they may choose up to two alternatives. If these attempts are unsuccessful, the custody officer has discretion to allow further attempts until a solicitor has been contacted and agrees to provide legal advice. Apart from carrying out these duties, an officer must not advise the suspect about any particular firm of solicitors.

6C   Not Used

6D   A detainee has a right to free legal advice and to be represented by a solicitor. The solicitor's only role in the police station is to protect and advance the legal rights of their client. On occasions this may require the solicitor to give advice which has the effect of the client avoiding giving evidence which strengthens a prosecution case. The solicitor may intervene in order to seek clarification, challenge an improper question to their client or the manner in which it is put, advise their client not to reply to particular questions, or if they wish to give their client further legal advice. Paragraph 6.9 only applies if the solicitor's approach or conduct prevents or unreasonably obstructs proper questions being put to the suspect or the suspect's response being recorded. Examples of unacceptable conduct include answering questions on a suspect's behalf or providing written replies for the suspect to quote.

6E   An officer who takes the decision to exclude a solicitor must be in a position to satisfy the court the decision was properly made. In order to do this they may need to witness what is happening.

6F   If an officer of at least inspector rank considers a particular solicitor or firm of solicitors is persistently sending non-accredited or probationary representatives who are unsuited to provide legal advice, they should inform an officer of at least superintendent rank, who may wish to take the matter up with the Law Society.

6G   Subject to the constraints of Annex B, a solicitor may advise more than one client in an investigation if they wish. Any question of a conflict of interest is for the solicitor under their professional code of conduct. If, however, waiting for a solicitor to give advice to one client may lead to unreasonable delay to the interview with another, the provisions of paragraph 6.6(b) may apply.

6H   In addition to a poster in English, a poster or posters containing translations into Welsh, the main minority ethnic languages and the principal European languages should be displayed wherever they are likely to be helpful and it is practicable to do so.

6I   Paragraph 6.6(d) requires the authorisation of an officer of inspector rank or above to the continuation of an interview when a detainee who wanted legal advice changes their mind. It is permissible for such authorisation to be given over the telephone, if the authorising officer is able to satisfy themselves about the reason for the detainee's change of mind and is satisfied it is proper to continue the interview in those circumstances.

6J   Whenever a detainee exercises their right to legal advice by consulting or communicating with a solicitor, they must be allowed to do so in private. This right to consult or communicate in private is fundamental. Except as allowed by the Terrorism Act 2000, Schedule 8, paragraph 9, if the requirement for privacy is compromised because what is said or written by the detainee or solicitor for the purpose of giving and receiving legal advice is overheard, listened to, or read by others without the informed consent of the detainee, the right will effectively have been denied. When a detainee chooses to speak to a solicitor on the telephone, they should be allowed to do so in private unless this is impractical because of the design and layout of the custody area or the location of telephones. However, the normal expectation should be that facilities will be available, *unless they are being used, at all police stations to enable detainees to speak in private to a solicitor either face to face or over the telephone.*

6K   *A detainee is not obliged to give reasons for declining legal advice and should not be pressed to do so.*

7   Citizens of independent Commonwealth countries or foreign nationals

(a)   Action

7.1   Any citizen of an independent Commonwealth country or a national of a foreign country, including the Republic of Ireland, may communicate at any time with the appropriate High Commission, Embassy or Consulate. The detainee must be informed as soon as practicable of:

- this right;
- their right, upon request, to have their High Commission, Embassy or Consulate told of their whereabouts and the grounds for their detention. Such a request should be acted upon as soon as practicable.

7.2   If a detainee is a citizen of a country with which a bilateral consular convention or agreement is in force requiring notification of arrest, the appropriate High Commission, Embassy or Consulate shall be informed as soon as practicable, subject to *paragraph 7.4*. The countries to which this applies as at 1st April 2003 are listed in *Annex F*.

7.3   Consular officers may visit one of their nationals in police detention to talk to them and, if required, to arrange for legal advice. Such visits shall take place out of the hearing of a police officer.

7.4   Notwithstanding the provisions of consular conventions, if the detainee is a political refugee whether for reasons of race, nationality, political opinion or religion, or is seeking political asylum, consular officers shall not be informed of the arrest of one of their nationals or given access or information about them except at the detainee's express request.

(b)   Documentation

7.5   A record shall be made when a detainee is informed of their rights under this section and of any communications with a High Commission, Embassy or Consulate.

Note for guidance

7A   *The exercise of the rights in this section may not be interfered with even though Annex B applies.*

8   Conditions of detention

(a)   Action

8.1   So far as it is practicable, not more than one detainee should be detained in each cell.

8.2   Cells in use must be adequately heated, cleaned and ventilated. They must be adequately lit, subject to such dimming as is compatible with safety and security to allow people detained overnight to sleep. No additional restraints shall be used within a locked cell unless absolutely necessary and then only restraint equipment, approved for use in that force by the Chief Officer, which is reasonable and necessary in the circumstances having regard to the detainee's demeanour and with a view to ensuring their safety and the safety of others. If a detainee is deaf, mentally disordered or otherwise mentally vulnerable, particular care must be taken when deciding whether to use any form of approved restraints.

8.3   Blankets, mattresses, pillows and other bedding supplied shall be of a reasonable standard and in a clean and sanitary condition. See *Note 8A*

8.4   Access to toilet and washing facilities must be provided.

8.5   If it is necessary to remove a detainee's clothes for the purposes of investigation, for hygiene, health reasons or cleaning, replacement clothing of a reasonable standard of comfort and cleanliness shall be provided. A detainee may not be interviewed unless adequate clothing has been offered.

8.6   At least two light meals and one main meal should be offered in any 24 hour period. See *Note 8B*. Drinks should be provided at meal times and upon reasonable request between meals. Whenever necessary, advice shall be sought from the appropriate health care professional, see *Note 9A*, on medical and dietary matters. As far as practicable, meals provided shall offer a varied diet and meet any specific dietary needs or religious beliefs the detainee may have. The detainee may, at the custody officer's discretion, have meals supplied by their family or friends at their expense. See *Note 8A*

8.7   Brief outdoor exercise shall be offered daily if practicable.

8.8   A juvenile shall not be placed in a police cell unless no other secure accommodation is available and the custody officer considers it is not practicable to supervise them if they are not placed in a cell or that a cell provides more comfortable accommodation than other secure accommodation in the station. A juvenile may not be placed in a cell with a detained adult.

(b) *Documentation*

8.9   A record must be kept of replacement clothing and meals offered.

8.10   If a juvenile is placed in a cell, the reason must be recorded.

8.11   The use of any restraints on a detainee whilst in a cell, the reasons for it and, if appropriate, the arrangements for enhanced supervision of the detainee whilst so restrained, shall be recorded. See *paragraph 3.9*

Notes for guidance

8A   *The provisions in paragraph 8.3 and 8.6 respectively are of particular importance in the case of a person detained under the Terrorism Act 2000, immigration detainees and others likely to be detained for an extended period. In deciding whether to allow meals to be supplied by family or friends, the custody officer is entitled to take account of the risk of items being concealed in any food or package and the officer's duties and responsibilities under food handling legislation.*

8B   *Meals should, so far as practicable, be offered at recognised meal times, or at other times that take account of when the detainee last had a meal.*

9 Care and treatment of detained persons

(a) *General*

9.1   Nothing in this section prevents the police from calling the police surgeon or, if appropriate, some other health care professional, to examine a detainee for the purposes of obtaining evidence relating to any offence in which the detainee is suspected of being involved. See *Note 9A*

9.2   If a complaint is made by, or on behalf of, a detainee about their treatment since their arrest, or it comes to notice that a detainee may have been treated improperly, a report must be made as soon as practicable to an officer of inspector rank or above not connected with the investigation. If the matter concerns a possible assault or the possibility of the unnecessary or unreasonable use of force, an appropriate health care professional must also be called as soon as practicable.

9.3   Detainees should be visited at least every hour. If no reasonably foreseeable risk was identified in a risk assessment, see *paragraphs 3.6–3.10*, there is no need to wake a sleeping detainee. Those suspected of being intoxicated through drink or drugs or whose level of consciousness causes concern must, subject to any clinical directions given by the appropriate health care professional, see *paragraph 9.13*:

- be visited and roused at least every half hour
- have their condition assessed as in *Annex H*
- and clinical treatment arranged if appropriate

See *Notes 9B, 9C* and *9H*

9.4 When arrangements are made to secure clinical attention for a detainee, the custody officer must make sure all relevant information which might assist in the treatment of the detainee's condition is made available to the responsible health care professional. This applies whether or not the health care professional asks for such information. Any officer or civilian support staff with relevant information must inform the custody officer as soon as practicable.

(b)   Clinical treatment and attention

9.5 The custody officer must make sure a detainee receives appropriate clinical attention as soon as reasonably practicable if the person:

(a)   appears to be suffering from physical illness; or

(b)   is injured; or

(c)   appears to be suffering from a mental disorder; or

(d)   appears to need clinical attention.

9.5A This applies even if the detainee makes no request for clinical attention and whether or not they have already received clinical attention elsewhere. If the need for attention appears urgent, e.g. when indicated as in *Annex H*, the nearest available health care professional or an ambulance must be called immediately.

9.5B The custody officer must also consider the need for clinical attention as set out in Note for Guidance 9C in relation to those suffering the effects of alcohol or drugs.

9.6 *Paragraph 9.5* is not meant to prevent or delay the transfer to a hospital if necessary of a person detained under the Mental Health Act 1983, section 136. See *Note 9D*. When an assessment under that Act takes place at a police station, *see paragraph 3.16*, the custody officer must consider whether an appropriate health care professional should be called to conduct an initial clinical check on the detainee. This applies particularly when there is likely to be any significant delay in the arrival of a suitably qualified medical practitioner.

9.7 If it appears to the custody officer, or they are told, that a person brought to a station under arrest may be suffering from an infectious disease or condition, the custody officer must take reasonable steps to safeguard the health of the detainee and others at the station. In deciding what action to take, advice must be sought from an appropriate health care professional. See *Note 9E*. The custody officer has discretion to isolate the person and their property until clinical directions have been obtained.

9.8 If a detainee requests a clinical examination, an appropriate health care professional must be called as soon as practicable to assess the detainee's clinical needs. If a safe and appropriate care plan cannot be provided, the police surgeon's advice must be sought. The detainee may also be examined by a medical practitioner of their choice at their expense.

9.9 If a detainee is required to take or apply any medication in compliance with clinical directions prescribed before their detention, the custody officer must consult the appropriate health care professional before the use of the medication. Subject to the restrictions in *paragraph 9.10*, the custody officer is responsible for the safekeeping of any medication and for making sure the detainee is given the opportunity to take or apply prescribed or approved medication. Any such consultation and its outcome shall be noted in the custody record.

9.10 No police officer may administer or supervise the self-administration of controlled drugs of the types and forms listed in the Misuse of Drugs Regulations 2001, Schedule 1, 2 or 3. A detainee may only self-administer such drugs under the personal supervision of the registered medical practitioner authorising their use. Drugs listed in Schedule 4 or 5 may be distributed by the custody officer for self-administration if they have consulted the registered medical practitioner authorising their use, this may be done by telephone, and both parties are satisfied self-administration will not expose the detainee, police officers or anyone else to the risk of harm or injury.

9.11 When appropriate health care professionals administer drugs or other medications, or supervise their self-administration, it must be within current medicines legislation and the scope of practice as determined by their relevant professional body.

9.12 If a detainee has in their possession, or claims to need, medication relating to a heart condition, diabetes, epilepsy or a condition of comparable potential seriousness then, even though *paragraph 9.5* may not apply, the advice of the appropriate health care professional must be obtained.

9.13 Whenever the appropriate health care professional is called in accordance with this section to examine or treat a detainee, the custody officer shall ask for their opinion about:

• any risks or problems which police need to take into account when making decisions about the detainee's continued detention;

• when to carry out an interview if applicable; and

• the need for safeguards.

9.14 When clinical directions are given by the appropriate health care professional, whether orally or in writing, and the custody officer has any doubts or is in any way uncertain about any aspect of the directions, the custody officer shall ask for clarification. It is particularly important that directions concerning the frequency of visits are clear, precise and capable of being implemented. See *Note 9F*.

(c) Documentation

9.15 A record must be made in the custody record of:

(a) the arrangements made for an examination by an appropriate health care professional under *paragraph 9.2* and of any complaint reported under that paragraph together with any relevant remarks by the custody officer;

(b) any arrangements made in accordance with *paragraph 9.5*;

(c) any request for a clinical examination under *paragraph 9.8* and any arrangements made in response;

(d) the injury, ailment, condition or other reason which made it necessary to make the arrangements in (*a*) to (*c*), see *Note 9G*;

(e) any clinical directions and advice, including any further clarifications, given to police by a health care professional concerning the care and treatment of the detainee in connection with any of the arrangements made in (*a*) to (*c*), see *Note 9F*;

(f) if applicable, the responses received when attempting to rouse a person using the procedure in *Annex H*, see *Note 9H*.

9.16 If a health care professional does not record their clinical findings in the custody record, the record must show where they are recorded. See *Note 9G*. However, information which is necessary to custody staff to ensure the effective ongoing care and well being of the detainee must be recorded openly in the custody record, see *paragraph 3.8* and *Annex G, paragraph 7.*

9.17   Subject to the requirements of Section 4, the custody record shall include:

- a record of all medication a detainee has in their possession on arrival at the police station;

- a note of any such medication they claim to need but do not have with them.

Notes for guidance

9A   *A 'health care professional' means a clinically qualified person working within the scope of practice as determined by their relevant professional body. Whether a health care professional is 'appropriate' depends on the circumstances of the duties they carry out at the time.*

9B   *Whenever possible juveniles and mentally vulnerable detainees should be visited more frequently.*

9C   *A detainee who appears drunk or behaves abnormally may be suffering from illness, the effects of drugs or may have sustained injury, particularly a head injury which is not apparent. A detainee needing or dependent on certain drugs, including alcohol, may experience harmful effects within a short time of being deprived of their supply. In these circumstances, when there is any doubt, police should always act urgently to call an appropriate health care professional or an ambulance. Paragraph 9.5 does not apply to minor ailments or injuries which do not need attention. However, all such ailments or injuries must be recorded in the custody record and any doubt must be resolved in favour of calling the appropriate health care professional.*

9D   *Whenever practicable, arrangements should be made for persons detained for assessment under the Mental Health Act 1983, section 136 to be taken to a hospital. There is no power under that Act to transfer a person detained under section 136 from one place of safety to another place of safety for assessment.*

9E   *It is important to respect a person's right to privacy and information about their health must be kept confidential and only disclosed with their consent or in accordance with clinical advice when it is necessary to protect the detainee's health or that of others who come into contact with them.*

9F   *The custody officer should always seek to clarify directions that the detainee requires constant observation or supervision and should ask the appropriate health care professional to explain precisely what action needs to be taken to implement such directions.*

9G   *Paragraphs 9.15 and 9.16 do not require any information about the cause of any injury, ailment or condition to be recorded on the custody record if it appears capable of providing evidence of an offence.*

9H   *The purpose of recording a person's responses when attempting to rouse them using the procedure in Annex H is to enable any change in the individual's consciousness level to be noted and clinical treatment arranged if appropriate.*

10   Cautions

(a)   When a caution must be given

10.1   A person whom there are grounds to suspect of an offence, see *Note 10A*, must be cautioned before any questions about an offence, or further questions if the answers provide the grounds for suspicion, are put to them if either the suspect's answers or silence, (i.e. failure or refusal to answer or answer satisfactorily) may be given in evidence to a court in a prosecution. A person need not be cautioned if questions are for other necessary purposes, e.g.:

(a)   solely to establish their identity or ownership of any vehicle;

(b) to obtain information in accordance with any relevant statutory requirement, see *paragraph 10.9*;

(c) in furtherance of the proper and effective conduct of a search, e.g. to determine the need to search in the exercise of powers of stop and search or to seek cooperation while carrying out a search;

(d) to seek verification of a written record as in *paragraph 11.13*;

(e) when examining a person in accordance with the Terrorism Act 2000, Schedule 7 and the Code of Practice for Examining Officers issued under that Act, Schedule 14, paragraph 6.

10.2 Whenever a person not under arrest is initially cautioned, or reminded they are under caution, that person must at the same time be told they are not under arrest and are free to leave if they want to. See *Note 10C*

10.3 A person who is arrested, or further arrested, must be informed at the time, or as soon as practicable thereafter, that they are under arrest and the grounds for their arrest, see *Note 10B*.

10.4 A person who is arrested, or further arrested, must also be cautioned unless:

(a) it is impracticable to do so by reason of their condition or behaviour at the time;

(b) they have already been cautioned immediately prior to arrest as in *paragraph 10.1*.

(b) Terms of the cautions

10.5 The caution which must be given on:

(a) arrest;

(b) all other occasions before a person is charged or informed they may be prosecuted, see *section 16*,

should, unless the restriction on drawing adverse inferences from silence applies, see *Annex C*, be in the following terms:

"You do not have to say anything. But it may harm your defence if you do not mention when questioned something which you later rely on in Court. Anything you do say may be given in evidence."

See *Note 10G*

10.6 *Annex C, paragraph 2* sets out the alternative terms of the caution to be used when the restriction on drawing adverse inferences from silence applies.

10.7 Minor deviations from the words of any caution given in accordance with this Code do not constitute a breach of this Code, provided the sense of the relevant caution is preserved. See *Note 10D*

10.8 After any break in questioning under caution, the person being questioned must be made aware they remain under caution. If there is any doubt the relevant caution should be given again in full when the interview resumes. See *Note 10E*

10.9 When, despite being cautioned, a person fails to co-operate or to answer particular questions which may affect their immediate treatment, the person should be informed of any relevant consequences and that those consequences are not affected by the caution. Examples are when a person's refusal to provide:

• their name and address when charged may make them liable to detention;

• particulars and information in accordance with a statutory requirement, e.g. under the Road Traffic Act 1988, may amount to an offence or may make the person liable to a further arrest.

(c) Special warnings under the Criminal Justice and Public Order Act 1994, sections 36 and 37

10.10   When a suspect interviewed at a police station or authorised place of detention after arrest fails or refuses to answer certain questions, or to answer satisfactorily, after due warning, see *Note 10F*, a court or jury may draw such inferences as appear proper under the Criminal Justice and Public Order Act 1994, sections 36 and 37. Such inferences may only be drawn when:

(a) the restriction on drawing adverse inferences from silence, see *Annex C*, does not apply; and

(b) the suspect is arrested by a constable and fails or refuses to account for any objects, marks or substances, or marks on such objects found:
- on their person;
- in or on their clothing or footwear;
- otherwise in their possession; or
- in the place they were arrested;

(c) the arrested suspect was found by a constable at a place at or about the time the offence for which that officer has arrested them is alleged to have been committed, and the suspect fails or refuses to account for their presence there.

When the restriction on drawing adverse inferences from silence applies, the suspect may still be asked to account for any of the matters in (*b*) or (*c*) but the special warning described in *paragraph 10.11* will not apply and must not be given.

10.11   For an inference to be drawn when a suspect fails or refuses to answer a question about one of these matters or to answer it satisfactorily, the suspect must first be told in ordinary language:

(a) what offence is being investigated;

(b) what fact they are being asked to account for;

(c) this fact may be due to them taking part in the commission of the offence;

(d) a court may draw a proper inference if they fail or refuse to account for this fact;

(e) a record is being made of the interview and it may be given in evidence if they are brought to trial.

(d) Juveniles and persons who are mentally disordered or otherwise mentally vulnerable

10.12   If a juvenile or a person who is mentally disordered or otherwise mentally vulnerable is cautioned in the absence of the appropriate adult, the caution must be repeated in the adult's presence.

(e) Documentation

10.13   A record shall be made when a caution is given under this section, either in the interviewer's pocket book or in the interview record.

Notes for guidance

10A   *There must be some reasonable, objective grounds for the suspicion, based on known facts or information which are relevant to the likelihood the offence has been committed and the person to be questioned committed it.*

10B   *An arrested person must be given sufficient information to enable them to understand they have been deprived of their liberty and the reason they have been arrested, e.g. when a person is arrested on suspicion of committing an offence they must be informed of the suspected offence's nature, when and where it was committed. If the arrest is made under the general arrest conditions in PACE, section 25, the grounds for arrest must include an explanation of the conditions which make the arrest necessary. Vague or technical language should be avoided.*

10C　*The restriction on drawing inferences from silence, see Annex C, paragraph 1, does not apply to a person who has not been detained and who therefore cannot be prevented from seeking legal advice if they want, see paragraph 3.21.*

10D　*If it appears a person does not understand the caution, the person giving it should explain it in their own words.*

10E　*It may be necessary to show to the court that nothing occurred during an interview break or between interviews which influenced the suspect's recorded evidence. After a break in an interview or at the beginning of a subsequent interview, the interviewing officer should summarise the reason for the break and confirm this with the suspect.*

10F　*The Criminal Justice and Public Order Act 1994, sections 36 and 37 apply only to suspects who have been arrested by a constable or Customs and Excise officer and are given the relevant warning by the police or customs officer who made the arrest or who is investigating the offence. They do not apply to any interviews with suspects who have not been arrested.*

10G　*Nothing in this Code requires a caution to be given or repeated when informing a person not under arrest they may be prosecuted for an offence. However, a court will not be able to draw any inferences under the Criminal Justice and Public Order Act 1994, section 34, if the person was not cautioned.*

11　Interviews — general

(a)　Action

11.1A　An interview is the questioning of a person regarding their involvement or suspected involvement in a criminal offence or offences which, under *paragraph 10.1*, must be carried out under caution. Whenever a person is interviewed they must be informed of the nature of the offence, or further offence. Procedures under the Road Traffic Act 1988, section 7 or the Transport and Works Act 1992, section 31 do not constitute interviewing for the purpose of this Code.

11.1　Following a decision to arrest a suspect, they must not be interviewed about the relevant offence except at a police station or other authorised place of detention, unless the consequent delay would be likely to:

(a)　lead to:

- interference with, or harm to, evidence connected with an offence;
- interference with, or physical harm to, other people; or
- serious loss of, or damage to, property;

(b)　lead to alerting other people suspected of committing an offence but not yet arrested for it; or

(c)　hinder the recovery of property obtained in consequence of the commission of an offence.

Interviewing in any of these circumstances shall cease once the relevant risk has been averted or the necessary questions have been put in order to attempt to avert that risk.

11.2　Immediately prior to the commencement or re-commencement of any interview at a police station or other authorised place of detention, the interviewer should remind the suspect of their entitlement to free legal advice and that the interview can be delayed for legal advice to be obtained, unless one of the exceptions in *paragraph 6.6* applies. It is the interviewer's responsibility to make sure all reminders are recorded in the interview record.

11.3　Not Used

11.4   At the beginning of an interview the interviewer, after cautioning the suspect, see *section 10*, shall put to them any significant statement or silence which occurred in the presence and hearing of a police officer or civilian interviewer before the start of the interview and which have not been put to the suspect in the course of a previous interview. See *Note 11A*. The interviewer shall ask the suspect whether they confirm or deny that earlier statement or silence and if they want to add anything.

11.4A   A significant statement is one which appears capable of being used in evidence against the suspect, in particular a direct admission of guilt. A significant silence is a failure or refusal to answer a question or answer satisfactorily when under caution, which might, allowing for the restriction on drawing adverse inferences from silence, see *Annex C*, give rise to an inference under the Criminal Justice and Public Order Act 1994, Part III.

11.5   No interviewer may try to obtain answers or elicit a statement by the use of oppression. Except as in *paragraph 10.9*, no interviewer shall indicate, except to answer a direct question, what action will be taken by the police if the person being questioned answers questions, makes a statement or refuses to do either. If the person asks directly what action will be taken if they answer questions, make a statement or refuse to do either, the interviewer may inform them what action the police propose to take provided that action is itself proper and warranted.

11.6   The interview or further interview of a person about an offence with which that person has not been charged or for which they have not been informed they may be prosecuted, must cease when the officer in charge of the investigation:

(a)   is satisfied all the questions they consider relevant to obtaining accurate and reliable information about the offence have been put to the suspect, this includes allowing the suspect an opportunity to give an innocent explanation and asking questions to test if the explanation is accurate and reliable, e.g. to clear up ambiguities or clarify what the suspect said;

(b)   has taken account of any other available evidence; and

(c)   the officer in charge of the investigation, or in the case of a detained suspect, the custody officer, see *paragraph 16.1*, reasonably believes there is sufficient evidence to provide a realistic prospect of conviction for that offence if the person was prosecuted for it. See *Note 11B*

This paragraph does not prevent officers in revenue cases or acting under the confiscation provisions of the Criminal Justice Act 1988 or the Drug Trafficking Act 1994 from inviting suspects to complete a formal question and answer record after the interview is concluded.

(b)   Interview records

11.7   (a)   An accurate record must be made of each interview, whether or not the interview takes place at a police station

(b)   The record must state the place of interview, the time it begins and ends, any interview breaks and, subject to *paragraph 2.6A*, the names of all those present; and must be made on the forms provided for this purpose or in the interviewer's pocket book or in accordance with the Codes of Practice E or F;

(c)   Any written record must be made and completed during the interview, unless this would not be practicable or would interfere with the conduct of the interview, and must constitute either a verbatim record of what has been said or, failing this, an account of the interview which adequately and accurately summarises it.

11.8   If a written record is not made during the interview it must be made as soon as practicable after its completion.

11.9   Written interview records must be timed and signed by the maker.

11.10 If a written record is not completed during the interview the reason must be recorded in the interview record.

11.11 Unless it is impracticable, the person interviewed shall be given the opportunity to read the interview record and to sign it as correct or to indicate how they consider it inaccurate. If the person interviewed cannot read or refuses to read the record or sign it, the senior interviewer present shall read it to them and ask whether they would like to sign it as correct or make their mark or to indicate how they consider it inaccurate. The interviewer shall certify on the interview record itself what has occurred. See *Note 11E*

11.12 If the appropriate adult or the person's solicitor is present during the interview, they should also be given an opportunity to read and sign the interview record or any written statement taken down during the interview.

11.13 A written record shall be made of any comments made by a suspect, including unsolicited comments, which are outside the context of an interview but which might be relevant to the offence. Any such record must be timed and signed by the maker. When practicable the suspect shall be given the opportunity to read that record and to sign it as correct or to indicate how they consider it inaccurate. See *Note 11E*

11.14 Any refusal by a person to sign an interview record when asked in accordance with this Code must itself be recorded.

(c) *Juveniles and mentally disordered or otherwise mentally vulnerable people*

11.15 A juvenile or person who is mentally disordered or otherwise mentally vulnerable must not be interviewed regarding their involvement or suspected involvement in a criminal offence or offences, or asked to provide or sign a written statement under caution or record of interview, in the absence of the appropriate adult unless *paragraphs 11.1, 11.18 to 11.20* apply. See *Note 11C*

11.16 Juveniles may only be interviewed at their place of education in exceptional circumstances and only when the principal or their nominee agrees. Every effort should be made to notify the parent(s) or other person responsible for the juvenile's welfare and the appropriate adult, if this is a different person, that the police want to interview the juvenile and reasonable time should be allowed to enable the appropriate adult to be present at the interview. If awaiting the appropriate adult would cause unreasonable delay, and unless the juvenile is suspected of an offence against the educational establishment, the principal or their nominee can act as the appropriate adult for the purposes of the interview.

11.17 If an appropriate adult is present at an interview, they shall be informed:
*   they are not expected to act simply as an observer; and
*   the purpose of their presence is to:
    —   advise the person being interviewed;
    —   observe whether the interview is being conducted properly and fairly;
    —   facilitate communication with the person being interviewed.

(d) *Vulnerable suspects — urgent interviews at police stations*

11.18 The following persons may not be interviewed unless an officer of superintendent rank or above considers delay will lead to the consequences in *paragraph 11.1(a)* to *(c)*, and is satisfied the interview would not significantly harm the person's physical or mental state (see Annex G):
    (a) a juvenile or person who is mentally disordered or otherwise mentally vulnerable if at the time of the interview the appropriate adult is not present;

(b) anyone other than in (*a*) who at the time of the interview appears unable to:

- appreciate the significance of questions and their answers; or
- understand what is happening because of the effects of drink, drugs or any illness, ailment or condition;

(c) a person who has difficulty understanding English or has a hearing disability, if at the time of the interview an interpreter is not present.

11.19   These interviews may not continue once sufficient information has been obtained to avert the consequences in *paragraph 11.1(a)* to *(c)*.

11.20   A record shall be made of the grounds for any decision to interview a person under *paragraph 11.18*.

Notes for guidance

11A   Paragraph 11.4 does not prevent the interviewer from putting significant statements and silences to a suspect again at a later stage or a further interview.

11B   The Criminal Procedure and Investigations Act 1996 Code of Practice, paragraph 3.4 states 'In conducting an investigation, the investigator should pursue all reasonable lines of enquiry, whether these point towards or away from the suspect. What is reasonable will depend on the particular circumstances.' Interviewers should keep this in mind when deciding what questions to ask in an interview.

11C   Although juveniles or people who are mentally disordered or otherwise mentally vulnerable are often capable of providing reliable evidence, they may, without knowing or wishing to do so, be particularly prone in certain circumstances to provide information that may be unreliable, misleading or self-incriminating. Special care should always be taken when questioning such a person, and the appropriate adult should be involved if there is any doubt about a person's age, mental state or capacity. Because of the risk of unreliable evidence it is also important to obtain corroboration of any facts admitted whenever possible.

11D   Juveniles should not be arrested at their place of education unless this is unavoidable. When a juvenile is arrested at their place of education, the principal or their nominee must be informed.

11E   Significant statements described in paragraph 11.4 will always be relevant to the offence and must be recorded. When a suspect agrees to read records of interviews and other comments and sign them as correct, they should be asked to endorse the record with, e.g. 'I agree that this is a correct record of what was said' and add their signature. If the suspect does not agree with the record, the interviewer should record the details of any disagreement and ask the suspect to read these details and sign them to the effect that they accurately reflect their disagreement. Any refusal to sign should be recorded.

12   Interviews in police stations

(a)   Action

12.1   If a police officer wants to interview or conduct enquiries which require the presence of a detainee, the custody officer is responsible for deciding whether to deliver the detainee into the officer's custody.

12.2   Except as below, in any period of 24 hours a detainee must be allowed a continuous period of at least 8 hours for rest, free from questioning, travel or any interruption in connection with the investigation concerned. This period should normally be at night or other appropriate time which takes account of when the detainee last slept or rested. If a detainee is arrested at a police station after going there voluntarily, the period of 24 hours runs from the time of their arrest and not the time of arrival at the police station. The period may not be interrupted or delayed, except:

(a) when there are reasonable grounds for believing not delaying or interrupting the period would:

   (i)   involve a risk of harm to people or serious loss of, or damage to, property;

   (ii) delay unnecessarily the person's release from custody;

   (iii) otherwise prejudice the outcome of the investigation;

(b) at the request of the detainee, their appropriate adult or legal representative;

(c) when a delay or interruption is necessary in order to:

   (i)   comply with the legal obligations and duties arising under *section 15*;

   (ii) to take action required under section 9 or in accordance with medical advice.

If the period is interrupted in accordance with *(a)*, a fresh period must be allowed. Interruptions under *(b)* and *(c)*, do not require a fresh period to be allowed.

12.3   Before a detainee is interviewed the custody officer, in consultation with the officer in charge of the investigation and appropriate health care professionals as necessary, shall assess whether the detainee is fit enough to be interviewed. This means determining and considering the risks to the detainee's physical and mental state if the interview took place and determining what safeguards are needed to allow the interview to take place. See *Annex G*. The custody officer shall not allow a detainee to be interviewed if the custody officer considers it would cause significant harm to the detainee's physical or mental state. Vulnerable suspects listed at *paragraph 11.18* shall be treated as always being at some risk during an interview and these persons may not be interviewed except in accordance with *paragraphs 11.18* to *11.20*.

12.4   As far as practicable interviews shall take place in interview rooms which are adequately heated, lit and ventilated.

12.5   A suspect whose detention without charge has been authorised under PACE, because the detention is necessary for an interview to obtain evidence of the offence for which they have been arrested, may choose not to answer questions but police do not require the suspect's consent or agreement to interview them for this purpose. If a suspect takes steps to prevent themselves being questioned or further questioned, e.g. by refusing to leave their cell to go to a suitable interview room or by trying to leave the interview room, they shall be advised their consent or agreement to interview is not required. The suspect shall be cautioned as in *section 10*, and informed if they fail or refuse to co-operate, the interview may take place in the cell and that their failure or refusal to co-operate may be given in evidence. The suspect shall then be invited to co-operate and go into the interview room.

12.6   People being questioned or making statements shall not be required to stand.

12.7   Before the interview commences each interviewer shall, subject to *paragraph 2.6A*, identify themselves and any other persons present to the interviewee.

12.8   Breaks from interviewing should be made at recognised meal times or at other times that take account of when an interviewee last had a meal. Short refreshment breaks shall be provided at approximately two hour intervals, subject to the interviewer's discretion to delay a break if there are reasonable grounds for believing it would:

   (i)   involve a:

   •   risk of harm to people;

   •   serious loss of, or damage to, property;

   (ii) unnecessarily delay the detainee's release;

(iii)   otherwise prejudice the outcome of the investigation.

See *Note 12B*

12.9   If during the interview a complaint is made by or on behalf of the interviewee concerning the provisions of this Code, the interviewer should:

(i)   record it in the interview record;

(ii)   inform the custody officer, who is then responsible for dealing with it as in *section 9*.

(b) Documentation

12.10   A record must be made of the:

- time a detainee is not in the custody of the custody officer, and why
- reason for any refusal to deliver the detainee out of that custody

12.11   A record shall be made of:

(a)   the reasons it was not practicable to use an interview room; and

(b)   any action taken as in *paragraph 12.5*.

The record shall be made on the custody record or in the interview record for action taken whilst an interview record is being kept, with a brief reference to this effect in the custody record.

12.12   Any decision to delay a break in an interview must be recorded, with reasons, in the interview record.

12.13   All written statements made at police stations under caution shall be written on forms provided for the purpose.

12.14   All written statements made under caution shall be taken in accordance with *Annex D*. Before a person makes a written statement under caution at a police station they shall be reminded about the right to legal advice. See *Note 12A*

Notes for guidance

12A   *It is not normally necessary to ask for a written statement if the interview was recorded or taped at the time and the record signed by the interviewee in accordance with paragraph 11.11. Statements under caution should normally be taken in these circumstances only at the person's express wish. A person may however be asked if they want to make such a statement.*

12B   *Meal breaks should normally last at least 45 minutes and shorter breaks after two hours should last at least 15 minutes. If the interviewer delays a break in accordance with paragraph 12.8 and prolongs the interview, a longer break should be provided. If there is a short interview, and another short interview is contemplated, the length of the break may be reduced if there are reasonable grounds to believe this is necessary to avoid any of the consequences in paragraph 12.8(i) to (iii).*

13   Interpreters

(a) General

13.1   Chief officers are responsible for making sure appropriate arrangements are in place for provision of suitably qualified interpreters for people who:

- are deaf;
- do not understand English.

Whenever possible, interpreters should be drawn from the National Register of Public Service Interpreters (NRPSI).

(b) Foreign languages

13.2   Unless *paragraphs 11.1, 11.18* to *11.20* apply, a person must not be interviewed in the absence of a person capable of interpreting if:

(a)   they have difficulty understanding English;

(b)   the interviewer cannot speak the person's own language;

(c)   the person wants an interpreter present.

13.3   The interviewer shall make sure the interpreter makes a note of the interview at the time in the person's language for use in the event of the interpreter being called to give evidence, and certifies its accuracy. The interviewer should allow sufficient time for the interpreter to note each question and answer after each is put, given and interpreted. The person should be allowed to read the record or have it read to them and sign it as correct or indicate the respects in which they consider it inaccurate. If the interview is tape-recorded or visually recorded, the arrangements in Code E or F apply.

13.4   In the case of a person making a statement to a police officer or other police staff other than in English:

(a)   the interpreter shall record the statement in the language it is made;

(b)   the person shall be invited to sign it;

(c)   an official English translation shall be made in due course.

(c)   Deaf people and people with speech difficulties

13.5   If a person appears to be deaf or there is doubt about their hearing or speaking ability, they must not be interviewed in the absence of an interpreter unless they agree in writing to being interviewed without one or *paragraphs 11.1, 11.18 to 11.20* apply.

13.6   An interpreter should also be called if a juvenile is interviewed and the parent or guardian present as the appropriate adult appears to be deaf or there is doubt about their hearing or speaking ability, unless they agree in writing to the interview proceeding without one or *paragraphs 11.1, 11.18* to *11.20* apply.

13.7   The interviewer shall make sure the interpreter is allowed to read the interview record and certify its accuracy in the event of the interpreter being called to give evidence. If the interview is tape-recorded or visually recorded, the arrangements in Code E or F apply.

(d)   Additional rules for detained persons

13.8   All reasonable attempts should be made to make the detainee understand that interpreters will be provided at public expense.

13.9   If *paragraph 6.1* applies and the detainee cannot communicate with the solicitor because of language, hearing or speech difficulties, an interpreter must be called. The interpreter may not be a police officer or civilian support staff when interpretation is needed for the purposes of obtaining legal advice. In all other cases a police officer or civilian support staff may only interpret if the detainee and the appropriate adult, if applicable, give their agreement in writing or if the interview is tape-recorded or visually recorded as in Code E or F.

13.10   When the custody officer cannot establish effective communication with a person charged with an offence who appears deaf or there is doubt about their ability to hear, speak or to understand English, arrangements must be made as soon as practicable for an interpreter to explain the offence and any other information given by the custody officer.

(e)   Documentation

13.11   Action taken to call an interpreter under this section and any agreement to be interviewed in the absence of an interpreter must be recorded.

14   Questioning — special restrictions

14.1   If a person is arrested by one police force on behalf of another and the lawful period of detention in respect of that offence has not yet commenced in accordance with PACE, section 41 no questions may be put to them about the offence while they are in transit between the forces except to clarify any voluntary statement they make.

14.2   If a person is in police detention at a hospital they may not be questioned without the agreement of a responsible doctor. See *Note 14A*

Note for guidance

14A   *If questioning takes place at a hospital under paragraph 14.2, or on the way to or from a hospital, the period of questioning concerned counts towards the total period of detention permitted.*

15   Reviews and extensions of detention

(a)   Persons detained under PACE

15.1   The review officer is responsible under PACE, section 40 for periodically determining if a person's detention, before or after charge, continues to be necessary. This requirement continues throughout the detention period and except as in *paragraph 15.10*, the review officer must be present at the police station holding the detainee. See *Notes 15A* and *15B*

15.2   Under PACE, section 42, an officer of superintendent rank or above who is responsible for the station holding the detainee may give authority any time after the second review to extend the maximum period the person may be detained without charge by up to 12 hours. Further detention without charge may be authorised only by a magistrates' court in accordance with PACE, sections 43 and 44. See *Notes 15C, 15D* and *15E*

15.2A   Section 42(1) of PACE as amended extends the maximum period of detention for arrestable offences from 24 hours to 36 hours. Detaining a juvenile or mentally vulnerable person for longer than 24 hours will be dependent on the circumstances of the case and with regard to the person's:

(a)   special vulnerability;

(b)   the legal obligation to provide an opportunity for representations to be made prior to a decision about extending detention;

(c)   the need to consult and consider the views of any appropriate adult; and

(d)   any alternatives to police custody.

15.3   Before deciding whether to authorise continued detention the officer responsible under *paragraphs 15.1* or *15.2* shall give an opportunity to make representations about the detention to:

(a)   the detainee, unless in the case of a review as in *paragraph 15.1*, the detainee is asleep;

(b)   the detainee's solicitor if available at the time; and

(c)   the appropriate adult if available at the time.

15.3A   Other people having an interest in the detainee's welfare may also make representations at the authorising officer's discretion.

15.3B   Subject to paragraph 15.10, the representations may be made orally in person or by telephone or in writing. The authorising officer may, however, refuse to hear oral representations from the detainee if the officer considers them unfit to make representations because of their condition or behaviour. See *Note 15C*

15.3C   The decision on whether the review takes place in person or by telephone or by video conferencing (see Note 15G) is a matter for the review officer. In determining the form the review may take, the review officer must always take full account of the needs of the person in custody. The benefits of carrying out a review in person should always be considered, based on the individual circumstances of each case with specific additional consideration if the person is:

(a)   a juvenile (and the age of the juvenile); or

(b)   mentally vulnerable; or

(c)   has been subject to medical attention for other than routine minor ailments; or

(d)   there are presentational or community issues around the person's detention.

15.4   Before conducting a review or determining whether to extend the maximum period of detention without charge, the officer responsible must make sure the detainee is reminded of their entitlement to free legal advice, see *paragraph 6.5*, unless in the case of a review the person is asleep.

15.5   If, after considering any representations, the officer decides to keep the detainee in detention or extend the maximum period they may be detained without charge, any comment made by the detainee shall be recorded. If applicable, the officer responsible under *paragraph 15.1* or *15.2* shall be informed of the comment as soon as practicable. See also *paragraphs 11.4* and *11.13*

15.6   No officer shall put specific questions to the detainee:

•   regarding their involvement in any offence; or

•   in respect of any comments they may make;

— when given the opportunity to make representations; or

— in response to a decision to keep them in detention or extend the maximum period of detention.

Such an exchange could constitute an interview as in *paragraph 11.1A* and would be subject to the associated safeguards in *section 11* and, in respect of a person who has been charged, *paragraph 16.5*. See also *paragraph 11.13*

15.7   A detainee who is asleep at a review, see *paragraph 15.1*, and whose continued detention is authorised must be informed about the decision and reason as soon as practicable after waking.

(b)   Persons detained under the Terrorism Act 2000

15.8   In terrorism cases:

(a)   the powers and duties of the review officer are in the Terrorism Act 2000, Schedule 8, Part II;

(b)   a police officer of at least superintendent rank may apply to a judicial authority for a warrant of further detention under the Terrorism Act 2000, Schedule 8, Part III.

(c)   Telephone review of detention

15.9   PACE, section 40A provides that the officer responsible under section 40 for reviewing the detention of a person who has not been charged, need not attend the police station holding the detainee and may carry out the review by telephone.

15.9A   PACE, section 45A(2) provides that the officer responsible under section 40 for reviewing the detention of a person who has not been charged, need not attend the police station holding the detainee and may carry out the review by video conferencing facilities (see *Note 15G*).

15.9B   A telephone review is not permitted where facilities for review by video conferencing exist and it is practicable to use them.

15.9C   The review officer can decide at any stage that a telephone review or review by video conferencing should be terminated and that the review will be conducted in person. The reasons for doing so should be noted in the custody record.

See *Note 15F*

15.10 When a telephone review is carried out, an officer at the station holding the detainee shall be required by the review officer to fulfil that officer's obligations under PACE section 40 or this Code by:

(a) making any record connected with the review in the detainee's custody record;

(b) if applicable, making a record in (*a*) in the presence of the detainee; and

(c) giving the detainee information about the review.

15.11 When a telephone review is carried out, the requirement in *paragraph 15.3* will be satisfied:

(a) if facilities exist for the immediate transmission of written representations to the review officer, e.g. fax or email message, by giving the detainee an opportunity to make representations:

(i) orally by telephone; or

(ii) in writing using those facilities; and

(b) in all other cases, by giving the detainee an opportunity to make their representations orally by telephone.

(d) Documentation

15.12 It is the officer's responsibility to make sure all reminders given under *paragraph 15.4* are noted in the custody record.

15.13 The grounds for, and extent of, any delay in conducting a review shall be recorded.

15.14 When a telephone review is carried out, a record shall be made of:

(a) the reason the review officer did not attend the station holding the detainee;

(b) the place the review officer was;

(c) the method representations, oral or written, were made to the review officer, see *paragraph 15.11*.

15.15 Any written representations shall be retained.

15.16 A record shall be made as soon as practicable about the outcome of each review or determination whether to extend the maximum detention period without charge or an application for a warrant of further detention or its extension. If *paragraph 15.7* applies, a record shall also be made of when the person was informed and by whom. If an authorisation is given under PACE, section 42, the record shall state the number of hours and minutes by which the detention period is extended or further extended. If a warrant for further detention, or extension, is granted under section 43 or 44, the record shall state the detention period authorised by the warrant and the date and time it was granted.

Notes for guidance

15A *Review officer for the purposes of:*

- *PACE, sections 40 and 40A means, in the case of a person arrested but not charged, an officer of at least inspector rank not directly involved in the investigation and, if a person has been arrested and charged, the custody officer;*

- *the Terrorism Act 2000, means an officer not directly involved in the investigation connected with the detention and of at least inspector rank, for reviews within 24 hours of the detainee's arrest or superintendent for all other reviews.*

15B *The detention of persons in police custody not subject to the statutory review requirement in paragraph 15.1 should still be reviewed periodically as a matter of good practice. Such reviews can be carried out by an officer of the rank of sergeant or above. The purpose of such reviews is to check the particular power under which a detainee is held continues to apply, any associated conditions are complied with and to make sure appropriate action is taken to deal with any changes. This includes the detainee's prompt release when the power no longer applies, or their transfer if the power requires the detainee be taken elsewhere as soon as the necessary arrangements are made. Examples include persons:*

(a)   arrested on warrant because they failed to answer bail to appear at court or failed to answer street bail;

(b)   arrested under the Bail Act 1976, section 7(3) for breaching a condition of bail granted after charge;

(c)   in police custody for specific purposes and periods under the Crime (Sentences) Act 1997, Schedule 1;

(d)   convicted, or remand prisoners, held in police stations on behalf of the Prison Service under the Imprisonment (Temporary Provisions) Act 1980, section 6;

(e)   being detained to prevent them causing a breach of the peace;

(f)   detained at police stations on behalf of the Immigration Service.

The detention of persons remanded into police detention by order of a court under the Magistrates' Courts Act 1980, section 128 is subject to a statutory requirement to review that detention. This is to make sure the detainee is taken back to court no later than the end of the period authorised by the court or when the need for their detention by police ceases, whichever is the sooner.

15C   *In the case of a review of detention, but not an extension, the detainee need not be woken for the review. However, if the detainee is likely to be asleep, e.g. during a period of rest allowed as in paragraph 12.2, at the latest time a review or authorisation to extend detention may take place, the officer should, if the legal obligations and time constraints permit, bring forward the procedure to allow the detainee to make representations. A detainee not asleep during the review must be present when the grounds for their continued detention are recorded and must at the same time be informed of those grounds unless the review officer considers the person is incapable of understanding what is said, violent or likely to become violent or in urgent need of medical attention.*

15D   *An application to a Magistrates' Court under PACE, sections 43 or 44 for a warrant of further detention or its extension should be made between 10am and 9pm, and if possible during normal court hours. It will not usually be practicable to arrange for a court to sit specially outside the hours of 10am to 9pm. If it appears a special sitting may be needed outside normal court hours but between 10am and 9pm, the clerk to the justices should be given notice and informed of this possibility, while the court is sitting if possible.*

15E   *In paragraph 15.2, the officer responsible for the station holding the detainee includes a superintendent or above who, in accordance with their force operational policy or police regulations, is given that responsibility on a temporary basis whilst the appointed long-term holder is off duty or otherwise unavailable.*

15F   *The provisions of PACE, section 40A allowing telephone reviews do not apply to reviews of detention after charge by the custody officer or to reviews under the Terrorism Act 2000, Schedule 8, Part II in terrorism cases. When video conferencing is not required, they allow the use of a telephone to carry out a review of detention before charge. The procedure under PACE, section 42 must be done in person.*

15G   *The use of video conferencing facilities for decisions about detention under section 45A of PACE is subject to the introduction of regulations by the Secretary of State.*

16   Charging detained persons

(a)   Action

16.1   When the officer in charge of the investigation reasonably believes there is sufficient evidence to provide a realistic prospect of the detainee's conviction, see *paragraph 11.6*, they shall without delay, and subject to the following qualification, inform the custody officer who will be responsible for considering whether the detainee should be charged. See *Notes 11B* and *16A*. When a person is detained in respect of more than one offence it is permissible to delay informing the custody officer until the above conditions are satisfied in respect of all the offences, but see *paragraph 11.6*. If the detainee is a juvenile, mentally disordered or otherwise mentally vulnerable, any resulting action shall be taken in the presence of the appropriate adult if they are present at the time. See *Notes 16B* and *16C*

16.1A   Where guidance issued by the Director of Public Prosecutions under section 37A is in force the custody officer must comply with that Guidance in deciding how to act in dealing with the detainee. See *Note 16AB*.

16.1B   Where in compliance with the DPP's Guidance the custody officer decides that the case should be immediately referred to the CPS to make the charging decision, consultation should take place with a Crown Prosecutor as soon as is reasonably practicable. Where the Crown Prosecutor is unable to make the charging decision on the information available at that time, the detainee may be released without charge and on bail (with conditions if necessary) under section 37(7)(a). In such circumstances, the detainee should be informed that they are being released to enable the Director of Public Prosecutions to make a decision under section 37B.

16.2   When a detainee is charged with or informed they may be prosecuted for an offence, see *Note 16B*, they shall, unless the restriction on drawing adverse inferences from silence applies, see *Annex C*, be cautioned as follows:

'You do not have to say anything. But it may harm your defence if you do not mention now something which you later rely on in court. Anything you do say may be given in evidence.'

Annex C, paragraph 2 sets out the alternative terms of the caution to be used when the restriction on drawing adverse inferences from silence applies.

16.3   When a detainee is charged they shall be given a written notice showing particulars of the offence and, subject to *paragraph 2.6A*, the officer's name and the case reference number. As far as possible the particulars of the charge shall be stated in simple terms, but they shall also show the precise offence in law with which the detainee is charged. The notice shall begin:

' You are charged with the offence(s) shown below.' Followed by the caution.

If the detainee is a juvenile, mentally disordered or otherwise mentally vulnerable, the notice should be given to the appropriate adult.

16.4   If, after a detainee has been charged with or informed they may be prosecuted for an offence, an officer wants to tell them about any written statement or interview with another person relating to such an offence, the detainee shall either be handed a true copy of the written statement or the content of the interview record brought to their attention. Nothing shall be done to invite any reply or comment except to:

(a)   caution the detainee, *'You do not have to say anything, but anything you do say may be given in evidence.'*; and

(b)   remind the detainee about their right to legal advice.

16.4A   If the detainee:

•   cannot read, the document may be read to them

•   is a juvenile, mentally disordered or otherwise mentally vulnerable, the appropriate adult shall also be given a copy, or the interview record shall be brought to their attention

16.5   A detainee may not be interviewed about an offence after they have been charged with, or informed they may be prosecuted for it, unless the interview is necessary:

•   to prevent or minimise harm or loss to some other person, or the public

- to clear up an ambiguity in a previous answer or statement
- in the interests of justice for the detainee to have put to them, and have an opportunity to comment on, information concerning the offence which has come to light since they were charged or informed they might be prosecuted

Before any such interview, the interviewer shall:

(a) caution the detainee, *'You do not have to say anything, but anything you do say may be given in evidence.'*;

(b) remind the detainee about their right to legal advice.

See *Note 16B*

16.6 The provisions of *paragraphs 16.2* to *16.5* must be complied with in the appropriate adult's presence if they are already at the police station. If they are not at the police station then these provisions must be complied with again in their presence when they arrive unless the detainee has been released.

See *Note 16C*

16.7 When a juvenile is charged with an offence and the custody officer authorises their continued detention after charge, the custody officer must try to make arrangements for the juvenile to be taken into the care of a local authority to be detained pending appearance in court unless the custody officer certifies it is impracticable to do so or, in the case of a juvenile of at least 12 years old, no secure accommodation is available and there is a risk to the public of serious harm from that juvenile, in accordance with PACE, section 38(6). See *Note 16D*

(b) Documentation

16.8 A record shall be made of anything a detainee says when charged.

16.9 Any questions put in an interview after charge and answers given relating to the offence shall be recorded in full during the interview on forms for that purpose and the record signed by the detainee or, if they refuse, by the interviewer and any third parties present. If the questions are tape recorded or visually recorded the arrangements in Code E or F apply.

16.10 If it is not practicable to make arrangements for a juvenile's transfer into local authority care as in *paragraph 16.7*, the custody officer must record the reasons and complete a certificate to be produced before the court with the juvenile. See *Note 16D*

Notes for guidance

16A *The custody officer must take into account alternatives to prosecution under the Crime and Disorder Act 1998, reprimands and warning applicable to persons under 18, and in national guidance on the cautioning of offenders, for persons aged 18 and over.*

16AB *Where Guidance issued by the Director of Public Prosecutions under section 37B is in force, custody officers are entitled (notwithstanding section 37(1)) to take reasonable time to apply that Guidance in deciding how a detained person is to be dealt with in accordance with section 37(7), as amended by Schedule 2 of the Criminal Justice Act 2003, including where appropriate consultation with a Duty Prosecutor. Where in accordance with the Guidance the case is referred to the CPS for decision, the custody officer should ensure that an officer involved in the investigation sends to the CPS such information as is specified in the Guidance.*

16B *The giving of a warning or the service of the Notice of Intended Prosecution required by the Road Traffic Offenders Act 1988, section 1 does not amount to informing a detainee they may be prosecuted for an offence and so does not preclude further questioning in relation to that offence.*

16C *There is no power under PACE to detain a person and delay action under paragraphs 16.2 to 16.5 solely to await the arrival of the appropriate adult. After charge, bail cannot be refused, or release on bail delayed, simply because an appropriate adult is not available, unless the absence of that adult provides the custody officer with the necessary grounds to authorise detention after charge under PACE, section 38.*

16D   *Except as in paragraph 16.7, neither a juvenile's behaviour nor the nature of the offence provides grounds for the custody officer to decide it is impracticable to arrange the juvenile's transfer to local authority care. Similarly, the lack of secure local authority accommodation does not make it impracticable to transfer the juvenile. The availability of secure accommodation is only a factor in relation to a juvenile aged 12 or over when the local authority accommodation would not be adequate to protect the public from serious harm from them. The obligation to transfer a juvenile to local authority accommodation applies as much to a juvenile charged during the daytime as to a juvenile to be held overnight, subject to a requirement to bring the juvenile before a court under PACE, section 46.*

17   Testing persons for the presence of specified Class A drugs

(a)   Action

17.1   A sample of urine or a non-intimate sample may be taken from a person in police detention for the purpose of ascertaining whether he has any specified Class A drug in his body if:

(a)   he has been charged with a trigger offence, or

(b)   he has been charged with an offence and a police officer of inspector rank or above, who has reasonable grounds for suspecting that the misuse by him of any specified Class A drug caused or contributed to the offence, has authorised the sample to be taken.

17.2   The person from whom the sample is taken must have attained the minimum age for drug testing under the provisions in force in the police area or police station concerned (14 or 18 years of age). See *Note 17F*.

17.3   A police officer must have requested the person concerned to give the sample.

17.4   Before requesting a sample from the person concerned, an officer must:

(a)   inform him that the purpose of taking the sample is for drug testing under PACE. This is to ascertain whether he has a specified Class A drug present in his body;

(b)   warn him that if, when so requested, he fails without good cause to provide a sample he may be liable to prosecution;

(c)   where the taking of the sample has been authorised by an inspector or above in accordance with paragraph 17.1(b) of this Code, inform him that the authorisation has been given and the grounds for giving it;

(d)   remind him of the following rights, which may be exercised at any stage during the period in custody:

(i)   the right to have someone informed of his arrest [see *section 5*];

(ii)   the right to consult privately with a solicitor and that free independent legal advice is available [see *section 6*]; and

(iii)   the right to consult these Codes of Practice [see *section 3*].

17.5   In the case of a person who has not attained the age of 17—

(a)   the making of the request for a sample under paragraph 17.3 above;

(b)   the giving of the warning and the information under paragraph 17.4 above; and

(c)   the taking of the sample,

may not take place except in the presence of an appropriate adult. See *Note 17G*

17.6   Authorisation by an officer of the rank of inspector or above within paragraph 17.1(b) may be given orally or in writing but, if it is given orally, it must be confirmed in writing as soon as practicable.

17.7   Custody officers may authorise continued detention for up to six hours from the time of charge to enable a sample to be taken.

(b)   Documentation

17.8   If a sample is taken following authorisation by an officer of the rank of inspector or above, the authorisation and the grounds for suspicion must be recorded in the custody record.

17.9   The giving of a warning of the consequences of failure to provide a specimen must be recorded in the custody record.

17.10   The time of charge and the time at which the sample was given must be recorded in the custody record.

(c)   General

17.11   A sample may only be taken by a prescribed person. See *Note 17C*.

17.12   Force may not be used to take any sample for the purpose of drug testing.

17.13   The terms 'Class A drug' and 'misuse' have the same meanings as in the Misuse of Drugs Act 1971. 'Specified' (in relation to a Class A drug) and 'trigger offence' have the same meanings as in Part III of the Criminal Justice and Court Services Act 2000.

17.14   Any sample taken:

(a)   may not be used for any purpose other than to ascertain whether the person concerned has a specified Class A drug present in his body; and

(b)   must be retained until the person concerned has made his first appearance before the court.

Notes for guidance

17A   *When warning a person who is asked to provide a urine or non-intimate sample in accordance with paragraph 17.1, the following form of words may be used:*

'You do not have to provide a sample, but I must warn you that if you fail or refuse without good cause to do so, you will commit an offence for which you may be imprisoned, or fined, or both'.

17B   *A sample has to be sufficient and suitable. A sufficient sample is sufficient in quantity and quality to enable drug-testing analysis to take place. A suitable sample is one which by its nature, is suitable for a particular form of drug analysis.*

17C   *A prescribed person in paragraph 17.11 is one who is prescribed in regulations made by the Secretary of State under section 63B(6) of the Police and Criminal Evidence Act 1984. [The regulations are currently contained in regulation SI 2001 No. 2645, the Police and Criminal Evidence Act 1984 (Drug Testing Persons in Police Detention) (Prescribed Persons) Regulations 2001.]*

17D   *The retention of the sample in paragraph 17.14(b) allows for the sample to be sent for confirmatory testing and analysis if the detainee disputes the test. But such samples, and the information derived from them, may not be subsequently used in the investigation of any offence or in evidence against the persons from whom they were taken.*

17E   *Trigger offences include: from the Theft Act 1968 – theft, robbery, burglary, aggravated burglary, taking a motor vehicle (or other conveyance) without authority, aggravated vehicle-taking, obtaining property by deception, going equipped for stealing etc.; and from the Misuse of Drugs Act 1971 (but only if committed in respect of a specified Class A drug) – producing and supplying a controlled drug, possessing a controlled drug, and possessing a controlled drug with intent to supply.*

17F   Section 17 is applicable only within certain police areas, where the relevant provisions for drug testing under section 63B of PACE have been brought into force. The areas where testing for persons aged 18 or over has been introduced are listed at Annex I. The minimum age of 14 will apply only in those police areas where:

- *new provisions introduced by section 5 of the Criminal Justice Act 2003 to test persons aged 14 or over have been brought into force*

AND

- *the relevant chief officer of police has been notified by the Secretary of State that arrangements for the taking of samples from persons under the age of 18 have been made for the police area as a whole, or for a particular police station within that area and the notice has not been withdrawn.*

The police areas where section 5 of the Criminal Justice Act 2003 is in force and where drug testing of persons aged 14–17 applies, if such notification is in force, are set out in Annex J.

17G   Appropriate adult in paragraph 17.5 means the person's—

- *(a)   parent or guardian or, if he is in the care of a local authority or voluntary organisation, a person representing that authority or organisation; or*
- *(b)   a social worker of a local authority social services department; or*
- *(c)   if no person falling within (a) or (b) above is available, any responsible person aged 18 or over who is not a police officer or a person employed by the police.*

ANNEX A — INTIMATE AND STRIP SEARCHES

A   Intimate search

1.   An intimate search consists of the physical examination of a person's body orifices other than the mouth. The intrusive nature of such searches means the actual and potential risks associated with intimate searches must never be underestimated.

(a)   Action

2.   Body orifices other than the mouth may be searched only if authorised by an officer of inspector rank or above who has reasonable grounds for believing that:

    (a)   the person may have concealed on themselves

        (i)   anything which they could and might use to cause physical injury to themself or others at the station; or

        (ii)   a Class A drug which they intended to supply to another or to export; and

    (b)   an intimate search is the only means of removing those items.

2A.   The reasons an intimate search is considered necessary shall be explained to the person before the search begins.

3.   An intimate search may only be carried out by a registered medical practitioner or registered nurse, unless an officer of at least inspector rank considers this is not practicable and the search is to take place under *paragraph 2(a)(i)*, in which case a police officer may carry out the search. See *Notes A1 to A5*

3A.   Any proposal for a search under *paragraph 2(a)(i)* to be carried out by someone other than a registered medical practitioner or registered nurse must only be considered as a last resort and when the authorising officer is satisfied the risks associated with allowing the item to remain with the detainee outweigh the risks associated with removing it. See *Notes A1 to A5*

4.   An intimate search under:

- *paragraph 2(a)(i)* may take place only at a hospital, surgery, other medical premises or police station

- *paragraph 2(a)(ii)* may take place only at a hospital, surgery or other medical premises and must be carried out by a registered medical practitioner or a registered nurse

5. An intimate search at a police station of a juvenile or mentally disordered or otherwise mentally vulnerable person may take place only in the presence of an appropriate adult of the same sex, unless the detainee specifically requests a particular adult of the opposite sex who is readily available. In the case of a juvenile the search may take place in the absence of the appropriate adult only if the juvenile signifies in the presence of the appropriate adult they do not want the adult present during the search and the adult agrees. A record shall be made of the juvenile's decision and signed by the appropriate adult.

6. When an intimate search under *paragraph 2(a)(i)* is carried out by a police officer, the officer must be of the same sex as the detainee. A minimum of two people, other than the detainee, must be present during the search. Subject to *paragraph 5*, no person of the opposite sex who is not a medical practitioner or nurse shall be present, nor shall anyone whose presence is unnecessary. The search shall be conducted with proper regard to the sensitivity and vulnerability of the detainee.

(b) Documentation

7. In the case of an intimate search the custody officer shall as soon as practicable, record:
    - which parts of the detainee's body were searched
    - who carried out the search
    - who was present
    - the reasons for the search including the reasons to believe the article could not otherwise be removed
    - the result.

8. If an intimate search is carried out by a police officer, the reason why it was impracticable for a registered medical practitioner or registered nurse to conduct it must be recorded.

B Strip search

9. A strip search is a search involving the removal of more than outer clothing. In this Code, outer clothing includes shoes and socks.

(a) Action

10. A strip search may take place only if it is considered necessary to remove an article which a detainee would not be allowed to keep, and the officer reasonably considers the detainee might have concealed such an article. Strip searches shall not be routinely carried out if there is no reason to consider that articles are concealed.

The conduct of strip searches

11. When strip searches are conducted:
    (a) a police officer carrying out a strip search must be the same sex as the detainee;
    (b) the search shall take place in an area where the detainee cannot be seen by anyone who does not need to be present, nor by a member of the opposite sex except an appropriate adult who has been specifically requested by the detainee;
    (c) except in cases of urgency, where there is risk of serious harm to the detainee or to others, whenever a strip search involves exposure of intimate body parts, there must be at least two people present other than the detainee, and

if the search is of a juvenile or mentally disordered or otherwise mentally vulnerable person, one of the people must be the appropriate adult. Except in urgent cases as above, a search of a juvenile may take place in the absence of the appropriate adult only if the juvenile signifies in the presence of the appropriate adult that they do not want the adult to be present during the search and the adult agrees. A record shall be made of the juvenile's decision and signed by the appropriate adult. The presence of more than two people, other than an appropriate adult, shall be permitted only in the most exceptional circumstances;

(d)   the search shall be conducted with proper regard to the sensitivity and vulnerability of the detainee in these circumstances and every reasonable effort shall be made to secure the detainee's co-operation and minimise embarrassment. Detainees who are searched shall not normally be required to remove all their clothes at the same time, e.g. a person should be allowed to remove clothing above the waist and redress before removing further clothing;

(e)   if necessary to assist the search, the detainee may be required to hold their arms in the air or to stand with their legs apart and bend forward so a visual examination may be made of the genital and anal areas provided no physical contact is made with any body orifice;

(f)   if articles are found, the detainee shall be asked to hand them over. If articles are found within any body orifice other than the mouth, and the detainee refuses to hand them over, their removal would constitute an intimate search, which must be carried out as in *Part A*;

(g)   a strip search shall be conducted as quickly as possible, and the detainee allowed to dress as soon as the procedure is complete.

(b)   Documentation

12.   A record shall be made on the custody record of a strip search including the reason it was considered necessary, those present and any result.

Notes for guidance

A1   *Before authorising any intimate search, the authorising officer must make every reasonable effort to persuade the detainee to hand the article over without a search. If the detainee agrees, a registered medical practitioner or registered nurse should whenever possible be asked to assess the risks involved and, if necessary, attend to assist the detainee.*

A2   *If the detainee does not agree to hand the article over without a search, the authorising officer must carefully review all the relevant factors before authorising an intimate search. In particular, the officer must consider whether the grounds for believing an article may be concealed are reasonable.*

A3   *If authority is given for a search under paragraph 2(a)(i), a registered medical practitioner or registered nurse shall be consulted whenever possible. The presumption should be that the search will be conducted by the registered medical practitioner or registered nurse and the authorising officer must make every reasonable effort to persuade the detainee to allow the medical practitioner or nurse to conduct the search.*

A4   *A constable should only be authorised to carry out a search as a last resort and when all other approaches have failed. In these circumstances, the authorising officer must be satisfied the detainee might use the article for one or more of the purposes in paragraph 2(a)(i) and the physical injury likely to be caused is sufficiently severe to justify authorising a constable to carry out the search.*

A5   *If an officer has any doubts whether to authorise an intimate search by a constable, the officer should seek advice from an officer of superintendent rank or above.*

ANNEX B — DELAY IN NOTIFYING ARREST OR ALLOWING ACCESS TO LEGAL ADVICE

A Persons detained under PACE

1. The exercise of the rights in *Section 5* or *Section 6*, or both, may be delayed if the person is in police detention, as in PACE, section 118(2), in connection with a serious arrestable offence, has not yet been charged with an offence and an officer of superintendent rank or above, or inspector rank or above only for the rights in *Section 5*, has reasonable grounds for believing their exercise will:

   (i)   lead to:

   •   interference with, or harm to, evidence connected with a serious arrestable offence; or

   •   interference with, or physical harm to, other people; or

   (ii) lead to alerting other people suspected of having committed a serious arrestable offence but not yet arrested for it; or

   (iii) hinder the recovery of property obtained in consequence of the commission of such an offence.

2. These rights may also be delayed if the serious arrestable offence is:

   (i)   a drug trafficking offence and the officer has reasonable grounds for believing the detainee has benefited from drug trafficking, and the recovery of the value of the detainee's proceeds from drug trafficking will be hindered by the exercise of either right;

   (ii) an offence to which the Criminal Justice Act 1988, Part VI (confiscation orders) applies and the officer has reasonable grounds for believing the detainee has benefited from the offence, and the exercise of either right will hinder the recovery of the value of the:

   •   property obtained by the detainee from or in connection with the offence

   •   pecuniary advantage derived by the detainee from or in connection with it.

3. Authority to delay a detainee's right to consult privately with a solicitor may be given only if the authorising officer has reasonable grounds to believe the solicitor the detainee wants to consult will, inadvertently or otherwise, pass on a message from the detainee or act in some other way which will have any of the consequences specified under *paragraphs 1* or *2*. In these circumstances the detainee must be allowed to choose another solicitor. See *Note B3*

4. If the detainee wishes to see a solicitor, access to that solicitor may not be delayed on the grounds they might advise the detainee not to answer questions or the solicitor was initially asked to attend the police station by someone else. In the latter case the detainee must be told the solicitor has come to the police station at another person's request, and must be asked to sign the custody record to signify whether they want to see the solicitor.

5. The fact the grounds for delaying notification of arrest may be satisfied does not automatically mean the grounds for delaying access to legal advice will also be satisfied.

6. These rights may be delayed only for as long as grounds exist and in no case beyond 36 hours after the relevant time as in PACE, section 41. If the grounds cease to apply within this time, the detainee must, as soon as practicable, be asked if they want to exercise either right, the custody record must be noted accordingly, and action taken in accordance with the relevant section of the Code.

7. A detained person must be permitted to consult a solicitor for a reasonable time before any court hearing.

B Persons detained under the Terrorism Act 2000

8. The rights as in *sections 5* or *6*, may be delayed if the person is detained under the Terrorism Act 2000, section 41 or Schedule 7, has not yet been charged with an offence and an officer of superintendent rank or above has reasonable grounds for believing the exercise of either right will:

    (i)   lead to:

          •   interference with, or harm to, evidence connected with a serious arrestable offence;

          •   interference with, or physical harm to, other people; or

    (ii) lead to the alerting of other people suspected of having committed a serious arrestable offence but not yet arrested for it; or

    (iii) hinder the recovery of property:

          •   obtained in consequence of the commission of such an offence; or

          •   in respect of which a forfeiture order could be made under that Act, section 23;

    (iv) lead to interference with the gathering of information about the commission, preparation or instigation of acts of terrorism; or

    (v)   by alerting any person, make it more difficult to prevent an act of terrorism or secure the apprehension, prosecution or conviction of any person in connection with the commission, preparation or instigation of an act of terrorism.

9. These rights may also be delayed if the officer has reasonable grounds for believing:

    (a)   the detainee:

          (i)   has committed an offence to which the Criminal Justice Act 1988, Part VI (confiscation orders) applies;

          (ii) has benefited from the offence; and

    (b)   the exercise of either right will hinder the recovery of the value of that benefit.

10. In these cases *paragraphs 3 (with regards to the consequences specified at paragraphs 8 and 9), 4* and *5* apply.

11. These rights may be delayed only for as long as is necessary but not beyond 48 hours from the time of arrest if arrested under section 41, or if detained under the Terrorism Act 2000, Schedule 7 when arrested under section 41, from the beginning of their examination. If the above grounds cease to apply within this time the detainee must as soon as practicable be asked if they wish to exercise either right, the custody record noted accordingly, and action taken in accordance with the relevant section of this Code.

12. In this case *paragraph 7* applies.

C Documentation

13. The grounds for action under this Annex shall be recorded and the detainee informed of them as soon as practicable.

14. Any reply given by a detainee under *paragraphs 6* or *11* must be recorded and the detainee asked to endorse the record in relation to whether they want to receive legal advice at this point.

D   Cautions and special warnings

When a suspect detained at a police station is interviewed during any period for which access to legal advice has been delayed under this Annex, the court or jury may not draw adverse inferences from their silence.

Notes for guidance

B1   *Even if Annex B applies in the case of a juvenile, or a person who is mentally disordered or otherwise mentally vulnerable, action to inform the appropriate adult and the person responsible for a juvenile's welfare if that is a different person, must nevertheless be taken as in paragraph 3.13 and 3.15.*

B2   *In the case of Commonwealth citizens and foreign nationals, see Note 7A.*

B3   *A decision to delay access to a specific solicitor is likely to be a rare occurrence and only when it can be shown the suspect is capable of misleading that particular solicitor and there is more than a substantial risk that the suspect will succeed in causing information to be conveyed which will lead to one or more of the specified consequences.*

ANNEX C — RESTRICTION ON DRAWING ADVERSE INFERENCES FROM SILENCE AND TERMS OF THE CAUTION WHEN THE RESTRICTION APPLIES

(a)   *The restriction on drawing adverse inferences from silence*

1.   The Criminal Justice and Public Order Act 1994, sections 34, 36 and 37 as amended by the Youth Justice and Criminal Evidence Act 1999, section 58 describe the conditions under which adverse inferences may be drawn from a person's failure or refusal to say anything about their involvement in the offence when interviewed, after being charged or informed they may be prosecuted. These provisions are subject to an overriding restriction on the ability of a court or jury to draw adverse inferences from a person's silence. This restriction applies:

(a)   to any detainee at a police station, see *Note 10C* who, before being interviewed, see *section 11* or being charged or informed they may be prosecuted, see *section 16*, has:

(i)   asked for legal advice, see *section 6, paragraph 6.1*;

(ii)   not been allowed an opportunity to consult a solicitor, including the duty solicitor, as in this Code: and

(iii)   not changed their mind about wanting legal advice, see *section 6, paragraph 6.6(d)*

Note the condition in (ii) will

—   apply when a detainee who has asked for legal advice is interviewed before speaking to a solicitor as in *section 6, paragraph 6.6(a)* or *(b)*.

—   not apply if the detained person declines to ask for the duty solicitor, see *section 6, paragraphs 6.6(c)* and *(d)*;

(b)   to any person charged with, or informed they may be prosecuted for, an offence who:

(i)   has had brought to their notice a written statement made by another person or the content of an interview with another person which relates to that offence, see *section 16, paragraph 16.4*;

(ii)   is interviewed about that offence, see *section 16, paragraph 16.5*; or

(iii)   makes a written statement about that offence, see *Annex D paragraphs 4* and *9*.

(b)   *Terms of the caution when the restriction applies*

2.   When a requirement to caution arises at a time when the restriction on drawing adverse inferences from silence applies, the caution shall be:

'You do not have to say anything, but anything you do say may be given in evidence.'

3. Whenever the restriction either begins to apply or ceases to apply after a caution has already been given, the person shall be re-cautioned in the appropriate terms. The changed position on drawing inferences and that the previous caution no longer applies shall also be explained to the detainee in ordinary language. See *Note C2*

Notes for guidance

C1 *The restriction on drawing inferences from silence does not apply to a person who has not been detained and who therefore cannot be prevented from seeking legal advice if they want to, see paragraphs 10.2 and 3.15.*

C2 *The following is suggested as a framework to help explain changes in the position on drawing adverse inferences if the restriction on drawing adverse inferences from silence:*

    (a) *begins to apply:*

        'The caution you were previously given no longer applies. This is because after that caution:

        (i) *you asked to speak to a solicitor but have not yet been allowed an opportunity to speak to a solicitor.' See paragraph 1(a); or*

        (ii) *you have been charged with/informed you may be prosecuted.' See paragraph 1(b).*

        'This means that from now on, adverse inferences cannot be drawn at court and your defence will not be harmed just because you choose to say nothing. Please listen carefully to the caution I am about to give you because it will apply from now on. You will see that it does not say anything about your defence being harmed.'

    (b) *ceases to apply before or at the time the person is charged or informed they may be prosecuted, see paragraph 1(a);*

'The caution you were previously given no longer applies. This is because after that caution you have been allowed an opportunity to speak to a solicitor. Please listen carefully to the caution I am about to give you because it will apply from now on. It explains how your defence at court may be affected if you choose to say nothing.'

ANNEX D — WRITTEN STATEMENTS UNDER CAUTION

(a) *Written by a person under caution*

1. A person shall always be invited to write down what they want to say.

2. A person who has not been charged with, or informed they may be prosecuted for, any offence to which the statement they want to write relates, shall:

    (a) unless the statement is made at a time when the restriction on drawing adverse inferences from silence applies, see Annex C, be asked to write out and sign the following before writing what they want to say:

        'I make this statement of my own free will. I understand that I do not have to say anything but that it may harm my defence if I do not mention when questioned something which I later rely on in court. This statement may be given in evidence.';

    (b) if the statement is made at a time when the restriction on drawing adverse inferences from silence applies, be asked to write out and sign the following before writing what they want to say;

        'I make this statement of my own free will. I understand that I do not have to say anything. This statement may be given in evidence.'

3. When a person, on the occasion of being charged with or informed they may be prosecuted for any offence, asks to make a statement which relates to any such offence and wants to write it they shall:

(a)   unless the restriction on drawing adverse inferences from silence, see *Annex C*, applied when they were so charged or informed they may be prosecuted, be asked to write out and sign the following before writing what they want to say:

'I make this statement of my own free will. I understand that I do not have to say anything but that it may harm my defence if I do not mention when questioned something which I later rely on in court. This statement may be given in evidence.';

(b)   if the restriction on drawing adverse inferences from silence applied when they were so charged or informed they may be prosecuted, be asked to write out and sign the following before writing what they want to say:

'I make this statement of my own free will. I understand that I do not have to say anything. This statement may be given in evidence.'

4.   When a person, who has already been charged with or informed they may be prosecuted for any offence, asks to make a statement which relates to any such offence and wants to write it they shall be asked to write out and sign the following before writing what they want to say:

'I make this statement of my own free will. I understand that I do not have to say anything. This statement may be given in evidence.';

5.   Any person writing their own statement shall be allowed to do so without any prompting except a police officer or civilian interviewer may indicate to them which matters are material or question any ambiguity in the statement.

(b)   Written by a police officer or civilian interviewer

6.   If a person says they would like someone to write the statement for them, a police officer, or civilian interviewer shall write the statement.

7.   If the person has not been charged with, or informed they may be prosecuted for, any offence to which the statement they want to make relates they shall, before starting, be asked to sign, or make their mark, to the following:

(a)   unless the statement is made at a time when the restriction on drawing adverse inferences from silence applies, see *Annex C*:

'I, ..., wish to make a statement. I want someone to write down what I say. I understand that I do not have to say anything but that it may harm my defence if I do not mention when questioned something which I later rely on in court. This statement may be given in evidence.';

(b)   if the statement is made at a time when the restriction on drawing adverse inferences from silence applies:

'I, ..., wish to make a statement. I want someone to write down what I say. I understand that I do not have to say anything. This statement may be given in evidence.'

8.   If, on the occasion of being charged with or informed they may be prosecuted for any offence, the person asks to make a statement which relates to any such offence they shall before starting be asked to sign, or make their mark to, the following:

(a)   unless the restriction on drawing adverse inferences from silence applied, see *Annex C,*when they were so charged or informed they may be prosecuted:

'I, ..., wish to make a statement. I want someone to write down what I say. I understand that I do not have to say anything but that it may harm my defence if I do not mention when questioned something which I later rely on in court. This statement may be given in evidence.';

(b)   if the restriction on drawing adverse inferences from silence applied when they were so charged or informed they may be prosecuted:

'I, ..., wish to make a statement. I want someone to write down what I say. I understand that I do not have to say anything. This statement may be given in evidence.'

9.   If, having already been charged with or informed they may be prosecuted for any offence, a person asks to make a statement which relates to any such offence they shall before starting, be asked to sign, or make their mark to:

'I, ..., wish to make a statement. I want someone to write down what I say. I understand that I do not have to say anything. This statement may be given in evidence.'

10.   The person writing the statement must take down the exact words spoken by the person making it and must not edit or paraphrase it. Any questions that are necessary, e.g. to make it more intelligible, and the answers given must be recorded at the same time on the statement form.

11.   When the writing of a statement is finished the person making it shall be asked to read it and to make any corrections, alterations or additions they want. When they have finished reading they shall be asked to write and sign or make their mark on the following certificate at the end of the statement:

'I have read the above statement, and I have been able to correct, alter or add anything I wish. This statement is true. I have made it of my own free will.'

12.   If the person making the statement cannot read, or refuses to read it, or to write the above mentioned certificate at the end of it or to sign it, the person taking the statement shall read it to them and ask them if they would like to correct, alter or add anything and to put their signature or make their mark at the end. The person taking the statement shall certify on the statement itself what has occurred.

ANNEX E — SUMMARY OF PROVISIONS RELATING TO MENTALLY DISORDERED AND OTHERWISE MENTALLY VULNERABLE PEOPLE

1.   If an officer has any suspicion, or is told in good faith, that a person of any age may be mentally disordered or otherwise mentally vulnerable, or mentally incapable of understanding the significance of questions or their replies that person shall be treated as mentally disordered or otherwise mentally vulnerable for the purposes of this Code. See *paragraph 1.4*

2.   In the case of a person who is mentally disordered or otherwise mentally vulnerable, 'the appropriate adult' means:

(a)   a relative, guardian or other person responsible for their care or custody;

(b)   someone experienced in dealing with mentally disordered or mentally vulnerable people but who is not a police officer or employed by the police;

(c)   failing these, some other responsible adult aged 18 or over who is not a police officer or employed by the police.

See *paragraph 1.7(b)* and *Note 1D*

3.   If the custody officer authorises the detention of a person who is mentally vulnerable or appears to be suffering from a mental disorder, the custody officer must as soon as practicable inform the appropriate adult of the grounds for detention and the person's whereabouts, and ask the adult to come to the police station to see them. If the appropriate adult:

•   is already at the station when information is given as in *paragraphs 3.1 to 3.5* the information must be given in their presence

- is not at the station when the provisions of paragraph 3.1 to 3.5 are complied with these provisions must be complied with again in their presence once they arrive. See *paragraphs 3.15* to *3.17*

4. If the appropriate adult, having been informed of the right to legal advice, considers legal advice should be taken, the provisions of *section 6* apply as if the mentally disordered or otherwise mentally vulnerable person had requested access to legal advice. See *paragraph 3.19* and *Note E1*

5. The custody officer must make sure a person receives appropriate clinical attention as soon as reasonably practicable if the person appears to be suffering from a mental disorder or in urgent cases immediately call the nearest health care professional or an ambulance. It is not intended these provisions delay the transfer of a detainee to a place of safety under the Mental Health Act 1983, section 136 if that is applicable. If an assessment under that Act is to take place at a police station, the custody officer must consider whether an appropriate health care professional should be called to conduct an initial clinical check on the detainee. See *paragraph 9.5* and *9.6*

6. It is imperative a mentally disordered or otherwise mentally vulnerable person detained under the Mental Health Act 1983, section 136 be assessed as soon as possible. If that assessment is to take place at the police station, an approved social worker and registered medical practitioner shall be called to the station as soon as possible in order to interview and examine the detainee. Once the detainee has been interviewed, examined and suitable arrangements been made for their treatment or care, they can no longer be detained under section 136. A detainee should be immediately discharged from detention if a registered medical practitioner having examined them, concludes they are not mentally disordered within the meaning of the Act. See *paragraph 3.16*

7. If a mentally disordered or otherwise mentally vulnerable person is cautioned in the absence of the appropriate adult, the caution must be repeated in the appropriate adult's presence. See *paragraph 10.12*

8. A mentally disordered or otherwise mentally vulnerable person must not be interviewed or asked to provide or sign a written statement in the absence of the appropriate adult unless the provisions of *paragraphs 11.1* or *11.18* to *11.20* apply. Questioning in these circumstances may not continue in the absence of the appropriate adult once sufficient information to avert the risk has been obtained. A record shall be made of the grounds for any decision to begin an interview in these circumstances. See *paragraphs 11.1, 11.15* and *11.18* to *11.20*

9. If the appropriate adult is present at an interview, they shall be informed they are not expected to act simply as an observer and the purposes of their presence are to:
   - advise the interviewee
   - observe whether or not the interview is being conducted properly and fairly
   - facilitate communication with the interviewee

   See *paragraph 11.17*

10. If the detention of a mentally disordered or otherwise mentally vulnerable person is reviewed by a review officer or a superintendent, the appropriate adult must, if available at the time, be given an opportunity to make representations to the officer about the need for continuing detention. See *paragraph 15.3*

11. If the custody officer charges a mentally disordered or otherwise mentally vulnerable person with an offence or takes such other action as is appropriate when there is sufficient evidence for a prosecution this must be done in the presence of the appropriate adult. The written notice embodying any charge must be given to the appropriate adult. See *paragraphs 16.1* to *16.4A*

12. An intimate or strip search of a mentally disordered or otherwise mentally vulnerable person may take place only in the presence of the appropriate adult of the same sex, unless the detainee specifically requests the presence of a particular adult of the opposite sex. A strip search may take place in the absence of an appropriate adult only in cases of urgency when there is a risk of serious harm to the detainee or others. See Annex A, *paragraphs 5* and *11(c)*

13. Particular care must be taken when deciding whether to use any form of approved restraints on a mentally disordered or otherwise mentally vulnerable person in a locked cell. See *paragraph 8.2*

Notes for guidance

E1   The purpose of the provision at paragraph 3.19 is to protect the rights of a mentally disordered or otherwise mentally vulnerable detained person who does not understand the significance of what is said to them. If the detained person wants to exercise the right to legal advice, the appropriate action should be taken and not delayed until the appropriate adult arrives. A mentally disordered or otherwise mentally vulnerable detained person should always be given an opportunity, when an appropriate adult is called to the police station, to consult privately with a solicitor in the absence of the appropriate adult if they want.

E2   Although people who are mentally disordered or otherwise mentally vulnerable are often capable of providing reliable evidence, they may, without knowing or wanting to do so, be particularly prone in certain circumstances to provide information that may be unreliable, misleading or self-incriminating. Special care should always be taken when questioning such a person, and the appropriate adult should be involved if there is any doubt about a person's mental state or capacity. Because of the risk of unreliable evidence, it is important to obtain corroboration of any facts admitted whenever possible.

E3   Because of the risks referred to in Note E2, which the presence of the appropriate adult is intended to minimise, officers of superintendent rank or above should exercise their discretion to authorise the commencement of an interview in the appropriate adult's absence only in exceptional cases, if it is necessary to avert an immediate risk of serious harm. See paragraphs 11.1, 11.18 to 11.20

ANNEX F — COUNTRIES WITH WHICH BILATERAL CONSULAR CONVENTIONS OR AGREEMENTS REQUIRING NOTIFICATION OF THE ARREST AND DETENTION OF THEIR NATIONALS ARE IN FORCE AS AT 1 APRIL 2003

Armenia
Austria
Azerbaijan
Belarus
Belgium
Bosnia-Herzegovina
Bulgaria
China*
Croatia
Cuba
Czech Republic
Denmark
Egypt
France
Georgia
German Federal Republic
Greece

Hungary
Italy
Japan
Kazakhstan
Macedonia
Mexico
Moldova
Mongolia
Norway
Poland
Romania
Russia
Slovak Republic
Slovenia
Spain
Sweden
Tajikistan
Turkmenistan
Ukraine
USA
Uzbekistan
Yugoslavia

* Police are required to inform Chinese officials of arrest/detention in the Manchester consular district only. This comprises Derbyshire, Durham, Greater Manchester, Lancashire, Merseyside, North South and West Yorkshire, and Tyne and Wear.

ANNEX G — FITNESS TO BE INTERVIEWED

1. This Annex contains general guidance to help police officers and health care professionals assess whether a detainee might be at risk in an interview.

2. A detainee may be at risk in an interview if it is considered that:

    (a) conducting the interview could significantly harm the detainee's physical or mental state;

    (b) anything the detainee says in the interview about their involvement or suspected involvement in the offence about which they are being interviewed **might** be considered unreliable in subsequent court proceedings because of their physical or mental state.

3. In assessing whether the detainee should be interviewed, the following must be considered:

    (a) how the detainee's physical or mental state might affect their ability to understand the nature and purpose of the interview, to comprehend what is being asked and to appreciate the significance of any answers given and make rational decisions about whether they want to say anything;

    (b) the extent to which the detainee's replies may be affected by their physical or mental condition rather than representing a rational and accurate explanation of their involvement in the offence;

    (c) how the nature of the interview, which could include particularly probing questions, might affect the detainee.

4. It is essential health care professionals who are consulted consider the functional ability of the detainee rather than simply relying on a medical diagnosis, e.g. it is possible for a person with severe mental illness to be fit for interview.

5. Health care professionals should advise on the need for an appropriate adult to be present, whether reassessment of the person's fitness for interview may be necessary if the interview lasts beyond a specified time, and whether a further specialist opinion may be required.

6. When health care professionals identify risks they should be asked to quantify the risks. They should inform the custody officer:

    *   whether the person's condition:
        —   is likely to improve
        —   will require or be amenable to treatment; and
    *   indicate how long it may take for such improvement to take effect

7. The role of the health care professional is to consider the risks and advise the custody officer of the outcome of that consideration. The health care professional's determination and any advice or recommendations should be made in writing and form part of the custody record.

8. Once the health care professional has provided that information, it is a matter for the custody officer to decide whether or not to allow the interview to go ahead and if the interview is to proceed, to determine what safeguards are needed. Nothing prevents safeguards being provided in addition to those required under the Code. An example might be to have an appropriate health care professional present during the interview, in addition to an appropriate adult, in order constantly to monitor the person's condition and how it is being affected by the interview.

ANNEX H — DETAINED PERSON: OBSERVATION LIST

1. If any detainee fails to meet any of the following criteria, an appropriate health care professional or an ambulance must be called.

2. When assessing the level of rousability, consider:

    Rousability – can they be woken?
    *   go into the cell
    *   call their name
    *   shake gently

    Response to questions – can they give appropriate answers to questions such as:
    *   What's your name?
    *   Where do you live?
    *   Where do you think you are?

    Response to commands – can they respond appropriately to commands such as:
    *   Open your eyes!
    *   Lift one arm, now the other arm!

3. Remember to take into account the possibility or presence of other illnesses, injury, or mental condition, a person who is drowsy and smells of alcohol may also have the following:
    *   Diabetes
    *   Epilepsy
    *   Head injury
    *   Drug intoxication or overdose
    *   Stroke

ANNEX I — POLICE AREAS WHERE THE POWER TO TEST PERSONS AGED 18 AND OVER FOR SPECIFIED CLASS A DRUGS UNDER SECTION 63B OF PACE HAS BEEN BROUGHT INTO FORCE*

Avon and Somerset
Bedfordshire
Cambridgeshire
Cleveland
Devon and Cornwall
Greater Manchester
Humberside
Lancashire
Leicestershire
Merseyside
Metropolitan Police District
North Wales
Northumbria
Nottinghamshire
South Yorkshire
Staffordshire
Thames Valley
West Midlands
West Yorkshire

* The provisions are being implemented in selected police stations within these police areas.

ANNEX J — POLICE AREAS WHERE THE POWER TO TEST PERSONS AGED 14 AND OVER FOR SPECIFIED CLASS A DRUGS UNDER SECTION 63B OF PACE (AS AMENDED BY SECTION 5 OF THE CRIMINAL JUSTICE ACT 2003) HAS BEEN BROUGHT INTO FORCE*

Cleveland
Humberside
Greater Manchester
Metropolitan Police District
Nottinghamshire
Merseyside
West Yorkshire

This power is subject to notification by the Secretary of State that arrangements for the taking of samples from persons who have not attained the age of 18 (ie persons aged 14–17) are available in the police area as a whole or in the particular police station concerned. The minimum age of 14 will apply only following that notification and if the notice has not been withdrawn. Testing in the case of those aged 14–17 cannot be carried out unless such notification is in force.

* The provisions are being implemented in selected police stations within these police areas.

Police and Criminal Evidence Act 1984

Code D

Code of Practice for the Identification of Persons by Police Officers

Commencement — Transitional Arrangements

This code has effect in relation to any identification procedure carried out after midnight on 31 July 2004.

1   Introduction

1.1   This Code of Practice concerns the principal methods used by police to identify people in connection with the investigation of offences and the keeping of accurate and reliable criminal records.

1.2   Identification by witnesses arises, e.g., if the offender is seen committing the crime and a witness is given an opportunity to identify the suspect in a video identification, identification parade or similar procedure. The procedures are designed to:

- test the witness' ability to identify the person they saw on a previous occasion

- provide safeguards against mistaken identification.

While this Code concentrates on visual identification procedures, it does not preclude the police making use of aural identification procedures such as a "voice identification parade", where they judge that appropriate.

1.3   Identification by fingerprints applies when a person's fingerprints are taken to:

- compare with fingerprints found at the scene of a crime

- check and prove convictions

- help to ascertain a person's identity.

1.4   Identification by body samples and impressions includes taking samples such as blood or hair to generate a DNA profile for comparison with material obtained from the scene of a crime, or a victim.

1.5   Taking photographs of arrested people applies to recording and checking identity and locating and tracing persons who:

- are wanted for offences

- fail to answer their bail.

1.6   Another method of identification involves searching and examining detained suspects to find, e.g., marks such as tattoos or scars which may help establish their identity or whether they have been involved in committing an offence.

1.7   The provisions of the Police and Criminal Evidence Act 1984 (PACE) and this Code are designed to make sure fingerprints, samples, impressions and photographs are taken, used and retained, and identification procedures carried out, only when justified and necessary for preventing, detecting or investigating crime. If these provisions are not observed, the application of the relevant procedures in particular cases may be open to question.

2   General

2.1   This Code must be readily available at all police stations for consultation by:

- police officers

- detained persons

- members of the public

2.2   The provisions of this Code:
- include the *Annexes*
- do not include the *Notes for guidance*.

2.3   Code C, paragraph 1.4, regarding a person who may be mentally disordered or otherwise mentally vulnerable and the *Notes for guidance* applicable to those provisions apply to this Code.

2.4   Code C, paragraph 1.5, regarding a person who appears to be under the age of 17 applies to this Code.

2.5   Code C, paragraph 1.6, regarding a person who appears blind, seriously visually impaired, deaf, unable to read or speak or has difficulty orally because of a speech impediment applies to this Code.

2.6   In this Code:
- 'appropriate adult' means the same as in Code C, paragraph 1.7,
- 'solicitor' means the same as in Code C, paragraph 6.12

and the *Notes for guidance* applicable to those provisions apply to this Code.

2.7   References to custody officers include those performing the functions of custody officer.

2.8   When a record of any action requiring the authority of an officer of a specified rank is made under this Code, subject to *paragraph 2.18*, the officer's name and rank must be recorded.

2.9   When this Code requires the prior authority or agreement of an officer of at least inspector or superintendent rank, that authority may be given by a sergeant or chief inspector who has been authorised to perform the functions of the higher rank under PACE, section 107.

2.10 Subject to *paragraph 2.18*, all records must be timed and signed by the maker.

2.11 Records must be made in the custody record, unless otherwise specified. References to 'pocket book' include any official report book issued to police officers or civilian support staff.

2.12 If any procedure in this Code requires a person's consent, the consent of a:
- mentally disordered or otherwise mentally vulnerable person is only valid if given in the presence of the appropriate adult
- juvenile, is only valid if their parent's or guardian's consent is also obtained unless the juvenile is under 14, when their parent's or guardian's consent is sufficient in its own right. If the only obstacle to an identification procedure in *section 3* is that a juvenile's parent or guardian refuses consent or reasonable efforts to obtain it have failed, the identification officer may apply the provisions of *paragraph 3.21*. See *Note 2A*.

2.13 If a person is blind, seriously visually impaired or unable to read, the custody officer or identification officer shall make sure their solicitor, relative, appropriate adult or some other person likely to take an interest in them and not involved in the investigation is available to help check any documentation. When this Code requires written consent or signing, the person assisting may be asked to sign instead, if the detainee prefers. This paragraph does not require an appropriate adult to be called solely to assist in checking and signing documentation for a person who is not a juvenile, or mentally disordered or otherwise mentally vulnerable (see Note 2B and Code C *paragraph 3.15*).

2.14 If any procedure in this Code requires information to be given to or sought from a suspect, it must be given or sought in the appropriate adult's presence if the suspect is mentally disordered, otherwise mentally vulnerable or a juvenile. If the appropriate adult is not present when the information is first given or sought, the procedure must be repeated in the presence of the appropriate adult when they arrive. If the suspect appears deaf or there is doubt about their hearing or speaking ability or ability to understand English, and effective communication cannot be established, the information must be given or sought through an interpreter.

2.15   Any procedure in this Code involving the participation of a person (whether as a suspect or a witness) who is mentally disordered, otherwise mentally vulnerable or a juvenile, must take place in the presence of the appropriate adult. However, the adult must not be allowed to prompt any identification of a suspect by a witness.

2.16   References to:

- 'taking a photograph', include the use of any process to produce a single, still, visual image

- 'photographing a person', should be construed accordingly

- 'photographs', 'films', 'negatives' and 'copies' include relevant visual images recorded, stored, or reproduced through any medium

- 'destruction' includes the deletion of computer data relating to such images or making access to that data impossible.

2.17   Except as described, nothing in this Code affects the powers and procedures:

(i)   for requiring and taking samples of breath, blood and urine in relation to driving offences, etc, when under the influence of drink, drugs or excess alcohol under the:

- Road Traffic Act 1988, sections 4 to 11

- Road Traffic Offenders Act 1988, sections 15 and 16

- Transport and Works Act 1992, sections 26 to 38;

(ii)   under the Immigration Act 1971, Schedule 2, paragraph 18, for taking photographs and fingerprints from persons detained under that Act, Schedule 2, paragraph 16 (Administrative Controls as to Control on Entry etc.); for taking fingerprints in accordance with the Immigration and Asylum Act 1999; sections 141 and 142(3), or other methods for collecting information about a person's external physical characteristics provided for by regulations made under that Act, section 144;

(iii)   under the Terrorism Act 2000, Schedule 8, for taking photographs, fingerprints, skin impressions, body samples or impressions from people:

- arrested under that Act, section 41,

- detained for the purposes of examination under that Act, Schedule 7, and to whom the Code of Practice issued under that Act, Schedule 14, paragraph 6, applies ('the terrorism provisions')

See *Note 2C*;

(iv)   for taking photographs, fingerprints, skin impressions, body samples or impressions from people who have been:

- arrested on warrants issued in Scotland, by officers exercising powers under the Criminal Justice and Public Order Act 1994, section 136(2)

- arrested or detained without warrant by officers from a police force in Scotland exercising their powers of arrest or detention under the Criminal Justice and Public Order Act 1994, section 137(2), (Cross Border powers of arrest etc.).

Note: In these cases, police powers and duties and the person's rights and entitlements whilst at a police station in England and Wales are the same as if the person had been arrested in Scotland by a Scottish police officer.

2.18   Nothing in this Code requires the identity of officers or civilian support staff to be recorded or disclosed:

(a)   in the case of enquiries linked to the investigation of terrorism;

(b)   if the officers or civilian support staff reasonably believe recording or disclosing their names might put them in danger.

In these cases, they shall use warrant or other identification numbers and the name of their police station. See *Note 2D*

2.19   In this Code:

(a)   'designated person' means a person other than a police officer, designated under the Police Reform Act 2002, Part 4, who has specified powers and duties of police officers conferred or imposed on them;

(b)   any reference to a police officer includes a designated person acting in the exercise or performance of the powers and duties conferred or imposed on them by their designation.

2.20   If a power conferred on a designated person:

(a)   allows reasonable force to be used when exercised by a police officer, a designated person exercising that power has the same entitlement to use force;

(b)   includes power to use force to enter any premises, that power is not exercisable by that designated person except:

(i)   in the company, and under the supervision, of a police officer; or

(ii)   for the purpose of:

•   saving life or limb; or

•   preventing serious damage to property.

2.21   Nothing in this Code prevents the custody officer, or other officer given custody of the detainee, from allowing civilian support staff who are not designated persons to carry out individual procedures or tasks at the police station if the law allows. However, the officer remains responsible for making sure the procedures and tasks are carried out correctly in accordance with the Codes of Practice. Any such civilian must be:

(a)   a person employed by a police authority maintaining a police force and under the control and direction of the Chief Officer of that force;

(b)   employed by a person with whom a police authority has a contract for the provision of services relating to persons arrested or otherwise in custody.

2.22   Designated persons and other civilian support staff must have regard to any relevant provisions of the Codes of Practice.

Notes for guidance

2A   *For the purposes of paragraph 2.12, the consent required from a parent or guardian may, for a juvenile in the care of a local authority or voluntary organisation, be given by that authority or organisation. In the case of a juvenile, nothing in paragraph 2.12 requires the parent, guardian or representative of a local authority or voluntary organisation to be present to give their consent, unless they are acting as the appropriate adult under paragraphs 2.14 or 2.15. However, it is important that a parent or guardian not present is fully informed before being asked to consent. They must be given the same information about the procedure and the juvenile's suspected involvement in the offence as the juvenile and appropriate adult. The parent or guardian must also be allowed to speak to the juvenile and the appropriate adult if they wish. Provided the consent is fully informed and is not withdrawn, it may be obtained at any time before the procedure takes place.*

2B   People who are seriously visually impaired or unable to read may be unwilling to sign police documents. The alternative, i.e. their representative signing on their behalf, seeks to protect the interests of both police and suspects.

2C   Photographs, fingerprints, samples and impressions may be taken from a person detained under the terrorism provisions to help determine whether they are, or have been, involved in terrorism, as well as when there are reasonable grounds for suspecting their involvement in a particular offence.

2D   The purpose of paragraph 2.18(b) is to protect those involved in serious organised crime investigations or arrests of particularly violent suspects when there is reliable information that those arrested or their associates may threaten or cause harm to the officers. In cases of doubt, an officer of inspector rank or above should be consulted.

3   Identification by witnesses

3.1   A record shall be made of the suspect's description as first given by a potential witness. This record must:

(a)   be made and kept in a form which enables details of that description to be accurately produced from it, in a visible and legible form, which can be given to the suspect or the suspect's solicitor in accordance with this Code; and

(b)   unless otherwise specified, be made before the witness takes part in any identification procedures under *paragraphs 3.5 to 3.10, 3.21 or 3.23.*

A copy of the record shall where practicable, be given to the suspect or their solicitor before any procedures under *paragraphs 3.5 to 3.10, 3.21 or 3.23* are carried out. See *Note 3E*

(a)   Cases when the suspect's identity is not known

3.2   In cases when the suspect's identity is not known, a witness may be taken to a particular neighbourhood or place to see whether they can identify the person they saw. Although the number, age, sex, race, general description and style of clothing of other people present at the location and the way in which any identification is made cannot be controlled, the principles applicable to the formal procedures under *paragraphs 3.5 to 3.10* shall be followed as far as practicable. For example:

(a)   where it is practicable to do so, a record should be made of the witness' description of the suspect, as in paragraph 3.1(a), before asking the witness to make an identification;

(b)   care must be taken not to direct the witness' attention to any individual unless, taking into account all the circumstances, this cannot be avoided. However, this does not prevent a witness being asked to look carefully at the people around at the time or to look towards a group or in a particular direction, if this appears necessary to make sure that the witness does not overlook a possible suspect simply because the witness is looking in the opposite direction and also to enable the witness to make comparisons between any suspect and others who are in the area; See *Note 3F*

(c)   where there is more than one witness, every effort should be made to keep them separate and witnesses should be taken to see whether they can identify a person independently;

(d)   once there is sufficient information to justify the arrest of a particular individual for suspected involvement in the offence, e.g., after a witness makes a positive identification, the provisions set out from paragraph 3.4 onwards shall apply for any other witnesses in relation to that individual. Subject to *paragraphs 3.12* and *3.13*, it is not necessary for the witness who makes such a positive identification to take part in a further procedure;

(e)   the officer or civilian support staff accompanying the witness must record, in their pocket book, the action taken as soon as, and in as much detail, as possible. The record should include: the date, time and place of the relevant occasion the witness claims to have previously seen the suspect; where any identification was made; how it was made and the conditions at the time (e.g., the distance the witness was from the suspect, the weather and light); if the witness's attention was drawn to the suspect; the reason for this; and anything said by the witness or the suspect about the identification or the conduct of the procedure.

3.3   A witness must not be shown photographs, computerised or artist's composite likenesses or similar likenesses or pictures (including 'E-fit' images) if the identity of the suspect is known to the police and the suspect is available to take part in a video identification, an identification parade or a group identification. If the suspect's identity is not known, the showing of such images to a witness to obtain identification evidence must be done in accordance with *Annex E*.

(b)   Cases when the suspect is known and available

3.4   If the suspect's identity is known to the police and they are available, the identification procedures set out in paragraphs 3.5 to 3.10 may be used. References in this section to a suspect being 'known' mean there is sufficient information known to the police to justify the arrest of a particular person for suspected involvement in the offence. A suspect being 'available' means they are immediately available or will be within a reasonably short time and willing to take an effective part in at least one of the following which it is practicable to arrange;

- video identification;
- identification parade; or
- group identification.

Video identification

3.5   A 'video identification' is when the witness is shown moving images of a known suspect, together with similar images of others who resemble the suspect. See paragraph 3.21 for circumstances in which still images may be used.

3.6   Video identifications must be carried out in accordance with *Annex A*.

Identification parade

3.7   An 'identification parade' is when the witness sees the suspect in a line of others who resemble the suspect.

3.8   Identification parades must be carried out in accordance with *Annex B*.

Group identification

3.9   A 'group identification' is when the witness sees the suspect in an informal group of people.

3.10   Group identifications must be carried out in accordance with *Annex C*.

Arranging identification procedures

3.11   Except for the provisions in *paragraph 3.19*, the arrangements for, and conduct of, the identification procedures in paragraphs 3.5 to 3.10 and circumstances in which an identification procedure must be held shall be the responsibility of an officer not below inspector rank who is not involved with the investigation, 'the identification officer'. Unless otherwise specified, the identification officer may allow another officer or civilian support staff, see *paragraph 2.21*, to make arrangements for, and conduct, any of these identification procedures. In delegating these procedures, the identification officer must be able to supervise effectively and either intervene or be contacted for advice. No officer or any other person involved with the investigation of the case against the suspect, beyond the extent required by these procedures, may take any part in these procedures or act as the identification officer. This does not prevent the identification officer from consulting the officer in charge of the investigation to determine which procedure to use. When an identification procedure is required, in the interest of fairness to suspects and witnesses, it must be held as soon as practicable.

Circumstances in which an identification procedure must be held

3.12   Whenever:

(i)   a witness has identified a suspect or purported to have identified them prior to any identification procedure set out in paragraphs 3.5 to 3.10 having been held; or

(ii)   there is a witness available, who expresses an ability to identify the suspect, or where there is a reasonable chance of the witness being able to do so, and they have not been given an opportunity to identify the suspect in any of the procedures set out in paragraphs 3.5 to 3.10,

and the suspect disputes being the person the witness claims to have seen, an identification procedure shall be held unless it is not practicable or it would serve no useful purpose in proving or disproving whether the suspect was involved in committing the offence. For example, when it is not disputed that the suspect is already well known to the witness who claims to have seen them commit the crime.

3.13   Such a procedure may also be held if the officer in charge of the investigation considers it would be useful.

Selecting an identification procedure

3.14   If, because of paragraph 3.12, an identification procedure is to be held, the suspect shall initially be offered either a video identification or identification unless:

(a)   a video identification is not practicable; or

(b)   an identification parade is both practicable and more suitable than a video identification; or

(c)   paragraph 3.16 applies.

The identification officer and the officer in charge of the investigation shall consult each other to determine which option is to be offered. An identification parade may not be practicable because of factors relating to the witnesses, such as their number, state of health, availability and travelling requirements. A video identification would normally be more suitable if it could be arranged and completed sooner than an identification parade.

3.15   A suspect who refuses the identification procedure first offered shall be asked to state their reason for refusing and may get advice from their solicitor and/or if present, their appropriate adult. The suspect, solicitor and/or appropriate adult shall be allowed to make representations about why another procedure should be used. A record should be made of the reasons for refusal and any representations made. After considering any reasons given, and representations made, the identification officer shall, if appropriate, arrange for the suspect to be offered an alternative which the officer considers suitable and practicable. If the officer decides it is not suitable and practicable to offer an alternative identification procedure, the reasons for that decision shall be recorded.

3.16   A group identification may initially be offered if the officer in charge of the investigation considers it is more suitable than a video identification or an identification parade and the identification officer considers it practicable to arrange.

Notice to suspect

3.17 Unless *paragraph 3.20* applies, before a video identification, an identification parade or group identification is arranged, the following shall be explained to the suspect:

(i) the purposes of the video identification, identification parade or group identification;

(ii) their entitlement to free legal advice; see Code C, paragraph 6.5;

(iii) the procedures for holding it, including their right to have a solicitor or friend present;

(iv) that they do not have to consent to or co-operate in a video identification, identification parade or group identification;

(v) that if they do not consent to, and co-operate in, a video identification, identification parade or group identification, their refusal may be given in evidence in any subsequent trial and police may proceed covertly without their consent or make other arrangements to test whether a witness can identify them, see *paragraph 3.21*

(vi) whether, for the purposes of the video identification procedure, images of them have previously been obtained, see *paragraph 3.20*, and if so, that they may co-operate in providing further, suitable images to be used instead;

(vii) if appropriate, the special arrangements for juveniles;

(viii) if appropriate, the special arrangements for mentally disordered or otherwise mentally vulnerable people;

(ix) that if they significantly alter their appearance between being offered an identification procedure and any attempt to hold an identification procedure, this may be given in evidence if the case comes to trial, and the identification officer may then consider other forms of identification, see *paragraph 3.21* and *Note 3C*;

(x) that a moving image or photograph may be taken of them when they attend for any identification procedure;

(xi) whether, before their identity became known, the witness was shown photographs, a computerised or artist's composite likeness or similar likeness or image by the police; see *Note 3B*

(xii) that if they change their appearance before an identification parade, it may not be practicable to arrange one on the day or subsequently and, because of the appearance change, the identification officer may consider alternative methods of identification; see *Note 3C*

(xiii) that they or their solicitor will be provided with details of the description of the suspect as first given by any witnesses who are to attend the video identification, identification parade, group identification or confrontation, see *paragraph 3.1*.

3.18 This information must also be recorded in a written notice handed to the suspect. The suspect must be given a reasonable opportunity to read the notice, after which, they should be asked to sign a second copy to indicate if they are willing to co-operate with the making of a video or take part in the identification parade or group identification. The signed copy shall be retained by the identification officer.

3.19 The duties of the identification officer under *paragraphs 3.17* and *3.18* may be performed by the custody officer or other officer not involved in the investigation if:

(a) it is proposed to hold an identification procedure at a later date, e.g., if the suspect is to be bailed to attend an identification parade; and

(b) an inspector is not available to act as the identification officer, see *paragraph 3.11*, before the suspect leaves the station.

The officer concerned shall inform the identification officer of the action taken and give them the signed copy of the notice. See *Note 3C*

3.20   If the identification officer and officer in charge of the investigation suspect, on reasonable grounds that if the suspect was given the information and notice as in *paragraphs 3.17* and *3.18*, they would then take steps to avoid being seen by a witness in any identification procedure, the identification officer may arrange for images of the suspect suitable for use in a video identification procedure to be obtained before giving the information and notice. If suspect's images are obtained in these circumstances, the suspect may, for the purposes of a video identification procedure, co-operate in providing suitable new images to be used instead, see *paragraph 3.17(vi)*.

(c) *Cases when the suspect is known but not available*

3.21   When a known suspect is not available or has ceased to be available, see *paragraph 3.4*, the identification officer may make arrangements for a video identification (see Annex A). If necessary, the identification officer may follow the video identification procedures but using **still** images. Any suitable moving or still images may be used and these may be obtained covertly if necessary. Alternatively, the identification officer may make arrangements for a group identification. See *Note 3D*. These provisions may also be applied to juveniles where the consent of their parent or guardian is either refused or reasonable efforts to obtain that consent have failed (see *paragraph 2.12*).

3.22   Any covert activity should be strictly limited to that necessary to test the ability of the witness to identify the suspect.

3.23   The identification officer may arrange for the suspect to be confronted by the witness if none of the options referred to in paragraphs 3.5 to 3.10 or 3.21 are practicable. A "confrontation" is when the suspect is directly confronted by the witness. A confrontation does not require the suspect's consent. Confrontations must be carried out in accordance with Annex D.

3.24   Requirements for information to be given to, or sought from, a suspect or for the suspect to be given an opportunity to view images before they are shown to a witness, do not apply if the suspect's lack of co-operation prevents the necessary action.

(d) *Documentation*

3.25   A record shall be made of the video identification, identification parade, group identification or confrontation on forms provided for the purpose.

3.26   If the identification officer considers it is not practicable to hold a video identification or identification parade requested by the suspect, the reasons shall be recorded and explained to the suspect.

3.27   A record shall be made of a person's failure or refusal to co-operate in a video identification, identification parade or group identification and, if applicable, of the grounds for obtaining images in accordance with *paragraph 3.20*.

(e) *Showing films and photographs of incidents and information released to the media*

3.28   Nothing in this Code inhibits showing films or photographs to the public through the national or local media, or to police officers for the purposes of recognition and tracing suspects. However, when such material is shown to potential witnesses, including police officers, see *Note 3A*, to obtain identification evidence, it shall be shown on an individual basis to avoid any possibility of collusion, and, as far as possible, the showing shall follow the principles for video identification if the suspect is known, see *Annex A*, or identification by photographs if the suspect is not known, see *Annex E*.

3.29 When a broadcast or publication is made, see *paragraph 3.28*, a copy of the relevant material released to the media for the purposes of recognising or tracing the suspect, shall be kept. The suspect or their solicitor shall be allowed to view such material before any procedures under *paragraphs 3.5 to 3.10, 3.21 or 3.23* are carried out, provided it is practicable and would not unreasonably delay the investigation. Each witness involved in the procedure shall be asked, after they have taken part, whether they have seen any broadcast or published films or photographs relating to the offence or any description of the suspect and their replies shall be recorded. This paragraph does not affect any separate requirement under the Criminal Procedure and Investigations Act 1996 to retain material in connection with criminal investigations.

(f) Destruction and retention of photographs and images taken or used in identification procedures

3.30 PACE, section 64A, provides powers to take photographs of suspects detained at police stations and allows these photographs to be used or disclosed only for purposes related to the prevention or detection of crime, the investigation of offences or the conduct of prosecutions by, or on behalf of, police or other law enforcement and prosecuting authorities inside and outside the United Kingdom. After being so used or disclosed, they may be retained but can only be used or disclosed for the same purposes.

3.31 Subject to *paragraph 3.33*, the photographs (and all negatives and copies), of suspects not detained and any moving images, (and copies), of suspects whether or not they have been detained which are taken for the purposes of, or in connection with, the identification procedures in *paragraphs 3.5 to 3.10, 3.21 or 3.23* must be destroyed unless the suspect:

(a) is charged with, or informed they may be prosecuted for, a recordable offence;

(b) is prosecuted for a recordable offence;

(c) is cautioned for a recordable offence or given a warning or reprimand in accordance with the Crime and Disorder Act 1998 for a recordable offence; or

(d) gives informed consent, in writing, for the photograph or images to be retained for purposes described in *paragraph 3.30*.

3.32 When *paragraph 3.31* requires the destruction of any photograph or images, the person must be given an opportunity to witness the destruction or to have a certificate confirming the destruction if they request one within five days of being informed that the destruction is required.

3.33 Nothing in *paragraph 3.31* affects any separate requirement under the Criminal Procedure and Investigations Act 1996 to retain material in connection with criminal investigations.

Notes for guidance

3A *Except for the provisions of Annex E, paragraph 1, a police officer who is a witness for the purposes of this part of the Code is subject to the same principles and procedures as a civilian witness.*

3B *When a witness attending an identification procedure has previously been shown photographs, or been shown or provided with computerised or artist's composite likenesses, or similar likenesses or pictures, it is the officer in charge of the investigation's responsibility to make the identification officer aware of this.*

3C   The purpose of paragraph 3.19 is to avoid or reduce delay in arranging identification procedures by enabling the required information and warnings, see sub-paragraphs 3.17(ix) and 3.17(xii), to be given at the earliest opportunity.

3D   Paragraph 3.21 would apply when a known suspect deliberately makes themself 'unavailable' in order to delay or frustrate arrangements for obtaining identification evidence. It also applies when a suspect refuses or fails to take part in a video identification, an identification parade or a group identification, or refuses or fails to take part in the only practicable options from that list. It enables any suitable images of the suspect, moving or still, which are available or can be obtained, to be used in an identification procedure.

3E   When it is proposed to show photographs to a witness in accordance with Annex E, it is the responsibility of the officer in charge of the investigation to confirm to the officer responsible for supervising and directing the showing, that the first description of the suspect given by that witness has been recorded. If this description has not been recorded, the procedure under Annex E must be postponed. See Annex E paragraph 2

3F   The admissibility and value of identification evidence obtained when carrying out the procedure under paragraph 3.2 may be compromised if:

(a)   before a person is identified, the witness' attention is specifically drawn to that person; or

(b)   the suspect's identity becomes known before the procedure.

4   Identification by fingerprints

(A)   Taking fingerprints in connection with a criminal investigation

(a)   General

4.1   References to 'fingerprints' means any record, produced by any method, of the skin pattern and other physical characteristics or features of a person's:

(i)   fingers; or

(ii)   palms.

(b)   Action

4.2   A person's fingerprints may be taken in connection with the investigation of an offence only with their consent or if *paragraph 4.3* applies. If the person is at a police station consent must be in writing.

4.3   PACE, section 61, provides powers to take fingerprints without consent from any person over the age of ten years:

(a)   under section 61(3), from a person detained at a police station in consequence of being arrested for a recordable offence, see Note 4A, if they have not had their fingerprints taken in the course of the investigation of the offence unless those previously taken fingerprints are not a complete set or some or all of those fingerprints are not of sufficient quality to allow satisfactory analysis, comparison or matching.

(b)   under section 61(4), from a person detained at a police station who has been charged with a recordable offence, see Note 4A, or informed they will be reported for such an offence if they have not had their fingerprints taken in the course of the investigation of the offence unless those previously taken fingerprints are not a complete set or some or all of those fingerprints are not of sufficient quality to allow satisfactory analysis, comparison or matching.

(c)   under section 61(4A), from a person who has been bailed to appear at a court or police station if the person:

(i)   has answered to bail for a person whose fingerprints were taken previously and there are reasonable grounds for believing they are not the same person; or

(ii)   who has answered to bail claims to be a different person from a person whose fingerprints were previously taken;

and in either case, the court or an officer of inspector rank or above, authorises the fingerprints to be taken at the court or police station;

(d)   under section 61(6), from a person who has been:

(i)   convicted of a recordable offence;

(ii)   given a caution in respect of a recordable offence which, at the time of the caution, the person admitted; or

(iii) warned or reprimanded under the Crime and Disorder Act 1998, section 65, for a recordable offence.

4.4   PACE, section 27, provides power to:

(a)   require the person as in *paragraph 4.3(d)* to attend a police station to have their fingerprints taken if the:

(i)   person has not been in police detention for the offence and has not had their fingerprints taken in the course of the investigation of that offence; or

(ii)   fingerprints that were taken from the person in the course of the investigation of that offence, do not constitute a complete set or some, or all, of the fingerprints are not of sufficient quality to allow satisfactory analysis, comparison or matching; and

(b)   arrest, without warrant, a person who fails to comply with the requirement.

Note: The requirement must be made within one month of the date the person is convicted, cautioned, warned or reprimanded and the person must be given a period of at least 7 days within which to attend. This 7 day period need not fall during the month allowed for making the requirement.

4.5   A person's fingerprints may be taken, as above, electronically.

4.6   Reasonable force may be used, if necessary, to take a person's fingerprints without their consent under the powers as in *paragraphs 4.3* and *4.4*.

4.7   Before any fingerprints are taken with, or without, consent as above, the person must be informed:

(a)   of the reason their fingerprints are to be taken;

(b)   of the grounds on which the relevant authority has been given if the powers mentioned in *paragraph 4.3(c)* applies;

(c)   that their fingerprints may be retained and may be subject of a speculative search against other fingerprints, see *Note 4B*, unless destruction of the fingerprints is required in accordance with *Annex F, Part (a)*; and

(d)   that if their fingerprints are required to be destroyed, they may witness their destruction as provided for in *Annex F, Part (a)*.

(c) Documentation

4.8   A record must be made as soon as possible, of the reason for taking a person's fingerprints without consent. If force is used, a record shall be made of the circumstances and those present.

4.9   A record shall be made when a person has been informed under the terms of *paragraph 4.7(c)*, of the possibility that their fingerprints may be subject of a speculative search.

(B)   Taking fingerprints in connection with immigration enquiries

Action

4.10   A person's fingerprints may be taken for the purposes of Immigration Service enquiries in accordance with powers and procedures other than under PACE and for which the Immigration Service (not the police) are responsible, only with the person's consent in writing or if *paragraph 4.11* applies.

4.11   Powers to take fingerprints for these purposes without consent are given to police and immigration officers under the:

(a)   Immigration Act 1971, Schedule 2, paragraph 18(2), when it is reasonably necessary for the purposes of identifying a person detained under the Immigration Act 1971, Schedule 2, paragraph 16 (Detention of person liable to examination or removal);

(b)   Immigration and Asylum Act 1999, section 141(7)(a), from a person who fails to produce, on arrival, a valid passport with a photograph or some other document satisfactorily establishing their identity and nationality if an immigration officer does not consider the person has a reasonable excuse for the failure;

(c)   Immigration and Asylum Act 1999, section 141(7)(b), from a person who has been refused entry to the UK but has been temporarily admitted if an immigration officer reasonably suspects the person might break a condition imposed on them relating to residence or reporting to a police or immigration officer, and their decision is confirmed by a chief immigration officer;

(d)   Immigration and Asylum Act 1999, section 141(7)(c), when directions are given to remove a person:

- as an illegal entrant,
- liable to removal under the Immigration and Asylum Act 1999, section 10,
- who is the subject of a deportation order from the UK;

(e)   Immigration and Asylum Act 1999, section 141(7)(d), from a person arrested under UK immigration laws under the Immigration Act 1971, Schedule 2, paragraph 17;

(f)   Immigration and Asylum Act 1999, section 141(7)(e), from a person who has made a claim:

- for asylum
- under Article 3 of the European Convention on Human Rights; or

(g)   Immigration and Asylum Act 1999, section 141(7)(f), from a person who is a dependant of someone who falls into (b) to (f) above.

4.12   The Immigration and Asylum Act 1999, section 142(3), gives a police and immigration officer power to arrest, without warrant, a person who fails to comply with a requirement imposed by the Secretary of State to attend a specified place for fingerprinting.

4.13   Before any fingerprints are taken, with or without consent, the person must be informed:

(a)   of the reason their fingerprints are to taken;

(b)   the fingerprints, and all copies of them, will be destroyed in accordance with *Annex F, Part B*.

4.14   Reasonable force may be used, if necessary, to take a person's fingerprints without their consent under powers as in *paragraph 4.11*.

4.15   *Paragraphs 4.1 and 4.8* apply.

Notes for guidance

4A   References to 'recordable offences' in this Code relate to those offences for which convictions, cautions, reprimands and warnings may be recorded in national police records. See PACE, section 27(4). The recordable offences current at the time when this Code was prepared, are any offences which carry a sentence of imprisonment on conviction (irrespective of the period, or the age of the offender or actual sentence passed) as well as the non-imprisonable offences under the Street Offences Act 1959, section 1 (loitering or soliciting for purposes of prostitution), the Telecommunications Act 1984, section 43 (improper use of public telecommunications systems), the Road Traffic Act 1988, section 25 (tampering with motor vehicles), the Malicious Communications Act 1988, section 1 (sending letters, etc. with intent to cause distress or anxiety) and others listed in the National Police Records (Recordable Offences) Regulations 2000.

4B   Fingerprints or a DNA sample (and the information derived from it) taken from a person arrested on suspicion of being involved in a recordable offence, or charged with such an offence, or informed they will be reported for such an offence, may be subject of a speculative search. This means the fingerprints or DNA sample may be checked against other fingerprints and DNA records held by, or on behalf of, the police and other law enforcement authorities in, or outside, the UK, or held in connection with, or as a result of, an investigation of an offence inside or outside the UK. Fingerprints and samples taken from a person suspected of committing a recordable offence but not arrested, charged or informed they will be reported for it, may be subject to a speculative search only if the person consents in writing. The following is an example of a basic form of words:

> *"I consent to my fingerprints and DNA sample and information derived from it being retained and used only for purposes related to the prevention and detection of a crime, the investigation of an offence or the conduct of a prosecution either nationally or internationally.*

> *I understand that my fingerprints or this sample may be checked against other fingerprint and DNA records held by or on behalf of relevant law enforcement authorities, either nationally or internationally.*

> *I understand that once I have given my consent for the sample to be retained and used I cannot withdraw this consent."*

See Annex F regarding the retention and use of fingerprints taken with consent for elimination purposes.

5 Examinations to establish identity and the taking of photographs

(A) Detainees at police stations

(a) Searching or examination of detainees at police stations

5.1   PACE, section 54A (1), allows a detainee at a police station to be searched or examined or both, to establish:

   (a)   whether they have any marks, features or injuries that would tend to identify them as a person involved in the commission of an offence and to photograph any identifying marks, see *paragraph 5.5*; or

   (b)   their identity, see *Note 5A*.

A person detained at a police station to be searched under a stop and search power, see Code A, is not a detainee for the purposes of these powers.

5.2   A search and/or examination to find marks under section 54A(1)(a) may be carried out without the detainee's consent, see *paragraph 2.12*, only if authorised by an officer of at least inspector rank when consent has been withheld or it is not practicable to obtain consent, see *Note 5D*.

5.3   A search or examination to establish a suspect's identity under section 54A(1)(b) may be carried out without the detainee's consent, see *paragraph 2.12*, only if authorised by an officer of at least inspector rank when the detainee has refused to identify themselves or the authorising officer has reasonable grounds for suspecting the person is not who they claim to be.

5.4   Any marks that assist in establishing the detainee's identity, or their identification as a person involved in the commission of an offence, are identifying marks. Such marks may be photographed with the detainee's consent, see *paragraph 2.12*; or without their consent if it is withheld or it is not practicable to obtain it, see *Note 5D*.

5.5   A detainee may only be searched, examined and photographed under section 54A, by a police officer of the same sex.

5.6   Any photographs of identifying marks, taken under section 54A, may be used or disclosed only for purposes related to the prevention or detection of crime, the investigation of offences or the conduct of prosecutions by, or on behalf of, police or other law enforcement and prosecuting authorities inside, and outside, the UK. After being so used or disclosed, the photograph may be retained but must not be used or disclosed except for these purposes, see *Note 5B*.

5.7   The powers, as in *paragraph 5.1*, do not affect any separate requirement under the Criminal Procedure and Investigations Act 1996 to retain material in connection with criminal investigations.

5.8   Authority for the search and/or examination for the purposes of *paragraphs 5.2* and *5.3* may be given orally or in writing. If given orally, the authorising officer must confirm it in writing as soon as practicable. A separate authority is required for each purpose which applies.

5.9   If it is established a person is unwilling to co-operate sufficiently to enable a search and/or examination to take place or a suitable photograph to be taken, an officer may use reasonable force to:

(a)   search and/or examine a detainee without their consent; and

(b)   photograph any identifying marks without their consent.

5.10   The thoroughness and extent of any search or examination carried out in accordance with the powers in section 54A must be no more than the officer considers necessary to achieve the required purpose. Any search or examination which involves the removal of more than the person's outer clothing shall be conducted in accordance with Code C, Annex A, paragraph 11.

5.11   An intimate search may not be carried out under the powers in section 54A.

(b)   Photographing detainees at police stations

5.12   Under PACE, section 64A, an officer may photograph a detainee at a police station:

(a)   with their consent; or

(b)   without their consent if it is:

(i)   withheld; or

(ii)   not practicable to obtain their consent.

See *Note 5E*

and *paragraph 5.6* applies to the retention and use of photographs taken under this section as it applies to the retention and use of photographs taken under section 54A, see *Note 5B*.

5.13   The officer proposing to take a detainee's photograph may, for this purpose, require the person to remove any item or substance worn on, or over, all, or any part of, their head or face. If they do not comply with such a requirement, the officer may remove the item or substance.

5.14   If it is established the detainee is unwilling to co-operate sufficiently to enable a suitable photograph to be taken and it is not reasonably practicable to take the photograph covertly, an officer may use reasonable force:

(a)   to take their photograph without their consent; and

(b)   for the purpose of taking the photograph, remove any item or substance worn on, or over, all, or any part of, the person's head or face which they have failed to remove when asked.

5.15   For the purposes of this Code, a photograph may be obtained without the person's consent by making a copy of an image of them taken at any time on a camera system installed anywhere in the police station.

(c)   Information to be given

5.16   When a person is searched, examined or photographed under the provisions as in *paragraph 5.1* and *5.12*, or their photograph obtained as in *paragraph 5.15*, they must be informed of the:

(a)   purpose of the search, examination or photograph;

(b)   grounds on which the relevant authority, if applicable, has been given; and

(c)   purposes for which the photograph may be used, disclosed or retained.

This information must be given before the search or examination commences or the photograph is taken, except if the photograph is:

(i)   to be taken covertly;

(ii)   obtained as in *paragraph 5.15*, in which case the person must be informed as soon as practicable after the photograph is taken or obtained.

(d)   Documentation

5.17   A record must be made when a detainee is searched, examined, or a photograph of the person, or any identifying marks found on them, are taken. The record must include the:

(a)   identity, subject to paragraph 2.18, of the officer carrying out the search, examination or taking the photograph;

(b)   purpose of the search, examination or photograph and the outcome;

(c)   detainee's consent to the search, examination or photograph, or the reason the person was searched, examined or photographed without consent;

(d)   giving of any authority as in *paragraphs 5.2* and *5.3*, the grounds for giving it and the authorising officer.

5.18   If force is used when searching, examining or taking a photograph in accordance with this section, a record shall be made of the circumstances and those present.

(B)   Persons at police stations not detained

5.19   When there are reasonable grounds for suspecting the involvement of a person in a criminal offence, but that person is at a police station **voluntarily** and not detained, the provisions of *paragraphs 5.1* to *5.18* should apply, subject to the modifications in the following paragraphs.

5.20   References to the 'person being detained' and to the powers mentioned in *paragraph 5.1* which apply only to detainees at police stations shall be omitted.

5.21   Force may not be used to:

(a)   search and/or examine the person to:

(i)   discover whether they have any marks that would tend to identify them as a person involved in the commission of an offence; or

(ii)   establish their identity, see *Note 5A*;

(b)   take photographs of any identifying marks, see *paragraph 5.4*; or

(c)   take a photograph of the person.

5.22   Subject to *paragraph 5.24*, the photographs or images, of persons not detained, or of their identifying marks, must be destroyed (together with any negatives and copies) unless the person:

(a)   is charged with, or informed they may be prosecuted for, a recordable offence;

(b)   is prosecuted for a recordable offence;

(c)   is cautioned for a recordable offence or given a warning or reprimand in accordance with the Crime and Disorder Act 1998 for a recordable offence; or

(d)   gives informed consent, in writing, for the photograph or image to be retained as in *paragraph 5.6*.

5.23   When *paragraph 5.22* requires the destruction of any photograph or image, the person must be given an opportunity to witness the destruction or to have a certificate confirming the destruction provided they so request the certificate within five days of being informed the destruction is required.

5.24   Nothing in *paragraph 5.22* affects any separate requirement under the Criminal Procedure and Investigations Act 1996 to retain material in connection with criminal investigations.

Notes for guidance

5A   *The conditions under which fingerprints may be taken to assist in establishing a person's identity, are described in Section 4.*

5B   *Examples of purposes related to the prevention or detection of crime, the investigation of offences or the conduct of prosecutions include:*

(a)   *checking the photograph against other photographs held in records or in connection with, or as a result of, an investigation of an offence to establish whether the person is liable to arrest for other offences;*

(b)   *when the person is arrested at the same time as other people, or at a time when it is likely that other people will be arrested, using the photograph to help establish who was arrested, at what time and where;*

(c)   *when the real identity of the person is not known and cannot be readily ascertained or there are reasonable grounds for doubting a name and other personal details given by the person, are their real name and personal details. In these circumstances, using or disclosing the photograph to help to establish or verify their real identity or determine whether they are liable to arrest for some other offence, e.g. by checking it against other photographs held in records or in connection with, or as a result of, an investigation of an offence;*

(d)   *when it appears any identification procedure in section 3 may need to be arranged for which the person's photograph would assist;*

(e)   *when the person's release without charge may be required, and if the release is:*

(i)   *on bail to appear at a police station, using the photograph to help verify the person's identity when they answer their bail and if the person does not answer their bail, to assist in arresting them; or*

(ii)   *without bail, using the photograph to help verify their identity or assist in locating them for the purposes of serving them with a summons to appear at court in criminal proceedings;*

(f)   *when the person has answered to bail at a police station and there are reasonable grounds for doubting they are the person who was previously granted bail, using the photograph to help establish or verify their identity;*

(g)   *when the person arrested on a warrant claims to be a different person from the person named on the warrant and a photograph would help to confirm or disprove their claim;*

(h)   *when the person has been charged with, reported for, or convicted of, a recordable offence and their photograph is not already on record as a result of (a) to (f) or their photograph is on record but their appearance has changed since it was taken and the person has not yet been released or brought before a court.*

5C   *There is no power to arrest a person convicted of a recordable offence solely to take their photograph. The power to take photographs in this section applies only where the person is in custody as a result of the exercise of another power, e.g. arrest for fingerprinting under PACE, section 27.*

5D   *Examples of when it would not be practicable to obtain a detainee's consent, see paragraph 2.12, to a search, examination or the taking of a photograph of an identifying mark include:*

(a)   *when the person is drunk or otherwise unfit to give consent;*

(b)   *when there are reasonable grounds to suspect that if the person became aware a search or examination was to take place or an identifying mark was to be photographed, they would take steps to prevent this happening, e.g. by violently resisting, covering or concealing the mark etc and it would not otherwise be possible to carry out the search or examination or to photograph any identifying mark;*

(c)   *in the case of a juvenile, if the parent or guardian cannot be contacted in sufficient time to allow the search or examination to be carried out or the photograph to be taken.*

5E   *Examples of when it would not be practicable to obtain the person's consent, see paragraph 2.12, to a photograph being taken include:*

(a)   *when the person is drunk or otherwise unfit to give consent;*

(b)   *when there are reasonable grounds to suspect that if the person became aware a photograph, suitable to be used or disclosed for the use and disclosure described in paragraph 5.6, was to be taken, they would take steps to prevent it being taken, e.g. by violently resisting, covering or distorting their face etc, and it would not otherwise be possible to take a suitable photograph;*

(c)   *when, in order to obtain a suitable photograph, it is necessary to take it covertly; and*

(d)   *in the case of a juvenile, if the parent or guardian cannot be contacted in sufficient time to allow the photograph to be taken.*

6   Identification by body samples and impressions

(A)   *General*

6.1   References to:

(a)   an 'intimate sample' mean a dental impression or sample of blood, semen or any other tissue fluid, urine, or pubic hair, or a swab taken from a person's body orifice other than the mouth;

(b)   a 'non-intimate sample' means:

(i)   a sample of hair, other than pubic hair, which includes hair plucked with the root, see *Note 6A*;

(ii)   a sample taken from a nail or from under a nail;

(iii)   a swab taken from any part of a person's body including the mouth but not any other body orifice;

(iv)   saliva;

(v)   a skin impression which means any record, other than a fingerprint, which is a record, in any form and produced by any method, of the skin pattern and other physical characteristics or features of the whole, or any part of, a person's foot or of any other part of their body.

(B) Action

(a) *Intimate samples*

6.2 PACE, section 62, provides that intimate samples may be taken under:

(a) section 62(1), from a person in police detention only:

(i)   if a police officer of inspector rank or above has reasonable grounds to believe such an impression or sample will tend to confirm or disprove the suspect's involvement in a recordable offence, see Note 4A, and gives authorisation for a sample to be taken; and

(ii) with the suspect's written consent;

(b) section 62(1A), from a person not in police detention but from whom two or more non-intimate samples have been taken in the course of an investigation of an offence and the samples, though suitable, have proved insufficient if:

(i)   a police officer of inspector rank or above authorises it to be taken; and

(ii) the person concerned gives their written consent. See *Notes 6B* and *6C*

6.3 Before a suspect is asked to provide an intimate sample, they must be warned that if they refuse without good cause, their refusal may harm their case if it comes to trial, see *Note 6D*. If the suspect is in police detention and not legally represented, they must also be reminded of their entitlement to have free legal advice, see Code C, *paragraph 6.5*, and the reminder noted in the custody record. If *paragraph 6.2(b)* applies and the person is attending a station voluntarily, their entitlement to free legal advice as in Code C, *paragraph 3.21* shall be explained to them.

6.4 Dental impressions may only be taken by a registered dentist. Other intimate samples, except for samples of urine, may only be taken by a registered medical practitioner or registered nurse or registered paramedic.

(b) *Non-intimate samples*

6.5 A non-intimate sample may be taken from a detainee only with their written consent or if *paragraph 6.6* applies.

6.6 (a)   under section 63, a non-intimate sample may not be taken from a person without consent and the consent must be in writing

(aa) A non-intimate sample may be taken from a person without the appropriate consent in the following circumstances:

(i)   under section 63(2A) where the person is in police detention as a consequence of his arrest for a recordable offence and he has not had a non-intimate sample of the same type and from the same part of the body taken in the course of the investigation of the offence by the police or he has had such a sample taken but it proved insufficient.

(ii) Under section 63(3) (a) where he is being held in custody by the police on the authority of a court and an officer of at least the rank of inspector authorises it to be taken.

(b)   under section 63(3A), from a person charged with a recordable offence or informed they will be reported for such an offence: and

(i)   that person has not had a non-intimate sample taken from them in the course of the investigation; or

    (ii)   if they have had a sample taken, it proved unsuitable or insufficient for the same form of analysis, see *Note 6B*; or

(c)   under section 63(3B), from a person convicted of a recordable offence after the date on which that provision came into effect. PACE, section 63A, describes the circumstances in which a police officer may require a person convicted of a recordable offence to attend a police station for a non-intimate sample to be taken.

6.7   Reasonable force may be used, if necessary, to take a non-intimate sample from a person without their consent under the powers mentioned in *paragraph 6.6*.

6.8   Before any intimate sample is taken with consent or non-intimate sample is taken with, or without, consent, the person must be informed:

(a)   of the reason for taking the sample;

(b)   of the grounds on which the relevant authority has been given;

(c)   that the sample or information derived from the sample may be retained and subject of a speculative search, see *Note 6E*, unless their destruction is required as in *Annex F*, Part A.

6.9   When clothing needs to be removed in circumstances likely to cause embarrassment to the person, no person of the opposite sex who is not a registered medical practitioner or registered health care professional shall be present, (unless in the case of a juvenile, mentally disordered or mentally vulnerable person, that person specifically requests the presence of an appropriate adult of the opposite sex who is readily available) nor shall anyone whose presence is unnecessary. However, in the case of a juvenile, this is subject to the overriding proviso that such a removal of clothing may take place in the absence of the appropriate adult only if the juvenile signifies, in their presence, that they prefer the adult's absence and they agree.

(c)   Documentation

6.10   A record of the reasons for taking a sample or impression and, if applicable, of its destruction must be made as soon as practicable. If force is used, a record shall be made of the circumstances and those present. If written consent is given to the taking of a sample or impression, the fact must be recorded in writing.

6.11   A record must be made of a warning given as required by *paragraph 6.3*.

6.12   A record shall be made of the fact that a person has been informed as in *paragraph 6.8(c)* that samples may be subject of a speculative search.

Notes for guidance

6A   When hair samples are taken for the purpose of DNA analysis (rather than for other purposes such as making a visual match), the suspect should be permitted a reasonable choice as to what part of the body the hairs are taken from. When hairs are plucked, they should be plucked individually, unless the suspect prefers otherwise and no more should be plucked than the person taking them reasonably considers necessary for a sufficient sample.

6B   (a)   An insufficient sample is one which is not sufficient either in quantity or quality to provide information for a particular form of analysis, such as DNA analysis. A sample may also be insufficient if enough information cannot be obtained from it by analysis because of loss, destruction, damage or contamination of the sample or as a result of an earlier, unsuccessful attempt at analysis.

*   (b)   An unsuitable sample is one which, by its nature, is not suitable for a particular form of analysis.*

6C   Nothing in paragraph 6.2 prevents intimate samples being taken for elimination purposes with the consent of the person concerned but the provisions of paragraph 2.12 relating to the role of the appropriate adult, should be applied. Paragraph 6.2(b) does not, however, apply where the non-intimate samples were previously taken under the Terrorism Act 2000, Schedule 8, paragraph 10.

6D   *In warning a person who is asked to provide an intimate sample as in paragraph 6.3, the following form of words may be used:*

   "You do not have to provide this sample/allow this swab or impression to be taken, but I must warn you that if you refuse without good cause, your refusal may harm your case if it comes to trial."

6E   *Fingerprints or a DNA sample and the information derived from it taken from a person arrested on suspicion of being involved in a recordable offence, or charged with such an offence, or informed they will be reported for such an offence, may be subject of a speculative search. This means they may be checked against other fingerprints and DNA records held by, or on behalf of, the police and other law enforcement authorities in or outside the UK or held in connection with, or as a result of, an investigation of an offence inside or outside the UK. Fingerprints and samples taken from any other person, e.g. a person suspected of committing a recordable offence but who has not been arrested, charged or informed they will be reported for it, may be subject to a speculative search only if the person consents in writing to their fingerprints being subject of such a search. The following is an example of a basic form of words:*

   "I consent to my fingerprints/DNA sample and information derived from it being retained and used only for purposes related to the prevention and detection of a crime, the investigation of an offence or the conduct of a prosecution either nationally or internationally.

   I understand that this sample may be checked against other fingerprint/DNA records held by or on behalf of relevant law enforcement authorities, either nationally or internationally.

   I understand that once I have given my consent for the sample to be retained and used I cannot withdraw this consent."

   See Annex F regarding the retention and use of fingerprints and samples taken with consent for elimination purposes.

6F   *Samples of urine and non-intimate samples taken in accordance with sections 63B and 63C of PACE may not be used for identification purposes in accordance with this Code. See Code C note for guidance 17D.*

ANNEX A — VIDEO IDENTIFICATION

(a) General

1.   The arrangements for obtaining and ensuring the availability of a suitable set of images to be used in a video identification must be the responsibility of an identification officer, who has no direct involvement with the case.

2.   The set of images must include the suspect and at least eight other people who, so far as possible, resemble the suspect in age, height, general appearance and position in life. Only one suspect shall appear in any set unless there are two suspects of roughly similar appearance, in which case they may be shown together with at least twelve other people.

3.   The images used to conduct a video identification shall, as far as possible, show the suspect and other people in the same positions or carrying out the same sequence of movements. They shall also show the suspect and other people under identical conditions unless the identification officer reasonably believes:

   (a)   because of the suspect's failure or refusal to co-operate or other reasons, it is not practicable for the conditions to be identical; and

    (b)   any difference in the conditions would not direct a witness' attention to any individual image.

4. The reasons identical conditions are not practicable shall be recorded on forms provided for the purpose.

5. Provision must be made for each person shown to be identified by number.

6. If police officers are shown, any numerals or other identifying badges must be concealed. If a prison inmate is shown, either as a suspect or not, then either all, or none of, the people shown should be in prison clothing.

7. The suspect or their solicitor, friend, or appropriate adult must be given a reasonable opportunity to see the complete set of images before it is shown to any witness. If the suspect has a reasonable objection to the set of images or any of the participants, the suspect shall be asked to state the reasons for the objection. Steps shall, if practicable, be taken to remove the grounds for objection. If this is not practicable, the suspect and/or their representative shall be told why their objections cannot be met and the objection, the reason given for it and why it cannot be met shall be recorded on forms provided for the purpose.

8. Before the images are shown in accordance with *paragraph 7*, the suspect or their solicitor shall be provided with details of the first description of the suspect by any witnesses who are to attend the video identification. When a broadcast or publication is made, as in *paragraph 3.28*, the suspect or their solicitor must also be allowed to view any material released to the media by the police for the purpose of recognising or tracing the suspect, provided it is practicable and would not unreasonably delay the investigation.

9. The suspect's solicitor, if practicable, shall be given reasonable notification of the time and place the video identification is to be conducted so a representative may attend on behalf of the suspect. If a solicitor has not been instructed, this information shall be given to the suspect. The suspect may not be present when the images are shown to the witness(es). In the absence of the suspect's representative, the viewing itself shall be recorded on video. No unauthorised people may be present.

(b) Conducting the video identification

10. The identification officer is responsible for making the appropriate arrangements to make sure, before they see the set of images, witnesses are not able to communicate with each other about the case or overhear a witness who has already seen the material. There must be no discussion with the witness about the composition of the set of images and they must not be told whether a previous witness has made any identification.

11. Only one witness may see the set of images at a time. Immediately before the images are shown, the witness shall be told that the person they saw on a specified earlier occasion may, or may not, appear in the images they are shown and that if they cannot make a positive identification, they should say so. The witness shall be advised that at any point, they may ask to see a particular part of the set of images or to have a particular image frozen for them to study. Furthermore, it should be pointed out to the witness that there is no limit on how many times they can view the whole set of images or any part of them. However, they should be asked not to make any decision as to whether the person they saw is on the set of images until they have seen the whole set at least twice.

12. Once the witness has seen the whole set of images at least twice and has indicated that they do not want to view the images, or any part of them, again, the witness shall be asked to say whether the individual they saw in person on a specified earlier occasion has been shown and, if so, to identify them by number of the

image. The witness will then be shown that image to confirm the identification, see *paragraph 17.*

13. Care must be taken not to direct the witness' attention to any one individual image or give any indication of the suspect's identity. Where a witness has previously made an identification by photographs, or a computerised or artist's composite or similar likeness, the witness must not be reminded of such a photograph or composite likeness once a suspect is available for identification by other means in accordance with this Code. Nor must the witness be reminded of any description of the suspect.

14. After the procedure, each witness shall be asked whether they have seen any broadcast or published films or photographs, or any descriptions of suspects relating to the offence and their reply shall be recorded.

(c) Image security and destruction

15. Arrangements shall be made for all relevant material containing sets of images used for specific identification procedures to be kept securely and their movements accounted for. In particular, no-one involved in the investigation shall be permitted to view the material prior to it being shown to any witness.

16. As appropriate, *paragraph 3.30* or *3.31* applies to the destruction or retention of relevant sets of images.

(d) Documentation

17. A record must be made of all those participating in, or seeing, the set of images whose names are known to the police.

18. A record of the conduct of the video identification must be made on forms provided for the purpose. This shall include anything said by the witness about any identifications or the conduct of the procedure and any reasons it was not practicable to comply with any of the provisions of this Code governing the conduct of video identifications.

ANNEX B — IDENTIFICATION PARADES

(a) General

1. A suspect must be given a reasonable opportunity to have a solicitor or friend present, and the suspect shall be asked to indicate on a second copy of the notice whether or not they wish to do so.

2. An identification parade may take place either in a normal room or one equipped with a screen permitting witnesses to see members of the identification parade without being seen. The procedures for the composition and conduct of the identification parade are the same in both cases, subject to *paragraph 8* (except that an identification parade involving a screen may take place only when the suspect's solicitor, friend or appropriate adult is present or the identification parade is recorded on video).

3. Before the identification parade takes place, the suspect or their solicitor shall be provided with details of the first description of the suspect by any witnesses who are attending the identification parade. When a broadcast or publication is made as in *paragraph 3.28*, the suspect or their solicitor should also be allowed to view any material released to the media by the police for the purpose of recognising or tracing the suspect, provided it is practicable to do so and would not unreasonably delay the investigation.

(b) Identification parades involving prison inmates

4. If a prison inmate is required for identification, and there are no security problems about the person leaving the establishment, they may be asked to participate in an identification parade or video identification.

5. An identification parade may be held in a Prison Department establishment but shall be conducted, as far as practicable under normal identification parade rules. Members of the public shall make up the identification parade unless there are serious security, or control, objections to their admission to the establishment. In such cases, or if a group or video identification is arranged within the establishment, other inmates may participate. If an inmate is the suspect, they are not required to wear prison clothing for the identification parade unless the other people taking part are other inmates in similar clothing, or are members of the public who are prepared to wear prison clothing for the occasion.

(c)   *Conduct of the identification parade*

6. Immediately before the identification parade, the suspect must be reminded of the procedures governing its conduct and cautioned in the terms of Code C, paragraphs 10.5 or 10.6, as appropriate.

7. All unauthorised people must be excluded from the place where the identification parade is held.

8. Once the identification parade has been formed, everything afterwards, in respect of it, shall take place in the presence and hearing of the suspect and any interpreter, solicitor, friend or appropriate adult who is present (unless the identification parade involves a screen, in which case everything said to, or by, any witness at the place where the identification parade is held, must be said in the hearing and presence of the suspect's solicitor, friend or appropriate adult or be recorded on video).

9. The identification parade shall consist of at least eight people (in addition to the suspect) who, so far as possible, resemble the suspect in age, height, general appearance and position in life. Only one suspect shall be included in an identification parade unless there are two suspects of roughly similar appearance, in which case they may be paraded together with at least twelve other people. In no circumstances shall more than two suspects be included in one identification parade and where there are separate identification parades, they shall be made up of different people.

10. If the suspect has an unusual physical feature, e.g., a facial scar, tattoo or distinctive hairstyle or hair colour which cannot be replicated on other members of the identification parade, steps may be taken to conceal the location of that feature on the suspect and the other members of the identification parade if the suspect and their solicitor, or appropriate adult, agree. For example, by use of a plaster or a hat, so that all members of the identification parade resemble each other in general appearance.

11. When all members of a similar group are possible suspects, separate identification parades shall be held for each unless there are two suspects of similar appearance when they may appear on the same identification parade with at least twelve other members of the group who are not suspects. When police officers in uniform form an identification parade any numerals or other identifying badges shall be concealed.

12. When the suspect is brought to the place where the identification parade is to be held, they shall be asked if they have any objection to the arrangements for the identification parade or to any of the other participants in it and to state the reasons for the objection. The suspect may obtain advice from their solicitor or friend, if present, before the identification parade proceeds. If the suspect has a reasonable objection to the arrangements or any of the participants, steps shall, if practicable, be taken to remove the grounds for objection. When it is not practicable to do so, the suspect shall be told why their objections cannot be met

and the objection, the reason given for it and why it cannot be met, shall be recorded on forms provided for the purpose.

13. The suspect may select their own position in the line, but may not otherwise interfere with the order of the people forming the line. When there is more than one witness, the suspect must be told, after each witness has left the room, that they can, if they wish, change position in the line. Each position in the line must be clearly numbered, whether by means of a number laid on the floor in front of each identification parade member or by other means.

14. Appropriate arrangements must be made to make sure, before witnesses attend the identification parade, they are not able to:
    (i)   communicate with each other about the case or overhear a witness who has already seen the identification parade;
    (ii) see any member of the identification parade;
    (iii) see, or be reminded of, any photograph or description of the suspect or be given any other indication as to the suspect's identity; or
    (iv) see the suspect before or after the identification parade.

15. The person conducting a witness to an identification parade must not discuss with them the composition of the identification parade and, in particular, must not disclose whether a previous witness has made any identification.

16. Witnesses shall be brought in one at a time. Immediately before the witness inspects the identification parade, they shall be told the person they saw on a specified earlier occasion may, or may not, be present and if they cannot make a positive identification, they should say so. The witness must also be told they should not make any decision about whether the person they saw is on the identification parade until they have looked at each member at least twice.

17. When the officer or civilian support staff (see paragraph 3.11) conducting the identification procedure is satisfied the witness has properly looked at each member of the identification parade, they shall ask the witness whether the person they saw on a specified earlier occasion is on the identification parade and, if so, to indicate the number of the person concerned, see *paragraph 28*.

18. If the witness wishes to hear any identification parade member speak, adopt any specified posture or move, they shall first be asked whether they can identify any person(s) on the identification parade on the basis of appearance only. When the request is to hear members of the identification parade speak, the witness shall be reminded that the participants in the identification parade have been chosen on the basis of physical appearance only. Members of the identification parade may then be asked to comply with the witness' request to hear them speak, see them move or adopt any specified posture.

19. If the witness requests that the person they have indicated remove anything used for the purposes of *paragraph 10* to conceal the location of an unusual physical feature, that person may be asked to remove it.

20. If the witness makes an identification after the identification parade has ended, the suspect and, if present, their solicitor, interpreter or friend shall be informed. When this occurs, consideration should be given to allowing the witness a second opportunity to identify the suspect.

21. After the procedure, each witness shall be asked whether they have seen any broadcast or published films or photographs or any descriptions of suspects relating to the offence and their reply shall be recorded.

22. When the last witness has left, the suspect shall be asked whether they wish to make any comments on the conduct of the identification parade.

(d) *Documentation*

23. A video recording must normally be taken of the identification parade. If that is impracticable, a colour photograph must be taken. A copy of the video recording or photograph shall be supplied, on request, to the suspect or their solicitor within a reasonable time.

24. As appropriate, *paragraph 3.30* or *3.31*, should apply to any photograph or video taken as in *paragraph 23*.

25. If any person is asked to leave an identification parade because they are interfering with its conduct, the circumstances shall be recorded.

26. A record must be made of all those present at an identification parade whose names are known to the police.

27. If prison inmates make up an identification parade, the circumstances must be recorded.

28. A record of the conduct of any identification parade must be made on forms provided for the purpose. This shall include anything said by the witness or the suspect about any identifications or the conduct of the procedure, and any reasons it was not practicable to comply with any of this Code's provisions.

ANNEX C — GROUP IDENTIFICATION

(a) *General*

1. The purpose of this Annex is to make sure, as far as possible, group identifications follow the principles and procedures for identification parades so the conditions are fair to the suspect in the way they test the witness' ability to make an identification.

2. Group identifications may take place either with the suspect's consent and cooperation or covertly without their consent.

3. The location of the group identification is a matter for the identification officer, although the officer may take into account any representations made by the suspect, appropriate adult, their solicitor or friend.

4. The place where the group identification is held should be one where other people are either passing by or waiting around informally, in groups such that the suspect is able to join them and be capable of being seen by the witness at the same time as others in the group. For example people leaving an escalator, pedestrians walking through a shopping centre, passengers on railway and bus stations, waiting in queues or groups or where people are standing or sitting in groups in other public places.

5. If the group identification is to be held covertly, the choice of locations will be limited by the places where the suspect can be found and the number of other people present at that time. In these cases, suitable locations might be along regular routes travelled by the suspect, including buses or trains or public places frequented by the suspect.

6. Although the number, age, sex, race and general description and style of clothing of other people present at the location cannot be controlled by the identification officer, in selecting the location the officer must consider the general appearance and numbers of people likely to be present. In particular, the officer must reasonably expect that over the period the witness observes the group, they will be able to see, from time to time, a number of others whose appearance is broadly similar to that of the suspect.

7. A group identification need not be held if the identification officer believes, because of the unusual appearance of the suspect, none of the locations it would

be practicable to use satisfy the requirements of paragraph 6 necessary to make the identification fair.

8.   Immediately after a group identification procedure has taken place (with or without the suspect's consent), a colour photograph or video should be taken of the general scene, if practicable, to give a general impression of the scene and the number of people present. Alternatively, if it is practicable, the group identification may be video recorded.

9.   If it is not practicable to take the photograph or video in accordance with *paragraph 8*, a photograph or film of the scene should be taken later at a time determined by the identification officer if the officer considers it practicable to do so.

10. An identification carried out in accordance with this Code remains a group identification even though, at the time of being seen by the witness, the suspect was on their own rather than in a group.

11. Before the group identification takes place, the suspect or their solicitor shall be provided with details of the first description of the suspect by any witnesses who are to attend the identification. When a broadcast or publication is made, as in *paragraph 3.28*, the suspect or their solicitor should also be allowed to view any material released by the police to the media for the purposes of recognising or tracing the suspect, provided that it is practicable and would not unreasonably delay the investigation.

12. After the procedure, each witness shall be asked whether they have seen any broadcast or published films or photographs or any descriptions of suspects relating to the offence and their reply recorded.

(b) Identification with the consent of the suspect

13. A suspect must be given a reasonable opportunity to have a solicitor or friend present. They shall be asked to indicate on a second copy of the notice whether or not they wish to do so.

14. The witness, the person carrying out the procedure and the suspect's solicitor, appropriate adult, friend or any interpreter for the witness, may be concealed from the sight of the individuals in the group they are observing, if the person carrying out the procedure considers this assists the conduct of the identification.

15. The person conducting a witness to a group identification must not discuss with them the forthcoming group identification and, in particular, must not disclose whether a previous witness has made any identification.

16. Anything said to, or by, the witness during the procedure about the identification should be said in the presence and hearing of those present at the procedure.

17. Appropriate arrangements must be made to make sure, before witnesses attend the group identification, they are not able to:

    (i)   communicate with each other about the case or overhear a witness who has already been given an opportunity to see the suspect in the group;

    (ii)   see the suspect; or

    (iii) see, or be reminded of, any photographs or description of the suspect or be given any other indication of the suspect's identity.

18. Witnesses shall be brought one at a time to the place where they are to observe the group. Immediately before the witness is asked to look at the group, the person conducting the procedure shall tell them that the person they saw may, or may not, be in the group and that if they cannot make a positive identification, they should say so. The witness shall be asked to observe the group in which the suspect is to appear. The way in which the witness should do this will depend on whether the group is moving or stationary.

Moving group

19. When the group in which the suspect is to appear is moving, e.g. leaving an escalator, the provisions of *paragraphs 20 to 24* should be followed.

20. If two or more suspects consent to a group identification, each should be the subject of separate identification procedures. These may be conducted consecutively on the same occasion.

21. The person conducting the procedure shall tell the witness to observe the group and ask them to point out any person they think they saw on the specified earlier occasion

22. Once the witness has been informed as in *paragraph 21* the suspect should be allowed to take whatever position in the group they wish.

23. When the witness points out a person as in *paragraph 21* they shall, if practicable, be asked to take a closer look at the person to confirm the identification. If this is not practicable, or they cannot confirm the identification, they shall be asked how sure they are that the person they have indicated is the relevant person.

24. The witness should continue to observe the group for the period which the person conducting the procedure reasonably believes is necessary in the circumstances for them to be able to make comparisons between the suspect and other individuals of broadly similar appearance to the suspect as in *paragraph 6*.

Stationary groups

25. When the group in which the suspect is to appear is stationary, e.g. people waiting in a queue, the provisions of *paragraphs 26 to 29* should be followed.

26. If two or more suspects consent to a group identification, each should be subject to separate identification procedures unless they are of broadly similar appearance when they may appear in the same group. When separate group identifications are held, the groups must be made up of different people.

27. The suspect may take whatever position in the group they wish. If there is more than one witness, the suspect must be told, out of the sight and hearing of any witness, that they can, if they wish, change their position in the group.

28. The witness shall be asked to pass along, or amongst, the group and to look at each person in the group at least twice, taking as much care and time as possible according to the circumstances, before making an identification. Once the witness has done this, they shall be asked whether the person they saw on the specified earlier occasion is in the group and to indicate any such person by whatever means the person conducting the procedure considers appropriate in the circumstances. If this is not practicable, the witness shall be asked to point out any person they think they saw on the earlier occasion.

29. When the witness makes an indication as in *paragraph 28*, arrangements shall be made, if practicable, for the witness to take a closer look at the person to confirm the identification. If this is not practicable, or the witness is unable to confirm the identification, they shall be asked how sure they are that the person they have indicated is the relevant person.

All cases

30. If the suspect unreasonably delays joining the group, or having joined the group, deliberately conceals themselves from the sight of the witness, this may be treated as a refusal to co-operate in a group identification.

31. If the witness identifies a person other than the suspect, that person should be informed what has happened and asked if they are prepared to give their name and address. There is no obligation upon any member of the public to give these

details. There shall be no duty to record any details of any other member of the public present in the group or at the place where the procedure is conducted.

32. When the group identification has been completed, the suspect shall be asked whether they wish to make any comments on the conduct of the procedure.

33. If the suspect has not been previously informed, they shall be told of any identifications made by the witnesses.

(c) *Identification without the suspect's consent*

34. Group identifications held covertly without the suspect's consent should, as far as practicable, follow the rules for conduct of group identification by consent.

35. A suspect has no right to have a solicitor, appropriate adult or friend present as the identification will take place without the knowledge of the suspect.

36. Any number of suspects may be identified at the same time.

(d) *Identifications in police stations*

37. Group identifications should only take place in police stations for reasons of safety, security or because it is not practicable to hold them elsewhere.

38. The group identification may take place either in a room equipped with a screen permitting witnesses to see members of the group without being seen, or anywhere else in the police station that the identification officer considers appropriate.

39. Any of the additional safeguards applicable to identification parades should be followed if the identification officer considers it is practicable to do so in the circumstances.

(e) *Identifications involving prison inmates*

40. A group identification involving a prison inmate may only be arranged in the prison or at a police station.

41. When a group identification takes place involving a prison inmate, whether in a prison or in a police station, the arrangements should follow those in *paragraphs 37* to *39*. If a group identification takes place within a prison, other inmates may participate. If an inmate is the suspect, they do not have to wear prison clothing for the group identification unless the other participants are wearing the same clothing.

(f) *Documentation*

42. When a photograph or video is taken as in *paragraph 8* or *9*, a copy of the photograph or video shall be supplied on request to the suspect or their solicitor within a reasonable time.

43. *Paragraph 3.30* or *3.31*, as appropriate, shall apply when the photograph or film taken in accordance with *paragraph 8* or *9* includes the suspect.

44. A record of the conduct of any group identification must be made on forms provided for the purpose. This shall include anything said by the witness or suspect about any identifications or the conduct of the procedure and any reasons why it was not practicable to comply with any of the provisions of this Code governing the conduct of group identifications.

ANNEX D — CONFRONTATION BY A WITNESS

1. Before the confrontation takes place, the witness must be told that the person they saw may, or may not, be the person they are to confront and that if they are not that person, then the witness should say so.

2. Before the confrontation takes place the suspect or their solicitor shall be provided with details of the first description of the suspect given by any witness who is to attend. When a broadcast or publication is made, as in *paragraph 3.28*, the suspect

or their solicitor should also be allowed to view any material released to the media for the purposes of recognising or tracing the suspect, provided it is practicable to do so and would not unreasonably delay the investigation.

3. Force may not be used to make the suspect's face visible to the witness.

4. Confrontation must take place in the presence of the suspect's solicitor, interpreter or friend unless this would cause unreasonable delay.

5. The suspect shall be confronted independently by each witness, who shall be asked "Is this the person?". If the witness identifies the person but is unable to confirm the identification, they shall be asked how sure they are that the person is the one they saw on the earlier occasion.

6. The confrontation should normally take place in the police station, either in a normal room or one equipped with a screen permitting a witness to see the suspect without being seen. In both cases, the procedures are the same except that a room equipped with a screen may be used only when the suspect's solicitor, friend or appropriate adult is present or the confrontation is recorded on video.

7. After the procedure, each witness shall be asked whether they have seen any broadcast or published films or photographs or any descriptions of suspects relating to the offence and their reply shall be recorded.

ANNEX E — SHOWING PHOTOGRAPHS

(a) *Action*

1. An officer of sergeant rank or above shall be responsible for supervising and directing the showing of photographs. The actual showing may be done by another officer or civilian support staff, see *paragraph 3.11*.

2. The supervising officer must confirm the first description of the suspect given by the witness has been recorded before they are shown the photographs. If the supervising officer is unable to confirm the description has been recorded they shall postpone showing the photographs.

3. Only one witness shall be shown photographs at any one time. Each witness shall be given as much privacy as practicable and shall not be allowed to communicate with any other witness in the case.

4. The witness shall be shown not less than twelve photographs at a time, which shall, as far as possible, all be of a similar type.

5. When the witness is shown the photographs, they shall be told the photograph of the person they saw may, or may not, be amongst them and if they cannot make a positive identification, they should say so. The witness shall also be told they should not make a decision until they have viewed at least twelve photographs. The witness shall not be prompted or guided in any way but shall be left to make any selection without help.

6. If a witness makes a positive identification from photographs, unless the person identified is otherwise eliminated from enquiries or is not available, other witnesses shall not be shown photographs. But both they, and the witness who has made the identification, shall be asked to attend a video identification, an identification parade or group identification unless there is no dispute about the suspect's identification.

7. If the witness makes a selection but is unable to confirm the identification, the person showing the photographs shall ask them how sure they are that the photograph they have indicated is the person they saw on the specified earlier occasion.

8. When the use of a computerised or artist's composite or similar likeness has led to there being a known suspect who can be asked to participate in a video

identification, appear on an identification parade or participate in a group identification, that likeness shall not be shown to other potential witnesses.

9. When a witness attending a video identification, an identification parade or group identification has previously been shown photographs or computerised or artist's composite or similar likeness (and it is the responsibility of the officer in charge of the investigation to make the identification officer aware that this is the case), the suspect and their solicitor must be informed of this fact before the identification procedure takes place.

10. None of the photographs shown shall be destroyed, whether or not an identification is made, since they may be required for production in court. The photographs shall be numbered and a separate photograph taken of the frame or part of the album from which the witness made an identification as an aid to reconstituting it.

(b) Documentation

11. Whether or not an identification is made, a record shall be kept of the showing of photographs on forms provided for the purpose. This shall include anything said by the witness about any identification or the conduct of the procedure, any reasons it was not practicable to comply with any of the provisions of this Code governing the showing of photographs and the name and rank of the supervising officer.

12. The supervising officer shall inspect and sign the record as soon as practicable.

ANNEX F — FINGERPRINTS AND SAMPLES — DESTRUCTION AND SPECULATIVE SEARCHES

(a) Fingerprints and samples taken in connection with a criminal investigation

1. When fingerprints or DNA samples are taken from a person in connection with an investigation and the person is not suspected of having committed the offence, see *Note F1*, they must be destroyed as soon as they have fulfilled the purpose for which they were taken unless:

    (a) they were taken for the purposes of an investigation of an offence for which a person has been convicted; and

    (b) fingerprints or samples were also taken from the convicted person for the purposes of that investigation.

    However, subject to *paragraph 2*, the fingerprints and samples, and the information derived from samples, may not be used in the investigation of any offence or in evidence against the person who is, or would be, entitled to the destruction of the fingerprints and samples, see *Note F2*.

2. The requirement to destroy fingerprints and DNA samples, and information derived from samples, and restrictions on their retention and use in *paragraph 1* do not apply if the person gives their written consent for their fingerprints or sample to be retained and used after they have fulfilled the purpose for which they were taken, see *Note F1*.

3. When a person's fingerprints or sample are to be destroyed:

    (a) any copies of the fingerprints must also be destroyed;

    (b) the person may witness the destruction of their fingerprints or copies if they ask to do so within five days of being informed destruction is required;

    (c) access to relevant computer fingerprint data shall be made impossible as soon as it is practicable to do so and the person shall be given a certificate to this effect within three months of asking; and

(d) neither the fingerprints, the sample, or any information derived from the sample, may be used in the investigation of any offence or in evidence against the person who is, or would be, entitled to its destruction.

4. Fingerprints or samples, and the information derived from samples, taken in connection with the investigation of an offence which are not required to be destroyed, may be retained after they have fulfilled the purposes for which they were taken but may be used only for purposes related to the prevention or detection of crime, the investigation of an offence or the conduct of a prosecution in, as well as outside, the UK and may also be subject to a speculative search. This includes checking them against other fingerprints and DNA records held by, or on behalf of, the police and other law enforcement authorities in, as well as outside, the UK.

(b) Fingerprints taken in connection with Immigration Service enquiries

5. Fingerprints taken for Immigration Service enquiries in accordance with powers and procedures other than under PACE and for which the Immigration Service, not the police, are responsible, must be destroyed as follows:

(a) fingerprints and all copies must be destroyed as soon as practicable if the person from whom they were taken proves they are a British or Commonwealth citizen who has the right of abode in the UK under the Immigration Act 1971, section 2(1)(b);

(b) fingerprints taken under the power as in *paragraph 4.11(g)* from a dependant of a person in *4.11(b)* to *(f)* must be destroyed when that person's fingerprints are to be destroyed;

(c) fingerprints taken from a person under any power as in *paragraph 4.11* or with the person's consent which have not already been destroyed as above, must be destroyed within ten years of being taken or within such period specified by the Secretary of State under the Immigration and Asylum Act 1999, section 143(5).

Notes for guidance

F1 *Fingerprints and samples given voluntarily for the purposes of elimination play an important part in many police investigations. It is, therefore, important to make sure innocent volunteers are not deterred from participating and their consent to their fingerprints and DNA being used for the purposes of a specific investigation is fully informed and voluntary. If the police or volunteer seek to have the sample or fingerprints retained for use after the specific investigation ends, it is important the volunteer's consent to this is also fully informed and voluntary.*

Examples of consent for:

*   *DNA/fingerprints – to be used only for the purposes of a specific investigation;*
*   *DNA/fingerprints – to be used in the specific investigation **and** retained by the police for future use.*

*To minimise the risk of confusion, each consent should be physically separate and the volunteer should be asked to sign one or the other, **not both**.*

(a) DNA:

(i) DNA sample taken for the purposes of elimination or as part of an intelligence-led screen and to be used only for the purposes of that investigation and destroyed afterwards:

"I consent to my DNA/mouth swab being taken for forensic analysis. I understand that the sample will be destroyed at the end of the case and that my profile will only be compared to the crime stain profile from this enquiry. I have been advised that

the person taking the sample may be required to give evidence and/or provide a written statement to the police in relation to the taking of it".

(ii)   DNA sample to be retained on the National DNA database and used in the future:

"I consent to my DNA sample and information derived from it being retained and used only for purposes related to the prevention and detection of a crime, the investigation of an offence or the conduct of a prosecution either nationally or internationally."

"I understand that this sample may be checked against other DNA records held by, or on behalf of, relevant law enforcement authorities, either nationally or internationally".

"I understand that once I have given my consent for the sample to be retained and used I cannot withdraw this consent."

(b)   Fingerprints:

(i)   Fingerprints taken for the purposes of elimination or as part of an intelligence-led screen and to be used only for the purposes of that investigation and destroyed afterwards:

"I consent to my fingerprints being taken for elimination purposes. I understand that the fingerprints will be destroyed at the end of the case and that my fingerprints will only be compared to the fingerprints from this enquiry. I have been advised that the person taking the fingerprints may be required to give evidence and/or provide a written statement to the police in relation to the taking of it."

(ii)   Fingerprints to be retained for future use:

"I consent to my fingerprints being retained and used only for purposes related to the prevention and detection of a crime, the investigation of an offence or the conduct of a prosecution either nationally or internationally".

"I understand that my fingerprints may be checked against other records held by, or on behalf of, relevant law enforcement authorities, either nationally or internationally."

"I understand that once I have given my consent for my fingerprints to be retained and used I cannot withdraw this consent."

F2   The provisions for the retention of fingerprints and samples in paragraph 1 allow for all fingerprints and samples in a case to be available for any subsequent miscarriage of justice investigation.

Index